LEE'S MAVERICK GENERAL
Daniel Harvey Hill

D0916610

Major General Daniel Harvey Hill, courtesy of the Valentine Museum, Richmond, Virginia

LEE'S MAVERICK GENERAL

Daniel Harvey Hill

BY HAL BRIDGES

Introduction by Gary W. Gallagher

University of Nebraska Press
Lincoln and London

First Bison Book Printing: 1991
Most recent printing indicated by the last digit below:
10   9   8   7   6   5   4   3   2   1

Library of Congress Cataloging-in-Publication Data
Bridges, Hal, 1918–
Lee's maverick general, Daniel Harvey Hill / by Hal Bridges; introduction by Gary
W. Gallagher.
p. cm.
Reprint. Originally published: New York: McGraw-Hill, c1961. Includes biblio-
graphical references (p.   ) and index. ISBN 0-8032-6096-2 (paper)
1. Hill, Daniel Harvey.   2. Generals—Confederate States of America—Biography.   3. Confederate States of America. Army—Biography. I. Title.
E467.1.H563B65   1991
973.7′13′092—dc20
[B]
91-13093 CIP

Reprinted by arrangement with McGraw-Hill, Inc.

Quotations from the following books have been made with the permission of the publishers:

Robert E. Lee the Soldier, by Major-General Sir Frederick Maurice. Copyright 1925 by
the Houghton Mifflin Company.

Leonidas Polk: Bishop and General, by William M. Polk. Copyright 1893 by Longmans,
Green & Co., Inc.

Robert E. Lee, by Douglas S. Freeman. Copyright 1937 by Charles Scribner's Sons.

Lee's Lieutenants, by Douglas S. Freeman. Copyright 1942–44 by Charles Scribner's
Sons.

Lee's Dispatches to Jefferson Davis, edited by Douglas S. Freeman and Grady McWiney.
Copyright 1957 by G. P. Putnam's Sons.

Inside the Confederate Government: The Diary of Robert Garlick Hill Kean, edited by Edward Younger. Copyright 1957 by Oxford University Press, Inc.

One Hundred Years at V.M.I., by William Couper. Copyright by Carrett & Massie, Inc.,
in 1939.

A Son's Recollections of His Father, by W. W. Mackall. Copyright 1930 by E. P. Dutton &
Co., Inc.

The Americans at Home, by David Macrae. Copyright 1952 by E. P. Dutton & Co., Inc.

Reprint of petition to Jefferson Davis through the courtesy of the Virginia State Library.

∞

*To Lois, L. H., Alice,
Lois, and Stephanie Bridges*

ACKNOWLEDGMENTS

THIS BOOK, which is not a biography but a study, with some bio-graphical background, of Daniel Harvey Hill's Civil War career, is the result of a suggestion made to me in 1952 by Dr. William B. Hesseltine. For his guidance and his kind encouragement and help through the years, I am most grateful.

I owe a large debt of gratitude to Miss Pauline Hill of Raleigh and Mr. and Mrs. David R. Williams of Mulberry Plantation, South Carolina, who generously gave me unrestricted use of Daniel Harvey Hill papers and related manuscripts in their possession. Miss Isabel Arnold of De Land, Florida, also extended me many kindnesses in aid of my search for material.

For endless courtesies and unfailingly helpful assistance, I thank the staffs of the University of Colorado Library; the Southern His-torical Collection, University of North Carolina Library; the Duke University Library; the North Carolina Department of Archives and History; the Virginia State Library; the Library of Congress; the National Archives; the Union Theological Seminary Library, Rich-mond; the Davidson College Library; the Henry E. Huntington Li-brary; the New-York Historical Society; the New York Public Li-brary; the United States Military Academy Archives; the Virginia Historical Society; the Washington and Lee University Library; the University of Arkansas Library; the University of Virginia Library; and the South Caroliniana Library, University of South Carolina.

Many persons provided material or aided me in other ways. Espe-cially do I feel grateful to Mr. Manly Wade Wellman, Dr. James W.

Patton, Miss Mattie Russell, Dr. Chalmers G. Davidson, Dr. and Mrs. Frontis W. Johnston, Dr. Clifford P. Westermeier, Mr. William J. Van Schreeven, Mrs. Albert Drane Oliphant, Dr. H. M. Brimm, Dr. Boyd C. Shafer, Dr. Avery O. Craven, Dr. Harold C. Syrett, Dr. Allan Nevins, Mrs. Lilla M. Hawes, Dr. J. Cutler Andrews, Dr. and Mrs. John A. Carpenter, and Miss Martha R. Cullipher. Others who took a courteous interest in my work are too numerous to list here, but I take this means of thanking them.

My colleagues in American history at the University of Colorado have been helpful. Two in particular, Dr. Robert G. Athearn and Dr. Howard L. Scamehorn, have rendered material aid as counselors and critics, and I thank them sincerely for their generous services.

I also wish to thank Mrs. William Hunter De Butts, of Washington, D.C., for permission to examine and to quote from the Robert E. Lee Papers, Library of Congress.

Mrs. Eloise Pearson typed my manuscript so cheerfully, and with such conscientious accuracy, that working with her was a pleasure.

My wife, Alice, copied long documents for me and listened helpfully to the reading of each chapter as it was written. By assuming more than her share of family duties, she gave me the time necessary for research and writing. Her assistance has been invaluable. I am deeply grateful.

To the University of Colorado and its Council on Research and Creative Work, I am much indebted for two faculty fellowships and several grants-in-aid. The American Philosophical Society also has my thanks for a timely research grant.

Hal Bridges

University of Colorado

CONTENTS

ILLUSTRATIONS

Introduction by Gary W. Gallagher

Daniel Harvey Hill holds a prominent position on the roster of controversial Confederate military leaders. A man of obvious ability who excelled in combat, he inspired lavish praise from many contemporary witnesses. E. Porter Alexander observed after the war that Hill "had done as much hard fighting as any other general, and had also displayed great ability in holding his men to their work by supervision and example." "There was an earnestness about . . . [his] fighting which was like Jackson's at its best," thought Alexander, who added that had "opportunity come to him, he must have won greater fame." John Haskell of South Carolina, whose memoirs are sharply critical of many southern officers, described Hill as a man of "high and well deserved reputation as a hard fighter" who always "seemed to go from choice into the most dangerous place he could find on the field." Echoing Alexander's assessment, Haskell considered Hill "as earnest in his Puritan beliefs as was Stonewall Jackson, who was his brother-in-law, and greatly resembled Jackson in many other ways; perhaps he imitated him." James Wylie Ratchford, a South Carolinian on Hill's staff who knew the general intimately, spoke of his "qualities of leadership which inspired the utmost confidence and loyalty in his soldiers and made him the idol of the Carolinas." Stonewall Jackson "repeatedly declared in my hearing that there was not . . . a man in the Southern Army, superior in military genius to D. H. Hill," affirmed Ratchford, "and emphatically expressed his disgust at the politics and bickerings that prevented the repeated gallantry of Hill and the brilliant service rendered by him from being officially recognized and rewarded."[1]

Soldiers in both the Union and Confederate armies habitually demanded that officers earn respect through courageous performance in battle. Leaders understood that gallantry on their part often prompted reciprocal bravery in the ranks. As Gerald Linderman observes in his careful study of Civil War soldiers, it "was as if officers were required to bank courage, with their deposits compelling equal contributions by the men and the joint balances then becoming available to officers to draw down when they thought them required."[2] Testimony from men who watched Hill in combat demonstrates that his personal deposits of courageous behavior were amply large. Artillerist Robert Stiles wrote of Hill that "like Jackson he was, too, a born fighter—as aggressive, pugnacious and tenacious as a bull-dog, or as any soldier in the service, and he had a sort of monomania on the subject of personal courage." According to Stiles, Hill frequently rode among his skirmishers, and if he saw a man seeking protection or firing wildly he would "make him get right up and come and stand out in the open, by his horse, and load his musket and hand it to him." Hill would take his time selecting an enemy target, carefully aim and fire, then discuss with the hapless skirmisher whether or not he had scored a hit. "He would continue [along his skirmish line] and distribute these blood-curdling object-lessons," concluded Stiles, "until his men settled down to a style of fighting that suited him."[3]

A soldier in the Fifth Texas Infantry of Hood's Texas Brigade vividly remembered Hill's conduct amid the chaotic fighting at Malvern Hill. Conspicuously vulnerable on horseback throughout the fighting, Hill made a perfect target. Literally hundreds of shells exploded near him, thought this man, yet Hill "appeared to be as unconcerned as if there had not been an enemy in a hundred miles. . . ." The Texan marveled at Hill's "true bravery and nerve" under the most trying circumstances. Major James Nicolson Edmondston, a North Carolinian who served under Hill for part of the war, spoke to relatives about the general in May 1863, observing that "in action & under fire he commands the admiration & respect of every one." Another Tarheel, William Alexander Smith of the Fourteenth North Carolina Infantry, summed up the attitude of most of the men who fought in the ranks under Hill: "He was a skillful officer, intelligent and keen-eyed, stern to rebuke violation of orders and lack of discipline—a determined bulldog fighter—as the boys expressed it, 'A fighter from way-back.'"[4]

Heroism alone did not guarantee a universally favorable reputation, however, and Hill's complex and difficult personality invited criticism. G. Moxley Sorrel, an astute judge of character whose memoirs are filled with perceptive sketches of southern officers, gave Hill full credit as "positively about the bravest man ever seen." But despite Hill's bravery, Sorrel considered him deeply flawed: "His backbone seemed a trifle weak. He would take his men into battle, fight furiously for some time and then something weakened about him." Unless James Longstreet or another strong commander was nearby to help, Hill's attacks were "apt to fail and his first efforts go unrewarded." Sorrel also noted Hill's "sharp prejudice and intemperate language," mentioning especially unfair blasts against Josiah Gorgas's Confederate Ordnance Department and southern cavalry in general (on one occasion, Hill sneeringly remarked that he had "yet to see a dead man with spurs on"). Overall, Sorrel considered Hill a "marked and peculiar character."[5]

Josiah Gorgas mentioned Hill several times in his diary, usually with much bitterness. Whether his low opinion of Hill preceded the latter's criticism of the Ordnance Department is open to question, but by April 1863 Gorgas expressed clear disdain for Hill's abilities. "D. H. Hill is still before Washington, N.C., and has alarmed the enemy for the safety of [Gen. John G.] Foster," wrote Gorgas. "Did they know Hill as well as we do they would be little alarmed. He can never achieve a success, tho' he might, I suppose, blunder upon one, as other short-witted people do."[6] Robert Garlick Hill Kean of the Confederate War department employed similarly harsh language in his diary. "D. H. Hill has been made a lieutenant general and sent to Mississippi," observed Kean on July 14, 1863. "A worse appointment could hardly be made for a people whose loyalty is shivering under the pressure of expected occupation." Conceding Hill's bravery and devotion to the Confederacy, Kean nonetheless called him "harsh, abrupt, often insulting in the effort to be sarcastic" and predicted he would "offend many and conciliate none."[7]

Hill, in fact, lavishly commended those whose actions met his rigorous standards, but his sarcasm and extreme bluntness often made a more lasting impression. Catherine Ann Devereux Edmondston's reactions to the general illustrate his phenomenon. Married to a prominent North Carolina planter, Catherine Edmonston kept a voluminous diary in which she praised Hill warmly for his triumphs on the battlefield and gratefully recorded his efforts to secure promotions for members of her family. But in the spring of 1863, Hill penned a vitriolic letter to Edward Stanly, Lincoln's military governor of North Carolina, which the *Raleigh Register* subsequently published. "He has . . . written the *coarsest personal* letter I ever saw from the pen of a gentleman," stated Edmondston in her diary. "Perfectly unneccessary [sic] & entirely unmilitary, the document would disgrace an underbred school boy. . . . It is a pity to see him destroy with his pen the reputation he has won with his sword." Edmondston had knitted a pair of gloves for Hill "which were not sent, however, for want of his address. I am half glad of it now. His letter is *so* ungentlemanly and unnecessary."[8]

A letter to Porter Alexander in early 1862 revealed Hill's seeming inability to restrain his sarcastic and critical urges. In response to Hill's complaints about the quality of his engineering officers, Alexander, who was then chief signal officer and chief of ordnance in Joseph E. Johnston's army, had helped Hill improve some fortifications near Leesburg during the first winter of the war. Appreciative of Alexander's efforts, Hill insisted in January 1862 that he required still more assistance. "I need another engineer who has tact at governing men & making them work," explained Hill in a passage lauding Alexander's labors. "Can such an officer be sent here?" "The Fort will be finished at present rates in about seven years," continued Hill, dipping into his reservoir of sarcastic expression. "Any effort of yours to send us an *energetic* Engineer and to forward guns *promptly* will be most gratefully appreciated." In the end, Alexander must have been somewhat puzzled by the shifting tone of this communication—first praise, then sarcasm, and finally a scolding sentence in which Hill implied that Alexander would be less than diligent unless reminded of the urgent requirements at Leesburg.[9]

Hill's insistence on presenting unvarnished, often pessimistic opinions caused problems with Jefferson Davis, Braxton Bragg, and R. E. Lee. He and Bragg waged a vicious war of words in the wake of the Confederate victory at Chickamauga, during the course of which Davis entered the fray and cast his vote of confidence in favor of

Bragg. In addition to bringing a number of unfair charges against Hill, Bragg averred that his frequent "croaking" harmed morale. [10] The *Oxford English Dictionary* offers a nineteenth-century definition of croaking: "to speak in dismal accents, talk despondingly, forebode evil (like the raven)." Beyond question, Harvey Hill stood guilty of croaking not only during his time with Bragg and the Army of Tennessee but also throughout the rest of his Confederate career. A letter from Hill to Secretary of War George Wythe Randolph in June 1862, for example, railed against troops from Gloucester, Virginia; said that ordnance officer J. Thomas Goode "fell infinitely short of my confidence" and characterized his division as "terribly disorganized" because of losses at Seven Pines; dismissed Brigadier Generals Gabriel J. Rains and W. S. Featherston, respectively, as "too slow" and "political;" and closed with the observation that "the Quartermaster Dept. is the very embodiment of inefficiency & indifference."[11] The cumulative effect of such gloomy letters, together with oral statements of a similar nature, led civilians and fellow officers to dismiss even Hill's valid criticisms as nothing more than tedious carping.

R. E. Lee considered Hill "an excellent executive officer" who lacked higher administrative ability. "Left to himself," Lee wrote Jefferson Davis in August 1862, "he seems embarrassed and backward to act." Moreover, Lee apparently interpreted Hill's chronic complaining during the following winter as evidence of depression. In postwar interviews with William Allan, then a member of the faculty at Washington College, Lee voiced some candid thoughts about Hill. Allan took no notes while listening to Lee, but he recorded the conversations shortly after the fact and likely captured at least the gist of the general's comments. According to Allan, Lee stated on February 15, 1868, that "D. H. Hill had such a queer temperament he [Lee] could never tell what to expect from him, & that he croaked. This was the case around Petersburg in 1864 when Beauregard complained of it to Lee."[12] In May 1863, Lee recommended Hill's assignment to "command of the department between the James River & the Cape Fear." Hill had gone to North Carolina in early 1863 to improve the military situation in the Old North State, young Robert E. Rodes (who did not croak) had handled Hill's division effectively at Chancellorsville, and Lee seemed well pleased with the opportunity to detach Hill permanently from the Army of Northern Virginia.[13]

Robert K. Krick has suggested that Hill's snarling "so regularly and acerbically at the world around him" caused Lee—"perhaps the personally least contentious general officer commissioned on either side"—to form a negative opinion of him. Douglas Southall Freeman agrees that "Hill's disposition to find fault with his comrades helps to explain the difficulty of using to best advantage his undeniable qualities."[14] Also worth noting is that with Hill's departure Lee lost the most outspoken critic among his principal lieutenants. Perhaps Hill's blunt critiques of Lee's generalship at Malvern Hill and during the Maryland Campaign influenced the commander's decision to send his cantankerous divisional leader away from Virginia.[15]

Harvey Hill's exile from the Army of Northern Virginia placed him in the company of John Bankhead Magruder, Benjamin Huger, Gustavus W. Smith, and others whom Lee had eased out of the Army of Northern Virginia. His name subsequently appeared progressively less often in connection with great events of the war. Staunch service at Chickamauga and cameo roles at Petersburg and Bentonville closed out his part in the Confederate military story. Nearly a quarter century of life remained to him after Appomattox, during which he edited the short-lived periodicals *The Land We Love* and *The Southern Home,* held presidencies of colleges in Arkansas and Georgia, and wrote widely about the war. Abrasive to the end, he defended his record, assailed enemies on both sides of the Potomac, and glorified the antebellum South's "old noble type of civilization."[16]

There is no definitive biography of Daniel Harvey Hill. Certainly he deserves such a treatment, for examination of his antebellum and postwar careers as an educator and author would yield insights into the broader history of the South. A close study of his writings and editorial work with *The Land We Love* and *The Southern Home* might be particularly instructive about the process by which southerners attempted to come to grips with their shattering defeat. The materials exist for a full life, awaiting the attention of a biographer with the temperament to spend several years in Hill's prickly company.

Fortunately for students of the military history of the Civil War, Hal Bridges covers Hill's Confederate years in *Lee's Maverick General:*

Daniel Harvey Hill. A Texan trained at Columbia who taught successively at the University of Arkansas, the University of Colorado, and the University of California at Riverside, Bridges published a biography of Pennsylvania ironmaster and Republican diplomat Charlemagne Tower before turning his attention to Hill.[17] Bridges drew on extensive research in manuscript collections and a variety of printed materials to produce a vigorous, analytical narrative that portrays Hill in a generally positive light. Admitting his subject's many quirks of personality, Bridges convincingly demonstrates that most of Hill's critical forays stemmed from perceptive readings of military affairs. The chapters on Hill's relationship with Lee and the firestorm within the Confederate high command of the Army of Tennessee that followed Chickamauga are especially strong.

Reviewers accorded Bridges high praise for his handling of Hill's Confederate career (most also expressed disappointment at his decision not to sketch Hill's entire life). Bell I. Wiley cheered the closing of a "glaring gap" in the literature on the Civil War: "The research is thorough; the tone is sympathetic but judicious; the writing is always clear and at times is vivid and moving." James I. Robertson, Jr., spoke of Bridges's "painstaking research, as much into manuscript as printed sources," and found it heartening that *Lee's Maverick General* placed a previously misunderstood commander "closer to the lights of truth and objectivity."[18] The standard bibliography of the Civil War, published a few years after the appearance of *Lee's Maverick General,* called the book "well-researched, sympathetic, but controversial because of the author's opinionated text." Bridges's willingness to sustain Hill's unflattering estimates of R. E. Lee during the Seven Days and the Maryland Campaign likely explains these allusions to controversy and an "opinionated text."[19]

Publication of this reprint edition of *Lee's Maverick General* makes available to a new generation of readers an important title in Confederate biographical literature. In its pages readers will come to understand the actions and motivations of Daniel Harvey Hill. Enhanced understanding might not foster affection for this dour warrior, but it will clarify significant episodes in the history of southern military leadership.

NOTES

1. E. P. Alexander, *Military Memoirs of a Confederate* (1907; reprint, Dayton, Ohio, 1977), p. 367, n. 1; John Haskell, *The Haskell Memoirs: The Personal Narrative of a Confederate Officer,* ed. by Gilbert E. Govan and James W. Livingood (New York, 1960), p. 40; J. W. Ratchford, *Some Reminiscences of Persons and Incidents of the Civil War* (1909; reprint, Austin, Texas, 1971), pp. 8–9.

2. Gerald F. Linderman, *Embattled Courage: The Experience of Combat in the American Civil War* (New York, 1987), pp. 44–45.

3. Robert Stiles, *Four Years Under Marse Robert* (1903; reprint, Dayton, Ohio, 1977), pp. 65–66.

4. John W. Stevens, *Reminiscences of the Civil War* (1902; reprint, Powhatan, Va., 1982), p. 39; Beth Gilbert Crabtree and James W. Patton, eds., *"Journal of a Secesh Lady": The Diary of Catherine Ann Devereux Edmondston* (Raleigh, 1979), p. 393; William Alexander Smith, *The Anson Guards: Company C, Fourteenth Regiment North Carolina Volunteers, 1861–1865* (1914; reprint, Wendell, N.C., 1978), p. 120.

5. Gilbert Moxley Sorrel, *Recollections of a Confederate Staff Officer* (1905; reprint, Jackson, Tenn., 1958), pp. 54–55

6. Frank E. Vandiver, ed., *The Civil War Diary of General Josiah Gorgas* (University, Ala., 1947), p. 33. On October 16, 1863, Gorgas wrote that the "failure of the plan of battle before Chattanooga appears to rest with D. H. Hill, on the extreme right. He could not be found to receive the necessary orders in time, and was too late in playing his part, which was to attack the communications with Chattanooga, and draw the enemy down the river," Ibid., p. 66. Braxton Bragg had relieved Hill of his command in the Army of Tennessee the day before Gorgas made this entry.

7. Edward Younger, ed., *Inside the Confederate Government: The Diary of Robert Garlick Hill Kean* (New York, 1957), p. 81.

8. Crabtree and Patton, *"Journal of a Secesh Lady,"* p. 384.

9. Transcript of letter from D. H. Hill to Edward Porter Alexander, January 4, 1862, Petersburg National Battlefield Collections. See also Gary W. Gallagher, ed., *Fighting for the Confederacy: The Personal Recollections of General Edward Porter Alexander* (Chapel Hill, 1989), pp. 63–65.

10. See chapter XII below for a full discussion of the controversy involving Hill, Bragg, and Davis.

11. D. H. Hill to George Wythe Randolph, June 6, 1862, Compiled Military Service Record for George Burgwyn Anderson, General and Staff Officers' Papers, Record Group 109, National Archives and Records Service, Washington, D.C. (microfilm 331).

12. Clifford Dowdey and Louis H. Manarin, eds., *The Wartime Papers of R. E. Lee* (Boston, 1961), pp. 258, 388; transcript of conversation between William Allan and R. E. Lee, February 15, 1868, p. 3, William Allan Papers, Southern Historical Collection, University of North Carolina, Chapel Hill.

13. On Hill's assignment to North Carolina, see Dowdey and Manarin, *Wartime Papers of R. E. Lee,* pp. 386, 489.

14. Robert K. Krick, "The Army of Northern Virginia in September 1862: Its Circumstances during That Pivotal Month; Its Opportunities; and the Reasons It Should Not Have Been at Sharpsburg on September 15–18," transcript of lecture delivered at Mont Alto, Pennsylvania, June 10, 1988, p. 19; Douglas Southall Freeman, *Lee's Lieutenants: A Study in Command* (3 vols., New York, 1942–44), 2:275.

15. Hill's reports are in U.S. War Department, *The War of the Rebellion: A Compilation of the Official Records of the Union and Confederate Armies* (127 vols., index, and atlas; Washington, D.C., 1880–1901), ser. I, 11, pt. 2: 622–30 (Malvern Hill); ser. I, 19, pt. 1: 1018–30 (Maryland Campaign).

16. The quotation is from D. H. Hill to Charles H. McBlair, July 9, 1866, A. K. Smiley Public Library, Redlands, California.

17. For the outline of Bridges's career, see Jaques Cattell Press, ed., *Directory of American Scholars,* vol. I, *History* (7th ed., New York, 1978), p. 73.

18. *The American Historical Review* 68 (July 1962): 1129 (Wiley); *Civil War History* 8 (March 1962): 93–94 (Robertson).

19. Allan Nevins and others, eds., *Civil War Books: A Critical Bibliography* (2 vols., Baton Rouge, 1967, 1969), 2:41. Robert W. Johannsen prepared the biographical section of this bibliography.

"It is unfortunate to have views different from the rest of mankind. It secures abuse."
—*D. H. Hill*

I CANNOT CRITICIZE LEE NOW

O<small>N A WINTER'S DAY</small> in 1885, General Daniel Harvey Hill sat thinking of Robert E. Lee, and of what could rightly be said to the American people about the man who had become the idol of the conquered South.

Before Hill lay pen and paper; he faced the task of explaining to the editors of the *Century Magazine* why an article that he had written for their popular Civil War series contained no personal comment on Lee's conduct of the battle of Malvern Hill. The editors had complained because Hill, in passing adverse judgment on Lee's generalship at Malvern, had done so, not in his own words, but by quoting from the history of the war published by the Comte de Paris. This method, in addition to impairing the originality of the article, deprived the astute men in New York of the very ingredient that was booming the circulation of their magazine: blunt criticism of one famous Civil War general by another. A running dispute between P. G. T. Beauregard and Joseph E. Johnston over honors in their joint victory at Bull Run was already titillating the *Century's* nationwide reading audience. Why should not Hill freely express his opinion of Lee's shortcomings?

Certainly his knowledge of Lee entitled him to do so; he had led "D. H. Hill's Division" of Lee's army through hard fighting at Mechanicsville, Gaines' Mill, Malvern Hill, South Mountain, and Antietam. From his service under the great commander he had emerged with due respect for Lee, but not unstinted admiration or personal liking for him. Indeed a much warmer and higher place in his esteem was held by his brother-in-law, Stonewall Jackson, and by another of his commanding officers, Johnston. All this the *Century* editors knew. It gave weight to their request that he unsheathe his pen against Lee.

Hill was painfully aware that if he failed to comply with the request they might refuse to publish his article, which contained explanations of his own actions at Malvern that he had waited for years to get before the public. Moreover, there were other important battles that he wanted to write about—Seven Pines, for example, which he had fought under Johnston, and Chickamauga, in which he had commanded a corps under General Braxton Bragg. Each of these engagements bore directly upon something dearer to Hill than life itself—his military reputation. He had much to lose by refusing to cooperate with the *Century* editors.

Still it is not likely that he hesitated long in composing his reply. At sixty-three, with an erect soldierly bearing that belied his whitening hair and beard, he customarily dispatched work in quantities that might have appalled a younger man; and doubtless, since he lived by iron principle, he had never wavered in his decision. Dipping his pen, he wrote in a bold firm hand that was not only upright but leaned over backward:

"In my official reports . . . I criticized the management of Gen Lee at Malvern and South Mountain. He was then alive, my commander and in the full tide of success. He is dead now and failed in his efforts. What I could and did do, when in the meridian of his power, I cannot do now." [1]

This statement sums up two significant aspects of Hill's Civil War career: first, that he did clash sharply with Lee, as well as with Bragg and Jefferson Davis, and, second, that he steadfastly refused, after the war, to use his considerable literary talents in an all-out effort to demolish his enemies and build up his own military reputation. Historians of the war, lacking facts on his battles that he did not publish, have tended to assume that any general at odds with Lee could not have been very able, and so to minimize Hill's accomplishments. Yet when the dramatic events that Hill helped to shape are examined from his vantage point, with the aid of his private papers and other records, a number of intriguing questions arise. First and most obvious: Have his military achievements been underrated? But also: Did Lee allow himself undue delay in assum-

ing command of the Army of Northern Virginia? Did James Longstreet steal unmerited credit for Confederate success at Seven Pines?
What was Lee's role in the slaughter of Southern troops at Mechanicsville?

Further: Can the storied charge of John B. Hood and his Texas
Brigade at Gaines' Mill unquestionably be credited with effecting
the first breach in the Federal line? Did Lee overrule Jackson in
ordering him to lead an independent force to capture Harpers Ferry?
Was Hill responsible for the "Lost Dispatch" of Lee's Maryland
campaign of 1862? How well did J. E. B. Stuart perform his scouting
and guard duties at South Mountain? In the fall of 1862, did Jackson feel that Lee showed partiality toward Longstreet, and, on the
other side of the triangle, was Longstreet loyal to Lee? Did Lee, after
the war, write Jackson's widow an inaccurate account of a military
incident involving Jackson's, and his own, reputation? What does
the Confederate controversy over Chickamauga reveal about the
character of Jefferson Davis? Who really led the post-Chickamauga
opposition to Bragg among his generals? Who wrote and who signed
the famous generals' petition to Davis, calling for Bragg's removal
from command of the Army of Tennessee?

So the questions multiply, and the answers add up to a critical
minority report on some of the most important battles and leaders
of the war. It should be emphasized that the answers are often
tentative and that of course they are open to question, for they derive from the partial, conflicting evidence upon which military history necessarily rests. All that is categorically asserted is that Hill's
story does offer fresh and challenging evidence, which warrants attention. Let it be examined candidly as Harvey Hill—no perfect
warrior, but indisputably one of the bravest, hardest fighters of all
Civil War generals—rides into battle ahead of his troops.

I

THE ATTACKERS

In April, 1862, as Union General George B. McClellan slowly built up a pressure of ninety thousand men against the fifty-three thousand Confederates holding General Joseph E. Johnston's defense line in the lower Virginia Peninsula, between the York River and the James, two keenly interested observers of the unequal contest wrote letters home to their wives.

From Richmond, General Robert E. Lee, commander of the Confederate armies under the direction of President Jefferson Davis, warned Mary Lee on April 22 that her ancestral home, the White House, in the upper Peninsula, was endangered by McClellan's impending drive against Richmond, and that she ought to abandon it. "Suppose the Army is driven South of James river, you are encompassed in the enemy's lines," he wrote. "How are you to live? The Confederate money would be valueless. . . . it has been in view of these sad reverses, which God in his mercy forbid may happen, that I have recommended a more distant move to Carolina or even Georgia." He added a note of caution—"This is for your own consideration and not for public discussion which would only be mischievous"—and closed with an outburst that revealed his impatience with life-as-usual attitudes toward the war. "There is to be a wedding tonight. A poor young girl, Miss Addie Deans to Dr. Lyons, Son of the James. Did you ever hear of such a thing! In such times to think of such trivial amusements!" [1]

Two days later, when Major General Daniel Harvey Hill wrote Isabella Hill from his headquarters in Yorktown, where he commanded the left wing of Johnston's line, he was in an equally serious mood. If anything happened to him, he hoped that Isabella would bring up their children with gentle firmness, keeping them free from "high, fastidious and aristocratic notions," and teaching them that "The salt of the earth is in the lower ranks of life." His letter ended tenderly, "May God bless you my darling, ever, ever more," but it contained one sentence that must have struck poor Isabella like a club: "You have been virtually a widow for a year and you may be so very soon in fact." [2]

This blunt remark was typical of Harvey Hill, especially so of Hill the soldier. War accentuated the basic hardness of his character, a hardness that was intermixed, like granite in softer rock, with love for the wife and children who waited for him in Charlotte, North Carolina, with a profoundly mystical faith in God, and with the scholarly interests of a college professor who combined the teaching of science and theology with literary attainments, linguistics, and a wide knowledge of history and belles-lettres.

As a matter of fact, few generals either North or South were more erudite than Hill, though outwardly at Yorktown he revealed no trace of his academic background. Before the college campus he had also known West Point, the United States Army, and the Mexican War, and when he entered the Confederate service as a colonel in 1861 the military manner had settled over him again as snugly as his gray uniform. A slender, well-proportioned man not long past forty, of medium height and erect military posture, except when pain from a chronic spinal ailment forced him to bend slightly, he had the hard-bitten look of a combat infantryman. A big nose, clamped jaw, and heavy dark-brown beard gave strength to his face. The proud set of his head and the well-nigh baleful look that could slant from his long, narrow blue eyes seemed to say, "Fight me, if you dare."

Hill was, more than anything else, a fighter. In Mexico, Johnston had heard other young officers call him "the bravest man in the army," [3] and since taking up arms for the Confederacy he had been acquiring a new reputation for complete fearlessness under fire. Somewhat in contrast to his grim demeanor was the fund of dry wit hidden behind it, but even this often took the combative form of sarcasm, especially when directed at skulkers. Intensely patriotic toward the South, Hill regarded any man who could fight for Southern independence and would not as the lowest form of humanity.

As he rode along his Yorktown line, oblivious to the Federal shell-fire, encouraging men crouching wretchedly in rain-flooded trenches, he of course concealed from them his belief, shared with Johnston, that they were in a trap. The defenses stretching southward across the Peninsula were too long to be defended properly by Johnston's army; they had been poorly engineered under the direction of General John B. Magruder, and on both river flanks they were vulnerable to Union naval power. Even more ominous was the fact that McClellan, with his slow but thoroughgoing siege tactics, was wheeling into position a mass of rifled artillery that could outrange the smoothbore Southern guns and blast the Confederate line to pieces. Earlier that month when Johnston—a gray-whiskered little gamecock of a general—had first inspected his defenses he had asked Hill how long he could hold Yorktown after McClellan opened fire with all his artillery.

"About two days," replied Hill.

"I had supposed, about two hours," said Johnston.[4]

Johnston had kept his army on the Yorktown line only because President Davis had decided, on the advice of Lee and Secretary of War George W. Randolph, that he should hold the position, and with it the Norfolk navy yard, as long as possible. Disagreeing with the decision, as he so frequently disagreed with Davis's views, Johnston yielded to it in the belief that developments on the Peninsula would soon cause the Richmond authorities to see the wisdom of withdrawing the army and concentrating it near the Confederate capital. Through April, he worked at making his defenses as strong as possible, giving Magruder command of the right wing, General James Longstreet the center, and Hill the left, with General Gustavus W. Smith's division in reserve. Hill had a total divisional strength, including special detachments, of about eleven thousand; his four brigade commanders were Generals Jubal A. Early, Robert E. Rodes, Gabriel J. Rains, and W. S. Featherston.[5]

By the end of April, Johnston had decided that he would stay no longer on a line that he regarded as untenable, and, after notifying Lee that he was going to pull back, he did so. Although last-minute delays and confusion hampered the withdrawal from Yorktown, the retreat got under way on the night of May 3. Hill, whose division was designated as the infantry rear guard, stayed until after mid-

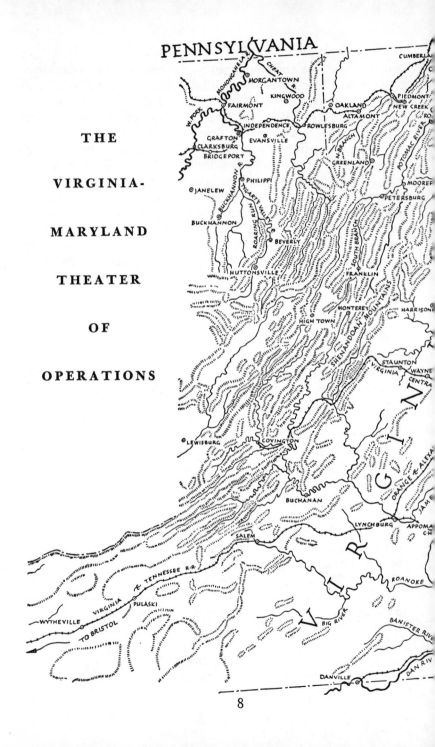

THE

VIRGINIA-

MARYLAND

THEATER

OF

OPERATIONS

18 MILES TO GETTYSBURG

BALTIMORE & OHIO R.R.

BALTIMORE

SCALE

0 5 10 15 20 25
MILES

N

MARTINSBURG
SHARPSBURG
FREDERICK
HARPERS FERRY
CHARLESTOWN
WINCHESTER
BERRYVILLE
LEESBURG
POTOMAC RIVER
ANNAPOLIS
STRASBURG
MIDDLEBURG
ALDIE
DRANESVILLE
FRONT ROYAL
UPPERVILLE
RECTORTOWN
CHANTILLY
WASHINGTON
WHITE PLAINS
SUDLEY SPGS.
FAIRFAX C.H.
SALEM
CENTERVILLE
FAIRFAX STA.
ALEXANDRIA
GROVETON
MANASSAS JUNC.
GREENWICH
BRISTOE STA.
WARRENTON
CATLETT STA.
OCCOQUAN
AMISSVILLE
BRENTSVILLE
LURAY
WARRENTON JUNC.
SPERRYVILLE
JEFFERSONTON
DUMFRIES
BEALETON STA.
RAPPANANNOCK STA.
BRANDY STA.
STAFFORD C.H.
CULPEPER
STEVENSBURG
MADDEN
AQUIA CREEK
RAPIDAN R.
BELLE PLAIN
RAPIDAN STA.
SALEM C.H.
FALMOUTH
CHANCELLORSVILLE
FREDERICKSBURG
ORANGE C.H.
VERDIERSVILLE
HAMILTON'S CROSSING
SKINKER'S NECK
SPOTSYLVANIA C.H.
PORT ROYAL
GORDONSVILLE
ORANGE SPGS.
GUINEY'S STA.
PORT TOBACCO
BRISCOE MINES
LAYTON
TREVILIAN STA.
BOWLING GREEN
MILFORD
LOUISA C.H.
FREDERICKS HALL
YANCEYVILLE
BEAVER DAM
CHESTERFIELD
MATTAPONI
TAPPANANNOCK
COLUMBIA
HANOVER JUNC.
AYLETT
SOUTH ANNA R.
HANOVER STA.
WALKERTON
ASHLAND STA.
HANOVER C.H.
KING WILLIAM C.H.
GOOCHLAND C.H.
HANOVERTOWN
KING & QUEEN C.H.
URBANNA
YELLOW TAV.
MECHANICSVILLE
SALUDA
JAMES RIVER
WEST POINT
RICHMOND
MANCHESTER
CHICKAHOMINY
GLOUCESTER C.H.
AMELIA C.H.
DREWRY'S BLUFF
DEEP BOTTOM
GLOUCESTER
FARMVILLE
CHARLES CITY C.H.
YORKTOWN
DANVILLE R.R.
PETERSBURG
FT. POWHATAN
WILLIAMSBURG
FT. MAGRUDER
HIGH BRIDGE
JAMESTOWN ISLAND
BURKVILLE
SOUTH SIDE R.R.
GLOBE TAV.
SURRY C.H.
BIG BETHEL
FIVE FORKS
REAM'S STA.
FT. MONROE
BLACK & WHITE'S
DINWIDDIE C.H.
BLACKWATER
NEWPORT NEWS
SEWELL'S PT.
STONY CREEK
PORTSMOUTH
NORFOLK
GOSPORT NAVY YARD
SUFFOLK
FRANKLIN
PETERSBURG & WELDON R.R.
NORTH CAROLINA
WELDON

MARYLAND

CHESAPEAKE BAY

APPOMATTOX RIVER

9

night while the last rounds were fired from the Yorktown batteries and the guns were spiked, and then with his staff and couriers rode away in the darkness toward Williamsburg.[6]

It had been raining hard, and the four divisions of Johnston's army crawled through deep mud. At Williamsburg, where they halted temporarily on May 4, the pursuing Federals caught up with them. Skirmishing began that afternoon, and the following day the fighting developed into a battle, with the Confederate rear guard, commanded by Longstreet, defending a line of fieldworks that Magruder had previously constructed just below the town. Running roughly east–west, the line consisted of a series of redoubts and rifle pits, and a central earthwork, Fort Magruder. It was anything but a strong defense position; and as the pressure of the Union attacks increased, Longstreet called for reinforcements that included Hill's division, while Johnston rode back from the van of his retreating army to observe the fighting.[7]

It was a battle marked by strange errors. Somehow, in their unfamiliarity with Magruder's fieldworks, Longstreet, Johnston, and their subordinates on the Confederate left failed to station troops in two redoubts on the east end of the defense line. About noon, Union General Winfield Scott Hancock took possession of these redoubts with two batteries, totaling ten guns, and approximately five regiments of infantry. Advancing west, he posted his guns and troops alongside and in front of the westernmost of the two redoubts, leaving a garrison in the one behind him. Although all this took place near the crest of an open, slanting plain, down which Hancock could look all the way to Fort Magruder, for some reason —perhaps the misty weather together with the smoke and confusion of intervening fighting—the Confederate commanders at the fort remained unaware of what he was doing.

Neither did Hancock's superiors grasp the opportunity his advance offered them. When he drove Confederate troops out of redoubts ahead of him and called for reinforcements to enable him to move forward again, he received instead orders to retire to his rear redoubt. But he stayed where he was, renewing his requests for reinforcements and opening fire on Fort Magruder.[8]

The shelling of the fort brought him to the attention of Hill's brigadier, Jubal Early. Approaching his commander while Hill waited on the left to see whether Longstreet would need his division, Early suggested that he be allowed to lead his four regiments against the enemy battery. Neither he nor Hill had any idea that the supposed battery was really Hancock's force. From their position they could not see the guns, only hear them. What caught their eye was a strip of dense woods to the north of that booming echo. Why not bypass the battery under cover of the woods and take the guns from the rear? This was the plan agreed upon, after they had hurriedly reconnoitered the ground immediately ahead and conferred with Johnston and Longstreet. Johnston enjoined caution in the attack and Longstreet directed Hill to help Early lead the brigade.[9]

The decision made, Hill and Early acted quickly, for it was approaching five o'clock. Under a sky heavy with dark rainclouds they deployed Early's brigade in a single battle line facing east toward the sound of the enemy guns. Hill led the right wing, composed of the Twenty-third and the Fifth North Carolina regiments; Early took charge of the left, comprising the Twenty-fourth and the Thirty-eighth Virginia regiments. Early, in his middle forties, was lean, long-bearded, badly stooped with Mexican War rheumatism, and full of the fire of battle. Hunched in the saddle in front of his men he warned them that the safest way to capture guns was to charge hard and fast. Then Hill gave the order and the brigade moved forward.[10]

Hill led his wing across a small stream and into the woods where the undergrowth shut out all view of Early's troops, and then halted his men with the intention of realigning the whole brigade. But Early plunged impetuously ahead without stopping. Leaving behind both Hill and his own Thirty-eighth Virginia, he swung south through the woods with the Twenty-fourth Virginia, burst into the open plain in front of Hancock's guns, pivoted the regiment left to face the enemy, and rode to the charge shouting, "Follow me!"

Hancock, seeing the charge shaping up at a distance of about one hundred yards, began complying with the order to retreat that he had previously received. As his artillery and men fell back toward the redoubt to the rear, the men of the Twenty-fourth Virginia took the movement for a rout, and rushed forward with taunting cries of "Bull Run!" But it was a fighting retreat; bullets cut through the Confederate ranks. One struck Early—a mere scratch, he noted—and then a Minié ball slammed against his shoulder like a sledgehammer and plowed a furrow of fire across his back. He stayed in the saddle but the pain almost paralyzed him, and soon he began to feel faint from loss of blood. Then he saw that his horse had been wounded too. There was no help for it, he would have to quit. With difficulty he reined his mount around and rode to the rear.[11]

Hill, meanwhile, had heard the uproar of the attack and had reached the edge of the woods, at a point where he was still unable to see what was happening. But soon one of Early's aides rode up with a request for reinforcements, and about the same time Major P. J. Sinclair of the Fifth North Carolina arrived with a message from the regimental commander, Colonel D. K. McRae. The Twenty-fourth Virginia was attacking the battery, said the major. Could the Fifth North Carolina join in the assault?

To Hill's trained military mind the word "battery" conveyed an image of unsupported artillery arrayed in the open field. He regretted that Early had left the protection of the woods, but thought that the best thing to do now was to support him. Yes, charge, he told the major, and do it quickly.[12]

Then, to protect McRae from flanking fire by Federal skirmishers in the woods, he rode back into it and found the two other regiments, the Thirty-eighth Virginia and the Twenty-third North Carolina, and sent them on an eastward sweep against the enemy marksmen in the timber and tangled underbrush. When he got back to the open he saw the tough mountaineers who made up the Twenty-fourth Virginia pressing forward along the edge of the woods through a wide, boggy wheat field, with the enemy retreating slowly before them. Off to the right, McRae's line was moving up as fast as the men could flounder through the green wheat, which reached half-way to their knees.

And now for the first time Hill could see the objective of the attack—and his eyes started wide with horror. Why, that was not just a battery! It was a brigade at least, and those guns and long blue lines on the crest of the slope were forming around one of Magruder's redoubts. A *battery!* My God—it was a death trap!

But it was too late to stop the charge. On went those thin, separate lines of Southern gallantry, through increasing infantry and artillery fire, past a cluster of farm buildings and up the long slope, converging at last behind a rail fence scarcely thirty yards from the enemy. At that point they faltered. Both regiments were being cut to pieces. McRae had sent his adjutant back to Hill asking for reinforcements, but, realizing that his position was "fatally destructive," as he later reported, he called off the charge without waiting for Hill's reply and ordered his men to take what cover they could behind the fence.

Hill, when McRae's adjutant reached him, was trying to push his other troops on through the woods to the rear of the Federal position and to prod the Sixth South Carolina regiment, which had come up from a Confederate redoubt, into charging the enemy flank under the crest of the slope. But seeing the attack stop at the fence he abandoned these efforts and sent back word to retreat. The order was promptly obeyed by the Virginians. Led by Major R. L. Maury, their one remaining field officer, they obliqued quickly into the woods on their left with small additional loss.

But now McRae's troops, alone before the enemy, caught the full force of the Union counterattack as they scrambled back into formation and retreated over a longer distance. Hancock advanced his infantrymen to the crest, where they fired two deliberate volleys at the helpless Carolinians. "The regiment was shot down like beeves," said Hill afterward, "the Yankees cheering and laughing as they fired at the poor fellows." The horror of that scene remained with him as long as he lived.[13]

When it was all over, casualties in Early's brigade were found to run at least as high as six hundred. It was poor consolation to know that the line at Williamsburg had been successfully defended, so that the battle could be claimed as a Southern victory. Total Federal losses that day were 2,239, as compared with Southern casualties of 1,560. But of the Confederate losses the attack against Hancock accounted for fully 38 per cent.[14]

Neither in official reports nor in postwar letters and publications did the officers involved in this costly assault agree as to how it had been initiated or why it failed. Hill stated in his report that Early had gone to Longstreet and obtained approval for the attack. Early reported that it was Hill who had obtained Longstreet's approval, and added many years later, in his autobiography, that he himself had first suggested the assault.

Longstreet in his report simply said that the movement was made and that Hill "was ordered to watch it. . . ." After the war, when he was at odds with Early over Gettysburg, Longstreet asserted in his memoirs that Hill had asked him to approve the attack, that he had opposed it because Early's brigade was "not in safe hands," and had given permission only on the condition that Hill go along to see that the troops were "properly handled." Johnston did not report the assault, but in his postwar *Narrative of Military Operations* he wrote that Early had sent to Longstreet for permission to make it, and that when Longstreet referred the message to him he approved the movement. The one thing that seems to emerge fairly clearly from all the conflicting testimony is that each of these officers, in one way or another, sanctioned the attack.[15]

Obviously the disastrous movement might never have taken place if the two redoubts that Hancock occupied had not been left vacant, or if his advance had been noted and properly opposed, or if Hill and Early had made a thorough reconnaissance before setting out to capture the supposed battery. Although Hill admitted in his report that he did not ascertain in advance the exact location of the enemy artillery, he emphasized his understanding with Longstreet that the movement was to be made through the woods to the Federal rear and his regret that Early had abandoned this plan. Longstreet laid the blame for failure on Early, very circumspectly in his report and very completely in his memoirs. Johnston's terse *Narrative* also made Early the chief architect of defeat.[16]

But Early maintained, in his report, in long postwar letters to Johnston and Jefferson Davis, and somewhat more cautiously in his autobiography, that the Twenty-fourth Virginia and the Fifth North Carolina routed Hancock's force and would have achieved complete victory had Hill sent reinforcements instead of ordering a retreat. Maury and McRae advanced similar arguments in historical papers published after the war, McRae apparently forgetting what he had written in his official report.[17]

The idea of a Union rout and a lost victory seems hard to accept in the light of all the evidence. Even in his historical paper McRae spoke of the "great precision" with which the Federals retired their guns, and the Federal reports state that Hancock withdrew to his rear redoubt, waited until the assault of the two regiments against his five broke under his artillery and infantry fire, and then counterattacked with deadly effect. All this supports Hill's contention, in a letter of 1866 to McRae: "I thought then and think now that aid sent to you would but have caused additional slaughter." [18]

Though Hill and Early held each other responsible for the failure against Hancock, both were discreet about making their views known, and they remained firm friends throughout the war and after. Early spent the days immediately following the battle in a hospital convalescing from his wound. Hill again had the unpleasant duty of rear guard in the continuing retreat of Johnston's army. He and Longstreet marched their divisions out of Williamsburg on May 6. Many of their men had found shelter from a rainstorm of the previous night in barns and outhouses, and driving them out into the mud to resume the march bordered on the impossible. Cold, dirty, hungry, and battle-worn, they answered Hill's orders with curses. Some fifteen hundred of them threw away their knapsacks and guns and straggled far in the rear of the main body of troops, slogging wearily through slush that oozed over their shoetops and made going difficult even for the horses. When Hill entreated them to march faster, lest they be captured by the pursuing enemy, they retorted: "I don't care if the Yankees do take me." Many of them fell prisoner to the Federal cavalry.[19]

Hill himself was suffering in the cold wet weather from chills, dysentery, and piles. "My bowels pained me so much that at times I was almost in despair," he said afterward. But constantly he rode up and down the marching column, trying to keep it closed up.

Once he came upon two surgeons in the act of abandoning an ambulance, heavily loaded with medical supplies, which was stalled in the mud. Hearing that the Federal cavalry was near, the frightened doctors had unhitched the horses and were about to ride off when Hill arrived. He ordered them to save their medical supplies—to hitch up again, take hold of the wheels of the ambulance, and push. They refused. Hill then hailed two of his cavalrymen, and ordered each man to tie a surgeon to his horse's tail and make him walk. As the order was being carried out the unhappy medical officers pleaded that because of the rain and the overcoat Hill was wearing they had not recognized him as their general. Given another opportunity, they pushed the ambulance out of the mud.[20]

Hill rode on, wrestling with the pain that stabbed through him. If it began in the spine you endured it as long as you could, and then sometimes you had to lie down. He had learned that in his boyhood....

II

WHENCE THE WARRIOR

For the boy Harvey, one of the intimate realities of life was pain; he had come to expect and accept it. Possibly it was poliomyelitis; the exact nature and time of the illness are not known, though in later years Hill sometimes made brief references to it in his letters. "I had a spell of sickness in my boyhood, which left me with a weak and suffering spine," he wrote on one occasion. And on another: "I have a very feeble frame and have been a great sufferer from boyhood." Whatever the nature of the disease, it permanently impaired his health but did not keep him from leading an active life. In fact he usually felt best when engaged in outdoor activity that involved vigorous exercise.[1]

As a boy he did hard farm work, for only four years after his birth on the family plantation in York District, South Carolina, July 12, 1821, his father, Solomon, died leaving the mother, Nancy, with debts that reduced the Hill estate to a relatively small tract of land. Harvey was the youngest of eleven children, of whom five boys and three girls lived to be of age. They grew up in genteel poverty; the thin red soil of that hilly region just below the North Carolina border did not produce abundant crops of corn and cotton.[2]

Both Nancy and Harvey Hill looked back joylessly upon the period of his formative years. "I have been a child of sorrow and anxiety," said the mother. Hill said, "I had no youth."

He remembered Nancy Hill as a loving mother, but one of fluctuating moods. She treated him with alternate tenderness and harshness, and to this he was inclined to attribute "many of the dark traits"

16

that he saw in his own character. "I had always a strong perception of right and wrong," he reflected, "and when corrected from petulance or passion, I brooded over it, did not forget it, and I am afraid did not forgive it." [3]

In the Hill household, where the oldest child, William Randolph, filled the role of father, and in so doing earned the lifelong admiration of Harvey, the watchwords through the week were honor, honesty, and piety, and the Sabbath was kept holy in both the spirit and the Presbyterian letter of the law. Hill's brother John, destined to be known as the "wild son," often declared in middle age that as a boy he invariably "took the blues on Thursday morning because Sunday was coming." Each boy in his turn was required to select from the Bible a prayer to read at breakfast to the assembled family, and John sometimes sent young Harvey into fits of laughter by reading the shortest verse he could find, regardless of how absurd it might sound to intone over the meal, "Jesus wept." [4]

Still the early religious training that Hill received went deep; he regarded his mother's teachings and example as the first source of the unquestioning faith that guided his mature life. Not until he was twenty-two did he join the Presbyterian church, but after that he became a ruling elder and an outstanding religious layman in the South. During the Civil War no other general—not even Stonewall Jackson—went into combat with a firmer faith in God.

Almost as strong in the Hill family as Presbyterianism was the Scotch tradition of education. College training had been provided for the older boys in more prosperous times, but for Harvey the only recourse seemed to be the free college degree offered by the United States Military Academy at West Point. No doubt he was also influenced in his decision to try for West Point by the family military tradition. In the American Revolution his paternal grandfather, William Hill, a well-known ironmaster and state political leader, had served with distinction as a lieutenant colonel of militia under General Thomas Sumter, and his maternal grandfather, Thomas Cabeen, had earned a reputation for extraordinary bravery as one of Sumter's scouts. In addition, two uncles on his father's side had been soldiers, one as an Indian fighter under Andrew Jackson and the other as adjutant general to General Arthur Hayne in the War of 1812.[5]

Hill applied for the Academy in 1838, being recommended for appointment by his Congressman, W. K. Clowney, and on June 1 he was admitted as a cadet. That he could be accepted despite his weak spine is an interesting commentary on the medical standards of the day. During his first year he suffered frequent illness, but then attained what he hoped was permanent good health, with the result that his grades rose from the lower to the middle bracket of the class standings. Through his years at West Point he made his highest marks in French, philosophy and ethics, the physical sciences, and infantry tactics, and his lowest in drawing, mathematics, English grammar, and engineering.

On July 1, 1842, he was graduated Number 28 in a class of 56 that teemed with future Civil War generals. Those who would gain the greatest fame were, in order of class rank, John Newton, William S. Rosecrans, Gustavus W. Smith, Mansfield Lovell, Alexander P. Stewart, Martin L. Smith, John Pope, Seth Williams, Abner Doubleday, Hill, George Sykes, Richard H. Anderson, Lafayette McLaws, Earl Van Dorn, and James Longstreet, who ranked a lowly 54.[6]

With Longstreet, Hill did not form a close friendship. Yet he seems to have made a number of friends at West Point, although to at least one cadet he appeared to be unsociable—morose at worst and at best coldly polite. His circle included Stewart, McLaws, and John D. Clark, a roommate of his plebe year, of whom he later said, "I could never meet him without a warm gush of feeling." He also liked George Sykes, who would fight against him in the battle of Gaines' Mill; he found Sykes an agreeable social companion, and admired him, as he said, for his "honor, courage, and frankness." [7]

These three qualities were dominant in Hill himself, and had been reinforced by Academy training. Especially did Hill, like many another West Pointer, value his professional honor. In combat, he would place it above his life, and fiercely would he defend it, at all times, against the slightest aspersion.

One other trait the Academy had instilled in him—patriotic pride in the United States, but not in sufficient quantity to outweigh his Southern nationalism. As a boy in South Carolina he had listened to endless stories of how Grandfather Hill and other Southerners had won the Revolutionary War, and of how Senator John C. Calhoun, whose father had been an intimate friend of Grandfather Hill, was defending states' rights against the Northerners; he had grown up in the unalterable conviction that within the larger nation Southern manhood was the bravest, Southern civilization the finest.

As part of this civilization he accepted the institution of Negro slavery. By the 1840s his mother and older brothers owned slaves, and he himself owned at least one young man, who worked on the home estate, read his Bible every day, and sent his love to "his dear Master Harvey," begging him to remember "poor Elias Frank . . . a poor low creature." [8]

Like Lee, then—like Johnston, Jackson, Longstreet, and so many other Southerners—he stepped from West Point into the United States Army with genuine loyalty for the flag he served, but with a stronger loyalty, not to become fully apparent until the Civil War, for the land of his birth and upbringing. A little more than a month after his graduation he accepted appointment as a brevet second lieutenant in the First Artillery and began several years of routine service in army posts up and down the coast from Fort Kent, Maine, to Savannah and Charleston. August of 1845 found him in Company E, Third Artillery, of General Zachary Taylor's command in Corpus Christi, Texas, where war was brewing between the United States and Mexico. [9]

At Corpus Christi Hill dined regularly in the officers' mess with his company commander, First Lieutenant Braxton Bragg, and the other two company officers, Lieutenants George H. Thomas and John F. Reynolds. All of the four were destined to become generals in the Civil War. Reynolds, Hill's tentmate and good friend, would fall prisoner to Hill in the Seven Days' battles; Thomas, who in Corpus Christi appeared to Hill to be "the strongest and most pronounced Southerner" of the four, would fight for the Union against Hill and Bragg at Chickamauga; and in a final strange interweaving of fate Bragg and Hill would become bitter personal enemies. [10]

Hill stayed in Texas just long enough to get an appalling first-hand view of the official blunders that beset Taylor's expedition. In January, 1846, he was promoted from brevet to full second lieutenant and sent back to Fort Monroe, Virginia, to fill a regimental vacancy in the Fourth Artillery. Here he wrote a scathing indictment of "the ignorance and imbecility of the War Department" that had caused so much suffering among the poorly supplied and equipped troops at Corpus Christi, and published it in the *Southern Quarterly Review* of April, 1846, under the heading, "The Army in Texas," by "H. S. Foote, Esq."

Historians have recognized the authenticity of this exposé and have cited it as a historical source without the obvious pseudonym. Justin H. Smith, who used it in his *War with Mexico*, suggested that it had probably been written by Bragg. The editor of the *Review*, Daniel K. Whitaker, stated privately that Hill wrote it, and that it produced a "profound sensation ... throughout the whole South and Southwest." [11]

It might also have produced a court-martial for the brash young author, had his identity become known; but his army career was not affected by what he had written, and in June, 1846, about a month after the start of open war between the United States and Mexico, he was sent back to Taylor with the Fourth Artillery to take part in Taylor's expedition against Monterrey. When in August he entered Mexico by river steamer, it was for the duration of the war. [12]

Throughout the war his regiment served as infantry, and only occasionally did he get to command gun batteries, but when the assault columns were formed he usually found a place in the lead. Under Taylor he helped to capture Monterrey. Under General Winfield Scott he fought at Vera Cruz, Cerro Gordo, Padierna (Contreras), and Chapultepec. For gallantry in leading a storming party at Padierna he was breveted captain, and for a similar exploit in the capture of Chapultepec, a fortress guarding Mexico City, he received the brevet rank of major. [13]

During the campaign against the City, Hill displayed to the full his fiery, reckless combativeness. Once while on reconnaissance he received two simultaneous and conflicting messages, one from his brigade commander ordering him to withdraw, the other, ordering him not to, from General Gideon J. Pillow, a military amateur who owed his high rank to his former law partner and political chieftain, President James K. Polk. Not knowing that Pillow had assumed command of his brigade in his absence, and thinking the political general was simply blundering again, Hill obeyed the order of his veteran colonel. On learning this, Pillow stood the young lieutenant before him and upbraided him in words that Hill considered "harsh and insulting."

The reaction was instantaneous. Hill drew his sword, shook it in the astonished general's face, and "forbade him," as he later put it, "to use such language again." Pillow placed him under arrest, but when his colonel promptly interceded he was released, and Pillow retracted the offensive language.[14]

Shortly after this, in the assault on Chapultepec, the volunteer storming party that Hill was helping to lead was temporarily pinned down in a roadside ditch by fire from enemy breastworks. Suddenly everyone's attention was riveted upon an Irish soldier from South Carolina's Palmetto Regiment who had gone berserk; he was standing in the road, in an advanced, exposed position, alternately cursing and shaking his fist at the Mexicans and trying to fire his musket, which kept snapping ludicrously upon a defective flint. As applause and shouts of laughter broke out among the troops, Hill stepped out into the storm of bullets singing around the fighting Irishman. Clapping him on the back he gave a hurrah for South Carolina. Then he helped him change the flint and fire a satisfying shot at the enemy.[15]

The fall of Chapultepec followed, giving Hill an opportunity for one more exploit. While the American troops that had closed in from three sides were crying "No quarter!" and shooting down unresisting Mexicans trying to drop from the walls or creep off through water passages—a spectacle that Hill termed "horrible in the extreme"—other enemy forces were streaming away from the fortress toward Mexico City. After them in hot haste went Hill, leading a handful of storm troopers. Up the Veronica causeway toward the San Cosme gate to the City they raced, leaving all support behind, driving the panicky Mexicans ahead of them by sheer audacity. Hill experienced what he called "a sublime and exalted feeling . . . chasing some five thousand men with little more than a dozen."

For more than a mile he and his men pursued alone. Then Lieutenant Barnard Bee overtook them with a small detachment of his own, and up galloped Lieutenant Thomas J. Jackson with two field guns, followed by his battery commander, Captain John B. Magruder. These reinforcements arrived just in time, for shortly afterward about fifteen hundred Mexican lancers came thundering down the causeway. Jackson opened fire with his guns, and the Mexican horsemen, unable to maneuver in the confines of the road, drew rein and retreated.[16]

Although the capture of the City, which took place the next day, spelled final defeat for Mexico, Hill had to remain in that country nearly six months longer, and did not get back to the United

States until March of 1848. He returned with the regular rank of first lieutenant, though his brevets gave him the title of major; and bitterness swept over him every time he thought of how volunteer officers without military training had been given high rank in the war, while volunteer troops received newspaper credit for fighting done by the regulars, whom President Polk referred to contemptuously as "hireling soldiers."

This feeling, plus shocked outrage over the way undisciplined volunteers wreaked robbery and rapine upon the Mexican people, had led him while in Mexico to write three slashing essays for the Charleston *Mercury*. Published in that newspaper in October and November, 1846, and February, 1847, over the signature "AN ACTOR," they flayed lawless volunteers, the volunteer system, and "mob-courting miscreants" like President Polk. Of course Hill was again risking court-martial, but again he went unscathed. For good measure, when he got back to the United States he fired one more round at the War Department in the form of another article in the *Southern Quarterly Review* entitled "The Army in Texas—No. 2," and signed this time by the single initial, "H." [17]

Professionally, his service in Mexico had not only enhanced his army reputation but had also given meaning to his West Point studies of military strategy and tactics. Under Scott he had seen the uses of entrenchments, concentration of force, massed artillery, the daring attack, and the turning movement. He would not forget these lessons in the Civil War.

Nor was war all that he had learned in Mexico. He had made friends among the people, had tried, despite his sharp Protestant disapproval, to understand their religion, and had seriously studied their literature and their language—this last with the aid of watchfully chaperoned señoritas, for like other young men of the army he had a keen eye for a pretty face behind a window grating. His most intense romance was with Mariana Ramos, beautiful daughter of the *alcalde* of Saltillo. She was betrothed and not allowed even to speak to him, but she did not mind exchanging glances, in church and from her room window, that caused him to record in his war diary how many times a day he had seen or silently bowed to her —his "little Bonita." When duty took him away from Saltillo, and he could not even tell her good-bye, he sighed, "So ends this farce. I have seldom been so much in love...." [18]

While on leave after his return to the United States, he met another brunette beauty who may have awakened haunting memories of Mexico. Isabella Morrison was the oldest daughter of the Reverend Robert Hall Morrison, a widely known Presbyterian church leader who was living in semiretirement at his farm residence, "Cottage Home," in Lincoln County, North Carolina. In the spring of 1848 Hill paid an extended visit to a married sister who lived near Cottage Home, and was introduced to the Morrisons and their numerous sons and daughters, including the charming Isabella.

Not only her sparkling brown eyes and vivacious manner appealed to Hill, but also her intelligence and her Presbyterian piety. Born January 28, 1825, at Fayetteville, North Carolina, and educated at the Salem Female Academy, she was a Southern belle who had enjoyed unusual social advantages. Her mother, Mary Graham Morrison, was the sister of William A. Graham, governor of North Carolina, and her uncle had introduced her to society at the executive mansion in Raleigh.[19]

Although his mother feared that Isabella might be a "proud, haughty girl," Hill courted her and they became engaged. They were married at Cottage Home, November 2, 1848, by the Reverend J. M. Anderson. Hill had two best men, the brothers John and Lardner Gibbon. Doubtless he would not have selected John had he known that his friend would become a Union general and march against him at South Mountain.[20]

At the time of his marriage Hill resigned from the army. His reasons were slow promotion, the boredom of peacetime service, and a reluctance to subject Isabella to the hardships of army life. "I cannot contemplate without horror her entrance into one of our wretched garrisons," he said.[21]

His resignation became effective February 28, 1849, by which time he had begun a new career as a college teacher. From December, 1848, to 1854 he taught mathematics at Washington College, Virginia, later to become Washington and Lee University, and from 1854 to 1859 he held the mathematics chair at Davidson College, North Carolina. At both of these small liberal-arts colleges his salary was low, hardly keeping pace with his growing family, but his prestige was high; he made a reputation as a strict disciplinarian and an excellent teacher, capable of eliciting the best from his students.[22]

At Davidson, a Presbyterian church college not far north of

Charlotte, he was the strong man of the faculty. The trustees employed him for the specific purposes of raising academic standards and tightening discipline, which under the presidency of the Reverend Samuel Williamson was an easygoing system punctuated by pistol shooting and rioting among the students. Hill accomplished both objectives, though not without difficulty. A power struggle quickly developed between him and Williamson, resulting in the ouster of the president. Then on the eve of the Christmas holidays, 1854, Hill personally quelled a riot by rushing into a mob of rock-throwing students with his Mexican War sword upraised. Next, when he and his colleagues convicted one young man of leading the riot, and suspended him, the other students protested that the evidence of guilt was inadequate, and went out on a protracted strike that virtually emptied the college classrooms.

But Hill weathered this campus tempest, aided by a rich legacy to Davidson from a wealthy Presbyterian merchant who had advocated strong discipline, and from then on his rule went unchallenged. A new college president, the Reverend Drury Lacy, came in after the riot, but it was Hill who continued to be recognized as the guiding force at Davidson.

"I learned from the boys at College that he [Hill] was the 'controlling spirit' in the institution, and afterwards by personal contact in the classroom that he was worthy to control," said one student who entered Davidson in 1858. Another remembered that Hill's "unsought primacy" was so completely "accepted by the faculty and students" that it "excited surprise and elicited comment from strangers." [23]

During these college years Hill formed friendships with two men who were to be closely associated with him in the Confederate service. One was J. W. Ratchford, a student at Davidson who would become his assistant adjutant general, or chief of staff. The other was Thomas J. Jackson, the future "Stonewall" of the South, who would be his commanding officer.

It was in Mexico, just before the Vera Cruz expedition, that Hill had first met Jackson, a rookie lieutenant from West Point with stiff manners and burning blue eyes, and had heard him say, "I want to be in one battle." Next he had fought alongside him in the brief engagement with the Mexican lancers before Mexico City, and then had lost touch with him. They renewed their acquaintance in the summer of 1851, when Jackson, having resigned from the army, began teaching at the Virginia Military Institute in Lexington.

Jackson owed his position at VMI largely to Hill, who had first recommended him for it, and he looked up to the older man as his mentor. When he confided in his earnest way that he was a religious seeker, Hill helped guide him into the Presbyterian church. When he began keeping company with Miss Elinor Junkin, who would become his wife, and naively asked Hill why her face, which he had once thought plain, now seemed to him "all sweetness," Hill laughingly explained that this was a common phenomenon known as love. For such counsel Jackson was grateful, and he did what he could to repay his friend. On one occasion he wrote Pillow, under whom he had served, asking him to furnish Hill with a statement that would clear his military record from any stigma that might arise from Pillow's arrest of him in Mexico. Apparently Pillow did not reply. On another occasion, Hill's little daughter, Eugenia, was dangerously ill with pneumonia, and in an effort to help her sleep Hill and Isabella had walked the floor with her until they were exhausted. One night there came a knock at the door. It was Jackson. Could he nurse the child while they got some rest? Gratefully the weary parents assented. He took Eugenia in his arms and began a measured pacing. All night he walked and prayed that she would get well, and she did.[24]

When Hill moved to Davidson his close association with Jackson was temporarily broken, but in July, 1857, they became brothers-in-law. Jackson's first wife, Elinor, had died, and he now married Isabella's younger sister, Mary Anna, whom he had known as a friend in Hill's home in Lexington. The Hills attended the wedding on July 16 at Cottage Home. Before the ceremony, a minor crisis arose when a slave who had been given Jackson's dress trousers to press brought them back to him beautifully creased the wrong way. Isabella came to the rescue by reironing the trousers.[25]

With the marriage, the lives of Hill and Jackson began once more to run parallel. Soon both would be Confederate officers, and on another July day, in 1861, Hill would write Isabella, with reference to Anna and herself: "If preachers' daughters fancy military men, they must expect all the uneasiness and anxiety incident to a state of war." [26]

The years 1857 to 1859 comprised a productive literary period in

Hill's life. In each year he published one book, first a textbook on college algebra and then two religious studies, A *Consideration of the Sermon on the Mount*, and *The Crucifixion of Christ*. None of these created any stir in the scholarly world, though the *Crucifixion* did go through a second edition. Both religious works, published by William S. and Alfred Martien of Philadelphia, revealed Hill's clear, forceful writing style and his erudition, his thorough knowledge of the Bible and Biblical criticism, his ability to utilize Latin, Greek, and Hebrew, and his familiarity with standard works of the time in history, belles-lettres, science, philosophy, and law. The *Elements of Algebra*, published by J. B. Lippincott and Company, showed Hill's mastery of his subject through the calculus, and also his Southern nationalism, which took the form of anti-Northern propaganda worked with sardonic humor into a number of the algebraic problems. For example:

The field of battle at Buena Vista is $6\frac{1}{2}$ miles from Saltillo. Two Indiana volunteers ran away from the field of battle at the same time; one ran half a mile per hour faster than the other, and reached Saltillo 5 minutes and $54\frac{6}{11}$ seconds sooner than the other. Required their respective rates of travel.

With similar ingenuity Hill managed to call attention in other problems to New England "treason" during the War of 1812, to the enslavement of the Pequot Indians in Connecticut, to the witchcraft persecutions in Massachusetts, and to the number of insane persons in New England and New York in a given year. He also gave data about Yankee traders who adulterated meat and milk, and about the accident rate on Northern-owned railroads. In contrast, Southerners in his problems invariably appeared in a favorable light. Doubtless the strong Southern bias of the book helped account for its limited sales. A friend warned Hill of this possibility, pointing out that Northern readers might well resent the slanted problems. Hill received the criticism pleasantly, but replied that he did not care.[27]

His attitude was typical of Southern intellectuals of the time, who had come to regard the South as an embattled nation, forced constantly to defend its agrarian way of life and its peculiar institution, slavery, against Northern criticism and political power. Hill felt that the growing hostility between North and South might eventually result in civil war, and he suggested as much in his *Sermon on the Mount.* So thinking, he gave his enthusiastic support to an accelerating movement for the establishment of military academies in the Southern states. For Southern strength, and if need be for Southern defense, more and more "West Points of the South." This was the concept, and Hill was one educator who helped to spread it. He longed to establish a Southern West Point in North Carolina.[28]

In 1858 he began to fulfill this desire. A group of influential men in Charlotte, led by Dr. Charles J. Fox, decided to found a military academy in that city, and asked both Hill and Jackson to undertake the project. Jackson preferred to remain at VMI, but Hill accepted the offer. Resigning from the Davidson College faculty, to the accompaniment of laudatory resolutions from his colleagues and the trustees, he moved to Charlotte and built an attractive two-story brick house at the corner of South Brevard and Liberty streets, conveniently near the site of the new North Carolina Military Institute.[29]

Fox and his associates incorporated the Institute with a capital stock of $75,000, and raised money by selling the stock in $50 shares. With the funds so realized they built, on a rise of land about half a mile from town, a three-story brick building designed by Hill in the West Point style. Everything else about the Institute was also modeled on West Point—the curriculum, the grading and demerit system, and the uniforms of the cadets. Hill served as superintendent, professor of mathematics and artillery, and president of the board of directors. The Institute opened its doors on October 1, 1859, with sixty cadets and three faculty members. Before it was eclipsed by the war, its faculty had increased to six and its student enrollment to more than one hundred and forty, with representatives from nearly every Southern state.[30]

When the war began, it was only a question of time until Hill, the rest of the teaching staff, and virtually all the cadets of military age were in the Confederate service. Throughout the South there was much boasting about licking the Yankees overnight, but Hill took up his sword in a sober mood. He had already warned his cadets that the North had superior military resources "both in men and means," and he foresaw a long and bloody conflict.[31]

His first duty was in the state service. On April 24, 1861, Governor John W. Ellis appointed him a colonel of North Carolina volunteers and put him in charge of a volunteer training camp near Raleigh. On May 11 he was elected colonel of the newly organized First Regiment of North Carolina Volunteers, a combat infantry unit, and early June found him with his men at Big Bethel Church, south of Yorktown, guarding entrenchments that he had devised as protection against Federal forces striking up the Peninsula from Fort Monroe at the tip.[32]

His commanding officer at Bethel was a comrade-in-arms of the Mexican War, John B. Magruder, now a colonel of Virginia volunteers in charge of defenses in the lower Peninsula. The theatrical Virginian, known as "Prince John" to his acquaintances, ranked low in the estimate of Hill, who on May 30 had written Isabella from Yorktown: "Col Magruder in command is always drunk and giving foolish and absurd orders. I think that in a few days the men will refuse to obey any order issued by him." Outwardly, however, no friction marred the cooperation of the two colonels at Bethel.[33]

Their troops numbered about fourteen hundred, consisting of Hill's well-trained regiment and about six hundred Virginians, including an artillery battalion of seven guns and a small company of cavalry. Moving to attack them were more than four thousand Federals under the over-all command of Major General Benjamin F. Butler. Magruder did not know the strength or whereabouts of the enemy, and apparently in an effort to find out he ordered his troops out of their entrenchments at 3 A.M. June 10, and sent them off under Hill's command along a road leading toward Fort Monroe. As J. W. Ratchford, who was serving as aide-de-camp to Hill, later said, it looked "as if Magruder was only sending us down to the vicinity of the fort as a dare to General B. F. Butler.... He no doubt thought we would have sense enough to get out of his way. I never heard of any order from Magruder instructing us how far to go, when we should turn back or whether or not we should capture the fortress, and I do not believe he gave any from what I heard Colonel Hill say and I was near him all the time." [34]

The uneasy march continued for a little more than three miles. Then Hill learned from a local resident that the Federals were just ahead of him in superior strength. Immediately he fell back to his entrenchments, and there beat off a number of inept Federal attacks in what came to be called the battle of Big Bethel, the first land battle of the war.

It lasted from about 9 A.M. to 1 P.M., costing the Federals 76 casualties, with 18 killed, out of about 4,400 men engaged, while the Confederates lost one man killed and 10 wounded. At one point in the fighting, when a thrust against the Confederate right was threatening to become dangerous, Hill encouraged his inexperienced troops with a bit of swashbuckling.

"Boys, you have learned to dodge already. I am an old hand at it," he called cheerfully to men who were falling back under enemy musketry and shellfire. So saying he ducked away from a whining projectile. Then, triumphantly, he shook his finger at the enemy. "You dogs! You missed me that time." [35]

The final Union assault resulted in the attackers being pinned down, with only partial cover, under the musket fire of Hill's regiment. Hill and two of his field officers supervised the shooting, giving individual men permission to fire when a good target offered. And targets, not fellow human beings, the bluecoats were to the excited young men behind the breastworks. "May I fire?" they would call out. "I think I can bring him." As Hill commented afterward, "They were all in high glee, and seemed to enjoy it as much as boys do rabbit-shooting." [36]

This was Hill speaking in his professional military role. The religious side of his nature appeared in the letters he wrote to Isabella after the battle. "I have to thank God for a great and decided Victory, and that I escaped with a slight contusion on the knee," he said in one. And in another: "It is a little singular that my first battle in this war should be at *Bethel*, the name of the church where I was baptised and worshipped until 16 years old. The Church of my Mother, was she not a guardian spirit in the battle averting the ball and the shell. Oh God give us gratitude to Thee and may we never dishonor Thee by a weak faith." [37]

From the Union point of view, the battle could only be called a blunder. In the North it created a newspaper furor that almost caused Butler to lose his confirmation as major general. In the South it made a hero of Hill, and also of Magruder, who as the over-all commander had given a few battle orders, while allowing Hill to control most of the fighting. Both officers were rewarded with promotions to brigadier general in the Provisional Army of the Confederate States. The effective date of Hill's new rank was July 10.[38]

There followed for Hill a series of administrative posts that were little to his liking. First, through the summer of 1861, he commanded at Yorktown under Magruder. Then late in September he was assigned to the District of the Pamlico, in North Carolina, where he spent about six weeks strengthening coastal defenses. Finally in November he was given command of a North Carolina brigade and stationed at Leesburg, in Joseph E. Johnston's Department of Northern Virginia.[39]

Shortly after arriving at Leesburg he added to his growing reputation as a general who seemed to consider himself shellproof. Across the Potomac River from his headquarters the Federals had a concentration of artillery, and he wanted to learn the type, caliber, and number of these guns. One day he placed himself at the head of a large escort and rode up and down the riverbank until the inviting target drew the fire of the Union batteries. The shrieking shells bursting all about soon made the members of the makeshift staff uncomfortable in the extreme, but Hill was too preoccupied to notice. He was down from his horse and busy with pick and shovel, digging a buried shell out of the riverbank for examination.[40]

His cavalry commander that winter was a rollicking young brigadier who also liked danger—James Ewell Brown Stuart, better known as "Jeb." Stuart's performance, in Hill's opinion, was not entirely satisfactory. In December, after Stuart had lost 194 men in an engagement with Federal forces at Dranesville, Hill wrote him: "From what I have been able to learn, the enemy knew your strength and destination before you started. . . . I would therefore respectfully suggest that when you start again, you should disguise your strength and give out a different locality from that actually taken." The letter ended, "Excuse the liberty I take, and believe me your sincere well wisher and friend."

It was the mildest of rebukes, but soon Hill became more dissatisfied with Stuart and wrote a sharper criticism of him that went through Johnston to Davis and caused the President to comment, "The letter of General Hill painfully impresses me with that which has heretofore been indicated—a want of vigilance and intelligent observation on the part of General Stuart." This was harsh language. The incidents at Leesburg may have provided the basis for the restrained dislike that Stuart and Hill entertained for each other during the war.[41]

Winter brought rain, sleet, disease, and gloom to Leesburg, and

Hill was vexed with many worries. In his brigade hospital the surgeons showed what he considered a "shameful indifference" to the welfare of their patients, and throughout his command there was a constant turnover of experienced personnel, owing to the bounty and furlough policies of the Confederate Congress and Secretary of War Judah P. Benjamin. With characteristic hyperbole Hill declared to Isabella that the army would be improved if "one half of our surgeons were hung." As for those men in Richmond: "The Sec. of War is a Jew politician and the Confederate Congress seems to be made up of fools. . . ." [42]

More distressing to him than the furloughing of scores of trained soldiers under the very guns of the enemy was the turn of wartime events against the Confederacy. The inspiring Southern victory of First Manassas, or Bull Run, which had brought fame and the nickname "Stonewall" to Jackson, belonged to the cheerful summer. Now in the bleak winter Hill clearly saw that the South was losing its war for independence, in England and on the battlefield.

On December 26, after learning that the North was about to appease angry Britain by releasing the two Confederate agents, James M. Mason and John Slidell, who had been seized from the English merchantman *Trent*, he wrote Isabella: "The news today is sad. The Yankees have backed out of the Mason and Slidell affair and all hope of English interference is at an end." In late January and February he was distressed by successive military reverses: the capture of Roanoke Island, North Carolina, by Union land and naval forces, the Confederate defeat at Mill Springs, Kentucky, the fall of Fort Henry on the Tennessee River, and the disastrous loss of Fort Donelson on the Cumberland, which cost the South some fourteen thousand men and precious guns and supplies, and opened much of Kentucky and Tennessee to the Northern armies. Surely it was time now, he thought, for the Southern people to abandon the false sense of security engendered by victory at Manassas. "We are in the midst of our national agony and the nation knows it not," he lamented. "Alas! Alas! Alas! Fiddling and dancing while the chains are forging for us. Army after Army beaten and captured, but the song and the dance go on."

He urged Isabella to convert some Confederate bonds she had bought into land: "The expenses of the Confederacy are a million a day and I fear that these Bonds will never be redeemed, even should we succeed, *which is doubtful.*" Still, despite such warnings, he clung to the hope that by prayer and renewed effort Southerners might yet save themselves. What was needed at once, in his opinion, was a great increase in the Confederate armies. "Can not our ladies drive into the field our worthless young men?" he suggested to Isabella. "The ladies ought to get up indignation meetings and force out the laggards. . . . I wish a draft was resorted to. . . ." [43]

On the subject of the draft he also wrote: "When our national existence is at stake, who has a right to be at home?" In part, no doubt, this was a reminder to Isabella of the duty that kept her husband from home, leaving her to care for the children and to give birth during his absence at Leesburg to a son, James Irwin. Hill longed to see the new baby. He deeply loved all his children, on whom he bestowed pet names: "Tell Eugenia she is my Comfort, Randolph my Hope, Nannie my Jewel, Harvey, my Pet-Boy, Irwin my Bright-Star."

Two-year-old Harvey had a special place in his affections. "I am always devoted to Babies," he explained, "and Harvey is my Baby, as poor little Irwin's baby hand has not been mine. I think of H constantly and when I am nervous at night and can't sleep, I fancy the little fellow lying in my arms and it soothes me to sleep." [44]

This simple, unrestrained love for his children contrasted somewhat with his attitude toward Isabella herself. He had terms of endearment for her, too, and sympathized eloquently with her trials when the children caught measles, but it seems clear that their marriage, like that of a more famous couple, Abraham and Mary Lincoln, was characterized both by mutual devotion and fairly frequent clashes of opinion and personality. Brief sentences and phrases in Hill's letters hint of discord: "I am not sure that home has appreciated me, as much as I have appreciated it." "The dear little children, who never saw any faults in their poor bungling Papa. . . ." "I believe that you will be happier without me. . . ." [45]

Such allusions doubtless referred in part to the quarrel that had begun between them when he first went into combat. Isabella suffered prostrating headaches for fear that he would be killed, and she constantly urged him to save himself for his family by resigning his commission, which he could honorably do because of his spinal trouble if for no other reason. This affliction caused him much suffering in the cold damp climate of Leesburg. [46]

Very few of Isabella's letters to him have come down through the years, but often his answers reflect what she wrote. On one occasion she angered him by indirectly accusing him of not being sociable toward Jackson and his wife. This was already a sore point, for Jackson, who had risen to major general and taken command of the Shenandoah Valley District under Johnston, seemed rather aloof. Early in February Hill remarked, "Genl Jackson's notes are strictly official. Well it is a funny world." When somewhat later Isabella implied that he should be friendlier to her sister and brother-in-law, she drew from him this revealing outburst:

God forgive me for all the wrong I have done. You are now distressed about my coldness to Anna and the General. Do you really think that I ought to seek a social correspondence with those, who entertain so contemptible an opinion of me? If you think that I ought, say so candidly. If not, why dwell upon a subject which you know to be painful. This is a time of great events, and we ought not to worry about small matters. My dear wife, I try to do right, and I do not wish to wrong any one of your family in the least, the very least. Why then do you always suspect me and dwell upon things which are distressing to me. I have just as much as I can bear now. I know that you mean always for the best and that your motives are pure and good, would that mine were half as much so. But your Father said truly that your excessive devotion to your family perverted your judgment. Well, my darling, forgive all that I have done wrong, all the sorrow that I have caused you. If I had my life to go over again, I would try to make you happier. . . . I have loved you truly and been faithful always, but I have not attended enough to your sensitive nature. This, you will have to overcome, trials and sorrows are before us. It is no time for sentimentality. . . . God bless you, my poor child. . . . Forgive all my errors, my poor dear wife.[47]

Hill's resentment of the Jacksons' social conduct toward him did not in the least reduce his admiration for his brother-in-law's military prowess, even though at this time Jackson's star had temporarily dimmed. In January Jackson had demoralized his troops by marching them through torturing cold to capture Romney, Virginia. Complaints had reached Richmond, President Davis had interfered with Jackson's troop dispositions, and in protest Jackson was in the act of resigning from the army, while Governor John Letcher of Virginia and other political friends carried on negotiations that would h him in.[48]

Referring to this situation in the

Jackson's "strictly official" notes, Hill said: "A report has reached us of Genl Jackson's resignation and it is thought to be due to Genl Johnston's rebuke of him for his march to Romney and Hancock." According to rumor in Winchester, Jackson's headquarters, "a thousand of his men had died from exposure on that march. Of course it will not do to speak of it. His loss from the Army at this critical time would be irreparable. He is more feared by the Yankees than any man in our Army." [49]

Jackson's esteem for Hill as a military commander did not run to such extremes; nevertheless he held him in high regard. On March 8, having learned that Hill that day had fallen back from Leesburg, he asked Johnston to send Hill to him. "I greatly need such an officer," he argued, "one who can be sent off as occasion may offer against an exposed detachment of the enemy for the purpose of capturing it." If he could not have Hill and his command, he hoped that "some other troops" might be sent him, to enable him to "inflict a terrible wound" on the enemy.[50]

But Johnston sent neither Hill nor any other reinforcements. He had begun a withdrawal of all his forces east of the Blue Ridge to new positions, first along the Rappahannock River and then south of the Rapidan, so that he might better defend Richmond against impending attack by McClellan's army.[51] Hill with his troops reached the Rapidan on March 19.

"We have abandoned the richest part of Virginia to the enemy," he reported to Isabella. "Millions of dollars worth of Government stores have been abandoned or burnt." The retreat in rainy weather over muddy roads had been a wretched affair of balking teams and breaking wagons, while the sight of the withdrawing army had terrified the loyal Confederates in the Potomac region. Many were fleeing from the advancing enemy. "Wives are deserted by their husbands, parents by their children," said Hill.

To have to abandon these good people, who had been so kind and hospitable, was saddening indeed, and his depressed state of mind was not improved by the spinal attacks that had put him in bed for three days during the retreat. "The affairs of our country are desperate, desperate," he exclaimed. "I have long foreseen how it would ... Those who heard me express my views, thought me a croaking ... views different from the rest of man-

By the time he reached the Rapidan, Hill had command of a division. The trouble was, as he informed Isabella, "I am acting a Major General without the rank, pay or consideration." But this situation was soon remedied. On March 25 he was formally assigned to the command of the division, and as of the next day he was promoted to major general. Both his spirits and his health improved.

"Freed from the labor and responsibility of an independent command, I sleep a great deal," he wrote home. "When the paroxysms of pain come on in my back, I can often get relief by lying down, which I could not do at Leesburg"—because of the constant official duties. What troubled him most now was the way "the poor soldiers suffer ... in this bleak climate. We have had a very heavy fall of sleet, the trees are breaking down with it and yet there are 10,000 soldiers without tents on this River. My own men are pretty well provided for, as I always give my personal attention to their comforts. But poor fellows, they have a hard time of it." [53]

From the Rapidan, Johnston's army moved on down into the lower Peninsula, where it absorbed Magruder's forces and spread out along the Yorktown line. As McClellan's bombardment of this position got under way and steadily increased, Hill was distressed by the poor quality of the Confederate guns and ammunition with which he was trying to fight back. The guns were made of flimsy metal and sometimes burst when fired. Many shells either exploded at the cannon mouth or failed to explode at all.

Hill was far removed from the organizational and supply difficulties with which the able and loyal Confederate chief of ordnance, Josiah Gorgas, had to contend, and apparently the fact that Gorgas had been born in Pennsylvania aroused his suspicions. To Secretary of War George W. Randolph, who had been his artillerist at Bethel and had succeeded Benjamin in office, he wrote: "There must be something very rotten in the Ordnance Department. It is a Yankee concern throughout, and I have long been afraid that there was foul play there." Randolph quickly assured him that the trouble in his opinion was not treachery but a shortage of good metal.[54]

When Johnston, whom Hill greatly admired, put an end to the unequal artillery duel by his strategic withdrawal up the Peninsula, Hill was more than pleased. Then at Williamsburg came the disastrous attack by Early's brigade, and no doubt, as he rode on through the rain toward Richmond, Hill was beset not only by physical pain but also by mental anguish over the slaughter of his troops. But if self-doubt arose, he resolutely put it aside, for he had in his complex make-up an abundance of the iron nerve so essential to a combat commander. The next time he attacked, it was the enemy who would retreat.

SEVEN PINES

Despite mud and Union pursuit, both by land and up the York River, Johnston made good his retreat up the Peninsula. By May 9 he had concentrated his army within less than thirty miles of Richmond. His headquarters were at New Kent Courthouse. The divisions of Hill and Longstreet were stationed on the right, near the Long Bridge over the Chickahominy River.[1]

Gratitude to God welled up in Hill's heart when he reflected on the hardship and danger he had survived. He wrote Isabella that "God has been wonderfully kind to me." Then he added: "Train our children to *love* God. Our gloomy Presbyterian ideas encourage *fear of God* not *love* for him. Let our children be taught *love, love, love.*"

He also told her that as a result of the retreat:

The Army is very much demoralized. Some five thousand threw away their guns and fled to Richmond to avoid a battle. There are thousands also scattered over the country engaged in plundering. When I ride along the ranks and hear the gross profanity and vulgarity of the soldiers, I cannot wonder at our reverses. I feel like retiring to some mountain home where I would see no more mankind in large and vicious collections.[2]

But if the military outlook was dark in the first part of May, it was soon alleviated by two cheering developments. On the fifteenth a Union naval force tried to advance up the James to Richmond and was repulsed at Drewry's Bluff. In addition, from the Shenandoah Valley came news of brilliant victories by Jackson over numerically superior Union forces—victories which so disturbed Abraham Lincoln that on May 24 he countermanded orders that would have sent General Irvin McDowell from Fredericksburg to Richmond with some forty thousand men.[3]

After the engagement at Drewry's Bluff, Johnston backed his army closer and closer to the suburbs of Richmond until it formed an eastward-fronting semicircle around the city. The main barrier between his forces and McClellan's was the Chickahominy River, a swampy, wooded stream that flowed down the Peninsula from the northwest to the southeast. By the end of May, McClellan had maneuvered his army to a position astride the Chickahominy. Three of his five corps were on the north bank of the river. The other two, under Generals Samuel P. Heintzelman and Erasmus D. Keyes, were on the south, or Richmond, side. Keyes, in fact, had advanced to the vicinity of Seven Pines, only seven miles from Richmond on the Williamsburg road, which ran east from the southeast suburbs of the city and crossed the Chickahominy at Bottom's Bridge.[4]

Opposite Keyes, at the Richmond end of the Williamsburg road, D. H. Hill was stationed. When Hill's reconnaissance revealed that the enemy had fortified the Seven Pines area, Johnston decided to take the offensive. Intelligence reports had assured him that McDowell was no longer a menace. Before him was the opportunity to concentrate the bulk of his army against the two Federal corps south of the Chickahominy and crush them before McClellan could send reinforcements across the rain-flooded stream.[5]

The final plan of attack which Johnston sought to put into operation on May 31 called for Hill to move his division down the Williamsburg road and assault the Federal left and center at Seven Pines, while simultaneously Longstreet threw his division against the right of the enemy position. Longstreet, who received oral orders, was given tactical command of operations in the Seven Pines area. His route to the battlefield was the Nine Mile Road, which wound eastward from the northeast suburbs of Richmond and then described a long southward bend, crossing the York River Railroad at Fair Oaks Station and continuing on for a distance of about one mile to join the Williamsburg road at Seven Pines. Longstreet was to be supported by W. H. C. Whiting's division, of G. W. Smith's command, while the remainder of Smith's forces guarded the upper Chickahominy against a Federal crossing. Magruder's troops, on the Nine

Mile Road, would be in reserve. To protect Hill's right flank during the attack, Johnston ordered General Benjamin Huger, who had come up from Norfolk, to march his three brigades about two miles east from Richmond on the Williamsburg road and then advance cautiously on the Charles City road, which forked off to the southeast. If he found no enemy troops in his front, he could aid Hill.[6]

Hill's division now had an effective strength of about 8,500 and comprised four brigades commanded by Generals Rodes, Rains, Featherston and Samuel Garland, Jr., who had the unit that had formerly been Early's. In the absence of Featherston because of illness, Colonel George B. Anderson was to lead his brigade in the attack on Seven Pines. Though most of the division was already on the Williamsburg route, Rodes was stationed on the Charles City road. He would have to march northward over three and one half miles of swampy terrain in order to join Hill at the point from which the attack would be launched. Hill was ordered by Longstreet not to move until Huger relieved Rodes.[7]

Once the attack was under way, Hill's men would have to press forward through pine woods and dense undergrowth interlaced with marshes and occasional clearings. The spongy, slightly undulating terrain was flooded by a violent rainstorm during the afternoon and night of May 30, and on the morning of the battle great pools of water gleamed among the trees. Here was ground to test all the skill and stamina of soldiers trying to advance in combat, but at least the thick green foliage would afford concealment from Union marksmen.[8]

The rain and the muddy roads slowed the troop movements that Johnston had scheduled for daybreak. But the chief obstacle to the smooth working out of the battle plan was a big, broad-shouldered general with long brown hair and expansive beard who appeared to be the very personification of massive dependability. James Longstreet, for reasons not clear even today, did not fight the battle as Johnston had conceived it.

Instead of moving to attack on the Nine Mile Road, he countermarched his troops off it, delaying Whiting in the process, and then took his division south toward the Williamsburg road. Just east of Richmond his men encountered Huger's division, at a make-shift bridge across rain-swollen Gillies Creek. By insisting on crossing the bridge first, single file, they completely stalled Huger, who was hardly in a position to protest, since Johnston had informed him neither of the over-all battle plan nor of Longstreet's tactical command. As the morning waned, Longstreet, Hill, and Huger held a conference at Hill's headquarters, during which Longstreet convinced Huger that he had authority over him.[9]

While the Confederate commanders talked, the Federals in the Seven Pines area waited to be attacked. Only Keyes's corps occupied this advanced and dangerously isolated position; Heintzelman's corps was five miles to the rear. Keyes had stretched his two divisions across the Williamsburg road in two defense lines. General Darius N. Couch's rear division was at Seven Pines, with flanking units to the north along the Nine Mile Road. About three fourths of a mile in advance was the division of General Silas Casey. Shallow rifle pits marked these recently occupied lines. Casey's men had also built a small pentangular redoubt, which was manned with six guns, and had begun felling trees to form an abatis in their front. Between the two lines another abatis had been constructed. The Federals had no illusions about the strength of their position, and they kept sharp watch of Confederate troop movements that might portend an attack. They were further alerted that morning when they captured a staff officer whom Johnston, mystified by the failure of his battle plan, had sent out in search of Longstreet.[10]

Eventually the tangle of troops that Longstreet had created was straightened out. But it took precious time, and as the hours passed Hill's impatience increased. He had been up all the previous night preparing for the battle; at dawn he had sent to Huger's camp an aide who, as Hill later said, "found Huger and all his people asleep, could with difficulty get them aroused." Hill had his own three brigades on the Williamsburg road ready to move by 6 A.M., and then waited for Huger to come up on the Charles City road and relieve Rodes's brigade.[11]

Longstreet recalled in his memoirs that as the hour approached noon Hill twice appealed to him to begin the battle. But he waited, said Longstreet, until Hill stated in his second appeal that Rodes was coming up from the Charles City fork and would be in on the attack. Then the long-delayed order was given. About 1 P.M. the signal guns were fired, and Hill's brigades commenced their eastward advance in column formation.

Garland's brigade moved on the left side of the Williamsburg road, preceded by a line of skirmishers and supported by G. B.

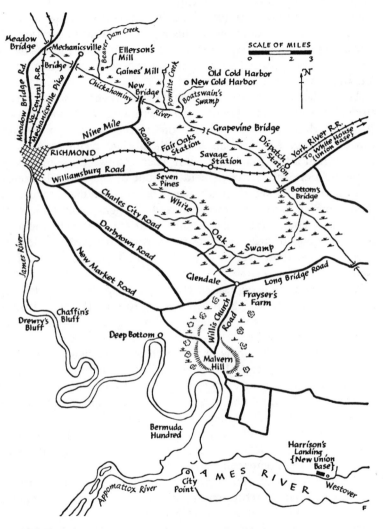

Scene of Seven Pines, and of the Seven Days' battles around Richmond.

Anderson. Rodes's brigade was assigned to the right side, with Rains in support. The heavy terrain and a washed-out bridge so delayed Rodes's march to join the rest of the division that when the signal for the attack sounded only two of his regiments were in position, the remaining units being sent into battle in echelon as they came up. As a result the two right-wing brigades fell behind the two on the left by about fifteen minutes.[12]

Alone, then, at the outset, Garland's and Anderson's men pushed through the woods and briery undergrowth, waded in pools of water, struggled through hip-deep bogs, and with a sputter of musketry drove the enemy pickets ahead of them. The regiments near the road overran a two-gun battery. But when the two brigades emerged from the trees into an open field in front of the Federal defenses, Casey's abatis blocked their advance. Concentrated enemy fire struck them, coming both from the front and the right flank. Officers fell before they could give orders. Confused attempts to turn the abatis to the left and to push through it met with little success. Help was needed, desperately, over there on the right. Where were Rodes and Rains? [13]

They were coming, as fast as Hill could hurry them. To take the Federal line in the rear, he ordered Rains to execute a wide flanking movement to the right. Rodes was directed straight forward and soon reached the abatis.

But although this timely arrival protected the right flank of the hard-pressed Confederate left wing, Rodes faced formidable opposition from a column of enemy troops double-quicking up the Williamsburg road. Hill sent Captain J. W. Bondurant's six-gun battery down the road to shell these reinforcements, but Bondurant was driven back by the Union artillery. Then Captain Thomas H. Carter asked permission to lead his five-gun battery, the King William Artillery, against the approaching Federals.

"I doubt if you can do anything," said Hill. "Bondurant has just been in and had to retire almost immediately. But if you conclude to try it go ahead and see where you can put your guns." He also instructed Carter to ignore the enemy artillery and concentrate his fire on the infantry column.

Carter and his men were eager to try—this was their first fight. Enthusiastically they pushed through the woods, wheeled their guns into battery at the edge of the open field, one piece in the road and four to the left, and opened fire. Immediately they became the target of the Federal artillery. But the enemy aim was high; the shells screamed overhead and landed behind them, almost blinding them with showers of mud and dirt.

Suddenly Carter's brother William, a first lieutenant of the battery, presented himself.

"I am very badly wounded," he said.

"Where?" asked Carter.

His brother opened his shirt and showed him a bullet hole in the middle of his chest as large as the end of his thumb.

It was a strange moment. There was hardly time for grief, nor opportunity amid the thunderous noise and falling debris to say more than, "I am afraid it is mortal. Mount your horse, find an ambulance and surgeon and go to Richmond. May God bless you," Carter added, as his brother rode away. He did not expect to see him alive again, but after the battle he learned that William would recover.[14]

The fire of Carter's battery—fast and accurate despite the difficulties under which the men worked—helped turn the tide of battle in favor of the Confederates. The concentrated shot and shell broke the enemy column, driving it back into the woods. Carter then turned his guns on Casey's redoubt, near the center of the Federal line. Behind the redoubt Rains had completed his flanking march, and his brigade now opened an effective fire from the rear. As the disconcerted Federals showed signs of evacuating their line, Rodes moved his regiments forward in a well-organized frontal attack.[15]

The Confederate left wing also surged forward. Anderson's Fourth North Carolina Regiment, commanded by Major Bryan Grimes, had advanced as far as a fence in front of the enemy works but had halted under heavy fire. One of Grimes's company officers, E. A. Osborne, sought him out in the battle confusion and found the major sitting calmly on his old gray horse with one leg thrown over the saddle bow. He called to Grimes, but his voice was lost in the uproar. He then seized his commander with one hand, and with the other pointed to the thinning ranks of the regiment, shouting at the top of his voice in Grimes's ear a request for an order to charge. All he could hear of Grimes's reply was, "Charge 'em! Damn 'em, charge 'em!"

It was enough for Osborne. He led his company pell-mell over the fence, straight toward the Union works. The entire regiment charged too, with Grimes riding in the lead. The next moment his horse's head was blown off by a cannon shot; the stricken animal fell so suddenly that Grimes's leg was caught under it. The men of the regiment, supposing their commander to be killed or wounded, faltered in the attack, but Grimes, still pinned under the horse, waved his sword and shouted, "Forward, forward!" Some of the men pulled the horse off him. He then led the attack on foot, carrying the regimental flag which he had found upon the ground.[16]

The Federals, assailed all along their line and in the rear, now gave way completely before the onrushing Confederates. Rodes took possession of the redoubt and turned the Union guns upon the retreating masses of blue-clad troops. Shortly afterward Carter galloped up with his battery. Rodes greeted his friend and former VMI classmate with blunt words:

"Carter, you are late. There's a battery at the edge of the woods on the road that's been giving the Yankees hell."

Carter laughed and bowed low. "Your right humble servant had the honor to command that battery!" All his life he remembered the look of surprise and pleasure that crossed Rodes's face.

Next, Hill rode up and brought Carter and his men to a new pitch of excitement by praising them for the expert way they had worked their guns under fire. "I would rather command that battery than be President of the Confederate States!" he exclaimed.[17]

There was good reason for exultation. Eight Federal guns and two hundred prisoners had been captured, together with the camp, tents, and stores of a brigade and the earthworks of the Union line. In about two hours of hard fighting, Hill's division had beaten Casey's division and all the reinforcements sent him.[18] But at this point in the battle at least two searching questions might have been asked: Where was Longstreet? What had he done with the six brigades of his division that Johnston had expected him to use in the assault alongside Hill?

In one way or another, he had kept every one of them out of the fighting. As the battle opened he had directed General George E. Pickett to move north with his brigade to cover the York River Railroad, even though that was the direction in which Johnston was waiting with the rest of the Confederate army. Three more of his brigades, under the over-all command of General Cadmus M. Wilcox, he sent with two brigades of Huger's division to the Charles City road, where for

more than an hour he kept them marching back and forth in obedi-
ence to indecisive orders and counterorders. The remaining two
brigades he held in reserve.[19]

Even such able military historians as Douglas S. Freeman, Gilbert E. Govan and James W. Livingood have had difficulty in dealing with Longstreet's strange troop dispositions. They have suggested
that Longstreet intended to send one or two of his six brigades into
the attack with Hill, and that Hill impatiently began the assault before these troops could reach him. This theory would seem to be untenable for several reasons. The evidence offered in support of it
consists of Hill's and Rodes's official reports, which show that Hill
urged Rodes to hurry to join him, that Rodes warned him he would
be late, and that the attack started before all of Rodes's regiments
were in position. But there is no intimation in any official report that
Longstreet meant to send part of his division with Hill in the initial
attack, or that Hill left such support behind through impetuosity.
Only two reports indicate who actually ordered the start of the fighting. Longstreet reported: ". . . I determined to move forward . . . and
gave orders to that effect to Maj. Gen. D. H. Hill." Pickett wrote
that the battle was "opened by Major-General Longstreet." Moreover, if any of Longstreet's troops were in fact left behind by an impatient Hill, one would suppose that Longstreet would have hurried
them on into the battle himself; but, as will be seen, he sent no support until Hill asked for it.[20]

Aid could have come from Johnston and the forces on the Confederate left, had Johnston known what was happening around Seven
Pines. Poor staff work, however, kept him ignorant of the attack, and
peculiar atmospheric conditions prevented him from hearing the
sounds of musketry that ordinarily would have told him that the
assault was in progress. While Hill was taking the first Union defense
line, Johnston was still waiting at his headquarters on the Nine Mile
Road for some indication that the battle had begun! [21]

Having thus captured the first defense line with no reinforcements
from any quarter, Hill decided it was time to ask for help. He knew
that he must press the Federals hard, before they could recover fully
from the demoralizing effects of their retreat. Numbers of them were
already counterattacking from the cover of the woods; bullets were
whistling into the redoubt and rattling like hail off the gun carriages
of Carter's battery. One member of the battery, an eighteen-year-old

boy named Tom Jones, fell dying at Carter's feet with blood gushing from a severed neck artery. Suddenly Hill noticed that his own uniform was wet with blood.

"I am wounded," he called to one of his couriers, young John Chamblin.

"General, a loose horse came by just now," said Chamblin. "I caught the bridle. It was very bloody and it swung against you."

"Oh, that's where the blood comes from," said Hill, and turned back to the business at hand, the dispatching of a courier to Longstreet with a request for reinforcements. The first courier who rode out with the dispatch had his horse shot from under him. Chamblin then took the message through.

As to what was said in it, the evidence conflicts. Hill wrote in his official report that he "asked for another brigade," and certainly this clear statement must take precedence over any recollection set down long after the event. But it is perhaps worth noting that Chamblin, in 1885, remembered that Hill asked for two brigades immediately, and that Longstreet replied: "Tell General Hill I have but two brigades in reserve. He shall have one of them." It would be helpful to have Longstreet's statement on this point; however, in neither his official report nor his memoirs does he indicate that Hill asked for aid. This silence seems to have influenced Freeman, the modern historian who has written most fully of the action around Seven Pines, for in his authoritative *Lee's Lieutenants* he also omits mention of any request for support.[22]

In response to Hill's message, Longstreet ordered General R. H. Anderson to move forward with his brigade. To guide Anderson, Hill sent back J. W. Ratchford, who was now serving, with the rank of major, as his chief of staff. Ratchford asked Longstreet whether he had any instructions for Hill and the answer was no. "Hill is on the ground and knows his business," said Longstreet, "and we can trust him to do the best under the circumstances."[23]

Before Anderson got into battle the Union counterattack had been repulsed. The Federals, beaten back by Carter's battery and the captured artillery, formed new lines in the woods to the right and left of Casey's redoubt—strong positions from which Hill determined to drive them. As soon as his reinforcements arrived he launched the attack on the left, by dividing Anderson's brigade into two forces. Colonel Micah Jenkins was sent wide to the left with two regiments, under orders to "scour along the railroad" and Nine Mile Road and get behind the enemy. Anderson with the remainder of the brigade was directed to assault the Federals to the immediate left of the redoubt.

Anderson led his men forward in the face of a withering fire from the woods and began to drive the Union forces, aided by Confederate guns brought up to enfilade the Federal lines. As the enemy fell back, portions of G. B. Anderson's brigade joined R. H. Anderson and Jenkins, and Captain James Dearing's battery, sent up by Longstreet, also went into action. The Confederate left pressed slowly ahead with repeated charges against the enemy.[24]

So far so good, but when Hill attacked the Federals in the woods on his right, he encountered stiff resistance. Attempting to repeat the tactics that had previously been successful, he ordered Rains to swing wide to the right while Rodes pushed straight ahead. But this time Rains did not go far enough to flank the enemy, and when Rodes advanced he ran into deadly infantry fire. During the savage combat that followed the Federals were reinforced from the rear, and though Hill called up reinforcements too in the form of Longstreet's other reserve brigade, under Colonel James L. Kemper, for some reason it did not engage the enemy. Part of Rodes's brigade was repulsed, Rodes himself receiving a painful arm wound that eventually forced him to turn his command over to Colonel John B. Gordon.

At one point in the contest Hill mounted his horse and with a cigar in his mouth rode slowly across the open field between the contending forces, completely exposed to the enemy fire. When he reached the safety of a copse where two of his officers were standing, they remonstrated with him for such recklessness. "I did it for a purpose," said Hill. "I saw that our men were wavering, and I wanted to give them confidence."

Whether inspired by this example or simply determined not to quit, many of Rodes's battle-weary soldiers did manage to fight their way up to the second abatis, which protected Couch's line at Seven Pines. And while they pinned down large numbers of Federal troops, the Confederate left continued to move forward, spearheaded by Jenkins and his Palmetto Sharpshooters, until, about 6 P.M., the Union resistance on this wing gave way completely, precipitating a general retreat on both sides of the road. Through the darkening woods Keyes's corps and Heintzelman's, which had come up in mid-afternoon, streamed back to a third line of defense about a mile and a half in the rear of Seven Pines. That night Hill's forces occupied the positions that had formerly been held by Casey and Couch.[25]

Hill's men had borne by far the heaviest burden of the fighting that day. Johnston, learning at last about 4 P.M. that a battle was raging around Seven Pines, had hurried his troops down the Nine Mile Road in an effort to salvage what he could of his plan of attack. Near Fair Oaks they encountered the Union corps of General Edwin V. Sumner, who had crossed the Chickahominy in refutation of Johnston's belief that it was impassable and had marched toward the sound of the guns. Fighting began, and in the fading afternoon light the contending forces engaged in an indecisive battle that saw about nine thousand men put into action on each side before darkness fell. Just at twilight Johnston was wounded, and his command devolved upon G. W. Smith.[26]

The next day, Sunday, June 1, Smith did not renew the battle on his front. Hill, however, had more fighting to do. Having spent the previous night in sleepless preparation for further combat, he welcomed Longstreet early Sunday morning when that commander rode up to Casey's tent, where he had established his headquarters. He learned from Longstreet that the Confederates had been checked at Fair Oaks and that Sumner's Federal corps had crossed the river. Suddenly, as they talked, musketry began crackling in the woods and three balls ripped through the tent. They finished their conversation while the skirmishing, which soon ended, was still in progress.

Not once during this visit did Longstreet give orders as to how the continuing battle should be conducted. Laconically he said to Hill, "You have taken the bull by the horns and must fight him out." And with that he rode away.[27]

But if this strange commander had no directions for his subordinate, at least during the previous afternoon and night he had ordered up additional reinforcements. By the time the intermittent skirmishing turned into serious fighting Hill's command had been augmented by Longstreet's other four brigades, under Generals Wilcox, Roger A. Pryor, R. E. Colston, and Pickett, together with two of Huger's brigades, under Generals Lewis A. Armistead and William Mahone. With four of these fresh brigades Hill formed his advance line, which stretched southeastward from Fair Oaks to the

Williamsburg road, with Armistead holding the left flank, Wilcox and Pryor the right, and Pickett the center. Just where the enemy lurked in that forested terrain Hill did not know; he could easily surmise, however, that Sumner's corps was off to his left, near Fair Oaks, and that Heintzelman and Keyes confronted him on the center and right.[28]

When Hill later wrote his official report of the action of June 1, he spoke of a Federal attack upon his advance brigades that morning, but did not mention a prior attack by his own forces. Yet it appears that before the Federals advanced, Hill ordered Pickett and Armistead to attack the enemy on the left, and that this attack began around 6 A.M. The Federals repulsed it and then launched a counterattack, under which Armistead's brigade broke and fled, with the exception of a few companies that rallied around their commander. This opened a gap on Pickett's left, exposing his brigade to the danger of a flank attack.[29]

To fill the gap Hill rushed forward Mahone's brigade, but these troops, fresh from garrison duty at Norfolk, were thrown into panic by a sudden volley from the enemy and began a precipitate retreat. Out to stop them rode Hill, shouting commands that went unheeded. He managed a partial rally of a North Carolina regiment by appealing to the men not to "disgrace the Old North State," but most of these green troops were Virginians who at the moment had little interest in the glory of North Carolina. As though a furious general were nowhere near them, they sought the safety of a roadside ditch.

Get out of that ditch, Hill ordered the men of the Ninth Virginia Regiment, and fight like soldiers of the Confederacy. They ignored him.

"Colonel Scales!"—He stood in his stirrups and at the top of his lungs addressed himself to the commander of the Thirteenth North Carolina Regiment, of Garland's brigade—"Colonel Scales, come and occupy the position that these cowardly Virginians have fled from!"

Immediately A. M. Scales moved forward. Obeying Hill's order to "run over the cowards" he marched his men over the backs of the prostrate Virginians, who retaliated by taunting, "Yes, go and fight like you did at Roanoke and Hatteras!" [30]

By this time William Mahone had reached Hill. Bone-thin "Little Billy," whose cavernous eyes and sweeping beard were the biggest things about him, did not like the epithets hurled at his troops. "You should not abuse my men," he protested, "for I ordered them out of the fight."

"Why did you do so?" demanded Hill. "Do you not see that you have left a gap open for the enemy to pass through and break our line in two? But if you ordered them out," he finished scathingly, "I beg the soldiers' pardon for what I have said to them and transpose it all to you."

The words stung Mahone to fury. So enraged was he that on the following day he asked Pryor to carry Hill a challenge to a duel, but Pryor warned him that this would merely damage his own reputation. The whole army, he explained, knew of Hill's courage in battle, and also of his moral scruples against dueling. Everyone would say that Mahone had made a cheap grandstand gesture, knowing in advance that Hill would not fight. Mahone saw the logic of this and dropped the idea of a duel, but from now on he would be Hill's enemy.[31]

Having failed to plug the gap on the left with Mahone's brigade, Hill next sent Colston into the danger area. Then, seeing that Colston's brigade was not engaging the Federals either, and mindful that the enemy strength now totaled three corps, he decided to pull back his advance line, and accordingly sent orders to Pickett, Pryor, and Wilcox to withdraw and reconcentrate around the captured works. Wilcox received his withdrawal order while holding off an enemy attack that had begun on the right. Though in later years he would regard Hill's decision as wise in view of the full tactical situation, he thought at the time that it was too cautious. Nevertheless he retreated promptly, ordering Pryor, who was also reluctant to withdraw, to come with him. The enemy pursued them only a short distance.[32]

Pickett meanwhile was holding his ground, reluctant to withdraw from strong defensive terrain. He also wanted to protect his wounded. So back he galloped to remonstrate with Hill and complain about not being properly supported.

"General, I have ordered your supports up but can't keep them there," said Hill. "You had better fall back."

With an oath Pickett rose in his stirrups and declared he would not fall back while he had a man remaining. Hill therefore, after further discussion of the situation, allowed him to put in two of

Colston's regiments on his left, and Mahone's brigade on his right. With this support Pickett held his position through the remainder of the morning against Federal forces that were not disposed to turn the fighting into a full-scale battle. The action of the afternoon consisted of desultory Union artillery fire which did no harm.[33]

While Hill used the quiet afternoon hours to collect 6,700 muskets and rifles from the battlefield, a strained little drama was taking place at Smith's headquarters on the Nine Mile Road—the transfer of command of the army from Smith to Lee, with Jefferson Davis as chief spectator. Davis and Lee had held a field conference with Smith on May 31 after Johnston had been wounded, and later that night as the President and his military adviser rode back to Richmond Davis told Lee that on reaching the city he would send him an order assigning him to command of the army. His instructions to Lee, as rendered by Lee's biographer, Freeman, were: "Make your preparations as soon as you reach your quarters." Yet not until about 1 P.M. on June 1 did Lee ride out from Richmond to relieve Smith.

Was this undue delay on Lee's part? Freeman does not suggest that it was. Lee, he remarks, could not attempt immediate direction of the battle, for that would have been "dangerous to the army" and "unfair to Smith." But surely the course of greater danger to the army was to leave the continuing battle to Smith, who in the conference of the thirty-first had revealed to Lee and Davis such extreme nervous strain (he suffered complete prostration on June 2) and such indecision in planning for the next day's fighting that Davis decided to transfer the command immediately to Lee. As for any question of unfairness to Smith, that might have been relevant in a mock battle, but in the middle of the bloody life-and-death struggle of Seven Pines it did not merit serious consideration.

How did Lee spend the morning of June 1, while Hill was attacking and being attacked, and Smith was holding the left wing of the army out of the battle? Before 5 A.M. he received a message from Smith explaining troop dispositions and asking for more men and engineers. He wrote back that he would do what he could to help and that he wished Smith success. Then, according to Freeman, who does not document the sequence of events, he received formal notice from Davis that he was in command of the army. After this, writes Freeman: "Other dispatches came; every hour brought new calls; time had to be found to draft an address for publication to the army when Lee took command; preparations had to be made to move the office." Surely such activities should have been postponed or left to other officers. On the basis of the visible evidence it is difficult to understand why Lee did not relieve Smith early that morning instead of waiting until about 1 P.M., as Freeman tells us, to start for the battlefield.[34]

Another question arises with regard to this changeover of command—so important to the fortunes of the Confederacy—and that is, exactly when and how did it finally take place? Freeman in his monumental *R. E. Lee* does not provide the answer, and the postwar narratives published by Davis in 1881 and by Smith in 1884 give two different versions of the episode. Davis's most exact reference to time is the statement that on the morning of June 1 he rode out to see Smith. "To relieve both him and General Lee from any embarrassment," he writes, "I preferred to make the announcement of General Lee's assignment to command previous to his arrival." He then states that he left Smith's headquarters after Lee arrived, and indicates that the command was transferred.

Smith gives more details of what happened and deals more precisely with the time element. About 1:30 P.M. that Sunday, he states, Davis rode up to his headquarters and asked for Lee. On being told that Lee was not there, the President "expressed so much surprise" that Smith asked him why he had expected to find Lee. Davis explained that "he had, early that morning, ordered General Lee to take command of the army at once." Then at Smith's invitation he took a seat to wait for his new commander. When Lee arrived, "about two o'clock P.M.," the command was transferred.

Smith, then, indicates that Davis on arriving at army headquarters expected to find Lee there in command; Davis, that he expected to reach Smith ahead of Lee. Thus Smith on this point is in conflict with Davis. In other respects his story fits the general pattern of evidence. He and Davis agree that Davis arrived in advance of Lee. His statement that Lee arrived about 2 P.M. accords with Freeman's establishment of 1 P.M. as the approximate time that Lee started with his staff for the battlefield. Smith's headquarters that day were about two miles from Richmond on the Nine Mile Road. To ride out of the city, over a muddy road crowded with ambulances and wagonloads of wounded, might well have taken Lee and his party about an hour. By similar reckoning Davis might have left Rich-

mond that morning, as he says, and have reached Smith about
1:30 P.M., as Smith says, for the President had some difficulty finding
Smith's headquarters and while en route stopped for a talk with
Whiting. Finally, Smith's account of Davis's surprise at not finding
Lee, and of his saying that early that morning he had ordered Lee
to take command at once, accords with these incidents related by
Freeman: (1) Davis's statement to Lee, as they rode back to Richmond the night of the thirty-first, that on reaching the city he would
send him an order giving him command of the army; (2) Davis's
instructions, "Make your preparations as soon as you reach your
quarters;" (3) Lee's receipt, some time after 5 A.M., June 1, of
Davis's formal notice that he was in command. This could have been
the early-morning order that Davis spoke of in Smith's narrative.

Even considering the long lapse of time involved, it is not likely
that Smith in 1884 wrote inaccurately of Davis's surprise and of his
remark about the order to Lee simply because of poor memory.
Either this part of the narrative is accurate or it is a fabrication designed to put Lee in a bad light. It is of course possible that Smith
nursed a grudge over the way he was shunted aside and did unfairly
disparage Lee. On the other hand it is also possible that Davis's
somewhat elliptical narrative of the transfer of command was designed to cover up initial dilatoriness on the part of Lee. By the
time Davis published his memoirs Lee was the dead hero of the
Lost Cause, and the former President of the Confederacy may well
have felt that his greatest general was entitled to immunity from any
revelations that would reflect upon his reputation.[35]

Lee's appraisal of the military situation, once he had assumed
command, convinced him that further effort to attack the enemy
was inadvisable. Accordingly he ordered a retreat to the lines the
army had occupied before the start of the battle. The order was
conveyed by Longstreet to Hill, and reached him after dark.

By now Longstreet had sent Hill the last of Huger's brigades. During the day's fighting Hill, with no guidance from Longstreet, had
controlled twelve of the thirteen brigades in the right wing of the
Confederate army; now he also had the thirteenth. The process by
which the actual tactical command of the right wing had devolved
upon him was complete.

He afterward wrote of the retreat that, "The thirteen brigades
were not got together until near midnight, and the delicate opera-

tion of withdrawing 30,000 men in the presence of a superior force of the enemy had to be performed before daylight." But despite the mud and the darkness the task was accomplished with no stragglers and no loss of equipment. At sunrise Hill's forces regained the old Confederate entrenchments.[36]

During the battle, Hill's division had sustained nearly three thousand casualties, most of which occurred in the three brigades that made the frontal attacks of May 31. G. B. Anderson lost 866 men; Garland, 740. Rodes took about 2,200 men into battle and came out with half that number. His loss of 50 per cent was one per cent more than that of the Light Brigade in its famous charge at Balaklava. The division as a whole fought remarkably well, especially so in view of the fact that the great majority of the men had never before been in combat. It bore nearly one half of the Confederate battle loss, which totaled 6,134. The Federals, fighting mainly on the defensive, lost 5,031.[37]

Had Hill been properly supported on May 31 in accordance with Johnston's plan, his brigades would doubtless have suffered fewer casualties, and in all likelihood the Confederate forces would have achieved a decisive victory. Instead the Southern army withdrew from the field with McClellan still threatening Richmond. Johnston later maintained that at least the battle "stopped the Federal advance and set McClellan to fortifying," thus affording Lee time to strengthen his army. Thomas H. Carter, after fighting through the war to Appomattox Court House, decided that the "one good result" of Seven Pines was the "splendid morale imparted to our men" by the successful attacks of May 31. To Hill he declared: "I consider the charge and capture of the works at Seven Pines by your command . . . the most difficult and dangerous that I saw during the war, except the charge of Pickett's Division at Gettysburg." [38]

That the battle improved Confederate morale was also asserted by Hill and Longstreet in their official reports. Hill's report made it plain, without explicitly saying so, that it was Hill rather than Longstreet who had conducted the fighting around Seven Pines; and no doubt Hill expected Johnston to commend him officially for his extraordinary services. He reckoned without Longstreet. That commander wrote a smooth report that blamed Huger for delaying the initial attack by slowness in getting into position, and effectively concealed the extent to which tactical command in the two-day battle had been thrown upon Hill. Longstreet did say that the "conduct of the attack was left entirely to Major-General Hill," and went on to praise Hill's "ability, courage, and skill." But read in the general context of the report this sounded as though Hill had done little more than lead the first assault, with Longstreet remaining in control of the battle as a whole. No hint was there of how long Hill fought unaided, nor of his requests for support, nor of the intermittent transfer of troops to him until in the end he commanded the entire right wing of the Confederate army.[39]

Johnston in his report accepted Longstreet's version of the battle at face value. On the assumption that Longstreet might have misunderstood his oral instructions, he refrained from pointing out how his plan of attack had been changed and got G. W. Smith to delete from his report passages that revealed Longstreet's failure to conform to the plan. Johnston also repeated Longstreet's assertions that Huger had delayed the initial attack on May 31. After describing the capture of the enemy works at Seven Pines he summed up: "The skill, vigor, and decision with which these operations were conducted by General Longstreet are worthy of the highest praise. He was worthily seconded by Major-General Hill, of whose conduct and courage he speaks in the highest terms." Thus Longstreet emerged as the hero of the battle, Huger as the scapegoat, and Hill—in view of what he had actually done—as the forgotten man.[40]

Huger protested repeatedly, and futilely, against the unfair statements made about him by Johnston and Longstreet, but Hill's personal credo forbade him from agitating merely for more recognition of his accomplishments. He stood silently, unhappily by while Longstreet basked in public acclaim as the hero of Seven Pines. Many years later he commented: "Longstreet very early got control of his superior officers and worked things to please himself. Thus at Seven Pines, he disregarded Johnston's order to attack on Nine Mile Road and put my division first, came behind me, was not on the field at all and got all the credit of the battle."

A similar view was expressed by another participant in the battle, Wilcox. Long after the war he wrote Hill that he had always "thought it a little strange you were not called the hero of Seven Pines. Longstreet I had reason then to think, had no knowledge of the fight, from personal observation.... I have always to restrain myself when I think of him as a soldier ... for I had a poor opinion of his ability and had ... a suspicion he was selfish, and indifferent to others." [41]

That he might yet be called the hero of Seven Pines was a hope to which Hill clung through the postwar years. Johnston's memoirs, published in 1874, were a disappointment; Johnston again portrayed him as second in the battle to Longstreet. But Longstreet was writing his memoirs, too, and at his request Hill in the late 1870s began helping him compile facts about their joint battles. Several times in the course of their correspondence Hill asked for a statement that would do full justice to his services at Seven Pines. Longstreet countered with the argument that he had already bestowed due recognition in his official report, but expressed a willingness to explain Hill's accomplishments more clearly in the memoirs.

"You certainly handled all of the troops on the Williamsburg road in that engagement and handled them successfully," he said. "I do not remember that I gave an order on that field other than to send you my brigades as you called for them. I hope you will allow me to suggest that you have your own extreme and quiet modesty to blame almost as much as General Johnston and myself for not receiving your just dues." [42]

This was encouraging. Hill continued to wait and hope. Then in 1885 he made an unpleasant discovery. On G. W. Smith's advice he examined a newly-published volume of official correspondence on Seven Pines, and there found a letter from Longstreet to Johnston about which he had heretofore known nothing. It had been written on June 7, 1862, six days after the close of the battle and three days prior to the date of Longstreet's official report. It briefly described the fighting with no mention of Hill or his division, and in it was this astonishing passage:

"The failure of complete success on Saturday [May 31], I attribute to the slow movements of General Huger's command. This threw perhaps the hardest part of the battle upon my own poor division."

Here was a much more explicit claim to preeminence in the battle than Longstreet had made in his official report. Hill wrote Smith: "The Longstreet letter to Joe Johnston is a reality. I am sorry, sorry, sorry that it is so." At least he now knew why Johnston had written a report about him that he had always deemed unfair, for "with such a letter from the supposed commander on the field, how could he report differently?" But since the discovery Hill had "not felt kindly" toward Longstreet: "I can't understand how he had the brass to write such a letter." [43]

Perhaps it was just as well for Hill's peace of mind that he did not live to read Longstreet's memoirs, which finally came out in 1896. For Longstreet in his account of Seven Pines again failed to give Hill his "just dues." Indeed he claimed as his own the withdrawal orders that Hill had issued to his brigadiers on the morning of June 1.[44] His portrait of himself in full tactical command is persuasive, and may help explain why Freeman in *Lee's Lieutenants* describes the fighting on the Confederate right as "Longstreet's battle." A more accurate version would seem to be that given by Wilcox in a post-script to his official report: "Seven Pines, the successful part of it, was D. H. Hill's fight." [45]

IV

RED FIELDS AROUND RICHMOND

AFTER SEVEN PINES, McClellan reverted to his favorite siege tactics. In Hill's words, he began "approaching Richmond with spade and shovel," expecting "to bombard it over our head with his long range guns." Lee in turn set his own men to digging, a duty still highly uncongenial to many Southern soldiers at that stage of the war. Hill confided to Isabella that he did not like to work the "brave fellows" of his "poor shattered and suffering Division." But the digging went on, despite stormy wet weather, and earthworks multiplied in front of Richmond.

Hill had many things to discuss with Isabella during this defensive lull. For instance, she really ought to get over her foolish fear that he would be killed in battle. So he told her with predestinarian firmness: "If my work is done, I will fall. If not, all the balls on earth cannot harm me. Never distrust God."

Somehow remarks of this nature did not comfort Isabella, nor terminate their running quarrel over his remaining a combat commander. Occasionally she would send him "a cold letter," and then he would ask for expressions of affection to match his own: "Poor sinner that I am, I want to hear you say that you love me. . . . God bless you darling and the dear little ones. Write often and kindly. Affectionately, Husband."

When Isabella informed him that McClellan was claiming victory in the recent battle he waxed indignant. "Surely, such a liar cannot be a great man," he exclaimed. "We drove him for three miles. . . . Had my boys been supported, his whole force would have been driven like chaff before the wind."

Proud of his achievements of May 31, he was inclined to overlook the Federal attacks of June 1 and blame Lee for not having ordered "a pursuit." The new commanding general, whose war record had so far been unimpressive, was much criticized at this time by his officers and men, the press, and the general public. His entrenching tactics were especially unpopular and earned him the derisive title, "King of Spades." Hill was among those who felt that swift aggressive action was necessary to stop the Federals from "burrowing along up to Richmond," as he expressed it, and in a letter home he complained: "Genl Lee is so slow and cautious. By a strange policy, the West Point Rail Road [York River Railroad] was not destroyed and the Yankees are bringing up heavy guns and mortars to destroy Richmond on a Rail Road built by its citizens." He also wrote Secretary of War Randolph, on June 10, expressing fear that Richmond would be taken by siege and urging that Beauregard be brought from Mississippi to take part in a "wide detour to the rear" of McClellan's army by 50,000 Confederates, the object being "to capture McClellan." [1]

Hill at this time had no way of knowing that Lee was the master planner of the daring Valley campaign that had made his friend Jackson, in his own admiring phrase, "emphatically the hero of the war." [2] Nor did he know that Lee was preparing to bring Jackson to Richmond for a combined assault on McClellan. From all he could see this engineer-general seemed wholly committed to entrenched defense. But at least it had to be conceded that Lee was successful in his efforts to enlarge the army by calling up reinforcements from the coastal states, and that he showed marked administrative talent in reorganizing the forces under his command.

The extensive reorganization that he carried out at this time was in part a diplomatic compliance with President Davis's desire to have army units brigaded by states; it was also an astute effort to weed out commanders of doubtful ability, eliminate personality conflicts, and bring promising young officers to the fore. In the process he transferred out of Hill's division two brigadiers, Rains and Featherston, who in Hill's opinion had not shown promise. Rains was replaced by Colonel Alfred H. Colquitt; Featherston, by George B. Anderson, who was promoted to brigadier general. A fifth brigade, newly arrived from South Carolina and commanded by Brigadier General Roswell S. Ripley, was also assigned to the division. [3]

Hill now had around him the brigade commanders who would fight beside him through some of the major battles of the war. Three of them, Rodes, Anderson and Garland, had demonstrated at Seven Pines that they could handle brigades effectively in close combat. Two of them, Colquitt and Ripley, were yet to be tried.

The five commanders made up a diverse group. Rodes, tall, thin and lantern-jawed, with a fierce brown handlebar mustache, was a native of Lynchburg, Virginia, who had graduated from VMI in 1848 and had been first a railroad civil engineer and then a mathematics professor at his alma mater. He was the able, self-assertive, and ambitious leader of five Alabama regiments, the First Brigade.[4]

Anderson, whose Second Brigade consisted of four regiments from his native state, North Carolina, was at thirty-one the very image of the ideal warrior. Big, athletic, and calmly alert, with blue-gray eyes and a golden, flowing beard, he rode his horse superbly and gave orders in a clear, musical voice. He had graduated tenth in his class at West Point and had served until the outbreak of the war in the Second Dragoons, United States Army.[5]

Garland, the thirty-two-year-old commander of the five North Carolina regiments that comprised the Third Brigade, had a background of personal tragedy—the recent deaths of his wife and only son—that may have made him deliberately reckless in battle. Like Rodes he had been born in Lynchburg and graduated from VMI. He had also studied law at the University of Virginia and until the war had practiced in Lynchburg, where he had enjoyed a reputation as a scholar unusually well versed in literature and drama. There was strength as well as sensitivity in his rough-hewn face, in which thoughtful, deep-set eyes bespoke the quiet integrity that endeared him to Hill.[6]

The lone colonel in the group, Colquitt, had taken over from Rains the Fourth Brigade, made up of one Alabama and four Georgia regiments. Colquitt lacked a formal military education. A Georgia lawyer, planter, and politician, with experience as a staff officer in the Mexican War, he had behind him at the age of thirty-eight a distinguished career as Congressman, Georgia legislator, and member of his state secession convention. After the war he would become one of Georgia's most powerful political leaders. But in his tightly buttoned gray uniform he was simply "Colonel Colquitt," a black-bearded, hook-nosed officer who had yet to prove that he could handle a brigade.[7]

Ripley's Fifth Brigade of two North Carolina and two Georgia regiments was commanded by—of all things—a Yankee. Ripley had been born in 1823 in Worthington, Ohio, and had been appointed to West Point from New York. Graduating a year after Hill, and ranking seventh in the class of 1843, in which U. S. Grant was twenty-first, he served in Mexico as an artillery officer and as aide to Hill's old enemy, General Pillow. In 1853 he resigned from the army and engaged in business in Charleston, South Carolina, the home of his wife, until the war crisis brought him into the military service of South Carolina and the Confederacy. He helped bombard Fort Sumter and for a time commanded the department of South Carolina under Lee. The oldest of the brigade commanders, he was balding, round-faced, bushy-bearded, and quarrelsome; in South Carolina he had denounced Lee so openly and bitterly that Governor F. W. Pickens of that state had protested to President Davis.[8]

The strength of these five brigades, plus four batteries of artillery and a company of cavalry, added up on paper to about fourteen thousand men. "But there are not more than 8,000 present," said Hill in a letter home. The rest were "sick, wounded or shamming." He was disturbed over the large numbers of "skulkers who are dodging off home or lying around the brothels, gambling saloons and drinking houses of Richmond."

Another serious concern, and one that probably cost Lee some sleepless nights, was the food problem. "How our large Army is to be fed is a mystery," Hill wrote Isabella on June 22. "There is great suffering among the soldiers for vegetables.... Scurvy is breaking out, bread and meat ... the only diet." He suggested that the ladies of North Carolina might be willing to send supplies of vegetables to their state regiments in his division.[9]

In the same letter he remarked, "We have a rumor that Genl Jackson is coming to Richmond." This information, which, despite Lee's efforts at tight security, was no secret in the capital, foreshadowed the impending attack on McClellan. Lee had been carefully studying his adversary. He had recently sent his cavalry commander, Stuart, on a reconnaissance that Stuart turned into a circuit of the entire Union army—"no more dashing thing done in the war," said Hill—and now finally he had decided that the time was ripe for Jackson to move his forces eastward and join him in assaulting the enemy.[10]

Toward noon of Monday, June 23, Hill received a summons to a conference at Lee's headquarters. It turned out to be a council of the generals who would lead the attack on McClellan. Longstreet was there. So was Ambrose Powell Hill, a recently promoted major general who was no relation to Harvey Hill. So also was Jackson, his brown beard and faded uniform begrimed from a long, fast horseback ride ahead of his troops.

As soon as his four lieutenants had assembled Lee closed the door of the conference room and began speaking in his quiet, deep voice. Except for his impeccable uniform this robust fifty-five-year-old Virginia gentleman with broad benevolent countenance, gentle brown eyes and whitening hair and beard looked more patriarchal than martial, but what he had to say revealed the audacity and aggressiveness that would help make him one of history's great generals.

He explained his strategy. By threatening Washington, D. C., with Jackson's little army, he had kept McDowell from joining McClellan. On June 11 he had sent reinforcements to Jackson and had let the Federals learn of this, so that presumably they would be expecting Jackson to renew his attacks toward Washington. Instead, Jackson had slipped away from the Valley, leaving only a masking force behind him. Under a heavy cloak of secrecy his main body of troops, 18,500 strong, was moving toward Richmond to spearhead the assault on McClellan.

McClellan's army was still astride the Chickahominy, holding just east of Richmond a generally north–south line that rested at the far south, or left, on White Oak Swamp. The left wing, comprising more than two thirds of the army, was south of the river. The right wing, some thirty thousand men under General Fitz John Porter, lay on the north bank, where it reached out toward McDowell, should he ever arrive, and protected the York River Railroad, the Federals' main line of supply from their base near the head of the York.

It was the right wing that Lee proposed to attack. While Magruder's and Huger's divisions demonstrated in front of the Richmond entrenchments, which he had constructed for just such a holding operation, he could cross the bulk of his Richmond forces to the north bank of the river and unite them with Jackson's troops coming down from the northwest. This would give him a striking force of about 56,000, or nearly two to one over Porter. Thus by swift maneuver of his total fighting force of about 85,500, he would achieve numerical superiority at the point of attack, even though he was confronted by a reinforced army of perhaps 105,000 under McClellan and by some 65,000 more Federals in the Valley. It must have been with an inner glow of pride that he unfolded before his generals a strategic plan worthy of Napoleon.

Porter's entrenchments curved northward along the east bank of the little Chickahominy tributary, Beaver Dam Creek, and would be hard to capture by frontal assault. Therefore Lee in his final battle orders, issued in writing on June 24, worked out a plan to turn the right flank, which Stuart considered vulnerable. This would drive Porter, and endanger the Union supply line, forcing McClellan to leave his entrenchments south of the river and either fight or retreat. It was of course possible for the Union general to allow his right wing to take care of itself while he marched the rest of his army straight into Richmond over the little Confederate holding force, but Lee counted on McClellan's well-known caution and on the speed and impetus of his own attack to prevent this.

When the attack began, Longstreet, Hill, and A. P. Hill would coordinate their movements with Jackson's. Lee's complex tactical plan, in main outline, called for Jackson to move his troops down through Ashland, sixteen miles north of Richmond, and then on the day of battle to strike southeastward along the north side of the river with the objective of swinging around Porter's right and continuing on toward Cold Harbor. As he advanced, and as the Federal defenders fell back from the Chickahominy bridges, A. P. Hill would cross the river at Meadow Bridge and Longstreet and D. H. Hill would cross at Mechanicsville Bridge. Then with Harvey Hill supporting Jackson, and Longstreet supporting A. P. Hill, the four divisions would sweep down the Chickahominy toward New Bridge and the York River Railroad.[11]

Before Jackson could open the battle he had to ride back to his troops and march them a good twenty-five miles through enemy-held country, over unfamiliar roads that might be blockaded by the Federals. When would he be in position to start the attack? This was the key question raised at the headquarters conference that afternoon of June 23. Lee rather oddly allowed it to be settled by discussion among his four lieutenants while he temporarily retired to another room to attend to some office work.

As to what was said in this discussion, varying accounts were given in after years by Longstreet and Harvey Hill. Longstreet, in a letter of 1877 in which he requested help in refreshing his memory of the conference, told Hill:

My recollection is that . . . I turned to Gen Jackson and suggested that as his troops had some distance to march he had better appoint the day of our attack, and he appointed Wednesday [June 25] when I suggested that he might encounter greater obstacles than then anticipated, and that I would in order to give him time suggest Thursday: which was accepted and agreed upon, and the orders given accordingly.

Some eight years after receiving this letter, Hill published his version of the conversation in a *Century Magazine* article. According to him, Longstreet asked Jackson to "fix the time for the attack to begin"; Jackson replied, "Daylight of the 26th"; and Longstreet then suggested that it might be well to "give yourself more time," but apparently went unanswered.

In naming the twenty-sixth instead of the twenty-fifth, the Jackson of Hill's narrative appears much less reckless and inept at logistics than the Jackson of Longstreet's letter. But when Longstreet published his memoirs in 1896 he adhered to his own version of the conversation—except that now he quoted himself as asking Jackson to appoint the "hour" for starting the attack, with Jackson responding, "The morning of the 25th," and then, after admonition, appointing "the morning of the 26th." Although this account is the one generally accepted by present-day historians, there is no certainty that it is more accurate than Hill's.[12]

When Lee returned to the conference room he agreed that the attack should begin on the twenty-sixth, and in his written orders he fixed the hour at 3 A.M. The conference lasted until dusk of the twenty-third. As soon as it ended Jackson set out on another long, hard ride to rejoin his troops, while the other commanders returned to their divisions to begin preparations for battle. On the very next day the scales of chance tipped toward the Federals: a deserter from the Valley army warned them that Jackson was on his way to Richmond.[13]

Unaware of the vital security leak, as were also Lee and Jackson, Harvey Hill readied his division for combat. One order that he issued was aimed at "hospital rats," the contemptuous army term for officers and men who sensed an impending battle and dodged it by feigning illness. Hill scored "the laziness and inefficiency" of the division surgeons, who in his opinion had permitted excessive absenteeism; laid down new rules for curbing the issuance of certificates of disability and discharge; and decreed: "Brigade and Regimental Commanders will institute a rigid inspection at once of the sick Camps and hospitals and drag out the drones and the Cowards." [14]

This order was dated June 24, and presumably was put into effect during the last two days before the battle in an effort to bring the division to maximum strength. When Hill started his march toward Mechanicsville Bridge, in the early morning darkness of the twenty-sixth, his five brigades and seven batteries, including three temporarily attached artillery units, totaled a little less than ten thousand men. By 8 A.M. they were in position, together with Longstreet's division, behind a crest of wooded hills overlooking the Chickahominy. The thick summer foliage concealed them from Union pickets across the river and from McClellan's far-off observation balloons, floating like silken bubbles in the bright morning sky.[15]

And now began a long wait for Jackson to advance—a wait that stretched on and on, until for the high command the tension became almost unbearable. A note from Jackson, received by Lee that morning, had warned that high water and mud were delaying the Valley forces, but surely they would appear before long. From a hilltop vantage point Lee, Longstreet, and Harvey Hill anxiously scanned the countryside beyond the river. After a while they were joined by President Davis, Secretary of War Randolph, and a number of other political leaders who had ridden out from Richmond.[16] As the hours passed, the wonder grew: what could possibly have thrown the hard-marching Valley army so far behind schedule? Lee made no effort to solve the mystery by sending out couriers to locate the missing attacking force.

The hour dragged past noon, past 3 P.M. Then suddenly the electrifying sound of musketry broke out upstream. A. P. Hill was driving down from Meadow Bridge, with the Yankees retreating before him! Jackson, then, must be on his way to flank Porter. The attack at last was under way and there might yet be time to carry it through to success. Hill and Longstreet hurried to alert their divisions for the crossing.

As Hill had his men nearer the bridge, Longstreet ordered him to cross first. The crossing was delayed by difficulty in repairing the bridge, which the enemy had partially destroyed. While repair crews were still at work President Davis and his followers hurried past them on their way to see the battle.[17]

By the time Hill could get his leading brigade, Ripley's, across the stream, A. P. Hill was engaged in a hot fight around Mechanicsville. Harvey Hill pushed Ripley's men forward, bolstered by five batteries of artillery, and helped drive the Federals out of the village. They retreated to the east side of Beaver Dam Creek, where from previously prepared positions their artillery and infantry poured a destructive fire across the stream.[18]

Hill must have learned about this time that A. P. Hill had not attacked in coordination with Jackson. The new major general, whose temperament was even fiercer than his luxuriant red beard, had waited for the Valley army until his patience was exhausted and then had struck out across the river on his own, in the belief, as he later explained, that further delay might ruin the whole offensive. Jackson was not turning the Union right as planned; his whereabouts was still unknown. No wonder Porter was standing so firm! Until the Valley army came up, he was safe behind Beaver Dam Creek.[19]

Flowing generally north–south into the Chickahominy, the creek served as a formidable natural barrier in front of the Union defense line. It ran waist-deep through a swampy-bottomed, steep-banked valley, approached on the western or Confederate side by open plains exposed to the Federal fire from across the stream. To the Union left, a destroyed bridge marked the point where the Cold Harbor road crossed the creek, a little more than a mile southeast of Mechanicsville. Here on the east bank stood a gristmill known as Ellerson's Mill. East of the mill, Federal artillery and infantry held entrenchments on a hill that formed a key strongpoint of this southern portion of the line.[20]

As A. P. Hill pushed his troops on past Mechanicsville, he formed them in battle line along the creek, with General William D. Pender's brigade opposite Ellerson's Mill, and the other brigades north of it. Lee by this time had crossed the Chickahominy and apprised himself of the confused military situation. Having been told that there was quicksand in the creek to the north, he sent orders to Powell Hill, as the action mounted in that direction, not to advance but to hold his ground. If A. P. Hill transmitted these orders to his brigadiers, neither he nor any of his generals mentioned it afterward in their official reports. From all indications, he had one central idea that day—attack! Meeting Ripley, of Harvey Hill's division, he requested him to cooperate in an assault on the Union left.[21]

Apparently without communicating with Harvey Hill, on that confused field of battle, Ripley started his brigade toward Ellerson's Mill, where Pender's troops were already engaged. He was complying with the request of Powell Hill, but before he reached his destination he received much higher authority for the attack than that aggressive young commander could give him. As he later reported, "While the troops were in motion I received orders to assault the enemy from General Lee and also from Maj. Gen. D. H. Hill. . . ."[22]

These orders resulted from an important change of plans on the part of Lee. Prior to the battle he had considered Porter's line along Beaver Dam Creek too strong to be taken by anything but a turning movement around the right flank. But now that his initial plans had gone awry, he had decided to support Powell Hill's attack against the Union left. He was haunted by fears that if he did not keep up his pressure against McClellan's army the Union general might take Richmond, or perhaps strike a disastrous blow against Jackson. Therefore, he ordered Harvey Hill to send a brigade forward to join in Pender's assault.[23]

Hill may have delayed in obeying because he thought the attack on the strong Federal position would prove costly and futile. He stated in his official report that he advanced with Ripley's troops after receiving "several messages from General Lee and one from the President of the Confederate States to send forward a brigade," but did not explain why so many orders to him were necessary. His son, D. H. Hill, Jr., further asserted in a postwar military history that Hill delayed ordering Ripley to attack because he was "adverse" to a "frontal waste of life," but it is not clear whether the younger Hill was repeating what his father had told him or simply drawing his own conclusions. At any rate Hill finally did move toward Ellerson's Mill with Ripley's brigade. Ripley may or may not have told him that he had already started toward that point at the suggestion of Powell Hill.[24]

In advancing with Ripley's brigade Harvey Hill met General Pender, who reported that his men had been roughly handled by the enemy. At Ellerson's Mill they had encountered a dam and a mill-race, had been unable to cross, and had been driven back by concentrated enemy fire. Still Pender thought that with two of Ripley's regiments joined to his brigade he could move to his right and turn the Union position while Ripley's other two regiments advanced in front of it. To this plan Hill agreed. He directed Ripley to co-operate with Pender.[25]

About dark the attack was made, and resulted in a bloody repulse. The regiments charging in front of Ellerson's Mill apparently escaped with comparatively few casualties because in the uncertain light the Federal defenders shot too high, but those attempting the turning movement farther downstream met a deadly hail of shell, canister, and musketry. Ripley's First North Carolina Regiment sustained 142 casualties, his Forty-fourth Georgia lost 335 out of 514, and the total loss in his brigade that day was 575. Pender's losses in the fighting around Mechanicsville were not reported separately. The total Confederate battle loss was about 1,350 as compared with a Federal loss of 361.[26]

And while so many Southern soldiers were charging to their death, where was Jackson? After slow marching had caused him to fall more and more behind schedule, he had finally arrived, about five o'clock that afternoon, at the point northeast of the headwaters of Beaver Dam Creek where he was supposed to join with the remainder of the army in the sweep down the Chickahominy. But finding no sign of any supporting forces, and no messenger from Lee to explain the situation, he bivouacked his troops for the night, without attempting to march to the sound of the firing that rolled up from the south, and without attempting to communicate with Lee.

Thus, although Confederate success on the twenty-sixth depended upon good liaison between Jackson and the rest of the army, so that all the tactical movements could be properly coordinated, there was no effective liaison whatever. Lee had detailed General L. O'B. Branch's brigade, of A. P. Hill's division, to march on the north side of the Chickahominy between Jackson and the river and serve as a communication link, but this device had not worked. In fact, neither Jackson, A. P. Hill, nor their subordinate commanders had shown awareness of the urgent need for constant communication. If their purpose had been to remain hidden from one another as they marched on the enemy through the swamps and woods, they could hardly have achieved it more completely.[27] Lee himself had inexplicably failed to break down the day-long wall of silence between himself and Jackson by sending out couriers to locate and direct his missing general. Had he done this, he could in all probability have avoided the slaughter at Ellerson's Mill.

The abortive attack at the mill did not end the day's fighting. Following the repulse of Ripley's and Pender's brigades, the opposing infantry and artillery units along Beaver Dam Creek continued to exchange fire until about 9 P.M. Fighting broke out again next morning as soon as objects grew visible through the rising mist, but after a while it became evident that the Federals' brisk cannonade was covering a withdrawal. They had learned that Jackson was in position to flank them and had begun a retreat down the Chickahominy toward Powhite Creek, about four miles distant.[28]

The way was now open for Lee to carry out the four-column sweep down the north side of the river that he had planned for the previous day. Near the stream, Longstreet and A. P. Hill could pursue the enemy and drive the Federals from New Bridge, thus reestablishing close communication with the troops defending Richmond, and ending the danger of a quick Union seizure of the capital. Farther north of the river, Jackson and Harvey Hill could march eastward to the vicinity of Old Cold Harbor. Their advance would turn Powhite Creek, another north–south tributary, where Lee thought Porter might try to stand as he had at Beaver Dam Creek. Also, from Old Cold Harbor they could strike at enemy communications with the York River Railroad or descend on Porter as he retreated before A. P. Hill and Longstreet.[29]

By nine o'clock of that clear, hot morning Longstreet and Powell Hill had their pursuit of the enemy well under way. Much earlier Harvey Hill had marched northeastward on the road from Mechanicsville to Bethesda Church, under orders, received from Lee the previous night, to cooperate on the left with Jackson. Before he could advance, he had to capture enemy entrenchments blocking his way. This he accomplished by sending Garland and Anderson on a turning maneuver that forced the Unionists to retreat from their earthworks.[30]

Moving ahead he effected a juncture with Jackson, coming down from the north, and then passed on to Jackson's left, taking a circuitous route by way of Bethesda Church to Old Cold Harbor. Jackson now had under his control the bulk of Lee's forces north of the Chickahominy, consisting of four divisions, Hill's, his own, led by General Charles S. Winder, and those of Generals Richard S. Ewell and William H. C. Whiting.[31] He and Hill that morning must have shared Lee's hope for a swift, decisive victory over Porter, but if so they reckoned without the handicaps that burdened the Army of Northern Virginia.

All the generals of the army from Lee down still had much to learn about the difficult art of maneuvering large bodies of troops; their marching techniques and their staff and courier systems needed improvement and development. Moreover, the crude maps they used were sadly inaccurate and lacking in place names north of the Chickahominy—a shocking fact that reflected little credit either on the engineer corps that had prepared them or upon the engineer-commanding general who had failed to see that they were done right. Without adequate maps, the Confederate commanders, although only a short distance from their national capital, were forced to grope blindly through unfamiliar terrain which the enemy knew much better than they.[32]

Not shown on their maps was the place selected by the Federals for a second defense line. It was not Powhite Creek as Lee had supposed, but another little watercourse just east of it. This stream, called Boatswain's Swamp by local residents because of the marshes along its lower reaches, began a short distance south of Old Cold Harbor, ran southwest for about two miles through a maze of trees and underbrush, and then curved southward into the Chickahominy. On an accurate map it formed an over-all pattern somewhat like a large capital "L" set upon the line of the river and tipped forward on its base. On high ground within the angle and along the stem of the L Porter had posted his infantry and artillery, so as to form a convex front. In some places men and guns stood three tiers deep behind hastily improvised breastworks.[33]

Hill, arriving in the vicinity of Old Cold Harbor early in the afternoon, came upon the right flank of this stout defense line, near the top of the L, and found that the Federals, facing north, blocked the only road by which he could advance his artillery. The enemy position, manned by Union regulars under his former West Point comrade, George Sykes, was too strong to be taken by a lone division, so he waited for the rest of Jackson's forces to come up—waited a long, long time, until nearly sunset. Part of this time he occupied a completely ineffective position, to which Jackson, who was confused about the military situation, withdrew him.

Jackson was having a bad afternoon. In his march to Old Cold Harbor he had been delayed by getting on the wrong road, a mishap that had forced him to reverse his column and follow Hill. After reaching his destination he was slow to grasp the Union position and his own relationship to it in the densely wooded terrain. Then, when he attempted to move Winder and Whiting into line on Hill's right, amateurish staff work resulted in further delay. No wonder Lee, when he encountered Jackson on the road that ran southwest from Old to New Cold Harbor, said: "Ah, General, I am very glad to see you. I had hoped to be with you before."

A commander of less tact and self-control might have said much more. For while Jackson had been floundering in his various difficulties, Confederate soldiers by the hundreds had been dying in futile attacks on the center of the Boatswain's Swamp line. A. P. Hill, leading the pursuit close to the river, had followed the enemy eastward past Powhite Creek, Gaines' Mill, and New Cold Harbor, and then about 2:30 P.M. had hurled his "Light Division," as he called it, against the main enemy position. Longstreet came up on the Federal left, but was held in reserve by Lee, who expected Jackson to attack the right flank at any moment and force Porter to extend his line. So Powell Hill fought alone until his division was exhausted, after which Lee replaced it with Ewell's division, brought over from the head of Jackson's column. Longstreet, too, was advanced against the Federal left. But piecemeal attacks would never win victory. Lee's orders to Jackson now were to get his remaining troops into line for a concerted charge.

Painfully, with much drifting of brigades in the swamps and tangled thickets, this was done; and at last as the sun, burning dim red through the battle smoke, dipped behind the horizon, the general advance got under way. Beginning on the extreme Confederate left with Harvey Hill, it continued to his right through Winder's, Ewell's, and Whiting's commands. On the far right, Longstreet's troops were pressing forward. The earth shook with the roar of musketry and belching guns.

Hill's five brigades struggled through a dense swamp and, emerging in considerable confusion on the southern edge, struck enemy troops and drove them back. Garland and Anderson surveyed the ground in their front. They were separated from the Federal ridge positions by some four hundred yards of open field, swept by fire from an enemy battery on their left. But over on their right Winder's and Lawton's brigades were advancing, and the Federal infantry opposing them was vulnerable to flank attack by Hill's division.

Hill rode up, and Garland and Anderson enthusiastically proposed a flanking charge across the plain. But what of the enemy battery on the left? "I don't think it can do much harm," said Garland, "and I am willing to risk it." Anderson answered in like spirit.

Hill then ordered a charge of the whole division, but not until he had sent five regiments to take the enfilading enemy guns from the front and rear. Only one regiment, the Twentieth North Carolina, reached the guns; and it held them only a short time before yielding them again to counterattacking Federals. But in that time the rest of Hill's troops at the swamp's edge, yelling like demons, rushed across the open space, mounted the ridge, and fell like a thunderbolt upon the Union flank.

The Federal line broke. As one soldier diarist of Anderson's brigade described it, "The Yank's run like turkeys. . . . Our forces formed a square and a whole Brigade of the Yanks run right in it. It was the most exciting scene imaginable . . . we forgot all fear and danger."

Victory! Rebel yells of triumph split the air, and were echoed off to the west, where other Confederate troops had breached the Federal positions. All along the line the enemy was retreating under cover of the gathering darkness. The battlefield, with its hideous carpet of dead and wounded, was in Southern hands. Some eight thousand men had fallen in Lee's army. The Federal toll was close to seven thousand.[34]

Victory even at so terrible a cost sent a thrill of pride through the Confederate army. General Lafayette McLaws of Magruder's command wrote his wife that, "General Lee is rapidly regaining, if he has not already regained entirely, the confidence of the Army and the people as a skilfull and even a dashing officer. . . ."[35] In the battlefield camps there was talk of individual deeds of heroism, and argument over which commander's troops had first pierced the enemy line. Harvey Hill claimed this honor, in his official report and ever afterward, but so did virtually every other Confederate commander except A. P. Hill. Southern journalists at the time wrote dramatically of Whiting's brigadier, John B. Hood, who had personally led his Fourth Texas Regiment in a charge on the Confederate right against enemy breastworks and guns. Later, Fitz John Porter stated that his line was penetrated in Hood's front and was not even shaken in any other place, an assertion that is not fully borne out by the reports of his subordinate commanders, much less by the Confederate reports. Among historians of Gaines' Mill, as the battle came to be called, Freeman is only one of many who have credited Hood with first breaking the Federal line.

But Harvey Hill's claim that his men were first cannot be completely discounted on the basis of the vague and conflicting official reports and postwar reminiscences; nor should modern students of the battle overlook Cadmus M. Wilcox, who commanded three of Longstreet's brigades on the right during the final action, and firmly believed all his life that his troops had reached the Federal guns ahead of Hood. In 1885, in a letter to Hill, Wilcox declared that "on our right the lines (Porters) were taken by my troops," and went on to describe an interesting post-battle conversation with Hood:

Several months after Gaines Mill, I had seen so much of Hood in the papers, and at the head of the 4th Texas taking so many guns, meeting Hood I said, You at the head of the 4th Texas were so busy, you could not see any of my men at the Yankee battery, he replied, Oh yes, you got there first but you could not hold them.

In view of the contradictory evidence, and of the very nature of the final action—a concerted charge in rugged, wooded terrain, obscured by battle smoke and approaching night—a widespread attack which no one saw as a whole but only in fragments, perhaps the best way to assign Confederate honors at Gaines' Mill is to accept the description of a general breakthrough that Lee gave in his official report. Indeed it is not improbable that the exhausted Federal defenders, their ranks thinned and their guns fouled by hours of fighting, broke simultaneously in several places along their line.[36]

As Hill's troops followed the retreating enemy on the twenty-seventh, they mingled with those of Winder and Lawton; and Hill, being the senior officer, took command of all the Confederate forces in his sector. With Lawton's concurrence, he halted the Confederate advance, reasoning that it was unsafe to attack an enemy of unknown reserve strength in the woods at night. This decision overruled Winder, who wanted to continue the pursuit. Later, when Hill had learned more about the difficulties with which the retreating Federals had to contend, he would say, "Winder was right; even a show of pressure must have been attended with great results." But that night he was content to bivouac his forces on the high ground captured from the enemy.[37]

About 9 P.M., a number of Union prisoners were brought to Hill's headquarters, a local residence known as the McGhee house. As Hill came forward to examine them, one major, crippled with a knee wound, let go the shoulder of the trooper supporting him and extended his hand.

"Hill, old fellow, how are you?"

To the surprise of his staff, Hill embraced the enemy officer like a brother. His prisoner was Henry B. Clitz, a friend of West Point and the Mexican War. Generals Anderson and Garland also knew Clitz well and greeted him warmly. Hill had the knee examined by his surgeon and was greatly relieved to learn that Clitz would not lose his leg. He and his friend slept on the same overcoat that night, and early the next morning he made preparations to send Clitz to Richmond in an ambulance.

Before the ambulance left, another prisoner was brought in—none other than John F. Reynolds, Hill's friend and tentmate at Corpus Christi, now one of Porter's brigadiers. His reaction at seeing an old army comrade was far different from Clitz's. He refused to recognize Hill! But at length, sitting in a proffered chair, his face covered with his hands, he said, "Hill, we ought not to be enemies."

There was no hard feeling on his part, Hill assured him, and urged him to think about his capture simply as the fortune of war.

Reynolds then explained that he did not so much mind being a prisoner as being captured asleep. As J. W. Ratchford, who was present, later remembered the embarrassed general's story: "He had been fighting and doing picket duty for several days and nights and was completely tired out, and the night before [his capture] when all was quiet he went to sleep in a little house on his line and was there captured by our men, his division [it was a brigade] having run away in the night."

On learning the cause of Reynolds' discomfiture, Hill told his de-

jected friend to cheer up, that everyone knew him to be a good soldier who "would do all that human nature could do."

At this Reynolds brightened and replied: "Hill, if you say that, I
will feel better about the matter. I know you would not mislead me,
and if you do not condemn me perhaps others will not. No man's
good opinion is more appreciated by me than yours is."

Hill then sent him off to Richmond in the same ambulance with
Clitz. There was no guard; Hill simply took his friends' word that
they would report themselves as prisoners. He also gave them his
wife's address, telling them to draw on her for any money they might
need, and to let him know if they needed any other assistance.
Reynolds was afterward released in a general exchange of prisoners,
returned to duty, rose to major general, and was killed at Gettysburg while commanding the left wing of the Union army.[38]

On that morning after Gaines' Mill, Hill's first concern was to
guard against a counterattack by the Federals, but soon after daylight it was discovered that they had retreated across the Chickahominy and burned the bridges. The question now which Lee had to
solve was: where was McClellan going? Not until the next morning,
Sunday, June 29, was he able to piece together enough information
from his scouts to make him reasonably certain that the Union
commander was retreating southward toward the James River, where
under the protection of Federal gunboats he could establish a new
base. Lee then issued swift orders: Jackson and D. H. Hill were to
march south across the Chickahominy at Grapevine Bridge and attack the Union rear guard north of White Oak Swamp. They
would support Magruder, who would come east from Richmond on
the Williamsburg road. Meanwhile Longstreet and A. P. Hill would
first move upriver and then swing southeast in a wide semicircle
designed to bring them against the Federal right flank south of the
swamp. By parallel roads from Richmond the troops of Generals
Benjamin Huger and Theophilus H. Holmes would also march southeast to complete what Lee hoped would be a winning concentration.[39]

But again unforeseen events outweighed careful planning. Jackson,
owing to the slowness of his men in repairing Grapevine Bridge, remained at that crossing until 3 P.M. Sunday. Then shortly after the
hour he received a message to the effect that Lee expected him to

resist Federal passage of the river until he was reinforced—an indication that Lee had fresh information that had renewed his uncertainty as to McCellan's intentions. Jackson now decided that he must hold his troops where they were until he was relieved by Lee. Accordingly, when Magruder encountered a strong enemy force at Savage Station, on the York River Railroad a short distance south of Grapevine Bridge, Jackson declined to assist him. Magruder launched a belated, timorous attack that was easily repulsed by the Federals, who continued their retreat after darkness.[40]

Despite this setback, Lee still could hope for success on Monday, the day he had set for the convergence of his full strength against the Union army, as it moved slowly under the burden of its abundant supplies from White Oak Swamp toward the James. He now ordered Magruder to circle back and support Longstreet and A. P. Hill in their eastward march against the Union right. Jackson was directed to pursue the Federals from the rear along the road, running southeast from Savage Station through the swamp, that they had used in retreat.[41]

At 1 A.M. Monday, Jackson, having been awakened by a drenching rain, rode out ahead of his troops to Savage Station, leaving orders for his special friend and staff member, the Reverend Major Robert L. Dabney, to march the infantry after him at dawn, with D. H. Hill's division in front. Dabney was greatly pleased when Hill led off promptly on time. Riding beside Hill at the head of the column he said:

"General Jackson can never get his brigades to move literally at dawn. . . . How do you do it?"

"By the force of hard scolding," Hill answered with a laugh.[42]

At Savage Station they rejoined Jackson, who had conferred with Magruder and Lee, and the march continued, with the advantage of the prompt start being gradually lost as Jackson took time to gather in Federal stragglers and abandoned supplies along the way. When, about noon, the column descended into White Oak Swamp, a curving ribbon of boggy woodland through which a muddy stream meandered, it was found that the enemy had already crossed the swamp and destroyed the bridge over the stream. On the south side, Union troops and guns stood ready to dispute a Confederate advance.

Jackson attacked this rear guard with a sudden salvo from massed artillery, but though the Federals retreated at first, they soon took up a stronger and better-protected position blocking the bridge crossing. Jackson then abandoned any serious attempt to get his troops over the stream. Sinking into an inertia caused, perhaps, by insufficient sleep and the mental strain of handling forces much larger than he was used to, in unfamiliar terrain, he did nothing to aid the futile efforts of Hill and other officers to launch some sort of attack. Not even a message from Longstreet, asking for help in attacking the enemy, could rouse him. Indifferent to the sound of Longstreet's guns, a short march off to the southwest, he allowed his eighteen thousand infantrymen to remain inactive through the afternoon.

Longstreet and A. P. Hill, the only two division commanders who got into proper position that day, fought the battle of Frayser's Farm, or Glendale, unaided, and suffered severe losses. After dark the enemy retreated some three miles farther southward to Malvern Hill, a commanding height close to the north bank of the James. Lee had lost his best opportunity to destroy the Federal army.[43]

Next morning he did not know exactly where his adversary had gone, but his orders to his commanders directed them to press the pursuit. Harvey Hill doubted the wisdom of such tactics in terrain largely unknown to the Confederates, and expressed his disapproval to Jackson, Longstreet, and Lee himself. Particularly was he disturbed by the thought that the Federals might mass their artillery and infantry on the Malvern plateau, which had been so graphically described to him by a local resident that he had become convinced it was an impregnable position.

"If General McClellan is there in force," he warned Lee, "we had better let him alone."

At this Longstreet laughed. "Don't get scared, now that we have got him whipped."

Hill later felt that it was this belief in the enemy's demoralization which outweighed his warning and led Lee to attempt one more attack when the Federals were discovered, as anticipated, on the Malvern heights. Cadmus Wilcox later explained the attack in similar terms. "Malvern Hill . . . was fought without reconnaissance, or rather without a detailed reconnaissance," he said. "The excuse . . . was, we were on a hot trail." [44]

However hot the trail may have been, the attack built up slowly. Jackson's column, leading the pursuit, struck the Federal outposts on the Willis Church road and drove them back to their main positions on Malvern. Then it took the rest of the morning for Hill and the other division commanders to deploy through swamp and dense woods and form a battle line facing south. As drawn by early afternoon at the base of the plateau, Lee's active line comprised, from the Confederate left to the right, Whiting's division, supported on its left rear by Isaac Trimble's brigade of Ewell's division; Hill's division; and Armistead's and Wright's brigades of Huger's division. Armistead, next to Hill, partially occupied ground that had been assigned to Magruder, who had taken the wrong road and was having a hard time reaching the battlefield. Longstreet's and A. P. Hill's battle-worn divisions were in reserve on the right. Reserved on the left were Jackson's division, and all of Ewell's except Trimble.[45]

Hill, like the other generals, moved his troops into line under fire from the Union artillery. While the brigades were advancing across an open field and fording a creek, the dead and wounded began to fall. Anderson got his brigade across the stream first, clashed with Federal pickets, and was wounded in the skirmish. Colonel C. C. Tew took over his command.[46]

In the woods beyond the creek, where the division halted by order of Jackson, there was more shelter from the shrieking shells, but they crashed through the trees and undergrowth with an unearthly din and sometimes with deadly effect. Hill saw one missile burst through a tree trunk behind which a soldier was seated and take off the man's head. When he himself chose a tree for a back rest, while he wrote some orders, he sat down on the side nearer the Federal batteries, calmly facing toward the big guns.

Here Colonel John B. Gordon approached him. This young officer, who was commanding Rodes's brigade while the general was absent on sick leave, had formed, as he later put it, "a most cordial and ... intimate" friendship with Hill, and was distressed to see him in such an exposed position. He urged him to get on the other side of the tree.

Hill replied, "Don't worry about me; look after the men. I am not going to be killed until my time comes."

Almost with the words a shell exploded near him, rolling him on the ground, ripping his uniform with metal fragments, and painfully bruising him. As Gordon recovered from the concussion, he saw his commander get shakily to his feet. Quietly, thoughtfully, Hill brushed the dirt from his torn uniform. Then he sat down on the other side of the tree.[47]

The halt in the woods was for the purpose of reconnaissance. Lee hoped to find good artillery positions from which to bombard the Federals. Riding up to Lafayette McLaws, who was waiting for Magruder to arrive, he ordered him to take part in the search for gun emplacements. McLaws rode about for some time on this mission, then returned to the rear to make his report. He found Lee asleep under a tree, with President Davis watching beside him. Davis admonished him not to wake Lee, explaining that he had been up all night. But at the sound of their voices Lee sat up and resolutely focused his weary mind on what McLaws had to say.[48]

Piecing together the varying descriptions of terrain reported by McLaws, Longstreet, and other officers, he decided that he would first pound the Federal positions with a converging artillery fire from his right and left and then, if the blue lines wavered, throw his infantry forward in a general charge. His assistant adjutant general, Colonel R. H. Chilton, was put to work drafting the necessary orders to the division commanders.

Hill meanwhile had been reconnoitering with his five brigade commanders and awaiting orders. About 2 P.M. he received, through Jackson, this brief message signed by Chilton: "Batteries have been established to rake the enemy's lines. If it is broken, as is probable, Armistead, who can witness the effect of the fire, has been ordered to charge with a yell. Do the same." [49]

The yell from Armistead's troops, then, would start the general charge. It was a weak signal; yells were all too common on battlefields; but Hill of course prepared to obey it. Showing the message to his brigade commanders, he went forward with several of them to a vantage point from which they could observe the effects of the Southern firing, which had already commenced.

Ahead of them, in the afternoon sunlight, the Willis Church road slanted up over the crest of the Malvern plateau, which loomed before them like a broad, low, grassy amphitheater, its upper tiers wreathed in smoke from flashing gun batteries. Guarding the guns, and partially visible behind trees, fences, and ravines, were two lines of blue-coated infantry, one behind the other. To reach the first line, Hill's troops would have to charge up an open slope 300 to 400 yards long swept by the enemy artillery and musketry. It would be a desperate venture—Hill already knew that from his earlier reconnaissance. If only he had some artillery of his own! But his guns had been ordered back to Seven Pines to refit, and no batteries to replace them had been sent by General William Nelson Pendleton, commanding Lee's reserve artillery.[50] So it was up to other generals to hammer those blue lines into confusion before the Southern infantry charged. Impatiently Hill waited for the mounting roar of Lee's massed guns.

It never came. Instead, to his amazement, a few divisional batteries challenged the concentrated power of the enemy and were quickly knocked to pieces by Federal fire. Hill may or may not have known that Jackson's chief of artillery, Colonel Stapleton Crutchfield, was absent sick, or that Lee was completely out of touch with General Pendleton, who had with him some ninety guns. But he could plainly see that the bombardment that was supposed to break the enemy lines was "of the most farcical character," and he so reported in a message to Jackson, asking what he should do under the circumstances.

Back came Jackson's reply: Charge when Armistead's men raised the yell.[51]

So Hill and his brigade commanders continued to watch and listen, while the shadows deepened at the base of the Malvern plateau, and the Union guns repeatedly overwhelmed the gallant but hopelessly outnumbered batteries that tried to keep up the Confederate bombardment. In the event of a general advance, Hill reasoned, he would have the support of Whiting on his left. On his right were Huger's brigades, and they were reinforced about 4 P.M. by the arrival of Magruder, who had finally found his way to the battlefield.

With six brigades of his own, and three of Huger's division, Magruder had a total of nine under his control on the right. In command of his First Brigade was a burly, quarrelsome brigadier for whom Hill had scant regard—Robert Toombs, former United States Senator from Georgia, former Secretary of State of the Confederacy, and now a political general and an unstinting critic of West Pointers in the army. West Pointers, Toombs had been known to proclaim with a characteristic burst of profanity, were generals with so much training they were scared to fight. When the Confederacy was dead, and it would be soon, its epitaph should read, "*died of West Point.*" [52]

But even the aggressive Toombs must have wondered, that afternoon, how Lee could hope to take Malvern Hill with an infantry charge. That he could not was the conclusion of Hill and his subordinates. After the beaten Confederate artillery had withdrawn and the hour had passed 6 P.M., the brigade commanders began leaving Hill to return to their men and prepare for the night.

At that moment, off to the right side of the Southern line, the shrill rebel yell arose, followed by the sound of musketry.

"That must be the general advance!" exclaimed Hill, and the others agreed with him. At his command they hurried to bring up their brigades.

Swiftly the battle lines were formed at the edge of the woods, and on either side of the Willis Church road the brigades went forward up the long, open slope of the plateau. On the crest above them, smoke and flame blossomed. The earth rocked to the crash of the guns. Exploding grapeshot and canister tore gaps in the advancing gray lines. Garland's men, immediately in front of Hill, pressed on through the storm of metal until volleys from the Union infantry began to cut through their ranks. Then, oblivious to Garland's efforts to keep the charge going, they threw themselves face down on the ground and began firing at the enemy. A breathless messenger brought back Garland's urgent call for help.[53]

On his heels arrived another messenger from Colonel Gordon. His men had broken the first line of Federal infantry, and had reached a point not much more than two hundred yards from the enemy batteries, when their ranks began thinning so rapidly that he had ordered them to lie down and open fire. To hold his position he must have support.[54]

Support—yes! The whole division was in desperate need of it. But where was it? Where were Magruder's troops, Huger's, Whiting's? In growing anger and dismay, Hill realized that the yell on the right had not been followed by the concerted advance called for in Lee's orders. So far as he could see, his division was fighting alone!

Hastily he sent word back to Jackson that he was in great need of reinforcements. Jackson would surely send up some of his reserve units. But they had fallen far back in the woods to escape the enemy shelling—too far; it would take time to bring them up through the swamps and undergrowth.[55] Meanwhile Hill would have to shift for himself.

Galloping over to a drifting regiment, he found it to be the Sixth Georgia, of Colquitt's brigade. He sent it to Garland's support.

Then, wheeling his horse, he saw a mass of Confederate troops by a fence to the rear. Back he dashed and queried the men. Whose brigade was this? Toombs's! That meant that Magruder must be attempting some kind of attack on the right. The brigade had veered in confusion from that side of the line.

As Toombs was not with his troops and had evidently lost control of them, Hill rallied the brigade and ordered it forward to the support of Garland. To hearten the men he led them in person up the slope, through the thickening smoke and the blinding, deafening geysers of dirt and noise thrown up by the exploding shells. They advanced with him as far as the brow of the hill, then broke under the enemy fire and retreated in disorder.

His own troops were breaking now. Colquitt's and Anderson's brigades were falling back; Ripley's men were streaming to the rear. Support had finally arrived from Huger and Jackson, but not soon enough nor in sufficient numbers to do any good. As night drew on, Garland and Gordon slipped back with the bloody remnants of their brigades.[56]

Then, between sunset and darkness, Hill watched the belated, futile charges of the bulk of Magruder's troops, thrown in piecemeal on the right. It was heart-stirring to see how those brave men rushed forward—and sickening to see how the relentless Union guns tore each brigade to pieces as it emerged from the woods. What could Southern courage avail to save a blundering, mismanaged battle? Nothing! The wages of gallantry, on this disastrous field, were death.[57]

Somewhere in the darkness and confusion of the lost battle, Hill encountered Robert Toombs. "Where were you when I was riding up and down your line rallying your troops?" he demanded. Then after angrily rebuking the unhappy brigadier for boasting about his desire to fight and failing to do so, he rode on.[58]

While pulling his shattered division together, and posting his brigades and the late-arriving supporting units in safe positions for the night, he began to learn details of what had happened on the right side of the Confederate line. A disheartening story it was, of misapprehension and disorganized effort. Magruder, on finally reaching the battlefield about 4 p.m., had found that Armistead had advanced three of his regiments to a sheltering roll of land part way up the slope of Malvern Hill. Perhaps to inform Lee of this—his exact purpose is not known—Magruder sent a staff officer, Captain A. G.

Dickinson, to the commanding general. Lee by this time had planned an infantry attack on his far left, but after receiving the news of Armistead's advance, coupled with reports from Whiting that indicated the Federals were retreating, he quickly reverted to his original plan for a general charge. Accordingly, he sent Dickinson back with directions to Magruder to "advance rapidly" and "follow up Armistead's successes." Magruder received this message just after reading, for the first time, Lee's earlier order outlining the plan for a general charge. Thus doubly galvanized into action, he launched a hasty, poorly organized attack which produced enough cheering at the outset to precipitate Hill's charge on the left, but was hampered throughout by delay and confusion, culminating finally in the slaughter that Hill had witnessed after sunset.[59]

Hill thought that Whiting should have moved to assist him on the left, but Jackson stated afterward in his official report that he had directed Whiting to form in support of the artillery on the left, and "to remain there until further orders." There is no indication, either in Jackson's report, Whiting's, or Lee's, that Whiting was ever directed to participate in the general charge, or released from duty with the artillery. Hill had obeyed orders by charging when the attack on the right commenced, but so apparently had Whiting by remaining where he was. Whether Lee had handled his forces wisely is another matter. Malvern Hill has been described as his "great tactical mistake." [60] *

Five thousand dead and wounded Confederate soldiers lay that night on the reddened slopes between the woods and the restless Union guns. Some seventeen hundred of them belonged to Hill's division. Lee's entire army was badly demoralized, in the opinion of Isaac Trimble. Had McClellan attempted a counterattack, he might have achieved a much greater victory than had already been won.

But retreat, not further fighting, was in the Union commander's mind that night. Across the dark battlefield, where men with flickering lanterns sought the piteously crying wounded, Hill and Trimble rode to within a hundred steps of the Union batteries and heard, away in the distance, a rumbling of wheels. The Federal retreat had begun.[61]

* *The Story of the Confederacy*, by Robert S. Henry, copyright 1931, 1936 by the Bobbs-Merrill Company, Inc., used by special permission of the publishers.

V

"LEE HAS MADE A GROSS MISTAKE"

I AM PERFECTLY WELL, never better. For eight days, I have not washed my face, have slept on the ground without bed or blanket, have not taken off boots or spurs, have been struck four times without being seriously hurt once. Surely, God even our God ought to be adored and worshipped."

So Hill wrote Isabella on July 3, 1862. Two days had elapsed since the battle of Malvern Hill. The Confederate army was following the enemy toward the James in a final, fruitless pursuit that would end on the fourth with Lee deciding that McClellan was in too strong a position under the protection of his gunboats to be attacked. Hill had been retained at the battlefield because, as Jackson told him in sober truth, "your division requires rest." His men spent a week burying the dead and collecting arms and other equipment; then he marched them back to Richmond. On July 8, Lee withdrew his army to the vicinity of the capital.[1]

During the Seven Days' fighting around Richmond the Southern forces had suffered more than 20,000 casualties, as against a Federal loss of close to 16,000. Hill had lost 4,000 of the slightly less than 10,000 men that he had taken into the field.[2] For his troops the battle on the slopes of the Malvern plateau had been, in his words, "the most bloody of all." His distress over the way his division had been cut up was mingled with regret that, as usual, the Richmond newspapers had overlooked the exploits of his men.

As a professional soldier, he was proud of his achievements in the Seven Days' campaign. No other of Lee's commanders had made a better record of sustained effort and accomplishment unmarred by personal failure. Both Lee and Jackson, in their official reports, would praise him without reservation. There was also satisfaction in the thought that while McClellan's army had not been destroyed it had been driven away from its siege lines in front of Richmond. Hill dismissed McClellan's claims to victory in the recent battles with the terse comment, "The art of lying can go no farther." [3]

In one respect the Malvern affair had not ended for Hill. Robert Toombs was seething over the way he had been rebuked the night of the battle, and on July 6 he sent Hill a demand for "such explanation of that language as you may choose to give." He made it plain that he felt that Hill had insulted both him and his brigade.

Hill replied on the same day that his remarks "were personal to yourself and not to your brigade. . . . What I said was in substance this: 'You have been wanting to fight, and now that you have one, you have got out of it.' " Then he elaborated:

It is notorious that you have a thousand times expressed your disgust that the commanding general did not permit you to fight. It is equally notorious that you retired from the field. These are the two facts of which I reminded you. . . . I made no comment upon them, and if the simple truth has been offensive, the interpretation of it has been your own.

On reading this, Toombs dashed off his second note of July 6, the gist of which was: "I now demand of you personal satisfaction for the insult you cast upon my command and myself on the battlefield . . . and for the repetition and aggravation thereof in your note of this day."

For some reason, Hill did not receive this message until July 11. On the twelfth he wrote his answer, again denying, at the outset, that he had reflected upon Toombs's brigade. Since Toombs evidently expected him either to apologize or to fight a duel, he continued, "I will state that I will make full, public, and ample concessions when satisfied that I did you injustice; and this I would do without any demand. I certainly thought that you had taken the field too late, and that you left it too early." Possibly, however, Toombs had done his "whole duty." If this proved to be so, Hill would be "gratified," and his "acknowledgment of error" would be "cordial and complete." But if Toombs meant his note to be a challenge, Hill rejected it on the grounds that "its acceptance, when we have a country to defend and enemies to fight, would be highly improper and contrary to the dictates of plain duty.... I will not make myself a party to a course of conduct forbidden alike by the plainest principles of duty, and the laws which we have mutually sworn to serve."

This unorthodox letter threw Toombs into the awkward position of having to argue that Hill ought to quit writing and start fighting. According to "common usage," correspondence between them should have ceased, he protested on July 13. He had certainly meant his previous note "as a peremptory demand for a hostile meeting." Dropping the charge that Hill had insulted his brigade, he declared:

Your allegations against me are now reduced to a tangible and clear certainty. You say, "I certainly thought you had taken the field too late and that you left it too soon." This statement impugns my honor as a gentleman and a soldier. It was and is your duty to see to it, that you were in full possession of my orders and all the facts and circumstances necessary to sustain this statement before you made it. I deny your right to cast upon me insulting imputations and then to demand of me the disproval of them as a condition to your either withdrawing them or giving me the satisfaction usual among gentlemen. . . .

Hill's reply, he went on, left him in doubt as to whether Hill would ever fight him. As for Hill's mention of laws they had mutually sworn to obey—

I have never sworn not to violate any of the rules and articles of war, but as those rules only forbid challenges between persons in the military service, if you will state that to be the only remaining difficulty I will remove it, by my resignation. I close, sir, by the simple renewal of my former demand and with the single additional remark that I do not consider a refusal to meet me as satisfaction.

But refusal was all the satisfaction that Toombs got. On July 15, Hill expressed regret that his last note, "which was intended to be conciliatory," had been "misunderstood or misappreciated," and put an end to the debate. "I take it for granted," he wrote, "that you know enough of my previous history to be aware that a hostile meeting under any circumstances would be abhorrent to my principles and character. At this time, it would be in the highest degree improper." He stated that he had already offered Toombs "the only redress which I could make even after a meeting, viz, the acknowledgement of error when convinced of that error"; declared that "no good can result from a continued correspondence"; and served notice that "it will close on my part with this communication."

Thus Toombs was left both frustrated and furious. He lost no time in denouncing Hill as a "poltroon," but his epithets bounced harmlessly off the shield of Hill's reputation for courage in battle.[4]

By mid-July Hill was concerned with a matter of much greater importance than a threatened duel. Lee, on the fourteenth, assigned him the duty of negotiating a cartel for the exchange of prisoners between the Confederate and the United States armies. President Lincoln and Secretary of War Edwin M. Stanton appointed Major General John A. Dix to serve as the Federal negotiator.

Hill and Dix, after several meetings at Haxall's Landing on the James, reached an agreement on July 22 that was designed to bring about the release of all prisoners of war. To meet the problem of an excess of captives on one side or the other, they decided that surplus prisoners would be released under parole and denied further military service, while prisoners exchanged on an even basis could again bear arms. The cartel was accepted by both sides, and for a time a brisk exchange of prisoners was carried on under its terms; but provocative military incidents and retaliatory governmental proclamations led to its breakdown by the end of 1863, after which systematic exchange was not resumed until the war was nearly over.[5]

Scarcely had Hill completed these cartel negotiations, which earned him the official thanks of Lee, than he was plunged once more into the difficulties of departmental administration. As the outstanding North Carolinian in the Confederate service, he was ordered on July 17 to assume command of the North Carolina district in place of General Holmes, who had been transferred to the Department of the Trans-Mississippi. In a farewell address to his division he declared that he was relinquishing command of it "with unfeigned pain and reluctance," commended it for its good moral conduct and fine combat record, and took the opportunity to point out that "alone and unsupported" it had driven the enemy from the fieldworks at Seven Pines. After his departure no one succeeded to his place, "in consequence of confusion among the major-generals," as Lee put it. The troops that Hill had led continued to be designated officially as "D. H. Hill's Division."[6]

Hill took command of the North Carolina district in orders dated

July 29. The department had been expanded to run from Cape Fear up to Drewry's Bluff on the James. This required Hill to cope not only with the Federals occupying the Sound region of North Carolina but also with McClellan, who was holding his army at Harrison's Landing under the protection of the James River gunboats. Lee, anxiously surveying the strategic scene from Richmond, felt himself vulnerable to attack on both sides of the river, and also from the Shenandoah Valley, where General John Pope had been put in charge of a Federal "Army of Virginia." Accordingly, he dispatched Jackson to hold Pope in check, and directed Hill to strengthen the defenses of his department and strike at the enemy along the James. "I rely greatly upon your intelligence, energy, and zeal," he wrote Hill.[7]

Confederate military strength in the Department of North Carolina, as of July 15, totaled on paper 17,217 men and 141 pieces of artillery. Hill disposed his troops for defense in three regions under his subordinate commanders: Major General R. H. Anderson at Drewry's Bluff, Brigadier General Samuel G. French at Petersburg, Virginia, and Brigadier General T. L. Clingman in charge of North Carolina from Weldon to Cape Fear. For his departmental headquarters he chose Petersburg.[8]

His administrative tour of duty turned out to be unexpectedly brief; he experienced a little less than a month of multiple problems and anxieties. One of his immediate concerns was to suppress enemy marauders in the coastal region along the North Carolina–Virginia border. He wrote Secretary Randolph suggesting that the government raise and arm guerrilla companies whose "special duty" it would be "to kill the murderers and plunderers wherever they show their villainous faces." Randolph approved the plan, and Hill put it into operation.[9]

Another urgent objective was the fortifying of Drewry's Bluff and Petersburg against the possibility of a Union advance south of the James. Under the guidance of Lee, who sent an army engineer to Petersburg, Hill detailed large numbers of troops to work on the fortifications. To speed the building of the Petersburg line he collected some one thousand Negro slaves, chiefly from the planters of North Carolina. The defenses thus begun would eventually be completed under General French, and would prove to be of vital importance in 1864, when they would enable the Confederate defenders of Petersburg to hold off Grant's army.[10]

A third objective, emphasized in the directives that Hill received from Lee, was to impair and perhaps even sever McClellan's river communications by shelling Union shipping from the south bank of the James, but Hill's offensive efforts disappointed the Confederate commander. After a brief surprise bombardment by forty-one guns had failed, on August 1, to do much damage to the Federal ships and camps at Harrison's Landing, Lee wrote Hill that "this does not satisfy the object I had in view." What was needed in the river offensive, he went on, was "continuous and systematic effort and a well-digested plan. . . . I wish you would see what can be done in this way." [11]

But attacking McClellan's powerful army and gunboats with the inferior Confederate artillery was not easy, and McClellan made the task more difficult by occupying the south bank of the river opposite his camps. Hill accomplished little more offensively, and in the first · weeks of August McClellan successfully evacuated his James River base, having been ordered to join Pope.[12] On August 17 Lee wrote Davis that McClellan had escaped. Feeling "greatly mortified," Lee passed quickly in his letter from painful reflections on the incomplete success of the Seven Days' campaign to criticism of Hill:

This induces me to say what I have had on my mind for some time. I fear General Hill is not entirely equal to his present position. An excellent executive officer, he does not appear to have much administrative ability. Left to himself he seems embarrassed and backward to act. If the people would think so, I really believe French would make the better commander of the department. This is only for you to think about, but I fear all was not done that might have been done to harass and destroy our enemies, but I blame nobody but myself.[13]

After reading this, Davis replied that he would "send General Hill to resume the command of his old division." Orders were issued accordingly, and on August 21 Hill left Petersburg to join Lee's forces in northern Virginia. At Hanover Junction he took command of Lafayette McLaws's division as well as his own before heading northwest on August 26 for Rapidan Station.[14]

On the march, he set a fast pace. Howell Cobb's brigade, of McLaws's division, covered sixty miles in three and a half days. This seemed much too swift to the portly Cobb, a general without formal military training who in civilian life had made an impressive political record as Congressman from Georgia, governor of Georgia, Secretary of the Treasury under President James Buchanan, and President of the Confederate Provisional Congress. On reaching Rapidan Station he wrote his wife that during Hill's poorly directed and "inhuman" march, "Men absolutely fell and died on the side of the road from the heat—one case I know of and I have heard of others." For Hill he had epithets more scorching than the weather: "a weak, self-conceited heartless and cruel ass . . . as despicable a wretch, as ever disgraced any army." [15]

Hill was pushing his troops in an effort to take part in Lee's campaign against Pope. This had begun on August 9, when Jackson repulsed a part of Pope's army at Cedar Mountain. It culminated, August 29–30, while Hill was marching northward from Rapidan, in the Confederate victory of Second Manassas, after which Lee moved his army in a fighting advance to Chantilly. Here on September 2 Hill caught up with him.[16]

Lee, having wrecked Pope's reputation and driven the Union forces back to the defenses of Washington, now decided to carry the war into Maryland. He knew that his army was not properly equipped for the invasion. His transportation was weak, his soldiers were in rags, and thousands of them had no shoes. With food in short supply the men would have to subsist mainly upon green corn plucked from the fields along the way. But an offensive across the Potomac would protect Virginia from invasion, perhaps until winter weather ended the year's fighting. It might also arouse the Southern sympathies of the Marylanders, and inspire them to support the Confederate cause.

In addition, broad strategic vistas extending as far north as Harrisburg, Pennsylvania, opened before Lee when he studied his maps. By crossing the Potomac east of the Blue Ridge and advancing to Frederick, Maryland, he could threaten Baltimore and Washington and cause the Federals to withdraw from the south bank of the Potomac. From Frederick he could strike northwestward, crossing first the Catoctin Mountains and then the portion of the Blue Ridge known as South Mountain, and arrive at Hagerstown, just south of the Pennsylvania border. Here he could threaten to take Harrisburg, and perhaps do so if the opportunity arose. At the least he might force McClellan, who had again taken command of the Union army, to come out from Washington and fight far from his base of supplies. His own line of supply and communication would run down into Virginia along the sheltered route of the Shenandoah Valley.[17]

With this strategy in mind he set out for Maryland, and on the march his barefoot, underfed soldiers straggled in appalling numbers. The army that crossed the Potomac near Leesburg between September 4 and 7 had melted away to about 53,000 men. It was divided informally into wings, with Jackson commanding the left wing and Longstreet the right. Hill, whose division was the first to cross, came under Jackson's control after reaching the Maryland side. As Jackson had been painfully bruised by a fall of his horse, he put Hill in temporary command of all his forces on September 6, and Hill directed the seizure of Frederick, near which Lee encamped his army.[18]

At Frederick, Lee soon realized that he would get few recruits and supplies from the Marylanders, who stared in shocked dismay at the ragged and hungry army that had "liberated" their prosperous land. He also learned that the Federals had not evacuated the Valley towns of Martinsburg and Harpers Ferry as he had expected them to do when he advanced beyond the Potomac. The Harpers Ferry garrison, with its military supplies and more than 11,000 men, was a tempting prize; moreover, Lee reasoned that the two Union posts, if not reduced, would menace his Valley supply line. In order to capture them with as little delay as possible while carrying out his previously planned movement toward Hagerstown, he decided to make use of his favorite maneuver: rapid division and reconcentration of force in the presence of the slow-moving enemy.

The operation was to start on September 10. Longstreet's command, with the reserve artillery, the supply and baggage trains, and D. H. Hill's division as rear guard, would march northwestward on the Hagerstown, or National, road as far as Boonsborough, at the western foot of South Mountain. Jackson with his three divisions was to hurry westward to Martinsburg and drive the enemy from that post, then move down the south side of the Potomac to invest the rear of Harpers Ferry. In reducing the arsenal town he would be supported by two other detachments under Generals McLaws and John G. Walker. McLaws, with his own division and that of R. H. Anderson, was to occupy Maryland Heights, on the north side of the Potomac, opposite Harpers Ferry. Walker with his small division was to take possession of Loudoun Heights, on the east side of the

Shenandoah River, across from the town. Harpers Ferry was to be captured on September 12, after which all the Confederate units would reconcentrate at Boonsborough or Hagerstown.[19]

The audacity of the plan was breath-taking. Lee was calmly preparing to divide his already small army into four separate pieces under McClellan's very nose. McClellan by September 8 had advanced twelve miles northwest of Washington with some 67,000 men, backed by as many more reserves, and was sending out reconnaissance parties to probe the cavalry screen that Stuart had established along the Monocacy River, just west of Frederick. By marching swiftly across the mountains he could get among the scattered fragments of Lee's army and crush them one at a time. But rapid movement was the last thing that Lee expected of his cautious adversary. Stuart reported that McClellan was "advancing very slowly with an extended front, covering the roads to Washington and to Baltimore." Lee felt sure that he would have his army safely reunited before McClellan crossed South Mountain.[20]

At a council of war with Longstreet and Jackson, held in his headquarters tent at Frederick about September 9, Lee outlined his plan for dividing his forces to capture Harpers Ferry. Since neither he nor Jackson wrote afterward of what was said in the council, Longstreet's postwar accounts of it have been an important source for historians of the Maryland campaign. According to Longstreet, Lee had earlier asked him to lead an independent attack on Harpers Ferry, and he had objected to dividing the army; but in the council he found both Lee and Jackson so "heartily" in favor of the dispersal plan, with Jackson now leading the attack, that he tempered his own opposition to the scheme.[21] Modern historians, in much the same manner, have portrayed Jackson as pleased with his independent mission and voicing no objection to Lee's plan.

Yet there is strong evidence to the contrary. As will appear in a subsequent chapter, Jackson, after the close of the Maryland Campaign, made a point of telling Harvey Hill that in the council of war he, Jackson, had opposed dividing the army to capture Harpers Ferry.* The conflict between this statement and Longstreet's narrative is obvious.

Whatever was or was not said in the council, Lee on September 9 issued the written order that put his plan into effect—Special Orders

* See above, p. 161.

No. 191, a directive that would have fateful consequences for the Confederate army and, in particular, for Harvey Hill. When Jackson received his copy of the order, he himself, with a view to complete secrecy, wrote out another copy and sent it to Hill, whose rear-guard assignment took him out of Jackson's corps and put him under Lee's immediate command. With like caution, Hill folded up the sheet of note paper covered with Jackson's atrocious but accurate scrawl and put it in his pocket rather than trust it among his office papers.[22] Later he would have every reason to be glad that he had handled it so carefully.

On the tenth, as scheduled, the army moved out on the National road. Except for irrepressible straggling on the macadamized turnpike, so cruel to shoeless feet, the march across the mountains was uneventful; but at Boonsborough Lee received a report that an enemy force was coming from the north toward Hagerstown. In order to hold this strategic point and protect military supplies said to be there, he ordered Longstreet to march on to Hagerstown, thirteen miles farther up the road. He accompanied Longstreet's brigades, taking with him most of the reserve artillery. Hill was left at Boonsborough with the supply train and one battalion of the reserve artillery. Lee directed him to guard the roads leading north from Harpers Ferry against any Federal troops that might escape from the town, and also to support the cavalry in guarding Turner's Gap, the main pass of South Mountain, against an enemy advance from the east.[23]

In compliance with these orders Hill spread his five brigades— still led by the commanders of the Seven Days' fighting, Rodes, Garland, G. B. Anderson, Colquitt, and Ripley—along the western base of the mountain, with his headquarters tent about three miles from Turner's Gap. His division was only a skeleton of what it had formerly been. Straggling, which in his own phrase "had been enormous," had reduced it to a total strength of less than five thousand men.[24] Not a very strong force, certainly. Yet he would soon be compelled to pit it against two corps of McClellan's army!

Lee, to be sure, had never dreamed of placing his rear guard in so desperate a predicament, but a number of factors that he had not foreseen were now to impede the smooth working out of his audacious plans. Most important, Jackson and his support were falling behind the rigid time schedule set for them. Harpers Ferry, which was supposed to be captured on September 12, would not surrender until the morning of September 15.[25] For a considerably longer period than Lee had estimated, McClellan would have an opportunity to defeat the widely separated Confederate forces in detail.

Neither was McClellan quite so passive or so baffled by Lee's movements as the Confederate commander had expected him to be. Lee, just before scattering his divisions westward, had assured General Walker—if Walker remembered correctly many years later—that McClellan would not assume offensive operations with his "demoralized" army "for three or four weeks." [26] Yet by September 12 McClellan had sifted from a steady stream of intelligence reports the fundamentally important fact that Lee had divided his forces, and at 10 o'clock that morning he telegraphed Washington: "My columns are pushing on rapidly to Frederick. I feel perfectly confident that the enemy has abandoned Frederick, moving in two directions, viz., on the Hagerstown and Harper's Ferry roads." [27]

McClellan also knew, as he concentrated his blue columns within easy striking distance of Harpers Ferry, that the Washington authorities held him responsible for the safety of the Ferry garrison. In the late afternoon and night of September 12 he directed his wing commanders to be ready to march to its relief. The next day he received a telegraph message from Governor A. G. Curtin of Pennsylvania that stated: "Longstreet's division is said to have reached Hagerstown last night. Jackson crossed Potomac at Williamsport to capture Martinsburg and Harper's Ferry." The message was underlined by the roar of the Harpers Ferry guns, which could be heard at Frederick, and told plainly that the arsenal town was under attack.[28]

Thus by September 13 McClellan was under the responsibility of acting to relieve Harpers Ferry, and from the ordinary sources of army intelligence he had gained sufficient knowledge of Lee's troop dispositions to enable him to move advantageously against the divided Confederates. Whether he would actually have done so, had nothing else occurred to spur him on, is a question that forever must remain conjectural. For something else did occur. An extraordinary source of intelligence fell right into his lap.

Toward noon of September 13, on campground near Frederick, Private B. W. Mitchell of the Twenty-seventh Indiana Volunteers found three cigars wrapped in a copy of Lee's Special Orders No. 191, a copy issued from Lee's headquarters, signed by his chief of staff,

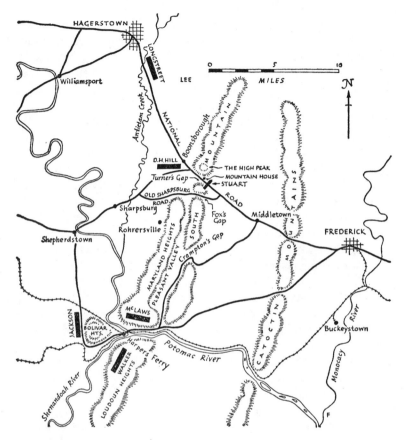

South Mountain and vicinity, and Lee's scattered army, about noon of
September 13, 1862.

Colonel R. H. Chilton, and addressed to D. H. Hill. Hurriedly this
exciting document was passed up the military hierarchy to McClellan,
who later recalled that it "was brought to me by some of my staff, as
having been found by some of the troops on ground vacated by the
camps of Genl Lee's army—recognizing Genl Chilton's signature I
was satisfied in regard to the genuineness of the order...." [29]

What actually satisfied him as to genuineness, at the time, was
doubtless not Chilton's signature alone, for surely he must have
realized that Chilton easily could have signed a false order, designed

as a ruse. A better proof of the genuineness of the order was the way it corroborated the information on Lee's movements that he already had. Exuberantly, at noon, he telegraphed President Lincoln that he had "all the plans of the rebels," and would "catch them in their own trap." "I think Lee has made a gross mistake, and that he will be severely punished for it." [30]

So the final unforeseen factor affecting Lee's strategy was the finding of the famous document known to history as the "Lost Dispatch." After McClellan had made use of it, stories of its discovery appeared in Northern newspapers, and speculation started on the intriguing question of how it had been lost. Irresponsible writers eventually charged Hill with losing it, and even with petulantly throwing it away.[31] Analysis of presently available evidence, however, leads to no conclusion so simple, but to a somewhat more complex mystery than has generally been associated with the Lost Dispatch.

Obviously, two copies of Special Orders No. 191 were prepared for Hill, one by Jackson and the other by Lee's office. As has already been seen, Hill received and carefully preserved Jackson's copy. He was able to produce it when speculation arose over the Lost Dispatch. As to the copy from Lee's office, Hill repeatedly declared that he never received it. His word on the matter was enough for certain of his colleagues; for example Charles Marshall, one of Lee's aides, wrote Hill shortly after the war, in regard to the Dispatch: "Your simple statement that you never saw it, puts an end to all conjecture as to the way you lost it." [32]

More convincing to the historian, who like the detective in the murder mystery must suspect everyone, is the fact that Hill's personal papers bear out his assertions that he never saw the Lost Dispatch. One of his letters to his wife indicates that at first he thought that Jackson's copy of Special Orders No. 191 was the only one that had been addressed to him. Even after McClellan's report had been published, reproducing the lost order with Hill's name at the bottom as the addressee, Hill clung to the hope that perhaps an error had been made in copying the document for the report. He carried on an extensive postwar correspondence trying to find out all circumstances surrounding the issuance of the Lost Dispatch. Finally in 1885 he conceded: "That an order from Lee directed to me was lost, I do not *now* doubt," but he coupled this with a reiteration that he had not received it.[33]

If Hill never saw the Lost Dispatch, what of his staff officers? His chief of staff, Major J. W. Ratchford, made affidavit after the war that the Dispatch had not been received at Hill's headquarters. Hill accepted this statement. Lee did not challenge it. In the absence of any evidence to the contrary, and in view of Ratchford's war record of honorable, efficient service, it would seem that his sworn word deserves credence.[34]

Writers on the subject of the Lost Dispatch have looked with suspicion upon Hill and his staff not only because Lee's order was addressed to Hill but also because in 1886 General Silas Colgrove, the former regimental commander of Private Mitchell, stated that Mitchell had discovered the Dispatch upon D. H. Hill's old campground. Yet Colgrove may have been mistaken. In 1868 General S. W. Crawford, a former division commander under McClellan, wrote Hill that he had arrived with his division at Frederick on the morning of September 13, and was informed by one of his staff officers that just prior to his arrival Lee's order had been discovered near the spot where he then stood. "He further informed me," wrote Crawford, "that we were then in A. P. Hill's old camp...."

For Hill's benefit Crawford cross-checked his own belief with McClellan's former chief of staff, R. B. Marcy. In answer to his query, Marcy replied on May 5, 1868:

I am of the opinion that the order of Lee that you inquire about was found in the camp which had been occupied by A. P. Hill and not D. H. Hill.

This has always been my impression from information obtained on the spot and it is hardly possible that I could be mistaken.[35]

Wishing not to reflect in any way on the reputation of A. P. Hill, who was killed in the war, Harvey Hill never published these statements.[36] Taken together they would seem to outweigh Colgrove's testimony of a later date.

Though he remained silent about A. P. Hill, Harvey Hill did defend himself after the war by pointing out that Lee's order to him could have been lost by Lee's own staff officers or couriers. Over these possibilities—in fact over virtually everything connected with the famous order—there was much inconclusive argument by Hill and others, in print, in letters, and in private memoranda. Of all the explanations of the mystery to be found in these writings, perhaps the most credible is the brief suggestion, made by both Hill and Ratchford, that one of Lee's couriers was acting as a Union spy.

One can arrive at the spy as the probable culprit by a process of elimination. On reflection, it is hard to believe that any staff officer of either Hill or Lee was so irresponsible as to keep, and use for cigar wrapping, a vital order meant only for Hill. It seems unlikely, also, that any of these picked, trusted men was disloyal. The couriers, though above average in intelligence, were not so select a group; and while no honest courier would be likely to wrap cigars in an important order given him to deliver, a spy might do so in order to conceal a stolen dispatch. To avoid exposure, the treacherous courier would need to submit to Lee's headquarters a false receipt of delivery, or possibly a failure to return the receipt could have been overlooked during the rush of preparations for the movement from Frederick. Finally the spy, or an accomplice to whom the innocent-looking cigar package had been passed, might have accidentally dropped it, or perhaps become frightened and discarded it.

All of which is speculation. But the treacherous courier was a war reality. Ratchford recalled that during the Maryland campaign "a spy acting as a Confederate courier was discovered near Harpers Ferry and was at once hung to a limb of a tree on the road-side." [37]

McClellan, of course, did not need to trouble himself with questions as to how Lee's order had failed to reach D. H. Hill. All that concerned him was its authenticity; having determined that, he sent his exultant telegram to Lincoln in full confidence that he now knew just how to move against Lee. The order told him why and how the Confederate army had been divided, and where it would reassemble. It was now plain beyond doubt that all he had to do, in order to relieve Harpers Ferry and wreak destruction upon Lee, was to push on through Crampton's Gap and Turner's Gap in that second range of rugged hills called South Mountain.

Yet in one important particular the order may have misled him. While it showed him correctly enough that forcing Crampton's Gap, on his left, would enable him to strike the rear of McLaws's forces on Maryland Heights, it also indicated that west of Turner's Gap, on his right, he would find both Hill and Longstreet. True, Governor Curtain had reported that Longstreet was said to have reached Hagerstown, but this was an uncertain message from a nervous civil official, and it may well have been outweighed in McClellan's mind by the fact that the order halted Longstreet at Boonsborough, just beyond Turner's Gap.[38]

Such a belief may help explain why McClellan did not take advantage of his best tactical move and rush the bulk of his army through Crampton's Gap. Only one corps was sent against this pass. The rest of the army was to march on the National road through Turner's Gap. The forcing of these mountain passes was scheduled for September 14. By the afternoon of the thirteenth, McClellan's foremost infantry troops were at Middletown, west of the Catoctin range. On the right and left his blue divisions were in position to reach Turner's Gap the next morning and Crampton's Gap by noon.[39] Before Harpers Ferry surrendered on the fifteenth, there would be ample time to do irreparable damage to Lee's divided army. Only one thing could save it. Somehow, the Confederates must hold the gaps against the oncoming blue host.

VI

HOLD AT ALL HAZARDS

AT BOONSBOROUGH, Harvey Hill got his first hint of danger on September 13. About noon, while he and Colquitt were engaged in reconnaissance around Boonsborough, a courier rode up with a message from Stuart. Two Federal brigades were pressing him back toward the eastern foot of South Mountain, wrote Stuart. Could Hill send one of his brigades up to Turner's Gap to help hold it? Hill ordered Colquitt to move immediately to the gap with his brigade and four guns, and because the brigades were now so small he also sent Garland's, together with another four-gun battery. To his other three commanders went orders to concentrate near Boonsborough.

While Hill watched, Colquitt formed his troops in marching column and led them from Boonsborough on the National road, which ran southeastward through the town and rose over the thousand-foot, northward coursing ridge of South Mountain, crossing it through Turner's Gap, a depression several hundred feet deep. About two miles from town Colquitt reached the Mountain House, a tollhouse at the apex of the gap, and here he found Stuart, calmly watching as his cavalry retreated up the mountain before the advancing enemy.[1]

Colquitt hurriedly disposed his troops to right and left of the turnpike, and the display of infantry and artillery stopped the Federals at the base of the mountain. Night approached, with no sign that they would attack. Colquitt discussed the situation with Stuart, and suggested that his infantry could continue to hold the turnpike while the cavalry guarded roads on either side of it. Many years later, he recalled Stuart's reply:

He informed me that he could not remain—that he should move with his cavalry towards Harpers Ferry—that I would have no difficulty in holding my position—that the enemy's forces, he thought, consisted of cavalry and one or two brigades of infantry.[2]

After this conversation, Stuart led his cavalrymen down the mountain to Boonsborough to spend the night. He did indeed plan to move toward Harpers Ferry the next morning—more specifically to Crampton's Gap, some five miles south of Turner's in a straight line. On the mountain, in the general vicinity of the turnpike, he had left his Jeff Davis Legion, together with Colonel Thomas L. Rosser and a detachment of cavalry and Stuart Horse Artillery, but apparently he did not inform Colquitt of this fact. Rosser was "annoyed," as he afterward put it, by the vagueness of his orders. Stuart directed him to occupy Fox's Gap, about a mile south of Turner's, but did not tell him to report to anyone. In Rosser's opinion, "Stuart did not expect the enemy would advance on Boonsboro, and was careless in guarding the roads leading that way." [3]

Earlier that afternoon Stuart had sent General Wade Hampton with most of his cavalry brigade to Crampton's Gap, to reinforce a cavalry detachment already there. Now he himself was headed that way; he was concentrating the bulk of his forces at Crampton's. One might ask whether this was in strict accordance with Special Orders No. 191, which directed Stuart to use "the main body of the cavalry" to "cover the route of the army." Since Lee with all the army except McLaws's and Walker's forces had marched up the National road through Turner's Gap, it would seem that this main pass was the one Stuart should have guarded with most of his men. Moreover, Lee later stated that part of Hill's duty at Boonsborough was "to support the cavalry," which could hardly mean anything but to assist Stuart in defending Turner's Gap. As will be seen, Lee expected the cavalry commander to remain at this pass.[4]

Stuart of course had reasons for his actions, and later in his official report to Lee he took pains to explain his movements up to the night of the thirteenth—especially his failure to realize that most of Mc-Clellan's army was preparing to march through Turner's Gap. "Every means was taken to ascertain what the nature of the enemy's movement was," he wrote, "whether a reconnaissance feeling for our whereabouts, or an aggressive movement of the army." But the Federals "studiously" avoided displaying more than part of one corps, and built no revealing campfires at Frederick. When September 12 passed, Stuart supposed that Harpers Ferry had been captured as scheduled, yet he still deemed it important to ascertain the nature of the Federal movement. He kept hoping that General Fitzhugh Lee (Lee's nephew), who had been ordered to scout behind the enemy, would report, but the expected information was not received. On the thirteenth, when he was driven from the Catoctin Mountains through Middletown to Turner's Gap, he was still able to discover no larger force of Federal infantry than two brigades, "so well did he [the enemy] keep his troops concealed." Turner's Gap struck him as "obviously no place for cavalry operations" because of the rugged terrain, so he left for Crampton's Gap, "which was now the weakest point of the line." All the information that he "had the means of possessing" had been reported to Hill and Lee.[5]

Whether this apologia satisfied Lee is hidden in his own reticent report. Colquitt was not satisfied, when Stuart left him at Turner's Gap, with the assurance that he would have to face only a small enemy force. Anxiously scanning the eastern plain below him, he saw in the distance, before darkness hid the view, heavy clouds of dust rising from the turnpike. He could not know that this was the division of Union General Jacob D. Cox, marching into Middletown, from which Stuart had been driven a few hours previously by General Alfred Pleasonton's cavalry division and General Isaac P. Rodman's division of infantry; nor could he know that the other two divisions of McClellan's Ninth Corps were not far behind Cox; but he was worried nonetheless. That billowing dust extended over an ominously long distance. He lost no time in reporting it to Hill, expressing in his message the opinion that "Genl Stuart must have been mistaken as to the strength of the enemy." [6]

Back came Hill's reply: Garland had instructions to join Colquitt, and the rest of the division would follow, "unless subsequent developments should seem to render it unnecessary." Garland, who had been stationed west of Boonsborough, did reach the mountain that night, bivouacking his men on the western slope, and seeking out Colquitt to confer on the military situation. The two commanders agreed that early the next morning Garland would deploy his men to the right of the turnpike.[7]

Hill meanwhile had to weigh Colquitt's opinion of Federal strength against Stuart's. Overestimation of the enemy's forces was a common military error, into which Stuart customarily tried to avoid falling. It is probable that Hill attached the greater weight to the opinion of the cavalryman, who had been in close contact with the Federals, and whose regular duty it was to appraise and report their strength. Nevertheless he dispatched a courier to Hagerstown to inform Lee of Colquitt's apprehensions, and sent Ripley to Stuart to obtain all the information that the cavalryman could give about the mountain roads and gaps.

Then Hill went to bed, but about midnight he was awakened. A courier had arrived with a message from Lee. Its exact content is not known, but evidently reports from Hill and Stuart had made Lee uneasy about Federal movements on the National road, and he suggested that Hill go in person the next morning to Turner's Gap and confer with Stuart about its defense. Probably he also informed Hill that Longstreet would march back the next day and take position on Beaver Creek, about two miles from Boonsborough on the Hagerstown side; for he gave this information to McLaws in a message written September 13 at 10 P.M.[8]

Late that night or very early the next morning, Stuart received information more revealing than any that had reached Hill. A Southern sympathizer who lived in Frederick rode into camp with a breathless warning: McClellan had found a copy of Special Orders No. 191![9]

Stuart doubtless forwarded this startling news to Lee as fast as a courier could gallop up the moonlit road to Hagerstown. Lee received the message early on the morning of September 14. It informed him, as he later recalled, that Stuart "had fallen back to the South Mountains; that Genl McClellan was pressing forward on the roads to Boonsborough and Rohersville [Turner's and Crampton's] gaps, and that he had learned from a citizen of Maryland, that he [McClellan] was in possession of the order directing the movement of our troops."[10]

Lee's chief concern, on reading this dismaying intelligence, was that McClellan would push through Turner's Gap. This would enable him to reach McLaws's rear and relieve Harpers Ferry,[11] while at the same time hurling overwhelming strength upon the isolated divisions of Hill and Longstreet. Visions of a shattered army must have flashed through Lee's mind. Possibly only Jackson and Walker, south of the Potomac, would escape disaster.

But it must not be allowed to happen! Awakening Longstreet, Lee

began to march back toward Boonsborough at daylight. He also sent
from Hagerstown two urgent messages, one to McLaws, the other to
Stuart. McLaws was told:

General Longstreet moves down this morning to occupy the Boonsborough Valley, so as to protect your flank from attacks from forces
coming from Frederick, until the operations at Harper's Ferry are finished.
I desire your operations there to be pushed on as rapidly as possible. . . .
General Stuart, with a portion of General D. H. Hill's forces, holds the
gap between Boonsborough and Middletown. . . .

To Stuart, Lee wrote:

I have received your note and also Capt Blackfords [sic] The gap must
be held at all hazards until the operations at Harpers Ferry are finished.
You must keep me informed of the strength of the enemy's forces moving
up by either route—Gen Longstreet is moving down this morning to
occupy the valley about Boonsboro'.

These messages [12] show that on the morning of September 14 Lee
knew Harpers Ferry had not fallen; that he thought Stuart was holding Turner's Gap with Hill's support; and that apparently he intended
to use Longstreet's troops in the vicinity of Boonsborough rather than
on South Mountain. As to the whereabouts of Stuart, Lee was mistaken. Early that morning the chief of cavalry had gone on to Crampton's Gap. He "had reason to believe," he later stated, that this pass
"was as much threatened as any other." Apparently on the morning
of the fourteenth he knew, with Lee, that Harpers Ferry had not yet
been captured; he believed "that the enemy's efforts would be against
McLaws, probably by the route of Crampton's Gap." Whether he
told Hill about the Harpers Ferry situation or about the discovery of
Lee's lost order, the records do not show.[13]

Evidently Stuart did not inform Hill on the night of the thirteenth
that he planned to leave the next morning for Crampton's Gap, nor
does Colquitt seem to have mentioned this in his message to Hill.
Perhaps Colquitt thought that Stuart himself would take care of the
matter. Stuart may have reasoned, however, that Hill might object
to his going, and that it might be better tactics to present the senior
general with a *fait accompli*. There is also the possibility that full and
free communication was lacking that night at Boonsborough because
of the strained relations between Hill and Stuart that had developed
early in the war at Leesburg.

Whatever the explanation, Hill on the morning of the fourteenth arose and breakfasted before day, and rode with his staff up the turnpike in the belief that Stuart was still defending Turner's Gap.[14] On reaching the Mountain House, before sunrise, he received a message from Stuart telling of his departure for Crampton's, but not of the posting of Rosser at Fox's Gap. For all Hill knew, his infantry troops now formed the sole defense of the mountain passes in the vicinity of the turnpike. Garland's brigade was on hand near the tollhouse, but where was Colquitt's? Hill discovered it at the eastern foot of the mountain. Colquitt had got over his fears of the previous night, and thought that the Federals were gone for good. Actually he knew nothing about the enemy, since no cavalry scouts were reporting to him.

Hill cast a disapproving West Point eye on the weak position Colquitt had selected, and promptly moved the brigade back to the top of the mountain, placing it astride the turnpike, a hundred yards or so east of the tollgate, in a strong position that could be held indefinitely against superior numbers.[15] His defensive preparations also included an early-morning examination of Turner's Gap, which struck him as "wholly indefensible" except by a large force. Accordingly, he ordered up Anderson's brigade and sent one regiment of Ripley's to guard a small pass about three miles north of the turnpike.[16]

The remainder of Ripley's brigade, together with Rodes's, he kept near Boonsborough, for he thought that while McClellan might feint against Turner's Gap his main thrust would come through Crampton's. If McClellan did throw the bulk of his army against this pass, as Stuart obviously expected him to do, then Hill had to guard against the possibility that enemy troops might pour through Crampton's and other lower gaps and strike north up the roads leading to Boonsborough. So he left Ripley and Rodes at the little town to protect the army supply train, guard the rear of his troops on the mountain, and reach out toward Lee and Longstreet. He had been notified that they were en route from Hagerstown, but he knew that it might well take Longstreet's men until after noon to march those thirteen hot and dusty miles.[17]

Having posted Colquitt and ordered up reinforcements, Hill went on a reconnaissance to his right with Major Ratchford. It was plain enough that the mountaintop would not be easy to defend. Its rounded slopes were cut by ravines and high ridges, and covered with woods and thick undergrowth, broken here and there by open patches of farmland bordered by low stone fences. At least two roads that might be usable by attacking forces curved up the mountain north of the turnpike and then ran down into it near Turner's Gap. To the south, the old Sharpsburg road passed through Fox's Gap, roughly paralleling the turnpike and connecting with it by means of several little roads and trails running along the mountain crest. Altogether, there were too many roads and knobby peaks that could be used for flanking maneuvers by enemy troops.[18]

Hill was especially concerned about Fox's Gap, and toward this point he and Ratchford made their way along a forest road through the early morning mist. A little less than a mile from the Mountain House they were startled by the sound of rumbling wheels and voices of command, coming from the direction of Fox's Gap. The woods hid the troops from them, and Hill naturally assumed that it was the enemy he heard, but evidently it was Rosser's detachment. The Federals, who had marched that morning from Middletown, were indeed getting ready to attack Fox's Gap: General Pleasonton was preparing to open artillery fire from below while Colonel E. P. Scammon of Cox's division started his brigade on a slow two-mile climb up the old Sharpsburg road; but the records indicate that no Federal troops reached the vicinity of the gap until about 9 A.M., whereas Hill's reconnaissance took place before 7 A.M.[19]

When Hill heard the alarming sounds from Fox's Gap, he turned back before he could be seen by the supposed enemy and hurried through the woods toward Turner's Gap to alert Colquitt and Garland. As the hour approached 7 A.M., he and Ratchford came upon a cabin in a clearing and stopped long enough to question the owner about the mountain roads. The mountaineer stood in his yard with his children clustered around him, answering all queries with taciturn amiability. He thought that Hill and Ratchford were Federals because Ratchford was wearing a blue cloak that he had found at Seven Pines.

Suddenly the conversation was interrupted by a shell that came crashing through the woods. Fear showed in the faces of the children; a little girl began crying. Hill thought of his own children. Today was Sunday; they would be going to Sunday school and church. No shells—thank God—would be falling around his home this morning.

He must get to his troops, but before leaving he spoke gently to the little girl and tried to soothe her tears.

On arriving at Turner's Gap he found that the continuing Federal bombardment had caused Garland to ready his troops for action. Hill briefly explained the military situation to the calm brigadier and gave him his orders: he was to lead his men—scarcely more than a thousand in all—through the woods to Fox's Gap and hold it at any cost, for on his success depended the safety of Lee's supply train.[20]

As Garland set out on his mission, Hill and several of his staff officers climbed to a lookout station near the Mountain House. The high point afforded a clear view of the eastern mountain base and the roads leading up to it through the Middletown valley. A heart-stopping view—for there below, spread out on the green and brown checkerboard of the sunlit plain, were the blue multitudes of McClellan's army: in front, the double lines of battle already formed, and behind, stretching far back toward the Catoctin Range, the marching columns bright with bayonets and regimental colors.

No feint this! Never before had Hill seen in full view so mighty an army. He looked down upon the great spectacle with admiration for the awesome military beauty of it, and satisfaction at the thought that McClellan was missing his best opportunity by concentrating against Turner's instead of Crampton's gap. There was also the blood-quickening realization that his own five little brigades were hopelessly outnumbered. But at least he was on a mountaintop; with luck and hard fighting he might be able to cling to it until Longstreet could come up and the army supply train could be moved to safety.[21]

Rodes and Ripley must be brought up at once. Hill sent off the necessary orders [22] and descended to the turnpike to prepare for the worst. About 9 A.M. a rattle of musketry from Fox's Gap told that Garland was in contact with the enemy. The sound fluctuated for a time, then gathered volume. Evidently the Federals were pressing their attack.

About this time Anderson came up [23] and moved quickly to the right, toward the sound of the firing. Hill sent an aide, J. F. Johnston, to him with an order to join the right of his brigade to Garland's left. Anderson replied with an objection. He could not obey the order, he said, because the Federals were between him and Garland.

Back to the command post with this answer hurried Johnston, and as he stood talking with Hill the chaplain of Garland's Thirteenth North Carolina regiment, hatless and excited, came galloping up, flung himself down from his horse, and blurted out shocking news: Garland was dead! His brigade was wavering under heavy attack.[24]

Here was a turn of events as desperate as it was unexpected. When Garland, earlier that morning, had arrived at the old Sharpsburg road he had found Rosser, who had occupied the road before sunrise and had sent word to Stuart that the enemy was moving on Fox's Gap. After conferring with Rosser, Garland posted his five North Carolina regiments across the old Sharpsburg road, stretching his line thin, with dangerous intervals between the regiments, in an effort to cover the smaller roads that forked out of the main one and offered good flanking opportunities to the enemy. From left to right the line consisted of the Thirteenth, the Twentieth, the Twenty-third, the Twelfth, and the Fifth regiments. Garland also had at his disposal one battery of artillery. On the right flank, Rosser took position with his force of about two hundred men.[25]

In all, the Confederates had about 1,200 men at Fox's Gap, and against their attenuated line the Federal brigade commander, Colonel Scammon, began an attack by Cox's division, which numbered in cavalry, artillery, and infantry a total strength of about 3,500. Early in the Federal advance a future President, Lieutenant Colonel Rutherford B. Hayes, was wounded while leading the Twenty-third Ohio Regiment.

The first heavy assault fell upon Garland's right, driving most of the Twelfth North Carolina's 92 men from the field. Garland apparently thought the next charge would strike his left. He made his way to the left flank, where Lieutenant Colonel Thomas Ruffin, Jr., was holding his ground with the men of the Thirteenth North Carolina. The two officers conferred briefly, but the fire was so heavy around them that Ruffin urged Garland to leave.

"General, why do you stay here? You are in great danger."

"I may as well be here as yourself," replied Garland.

Ruffin countered with an argument about the difference in their respective duties, but it was cut short by a bullet that struck him in the hip. Seconds later Garland was also wounded, mortally. He fell groaning and writhing in pain, but remained conscious long enough to send a message to Colonel D. K. McRae, of the Fifth North Carolina, devolving upon him the command of the brigade.[26]

On receiving the message, McRae hurried to the center of the line, where he discovered that Garland was dead and that he must now hold together a partially broken and demoralized brigade. He lost no time in sending several messages to Hill describing his plight—one of these by the chaplain of the Thirteenth regiment. He also offered to turn over his command to Colonel C. C. Tew, who came up with two of Anderson's regiments, but Tew declined the responsibility. Then, as Tew prepared to take position on the left flank, he received an order from Anderson that pulled him back toward Turner's Gap. Apparently Anderson was ignorant of the true military situation and determined to handle his brigade cautiously. In any event, McRae was left to meet as best he could the next Federal charge, which was shaping up against Colonel Alfred Iverson's Twentieth North Carolina.

The Federals had fired canister on the Twentieth from a four-piece battery until Iverson sent out a company of infantrymen who flanked and killed the Union gunners. Now there was silence; behind a sheltering ridge the blue troops were massing and fixing bayonets. Iverson's men waited with muskets leveled over a low rail fence. The Federals charged, shouting. A volley from the Southern muskets cut down their front ranks, but on they came. Iverson, McRae, the Twentieth, and the rest of the brigade were engulfed in an irresistible blue flood.

They ran. Bullets whined around Iverson, and commands of "Halt!" were shouted at him, but he bounded down the mountain in tremendous leaps, overtaking McRae and escaping with him. On the flanks, the Confederates fared better. Ruffin managed to cut his way out to the left, while on the right Rosser fell back with relatively small losses and took up a position more than a mile to the rear from which he could maintain artillery fire against the gap. McRae rallied parts of some regiments in support of Rosser, but the effectiveness of Garland's command as a fighting unit had been destroyed.[27]

Hill quickly received news of the disaster. Although the chaplain's message had prepared him for it, this did not prevent him from experiencing what he later described as the greatest feeling of "loneliness" he had ever known. At hand were only Colquitt's and Anderson's brigades and the small force of Rosser, who by now had reported to Hill. Colquitt could not be shifted from the turnpike except as a last resort. Anderson alone must now try to check the force that had shattered Garland's command. Meanwhile, as Anderson moved to the counterattack, supported by Bondurant's battery, Hill would do all he could to put up a good front. He ran two guns down from the Mountain House, massed dismounted staff officers, couriers, teamsters, and cooks behind them to give the appearance of infantry support, and opened rapid fire on the enemy.

At the same time he made an effort to keep the Federals from reaching a commanding peak north of the turnpike. With no infantry to spare, he employed for this purpose a large number of guns from the reserve artillery battalion, directing the inexperienced gunners to sweep the approaches to the peak. They responded energetically and with good intent, but their ineptitude wrung Hill's artillerist heart.[28]

Anderson advanced on the Federals with what Cox himself later described as "great obstinancy and boldness," and though the counterattack was repulsed, it helped to convince the Union commanders that the woods and rugged terrain in their front concealed strong Confederate forces. No doubt the illusion was enhanced by Hill's artillery show. Confederate prisoners did their bit by solemnly assuring their captors that D. H. Hill was before them with five brigades, closely supported by Longstreet's command. The Federal commanders, accordingly, called a halt to wait for reinforcements. To Hill's immeasurable relief, the advance that had threatened to crush his handful of troops ground to a stop, and a lull settled over the battlefield.[29]

About 11 A.M., Rodes and Ripley arrived.[30] Hill sent Rodes to the left, to guard against a Federal advance north of the turnpike, and sent Ripley to the right to support Anderson. Through midday and early afternoon the lull in the battle continued, except for artillery fire and skirmishing by reconnaissance parties. The Federals were in the process of deploying at Fox's Gap the rest of General Jesse L. Reno's Ninth Corps, while north of the turnpike General Joseph Hooker's First Corps moved slowly into position. Thus seven Federal divisions, four under Reno and three under Hooker, were ponderously concentrating against one, if Hill's depleted and damaged little force could be called a full division. Only the slow caution of the Federal commanders kept them from driving forward to victory.[31]

Hill of course was tormented by the thought that the unequal contest might be renewed at any moment. As his lookouts reported steadily increasing numbers of bluecoats moving up on both sides of the turnpike, his anxiety increased. Word came from Longstreet that he was nearing Boonsborough, and Hill sent back a message urging him to hurry forward reinforcements.[32]

About 3 P.M., the first of Longstreet's troops came up—General Thomas F. Drayton's and Colonel G. T. Anderson's brigades—hot, dusty, tired, their ranks depleted by their exhausting forced march. But there was no time for rest. Hill hoped that by attacking on his right he could beat the Federals at Fox's Gap before the Union commanders began a concerted advance. Meeting Drayton and Anderson at the Mountain House, he conducted them to the right, called up Ripley, and instructed the three commanders to form battle line and sweep the woods before them. Ripley as senior officer was given command of the operation. To prepare the way, Hill brought up a battery and had it shell the woods.

But Ripley bungled the attack. First he gave hasty orders that threw his battle line into confusion, and then he took his own brigade on a weird, wandering trip through the mountain laurel—away from the scene of action! He marched it to the western base of the mountain, held it there for a time, and did not take it back up again until after dark. His brigade did no fighting that day.[33]

The other two commanders, isolated from each other by Ripley's faulty orders, were soon in retreat. Three Union brigades struck Drayton's troops and drove them to the rear. G. T. Anderson fell back just in time to avoid being cut off by the enemy. In the Confederate defense line, only G. B. Anderson's and Rosser's forces on the far right held firm. Once again disaster threatened Harvey Hill, but fortunately General John B. Hood of Longstreet's command had reached Turner's Gap with two brigades. Rushed to the right, Hood's men attacked vigorously and filled the gap in the Confederate defenses.[34]

By the time this emergency had been met, Hill was faced with a growing crisis on his left, where Rodes had come under attack about 3 P.M. The key to this region, and to Turner's Gap, was the commanding peak, about three fourths of a mile north of the turnpike, that Hill had sought to defend that morning with the reserve artillery. Rodes had been ordered to hold this high ground, and he was now clinging to it with great tenacity, although his little brigade of twelve hundred men was under heavy pressure from the Federal division of

General George G. Meade, who had been an instructor at West Point while Hill was there. To make matters worse, another Federal division under General John P. Hatch was heading for the wide gap in Hill's defenses between Rodes's right flank and the turnpike.

As Hatch's troops emerged from the woods on the lower slopes, and marched up the mountain in three precise lines, their officers on horseback, their colors flying, the scene engraved itself upon Hill's mind. Late in life he recaptured it in a Biblical phrase—"terrible as an army with banners." Not a Confederate infantryman did he have to oppose to this new force, and although the men of the reserve artillery battalion worked their guns as valiantly as ever, their poor aim was made even worse by the wide angles of depression they had to employ. The Federals came on without flinching as the ineffective missiles flew around them.

But the advance, for all its impressiveness, was no precipitate charge. The blue lines moved slowly up the increasingly rugged slope, and before they could outflank Rodes, Longstreet arrived at Turner's Gap with three brigades—badly depleted by straggling, to be sure, but a joyous sight to Hill. Then, to Hill's chagrin, Longstreet stood on his seniority and immediately assumed command of the battle. One brigade he sent to the aid of Rodes; the two others were put in on Rodes's right. These reinforcements did not fight well. The trouble, it seemed to Hill, was that they were exhausted, and that because of Longstreet's unfamiliarity with the terrain they were posted on weak ground.[35]

But this was no time for a dispute with Longstreet. The Federals were developing their attack all along the mountain crest, and Hill, riding up and down the line between Turner's and Fox's gaps, had all he could do to keep his weary troops in the battle.

The men of one regiment protested excitedly that the bluecoats were getting behind them.

Never mind, said Hill, the front was where the enemy appeared, and muskets would carry as well in one direction as another.

Then, from another regiment, the dismayed cry: no more ammunition, General!

"Well, what of it?" snapped Hill. "Here are plenty of *rocks!*"

The answers were inconsequential. What counted was the gritty composure, the sheer will of the man, as he sat his horse on the firing line while other men crouched behind shelter. A captain in George

B. Anderson's brigade who saw Hill in action that day wrote afterward:

Hill's presence was always sufficient to give full assurance that we were in the right place, and we had only to fight to win. There was never a better soldier, or a man better qualified to judge of the merits of one. The clash of battle was not a confusing din to him, but an exciting scene that awakened his spirit and his genius.[36]

Yet, more than inspiration, the Confederates needed numbers to hold their ground until darkness brought relief. Just before sunset, General Reno was killed near the same spot where Garland had fallen that morning, and his corps did not achieve a breakthrough. But north of the turnpike, where a fourth brigade of Longstreet's command was put in at dusk, the reinforcements that had made the hard march from Hagerstown were broken and scattered, and Rodes, forced back half a mile, had to yield the high peak to the enemy. From this point, when morning came, the Federals could move down and seize the turnpike.[37]

Fortunately for the Confederates, the Union attack was not pressed after dark except on the turnpike. Here a detached Federal brigade under Hill's former groomsman, General John Gibbon, began a late afternoon assault on Colquitt's brigade that continued for several hours into the night. The Georgians, who had held their strong position all day with not much more than heavy skirmishing, now repulsed every attempt to drive them. After each success they would raise the rebel yell, and at the Mountain House the young men of Hill's staff would laugh and clap their hands and exclaim, "Hurrah for Georgia! Georgia is having a free fight." [38]

Before this action ended, Hill and Longstreet were summoned to Lee's headquarters west of the mountain for a council of war. There Lee, his impassive dignity concealing his anxiety, asked them whether they could hold their positions the next day.

No, said Hill. From heavy batteries placed on the Confederate right and on the high peak north of the turnpike the Federals could mount a crossfire that would make the mountaintop untenable.

Longstreet concurred. Hill knew the situation better than he did, he remarked.

Lee stoically accepted this disheartening appraisal. There was no alternative, then. He would have to retreat. He dismissed his lieutenants and set about the business of preparing the necessary orders.

As Hill rode wearily back up the mountain, toward the sporadic firing and triumphant rebel yells that marked the end of Colquitt's fight, he must have had mixed feelings—of regret that the field had been lost, and pride that it had been held so long. The slowness and extraordinary caution of the enemy had helped to save him, but so had his own generalship and the gallantry of his men. For six hours, from 9 A.M. to 3 P.M., they had held the gaps unaided, and then with the help of Longstreet's troops they had continued to hold into the night. Though they must now yield to superior numbers, for one long, vital day they had blocked an enemy drive that could have spelled disaster to Lee's army. Hill had good reason to feel then what he later asserted in his report—that his division had fought "one of the most remarkable and creditable" battles of the war.[39]

As for Lee, there soon came to him additional bad news: the Federals, toward nightfall, had forced Crampton's Gap; McLaws was in danger of being cut off. But later came a message from Jackson indicating that Harpers Ferry would be captured the next morning, and on the basis of this hopeful turn of events Lee began formulating typically daring and aggressive new plans. Perhaps he need not retreat across the Potomac. He would move southwest, toward Antietam Creek and Sharpsburg. At that town, some twelve miles north of Harpers Ferry by the shortest route, he might be able to reunite his army for further campaigning in Maryland.[40]

He had already ordered Hill and Longstreet to fall back from South Mountain on the road to Sharpsburg, and about 10 P.M. the withdrawal from the now quiet battlefield began. In the chill darkness Ratchford and other staff officers went out along the battle line, where some eighteen hundred Federals and perhaps as many Confederates lay dead or wounded,[41] and the living huddled among rocks and bushes in the overpowering sleep of exhaustion. Crawling cat-like on hands and feet, they shook officers awake and gave the order in a whisper. The men in turn were stealthily roused and brought down the mountain.[42]

Then, while the enemy in all the power of his numbers slept, Lee's ragged columns moved toward Sharpsburg.

VII

"THE LONGEST, SADDEST DAY"

AFTER THE seemingly endless night march from South Mountain, Sharpsburg stood out in the morning light like a white beacon in the autumn-tinted hills. With a last surge of energy the exhausted veterans of Hill and Longstreet crossed to the west side of Antietam Creek and took positions between it and the town, on either side of the Boonsborough road. Together the two battleworn divisions had a strength of only eighteen thousand, and that afternoon the pursuing Federals began massing on the east side of the Antietam, preparing for the final hammerstroke. Still Lee stood his ground, for about midday he received definite word that Harpers Ferry had fallen, and he was now confident that he could reconcentrate his scattered army before the ever-cautious McClellan attacked in full force.

Two days passed. Toward noon of September 16 Jackson and Walker arrived; at sundown Hill helped Hood check a Union advance that carried Hooker's corps across the Antietam, north of Sharpsburg; and by daylight of the seventeenth Lee had the welcome news that McLaws and R. H. Anderson were approaching. When they arrived his reconcentration would not be complete, for A. P. Hill's division, left behind by Jackson to parole prisoners and care for captured stores, still had to come up from Harpers Ferry. With it on hand, when and if it arrived, Lee would have a grand total of less than forty thousand men to oppose to McClellan's seventy-odd thousand.

As Lee faced east, calmly watching the blue masses building up across the Antietam, he was standing with his back to the Potomac. Snakelike it coiled behind him scarcely two miles west of Sharpsburg, and while it protected his flanks it threatened to trap his army should he be forced to retreat across the one good ford, near Shepherdstown, that was available to him. Lee, however, did not intend to retreat. He was used to being outnumbered by the Federals, and to driving them back when he fought them.[1]

His battle line, which roughly paralleled the meandering north–south course of Antietam Creek, was drawn along a range of hills between the creek and Sharpsburg. Harvey Hill held the center. On his left, Jackson's forces occupied positions that ran north and west, blocking Hooker to the north. On his right, Longstreet held heights to the east and south of Sharpsburg, and farther south Walker's two brigades were stationed. From Walker's small cavalry force on the right flank to Stuart's cavalry on the left, the Confederate positions covered a distance of about four miles. There were no breastworks, and the relatively open, rolling farm country did not provide much cover. Backing the line were about two hundred guns which were outnumbered and outranged by the Union artillery.

Hill's five depleted brigades, totaling now about three thousand men, occupied flat ground in the angle of a V formed by two turnpikes, the Hagerstown pike, running north–south into Sharpsburg, and the Boonsborough pike, which slanted into the town on a northeast–southwest axis. G. B. Anderson, on Hill's right, had his troops astride the Boonsborough pike, and from this point Hill's line ran northwest through Rodes's brigade, Garland's, commanded now by McRae, Colquitt's and Ripley's. The three center brigades were spread along the zigzag line of a sunken farm road which connected the two pikes. It would soon acquire the name of "Bloody Lane."

All in all, it was not a very strong position that Hill had to defend. He blamed Longstreet, who exercised tactical command over him, for having stationed him "on the flats," as he put it, while taking favorable high ground for his own division,[2] but of course this was the senior general's prerogative. It was now up to Hill to make the best of a difficult assignment by carefully studying the terrain over which his men must fight.

With this in mind he called Ratchford to him at daybreak on the seventeenth and rode out with him on reconnaissance. Under their horses' hooves the ground was spongy with rain that had fallen in the night. Gray clouds still lingered overhead and mist floated wraith-like in the valley of the Antietam. From the north came the staccato sound of skirmishing, while all along the battle line the intermittent crash of artillery greeted the somber dawn.

Hill rode toward the sound of the musketry until he came to a field of tall corn that separated the contending forces. A rail fence, running parallel with the skirmish lines, kept him from observing the exact position of the enemy, so he crossed it and walked his horse along it for a quarter of a mile while the Federal skirmishers shot at him. Ratchford, an unwilling escort on this expedition, considered it unnecessary. Had he been versed in Freudian psychology he might have wondered whether Hill harbored a subconscious death wish. After they had somehow got back unharmed, he put some searching questions to his chief.

Did Hill never have the sensation of fear? he asked.

Hill answered that he "realized the danger of being killed."

Then why did he expose himself as he had in that ride along the fence?

Hill replied that he would not ask his men to go where he would not go himself, nor would he send them to fight in any place that he did not know thoroughly, both as to the nature of the terrain and the strength of the enemy. As for death, he had no fear of it if it came in the line of duty, and he believed that his Heavenly Father would take care of him as well in battle as at home.

But surely he would rather live than die, Ratchford persisted.

"Oh yes," said Hill, "when I think of my wife and babies I would, but God will take care of them, if he allows anything to happen to me." [3]

Hardly had the two riders returned to the center of the Confederate line before the skirmishing on the left roared into full-scale battle. Hooker's corps attacked with overwhelming power and fairly tore Jackson's line apart, opening a great gap to the left of Hill. Into the breach rushed Hood's division, which had come up from a reserve position, and for a time the Texans drove the Federals back. To aid Hood, Jackson sent in Jubal Early's brigade from the far left, while Hill threw in Ripley, Colquitt, and McRae.

Confused and furious, the battle raged, surging back and forth through the cornfield that Hill had reconnoitered and through woods on either side of it, turning the whole area into a bloody shambles.

The Federals brought up a second corps, and then a third, and Hood and Hill were forced back, although Lee reinforced them with G. T. Anderson's brigade and Walker's division. But fortunately McLaws's men had reached the scene of action; they bolstered the Confederate line and held it against the uncoordinated Union attacks until at last they subsided.[4]

While McLaws's fight was in progress, Lee rode to the center, for an ominous massing of blue divisions in the distance indicated that the next heavy Union attack would fall upon Harvey Hill. Having used up three brigades in the defense of Jackson's area, Hill now had only two fresh units, Rodes's and G. B. Anderson's, with which to meet the impending assault. These he had stationed in the sunken road.

Together he and Lee rode along the line of troops waiting grimly in the trenchlike little lane, urging them to stay calm and hold fast when the attack began. A break in the center would endanger the whole army, they warned the men. As they moved past the Sixth Alabama, Hill's friend Colonel John B. Gordon spoke out resolutely: "These men are going to stay here, General, till the sun goes down or victory is won." [5]

Of such fine moments in war would the developing Lee legend be built. The tableau was complete: Lee in all his gray dignity on his famous mount, Traveller; the thin line of faithful rebel soldiers ready to do battle for "Marse Robert"; the gallant young colonel with ringing words for the occasion. But since battlefields invariably inspire fear as well as bravery, even a Lee occasionally had to unbend and cope in mundane fashion with the lesser heroes of his army. During the hard fighting on the left, McRae's men—still holding vivid recollections of the flank fire that had riddled their brigade at South Mountain—had suddenly broken and fled in panic when one of their captains cried, "They are flanking us." At a safe distance to the rear the more shameless fugitives had burrowed into convenient haystacks, and Lee spent some of his time in Hill's sector helping McRae root these unnerved soldiers out of their hiding places.[6]

After the ride along Hill's line, Lee and Hill were joined by Longstreet, and together the three generals climbed a ridge to study the enemy concentration. Lee and Longstreet dismounted, but Hill stayed in the saddle.

"If you insist on riding up there and drawing the fire," said Long-

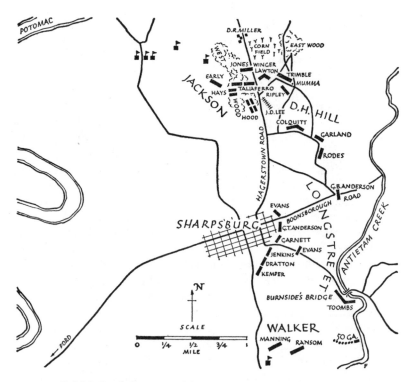

Initial Confederate positions in the battle of Antietam.

street, "give us a little interval so that we may not be in the line of the fire when they open upon you."

Then, as his field glass picked up a puff of white smoke from a distant cannon, he called to Hill, "There is a shot for you."

Moments later the missile cut off the forelegs of Hill's horse, dropping the unfortunate animal upon its stumps. "The horse's head was so low and his croup so high that Hill was in a most ludicrous position," Longstreet said afterward. "With one foot in the stirrup he made several efforts to get the other leg over the croup, but failed. Finally we prevailed upon him to try the other end of the horse, and he got down." [7]

It was the second horse that had been shot under Hill since the start of the battle. Putting the crippled beast out of its misery, he obtained another mount and hurried back to his men. As he had seen all too plainly from the ridge, the Union columns down in the creek valley had forded the stream and were deploying in battle line and coming straight toward his center position. There was a full division of those bluecoats, and beyond the creek to the south another Federal division was coming up.

Heavy odds—he would have to stop them at first with Rodes and Anderson, plus a regiment of McRae's that had held together and some stragglers that he had herded into the sunken road. Lee had brought word that R. H. Anderson had been ordered to the center with his division of about four thousand. That would help immeasurably, if only Anderson would hurry. Support over on the left was weak, consisting of mingled elements of Walker's and Ripley's broken commands. And the worst thing of all was, no artillery! The division batteries had been moved away during the desperate struggle on the left, and about 10 A.M. Colonel Stephen D. Lee had withdrawn his artillery battalion from Hill's sector in order "to refit," as he later said. Lieutenant J. A. Reid and Hill's other aides were out now, trying to bring up some batteries.

In some respects the sunken road was a stout defense point. A ridge in front of it protected it from the Federal artillery, and over and down this ridge the attacking infantry would have to come, marching into the fire of Hill's men, who had improved their position with breastworks made from fence rails. The weak points of the defense line were the flanks. Enfilade fire from the enemy could turn this improvised trench into a Confederate tomb.

All was in readiness now, and beyond the ridge the Federals were coming on steadily, driving back the outlying skirmishers. Three blue lines mounted the crest, halted while the officers dressed ranks, and again advanced. Against a sunny sky burned clear of clouds it was like a parade—flags fluttering, bayonets flashing, blue-uniformed soldiers keeping perfect, white-gaitered step—fresh regiments, some of these, new to the dirty business of war.

They would learn, now, how parades ended. "Fire!" A sheet of flame leaped out from the rail breastworks, and the first blue line dissolved in thunderous noise and black smoke. But the gaps closed as the men behind came on, stepping over their dead and wounded. They were blasted again, and they reeled from the terrible shock of it, and retreated. But that was only the first charge. Another followed, and another. It was hard, relentless fighting, as savage as any in the war.

Through the smoke Lieutenant Reid came dashing up, painfully wounded, but bringing with him a battery. Hill rushed it into position, and the gunners raked the Federal front, helping to break the persistent attacks and drive the Union forces back behind the crest of the ridge, where they lay down and began a steady return fire.

Longstreet now took a hand in the battle, ordering Rodes to charge the enemy. The tall, ardent brigadier promptly obeyed, but to no avail. The first Federal division, under General William H. French, had been reinforced by the second, under General Israel B. Richardson. Rodes and his men—no more than seven hundred, he estimated—were quickly beaten back to the shelter of the sunken road.

By now R. H. Anderson had arrived, and Hill had posted his men in a second line. Against Rodes, on the left, the Federal pressure seemed to be slackening, but G. B. Anderson, whose men were spread along the zigzag road to the right of Rodes's forces, was having trouble holding back Federals trying to get into flanking position between the two brigades.

Then it happened. Rodes's men suddenly abandoned their positions and marched to the rear!

The explanation, Hill later learned, was that Rodes had attempted to pull back the right of his line to face the men toward the increasing Federal flank fire, and Lieutenant Colonel J. N. Lightfoot of the Sixth Alabama had mistakenly transmitted his instructions as an order for a general retreat. The regular commander of the Sixth, Colonel Gordon, lay unconscious with five wounds as Lightfoot countermarched the regiment, with the other units following suit. Rodes, who might otherwise have stopped the movement, was in those ill-fated moments preoccupied with an aide who had been shot in the face, and with a wound of his own in the thigh. Before he realized what was happening his brigade disintegrated, the initial retreat quickly turning into a rout.

Disaster followed. With triumphant yells the Federals closed in on the unprotected left flank of G. B. Anderson's brigade. Murderous enfilade fire swept the sunken road, piling Confederates in it like cordwood. Anderson himself received a wound that proved to be fatal. The survivors of the shattered brigade fled.

Over the sunken road ("Bloody Lane" now, forevermore) plunged the victorious Federals, driving on toward the Hagerstown road. R. H. Anderson's little division—which had suffered heavy casualties and lost its effectiveness after Anderson had been severely wounded —failed to stop them. Hill's center defenses were in shreds.

In the emergency he found Captain Robert Boyce's South Carolina battery in a cornfield, got it out, and set it to firing grape and canister on the advancing blue infantry. Longstreet, too, found a battery and threw it into the fight, while from the left two isolated regiments of Walker's division, the Third Arkansas and the Twenty-seventh North Carolina, poured out a swelling volume of musketry.

The Federals halted, fell back. Now was the time to drive them into the Antietam! Hill, eyes aflame with battle ardor, appealed to the stragglers around him. Who would charge the Yankees? About two hundred were willing, if the general would lead them.

Good enough. Hill seized a musket and off they went in a forlorn-hope charge if ever there was one. They drove some of the Federals a short distance, but soon ran into heavy counterfire that forced them to disperse. A similar fate met the men of the Third Arkansas and the Twenty-seventh North Carolina when they advanced on the left.

Hill returned unharmed from his charge and found that another two hundred brave men had been rounded up by his officers. He sent this little force out in a flank attack that had some success before being repulsed.

These bold advances and counterattacks, together with the rapid fire of the two Confederate batteries, seem to have convinced the Federal commanders that strong forces still opposed them in the center. With victory in their grasp, and with a fresh corps in position to complete the destruction of Lee's army, Generals Sumner and McClellan took counsel of their heavy casualties and their fears and agreed that the center attack should end. To the vast relief of Hill and his men, the pressure against their sector dwindled away, and after noon the main Union effort shifted to the Confederate right.[8]

Here the heights between Sharpsburg and Antietam Creek were held by about two thousand infantry under General David R. Jones of Longstreet's command, for Lee had been compelled, during the morning's fighting, to strip this mile and more of battlefront of all other defending forces. Confronting Jones was General Ambrose E.

Burnside, in command of some thirteen thousand Union troops. Through the morning the Confederate defenders had held back Burnside's men at a stone bridge that spanned the Antietam southeast of Sharpsburg, but by about 1 P.M. the Federals had taken the bridge and made two other crossings north and south of it.

For two hours they halted to reorganize and replenish ammunition. Then, about 3 P.M., the powerful blue lines and columns began moving up the slopes toward Sharpsburg. The attack developed slowly in the face of hot defensive fire, but it ground forward irresistibly. Within an hour it was threatening to envelop the town and roll up the Confederate right flank. Once more a Union victory was in the making. The destruction of Lee's army and the end of the Confederacy were in sight.[9]

Hill, from his position north of Sharpsburg and the Boonsborough pike, watched this steadily worsening crisis and did what he could to stop the Federal advance. Seeing a strong enemy column coming up the pike he stationed three of his division batteries on a commanding hill just north of the road, waited until the bluecoats got within close range, and then with a sudden storm of grape and canister drove them back in confusion.[10]

Lee and Longstreet were also using artillery to stave off disaster. On the heights in front of Sharpsburg they gathered every battery they could find, including twelve guns that Colonel Stephen D. Lee had refitted and brought back to the front. Time and again blasts of grape and canister broke up Union charges, but still the blue tide edged closer and closer to Sharpsburg. A. P. Hill had at last come up from Harpers Ferry with five brigades, and Lee had ordered him to attack on the Confederate right as soon as he could get his troops into position. Already Hill's batteries were engaging, and as the hour neared 4 P.M. his infantry moved against the left flank of the attacking Federal line.[11]

Then Harvey Hill, from the high ground he had occupied, beheld a dismaying sight. As a Confederate force that appeared to be the right wing of A. P. Hill's division took the field, south of Sharpsburg, a heavy Federal column drove toward it and threw it back! A few hundred yards more and the Federals would cross the Confederate escape route leading to the Shepherdstown ford. Quickly Hill pointed out the danger to Captain Thomas H. Carter, the artillerist who had fought so ably at Seven Pines, and Carter opened fire with three guns.

Over a distance of some twelve hundred yards the shells arched, and with deadly accuracy found their target. Two more of Hill's guns joined in the firing. The blue column broke, as the Federals sought cover from the shells that seemed to come from nowhere.[12]

A. P. Hill's brigades were charging now, and David Jones's men rushed forward with wild rebel yells, while the batteries defending Sharpsburg, reinforced by those of the Light Division, poured a withering steel hail upon the Federals. The Union left wavered under Hill's flank attack. The long blue line halted and then retreated, the Union field commanders withdrawing their men to the cover of a ridge near the creek.[13]

To the west an appropriately blood-red sun set behind the Maryland hills. Wednesday, September 17, the bloodiest day of battle on the American continents, "the longest, saddest day" that Captain Henry King of Lafayette McLaws's staff had ever known, had ended at last. Only the artillery—the long-range Federal guns that since early morning had created for the Southerners what Stephen Lee called "Artillery Hell," and the Confederate batteries that still roared defiance—continued the fight for a time; and then they too subsided and the cries of the wounded rose up and filled the night.

The Confederate army had suffered more than ten thousand casualties; the Federal, more than twelve thousand. Lee's battle line, where the men slept on their arms, was only a thread, but Lee was as resolute as ever. Boldness had been his watchword on the Antietam; earlier that day he would have tried to attack around the Union right, had not Jackson reported that enemy artillery barred the way; and now he was not disposed to yield the battlefield to his adversary. Quietly, firmly, he issued his orders. Cook rations and deliver them to the front. Round up all stragglers, replenish ammunition, and stand ready for combat on the morrow.[14]

Perhaps Lee reasoned that McClellan would not dare to attack again, and if so he judged correctly. The eighteenth passed with neither army taking offensive action. Although Lee again explored the possibility of turning the Union right, he and Jackson could find no way around the strongly posted Federal artillery.[15]

During the quiet day there was time for the weary Confederate fighters to recover somewhat from the shock of battle, to relax and smoke and congratulate themselves on their near escape from disaster. A. P. Hill's timely arrival was much discussed. He had left Harpers

Ferry on the seventeenth at 7:30 A.M., one hour after receiving a message from Lee ordering him to come up, had driven his division furiously over some sixteen hot and dusty miles, and had ridden up to Lee at Sharpsburg at 2:30 P.M., proudly reporting that three thousand men were straining forward on the road behind him.

Historians have since written vivid descriptions of that dramatic march; of how Powell Hill in his red battle shirt raged up and down his line urging laggards onward with the point of his sword; and of how he reached the battlefield just when his comrades needed him most; but Freeman and other authorities on Lee's army have not asked a rather anticlimactic question: Should Hill have left Harpers Ferry sooner and arrived at Sharpsburg earlier than he did? Although the question cannot be answered definitely, the facts seem to warrant its consideration.

On the morning of the surrender of Harpers Ferry, September 15, Jackson had written Lee that Hill would "be left in command until the prisoners and other public property shall be disposed of, unless you direct otherwise." Jackson later stated in his official report that he had left Hill "to receive the surrender of the Federal troops and take the requisite steps for securing the captured stores," and mentioned no further orders to the commander of the Light Division. Hill reported: "By direction of General Jackson, I remained at Harper's Ferry until the morning of the 17th, when, at 6:30 A.M., I received an order from General Lee to move to Sharpsburg."

All of which might indicate that no one expected Hill to march earlier than he did. Yet Lee wrote President Davis on September 18 that he had hoped A. P. Hill would arrive *the night of the sixteenth.* Evidently Jackson, who reached Sharpsburg the morning of the sixteenth, did not tell Lee anything to make him think otherwise, and surely the two generals discussed the probable time of Hill's arrival. Did both Lee and Jackson, then, expect Hill to complete his duties at Harpers Ferry in time to march for Sharpsburg on the sixteenth and arrive that night? If so, why was Hill still at Harpers Ferry on the morning of the seventeenth, and apparently even then not preparing to move until he received what must have been an urgent order from Lee? Evidence available at present points to but does not penetrate the mystery. In their official reports, neither Lee, Jackson, nor Hill dealt with such questions.[16]

It was probably on this quiet September 18, while other soldiers were finishing meager meals of bread and meat, or penciling letters home, that Calvin Leach found time to bring his war diary up to date. Leach was a private in Ripley's brigade, and had been through the fighting on the Confederate left. It was hard for him to write about it because the words did not come easily and he had some trouble with spelling and grammar, but laboriously he set down one man's limited view of a great battle:

Our brigade was firs in, soon in the morning the fireing commenced, and very soon our Reg was under fire the balls whisin over us. . . . Here our gallant and much loved capt Boushell got severely wounded in the mouth. . . . Olso Lieut Peden was wound. . . . I commenced loading and shooting with all my might but my gun got chooked the first round, and I picked up a gun of one of my comrades who fell by my side and continued to fire. Here I could see the second line of battle of the enemy and when their men would fall, the rest would close in and fill their places. Their first line was lying by a fence. . . . I fired as near as I could aim. . . . I do not know whether I killed any one or not.

There were other things, too, that Leach did not know, did not understand at all, and under the heading "Thus 18" he made an entry that pronounced a kind of final judgment upon those long, sad hours of carnage along Antietam Creek:

Today we were in line of battle all day, and all night last night. Our men sent over a flag of truce asking permission to bury our dead and it was granted. It seemed very curious to see the men on both sides come together and talk to each other when the day before were fireing at each other.[17]

⟶⟶⟨⊙⟩ VIII ⟨⊙⟩⟶⟶

A CONFLICT OF TESTIMONY

AFTER FACING DOWN McCLELLAN on September 18, Lee decided that it was wiser to retreat to Virginia than to stand longer in a position that he knew to be "a bad one to hold with the river in rear." Although he had acquired a few fresh troops, they were only a handful compared to the reinforcements the Federals were bringing up. So in the night and morning of September 18–19 he withdrew, crossing the Potomac at Boteler's Ford, just below Shepherdstown. To check enemy pursuit, Stuart was sent back to threaten the Federal right and rear, and Chief of Artillery Pendleton was stationed on the south bank of the river with forty-four guns of the reserve artillery and two fragmentary brigades totaling about six hundred men. The rest of the army moved on toward Martinsburg and camped for the night at various points from two to five miles beyond the Potomac.[1]

No doubt Harvey Hill and his men, like Lee and all the others of that weary band, lay down to sleep on the nineteenth in the hope that now at last they were safe. Hill felt that the recent hard marching and fighting had not only reduced the army to a shadow of its former strength but had also demoralized those divisions that had seen the most action. A breathing spell, in his opinion, was badly needed. He was all the more dismayed, then, when he was awakened about midnight by a distraught General Pendleton, who told him that the enemy had forced the river crossing—and captured thirty of the reserve guns!

Here was a stroke of ill luck, to put it mildly. Thoughts of a weakened Confederate army, with few reserve guns, having to fight another terrible battle must have raced through Hill's mind. Pendleton went off to report to Jackson and Lee, and it is safe to assume that no one who heard his dismal news got much more sleep that night.

Hill looked to Jackson for orders, having been reassigned to Jackson's command during the retreat. But when the orders came, they were puzzling: Hill was to follow Jubal Early to Boteler's Ford. Hill did not recognize this as the ford the army had so recently crossed; he apparently knew the place only by the more general name of Shepherdstown Ford.

Lee had the same difficulty. About daybreak, he came to Hill's tent and asked where Jackson was. Hill replied that he did not know, and then told of the order sending him to Boteler's Ford. Lee was mystified. It must be a mistake, he said.

To Hill and to Ratchford, who was also present, Lee seemed unable to summon his usual powers of decision. Possibly, like Jackson during the Seven Days, he was suffering from exhaustion brought on by inadequate rest and nervous tension. More than once Hill asked him for other orders, since Jackson's seemed erroneous, but Lee gave none. Finally he said, "I do not know what to tell you, but follow Jackson."

But that was just the point. Where was Jackson?

"I do not know, follow him," said Lee.

At least, this was the way that Ratchford, long after the war, recalled the conversation, and he further said of Lee, "I never saw a man more confused." Hill as early as 1864 wrote the Reverend R. L. Dabney an account of this incident, to aid him in preparing his biography of Jackson; and although Hill did not quote anything that Lee said, he did remark, after telling of Lee's perplexity over Jackson's order, "I have never seen him exhibit such indecision and embarrassment."

Leaving Hill to solve the Boteler's Ford riddle for himself, Lee went off to find Longstreet. Hill then sought out Early, who had succeeded to the command of Ewell's division, and found that he also had orders to go to Boteler's Ford but did not know where it was. Neither could Jackson's chief of staff, Major Elisha Paxton, say where the ford was located, or where Jackson was, but he could point out the direction in which the general had ridden away.

Since Jackson had headed back toward the crossing below Shepherdstown, Early and Hill started their divisions toward that point, with Early in the lead. Hill noted that Longstreet, meanwhile, had formed his troops in battle line. Apparently he and Lee had decided to stand on the defensive, awaiting any attack the Federals might launch. To Hill this seemed tantamount to inviting destruction; he firmly believed that the battered Confederate forces were in no condition to withstand another battle with McClellan's reinforced army.

On the way to the ford, he met Ratchford, whom he had ordered to ride ahead and locate Jackson. Ratchford reported that he had found the general at the river crossing, entirely without escort, reconnoitering the Federal position. Jackson had said that he wanted to see Hill.

In compliance with this order, Hill rode straight to Jackson's command post, and found that his brother-in-law had things well in hand. "With the blessing of God they will soon be driven back," said Jackson. He had ordered A. P. Hill to the ford to spearhead the counterattack with his relatively fresh troops, and Hill's men, charging gallantly into heavy artillery fire from Union batteries on the Maryland shore, were driving the Federal troops on the Virginia side back across the river. Although Early stood ready to join in the fight, Powell Hill needed no assistance. The danger was over.[2]

Actually it had not been as great as General Pendleton thought, although it might have become serious in the extreme but for Jackson's prompt action. After the fighting had ended and the ford was once more under Southern control, Pendleton discovered that when he had been driven away from it the night of the nineteenth, by a Federal assault party from Porter's corps, he had lost only four guns. In the darkness, without his knowing it, Major William Nelson and other officers of his command had saved all the rest. Moreover, Porter had shown little initiative. Instead of crossing his entire corps during the night, a move that might have put Lee in grave difficulty, he had recalled the assault party and waited until about seven o'clock the next morning to start two of his three divisions across the ford. It was the advance guards of these divisions that Powell Hill had driven back.[3]

So in the end the affair at Boteler's Ford went down in the records as a minor engagement for both sides. The sequel was a postwar conflict of testimony about it, involving Harvey Hill and Lee, and to some extent the reputation of Jackson, who had died in May, 1863, after being wounded at Chancellorsville. Dabney apparently accepted the account that Hill sent him in 1864 and told in his biography how Jackson, acting on his own initiative, had ended the threat at Boteler's Ford while Lee and Longstreet stood on the defensive. Before publication the manuscript was submitted by Mrs. Jackson to Lee, for his comment, and on January 25, 1866, he wrote her a letter in which he disagreed with a number of Dabney's statements. Regarding Boteler's Ford, he said:

After crossing the Potomac, Gen. Jackson was charged with the command of the rear, and he designated the brigades of infantry to support Pendleton's batteries. I believed Gen. McClellan had been so crippled at Sharpsburg, that he could not follow the Confederate army into Virginia, immediately.... Near daylight the next morning, Gen. Pendleton reported to me the occurrence at Shepherdstown the previous evening, and stated that he had made a similar report to Gen. Jackson, who was lying near me on the same field. From his statement, I thought it possible, that the Federal Army might be attempting to follow us; and I sent at once to Gen. Jackson to say, that in that event, I would attack it; that he must return with his whole command if necessary; that I had sent to Longstreet to countermarch the rest of the army; and that upon his joining me, unless I heard from him to the contrary, I should move with it to his support. Gen. Jackson went back with Hill's Division, Gen. Pendleton accompanying him, and soon drove the Federals into Maryland with loss. His report which I received on my way towards the river relieved my anxiety, and the order of the march of the troops was again resumed.[4]

Now, no statement written by Robert E. Lee can be lightly set aside, yet it must be said that this narrative is difficult indeed to reconcile with other evidence bearing upon the Boteler's Ford incident. Since neither Freeman nor any other historian has tried fully to explore this truly remarkable conflict of testimony, a point by point analysis is in order.[5]

1. Lee states that Jackson "was charged with the command of the rear," and that he "designated the brigades." This makes Jackson responsible for the loss of the ford, and also for providing Pendleton, who had never before commanded infantry, with a small and weak infantry support. The two brigades stationed at the ford were those of Armistead and A. R. Lawton, but both these generals were absent at the time, and the two units—remnants of brigades only, since they totaled no more than six hundred men—were commanded at

the ford by relatively inexperienced colonels.[6] Early stated in his official report that it was Lawton's brigade that "gave way" on the nineteenth. The brigade, he explained, had "suffered terribly on the 17th, and a considerable number of the men, being just returned from the hospitals, were without arms...." [7] In short, a position vital to the safety of the army was entrusted to a rear guard compounded of strange elements of inexperience and weakness.

But the official reports do not indicate that Jackson was either the commander of the rear or the designator of Pendleton's infantry support. Lee did not report that he gave Jackson such duty; in fact, the few sentences that he devoted to the Boteler's Ford incident are quite reticent. Jackson did not report such duty either, although usually he mentioned each assignment given him by Lee. A. P. Hill reported that, "as directed by General Lee," his division covered the retirement of the army from Sharpsburg, but added that after crossing the ford he moved on and "bivouacked that night (19th) about 5 miles from Shepherdstown." He did not indicate that he had rear-guard duty in Virginia.[8]

Longstreet reported that after crossing the river in the van of the army he guarded the ford for a time with part of his command. When all the army had crossed he proceeded, "as directed by the commanding general ... to form his line. As this was completed, it became evident that the enemy was not pursuing, except with some of his batteries and some small force. The various commands were then marched off to their points of bivouac." Longstreet reported nothing else about Boteler's Ford. In his memoirs, after describing how the army crossed, he said: "As the pursuit was not threatening, General Lee ordered his army to continue the march to proper points of bivouac, holding the artillery reserve under General Pendleton and an infantry detail ... as guard at the ford." [9]

Pendleton wrote in his report to Lee, dated September 24, 1862:

From yourself, I received instructions to hold the position [the ford] all that day [the nineteenth] and the night succeeding, unless the pressure should become too great, in which event I was, at my discretion, to withdraw after dark.... I was informed also that two brigades of infantry would remain as a support.... I was, by General Longstreet, requested to take charge of these brigades.

Pendleton further reported that after he had been driven from the ford he sought help from Generals Roger A. Pryor and Hood of Longstreet's command. Pryor declined to accept the responsibility of taking action, and referred Pendleton to Hood, but Hood could not be found. Pendleton then wrote: "No one could inform me where General Longstreet was. To find yourself, then, was clearly my next duty." And he did find and report to Lee, after more wandering in the darkness, during which he could have encountered Harvey Hill as well as Jackson.[10]

Thus Pendleton's report states that Lee stationed him at the ford, and that Longstreet requested him to take charge of the two infantry brigades. His effort to get help from Pryor and Hood seems to have been the result of their proximity more than anything else, but next he sought Longstreet and then Lee. Not once, in all this, does he mention Jackson. On this first point, his report weighs heavily against Lee's narrative.

2. In the narrative, Lee does not mention giving discretionary orders to Pendleton, but, as the foregoing quotation shows, Pendleton reported that Lee instructed him to retire after dark on the nineteenth if the enemy pressure became too great. A letter in the official records corroborates Pendleton. Addressed to him on September 19, and signed by R. H. Chilton, it reads: "The commanding general says that if the enemy is in force in your front you must retire to-night." If the enemy was not in strength, Pendleton was to "withdraw the infantry forces" and continue to guard the ford with "a few guns and a small cavalry force." [11]

Thus on the nineteenth Lee intended, if too much enemy pressure developed, to yield the ford after dark, and in retreating at dusk Pendleton came very close to complying with orders. Moreover, this note of the nineteenth came direct from Lee's headquarters to Pendleton. One would think that if Jackson had been in command of the rear the message would have come from or through his headquarters.

3. Lee states that "near daylight" on the twentieth Pendleton told him of "the occurrence at Shepherdstown" and said that he had also informed Jackson, who was lying near Lee. Then, Lee says, "I sent at once to Gen. Jackson. . . ." Pendleton did not report that Lee did this. He wrote that after he had told Lee his troubles, "I was instructed to do no more till morning, when measures would be taken suited to circumstances, and meantime to secure a few hours of necessary rest." [12] More significant than this statement in the official

report, however, is a letter that Pendleton wrote to his wife on September 22. Describing the events of the twentieth, he told her that "past midnight I reached General Lee. He was of course disturbed, but determined to do nothing till next morning, and I lay down [to sleep]." [13] Here again there is no indication that Lee "sent at once" to Jackson.

4. If Lee did "at once" send a message to Jackson, who was near him, why did not Jackson receive it? Much evidence indicates that he did not receive such a message and that he went to Boteler's Ford on his own initiative. Although it might be inferred from Lee's narrative that Jackson got such a message, Lee does not actually say this. He says that after hearing Pendleton's report he thought that possibly the Federal army was pursuing—"and I sent at once to Gen. Jackson to say, that in that event, I would attack it; that he must return with his whole command if necessary; that I had sent to Longstreet to countermarch the rest of the army; and that upon his joining me, unless I heard from him to the contrary, I should move with it to his support. Gen. Jackson went back with Hill's Division, Gen. Pendleton accompanying him. . . ."

Here, in regard to Jackson, there are two separate statements; first, that Lee sent to Jackson *to say* what should be done; second, that Jackson went back. Lee does not say that Jackson received the message and went back in compliance with it, although the two statements, when read in sequence, strongly imply this. There is here a singular ambiguity, to say the least, in a statement written for purposes of clarification by a master of precise military prose.

Longstreet, in his memoirs, does say that "General Lee ordered General Jackson to send his nearest division back to the ford early in the morning," and adds that A. P. Hill was sent. But there is no indication that Longstreet wrote this from personal knowledge. The context in which it appears indicates that it is based upon the official reports, which do not in fact support it.[14]

Pendleton, in his letter to his wife, wrote: "Next morning General Jackson's force was sent back to Shepherdstown. I accompanied him." In his official report he said: "Early the next morning I had the privilege of accompanying a force, under General Jackson, sent to punish the enemy. . . ." Each of these statements can be taken to mean either that Lee sent Jackson's force, or that Jackson sent it. Lee himself reported in the passive voice that "A. P. Hill was ordered to return. . . ." Jackson reported: "Orders were dispatched to Generals Early and Hill . . . to return and drive back the enemy." Again the passive voice conceals who gave the orders, but in a report by the meticulous Jackson the fact that no mention is made of orders from "the commanding general" is fairly weighty evidence that Jackson received none.

Moreover, to the foregoing negative evidence must be added the positive testimony of others involved in the Boteler's Ford incident. D. H. Hill believed that Jackson went back to the ford on his own initiative, and praise of Jackson for his swift, independent action was the main theme of Hill's letter to Dabney in 1864. This makes it even harder to understand why Lee wrote so ambiguously to Mrs. Jackson on this point. Ratchford also said that Jackson acted independently: "Gen. Jackson hearing of the capture of the artillery did not wait for Gen. Lee's orders but double-quicked Gen. A. P. Hill's division to the river. . . ." Jackson's medical director, Dr. Hunter McGuire, who usually camped near his commander, held the same opinion.[15] The weight of evidence indicates that Jackson did act on his own initiative, without receiving orders from Lee.

5. In comparing Lee's narrative with the recollections of Hill and Ratchford, one should keep in mind the fact that Ratchford did not write his undated recollections until after Hill's death—that is, not until 1889 or after. By this time his memory of events could easily have become blurred. The beginning of his story conflicts with Hill's, for he wrote that on the morning of the twentieth "Gen. Hill reported to Gen. Lee for orders, not knowing anything about the captured artillery"; whereas Hill in 1864 stated that "about midnight" Pendleton had visited him "in search of Gen. Lee" and that "Genl. Lee came over to my tent at daylight after Pendleton saw him and inquired for Jackson." On the more important points, however, Ratchford either does not conflict with Hill, or agrees with him. Since he apparently did not know of Hill's letter of 1864, his narrative, on the whole, is strong corroborative testimony.

From Lee's narrative one gains the impression that Lee reacted to Pendleton's alarming news swiftly, decisively, and aggressively, ordering Jackson back to the ford to attack the Federal army if it was pursuing, ordering Longstreet to countermarch the rest of the army, and planning to lead it back to support Jackson unless Jackson notified him to the contrary. True, this was the way Lee usually did react to military emergencies. But according to Hill, when Lee came to his tent asking for Jackson and was told of the Boteler's Ford order, Lee's reaction was most untypical: "He said that this [Jackson's order] must be a mistake and was much perplexed. I have never seen him exhibit such indecision and embarrassment. He then went off to find Longstreet."

Ratchford described Lee as "confused." He wrote: "Gen. Lee was very much confused by conflicting reports and gave no orders although Gen. Hill asked for orders more than once, finally he said I do not know what to tell you, but follow Jackson: he [Hill] then asked where Jackson went. Gen. Lee replied 'I do not know, follow him.' (I never saw a man more confused)."

Granted that Ratchford may not have recalled the conversation exactly over so many years, there is still convincing agreement in these two narratives. In both accounts Lee acts not at all decisively. Naturally, if he was unfamiliar with the name Boteler's Ford, Jackson's order puzzled him, but why did he not tell Hill of the messages that, according to his narrative, he had sent to Jackson and Longstreet? Why, if he had been planning to attack the Federals at the ford, did he not order Hill to join Longstreet and march back with all possible speed? Taken together, Hill's and Ratchford's descriptions of Lee convey the strong impression that he was not his usual self, that probably he was suffering from exhaustion.

6. In regard to Lee's plans for attacking the Federals, one should note, in the official reports, a letter from Lee to Davis, dated September 20, 1862, in which Lee speaks of returning to attack. After relating why and how he had crossed the river, Lee said:

At night [of the nineteenth] the infantry sharpshooters, left, in conjunction with General Pendleton's artillery, to hold the ford below Shepherdstown, gave back, and the enemy's cavalry took possession of that town, and, from General Pendleton's report after midnight, I fear much of his reserve artillery has been captured. I am now obliged to return to Shepherdstown, with the intention of driving the enemy back if not in position with his whole army; but, if in full force, I think an attack would be inadvisable, and I shall make other dispositions.[16]

If only an early hour of writing were marked on this letter it would strongly corroborate Lee's narrative, but unfortunately the hour was not set down along with the date. The letter could have

been written on the twentieth after Lee had finally learned that
Jackson had gone to the ford.

7. Lee in his narrative appears more disposed to aggressive action
against the Federal army than he does in any other document bearing upon the Boteler's Ford incident. If "the Federal army" was
trying to follow him, he planned to attack it, and apparently considered no other alternative. But in his letter to Davis of September
20 he said that if the enemy was "in full force" at the ford, he would
not attack but "make other dispositions." This is more in keeping
with his message of the nineteenth to Pendleton, ordering him to
retreat that night if the enemy was "in force" at the ford. The letter
and the message also harmonize with Hill's letter of 1864 to Dabney,
in which he recalled that by the time he and Early had started their
divisions toward the ford, "Longstreet had got his drawn up across
the Charlestown Pike"—that is, in a defensive battle line. Hill added:
"From the dispositions made by Lee and Longstreet, I am satisfied
that they intended to *wait* an attack."

8. Now that all the pertinent documents have been brought into
the discussion, a further analysis can be made of the time question,
which involves the time that Lee heard Pendleton's report and the
time that Jackson's commanders received orders to march to the
ford. In Lee's narrative, little time appears to elapse between Pendleton's report and Jackson's return to the ford with A. P. Hill: Lee
hears Pendleton's report "near daylight," sends orders "at once" to
Jackson and Longstreet, and Jackson goes back with Hill's division.
How well does this harmonize with the two points of time involved?

The time that Jackson's commanders received orders seems clear
enough. Although Early did not report the hour, and D. H. Hill did
not mention the Boteler's Ford incident in his report, A. P. Hill reported that "at 6.30 o'clock" Jackson ordered him to attack. This
harmonizes with the fact that when Powell Hill reached the ford he
met the advance guards of the Federal divisions that had, according
to Porter, started to cross "about 7 A.M." [17]

If 6:30 A.M. be taken as the approximate time Early and both
Hills received Jackson's orders, this will be seen to agree fairly well
with the narratives of Lee and D. H. Hill. Lee states that he sent
his message to Jackson right after Pendleton reported to him "near
daylight," and from "near daylight" to 6:30 A.M. seems to encompass
a reasonably fast transmission of orders from Lee to Jackson to

Jackson's commanders. Hill wrote that he had Jackson's order when Lee came to his tent "at daylight."

But if Lee's narrative is in accord with the other evidence as to the time Jackson's orders were received, there is less agreement with regard to the time that Lee heard Pendleton's report. Lee states that Pendleton reported to him "near daylight," and in the foregoing paragraph this phrase has been interpreted as meaning not long before 6:30 A.M. But the statements in all the rest of the evidence turn upon the word "midnight." Lee in his letter of September 20 to Davis referred to "General Pendleton's report after midnight." Hill said that Pendleton came to his tent in search of Lee "about midnight," and Pendleton wrote his wife on the twenty-second that he reached Lee "past midnight," a statement that dovetails with Hill's.

Thus the phraseology used by three different witnesses, including Lee himself in his letter to Davis, indicates that Lee heard Pendleton's report perhaps as much as six hours before orders reached Jackson's commanders about 6:30 A.M. This certainly does not harmonize with the picture of immediate action to meet the emergency that is conveyed by Lee's narrative. It does harmonize with the previously noted passage of Pendleton's report which states that, after Pendleton reached Lee, "I was instructed to do no more till morning, when measures would be taken suited to circumstances, and meantime to secure a few hours of necessary rest." It also harmonizes with Pendleton's previously noted statement to his wife on September 22— "past midnight I reached General Lee. He was of course disturbed, but determined to do nothing till next morning, and I lay down [to sleep]."

From this analysis of conflicting testimony, conclusions as to the reliability of the chief witnesses can be drawn. Pendleton emerges as a reliable witness. Although his official report reveals him as a rather laughably pompous gentleman, and as an infantry commander no less inept than inexperienced, he seems both honest and accurate. D. H. Hill also appears reliable, and by using his narrative to supplement Pendleton's one can reconstruct the Boteler's Ford incident so as to harmonize nearly all the evidence, as follows:

After the Confederate army had completed its retreat across the Potomac on the morning of September 19, Lee ordered Pendleton to guard the ford with forty-four guns of the reserve artillery, supported by infantry. Longstreet designated the supporting force of about six hundred, the remnants of Lawton's and Armistead's brigades. Since neither Lee nor Longstreet thought that the enemy would immediately attempt serious pursuit, their defense arrangements were weak. Not only were Pendleton and the colonels who commanded the infantry inexperienced, but the shattered brigades were low in morale, and some of Lawton's men, who had just returned from the hospital, lacked muskets.

During the day Lee exercised command of the rear, in that he sent a message direct to Pendleton, instructing him to retreat that night if the enemy pressure became too great. Pendleton, the amateur, failed to count his infantry and dispersed it up and down the river until he had scarcely three hundred men at the ford. At dusk these men retreated before Porter's assault party. According to Jackson's report as well as Early's, it was Lawton's brigade that gave way. Hill told Dabney that the men of Lawton's brigade threw down their arms and "fled without firing a shot."

In the confusion, Pendleton thought that he had lost many more guns than the four that were actually captured. Wandering through the darkness he talked with Pryor, tried futilely to find Hood and then Longstreet, and about midnight arrived at Hill's tent in search of Lee. As Hill remembered, Pendleton "told me that the Yankees had crossed in force and that he had lost 30 pieces of artillery."

From Hill Pendleton made his way to Jackson, who was lying near Lee, and finally after midnight reported to Lee himself. The commanding general, as Pendleton wrote his wife two days later, "was of course disturbed, but determined to do nothing till next morning. . . ." Lee instructed Pendleton to "secure a few hours of necessary rest," as Pendleton expressed it in his official report, and Pendleton did as he was told.

At this point direct evidence and testimony fails, and the reconstruction must rest upon conjecture. Probably Lee, when Pendleton left him, lay down again to get a little more rest and pull his thoughts together. The reported loss of the artillery was unexpected and dismaying, but Lee could hardly have been completely surprised by news that the Federals had crossed the ford. He had realized that they might do so, and in his message to Pendleton on the nineteenth had directed that, "if the enemy is in force in your front you must retire to-night." Evidently, on the nineteenth, he was formulating a defensive plan that contemplated yielding the ford.

On the 20th, he probably meant to act on this plan at daylight. There were numerous reasons for not acting at once. Getting the army together in darkness would be extremely difficult, and might cause panic among troops already low in morale. Moreover, despite Pendleton's report it was not certain that McClellan was pursuing in force. Stuart had not reported that he was, and there was always the possibility that Pendleton had overestimated the enemy numbers. Even if the Federals were pursuing in strength, Stuart might be counted upon to hinder them, for he had been ordered, as Lee later reported, "to operate upon the right and rear of the enemy should he attempt to follow us." In any event, it was highly probable that pursuing Federal forces would not leave the river until daylight, at the earliest, and would then move slowly and cautiously on the Confederate trail.

So Lee may have reasoned and waited, and Jackson, too, evidently waited through the hours of darkness before taking action. Then, at 6:30 A.M., as A. P. Hill later reported, Jackson ordered Hill to return to the ford and attack the Federals. According to Lee and Pendleton, Jackson also went back, taking Pendleton with him.

Now Harvey Hill becomes the chief witness. In his letter to Dabney he portrayed Jackson as acting on his own initiative, and as riding out ahead of his escort to reconnoiter the enemy, in which dangerously exposed position Ratchford found him. Hill said that Jackson also ordered Early to the ford, a statement borne out by Jackson's and Early's reports, and that he himself received an order to "follow Early to Boteler's Ford." This is not mentioned in any official report, but since Hill's division was not employed even as a reserve in the attack on the Federals, the omission seems natural enough.

At daylight, said Hill, Lee came to his tent looking for Jackson, was told of the Boteler's Ford order, replied that it must be a mistake, was "much perplexed," exhibited singular "indecision and embarrassment" (corroborated by Ratchford), and went off to find Longstreet, leaving Hill to find Boteler's Ford for himself. Lee's unusual manner seems best explained by the theory that he was exhausted.

That Jackson referred to the ford by a precise name that was unknown to his associates seems believable when it is remembered that the Valley was Jackson's favorite military arena, and that his march to Martinsburg and Harpers Ferry and back again to Sharpsburg had given him occasion to acquire a thorough knowledge of Potomac crossings. The fact that one of his close friends was the Confederate Congressman Colonel A. R. Boteler may also have served to fix the precise name of the ford in his mind.

According to Hill, Early did not know the position of Boteler's Ford and neither did Jackson's chief of staff, Major Paxton. But after Paxton had pointed out the direction Jackson had taken, Early and Hill marched their divisions to the ford, where Hill witnessed the attack of A. P. Hill, talked with Jackson, and of course had ample opportunity to learn whether Jackson had acted under Lee's orders.

Since Hill also wrote that while he was starting his division toward the ford he saw Longstreet forming a defense line, it may be supposed that Lee at that time was still thinking in defensive terms, as on the nineteenth. One may also conjecture that before long Lee received word that Jackson had gone to the ford; that he then directed Longstreet to re-form his troops in marching column and move to Jackson's support; and that while this was being done he dispatched his letter to Davis, saying that he was "obliged to return to Shepherdstown," and intended to drive the Federals back if their whole army was not in position. Finally, according to Lee's narrative, on his way to the river Lee received Jackson's report of a successful attack, "and the order of the march of the troops was again resumed."

Partially conjectural though it is, this reconstruction does seem to harmonize the great bulk of the evidence in a logical manner. It appears to support the conclusions that Pendleton and Hill are reliable witnesses.

The final conclusion to be drawn from the analysis of testimony is a corollary of the first two, and is simply that Lee's narrative is less reliable than Pendleton's or Hill's. The numerous conflicts between it on the one hand, and Pendleton, Hill, and the rest of the harmonizing evidence on the other, mark it as inaccurate.

That Dabney was not fully satisfied with it is shown by the way he handled it in his biography of Jackson. Although he followed it, essentially, in his key paragraph on Boteler's Ford, he enclosed the whole paragraph in quotation marks, and published it without giving the source of the quoted statements.[18]

After the book had appeared, he wrote Hill:

On the affair at Boteler's ford ... I derived some interesting facts and opinions from you. If my narrative as printed is not exactly conformed to your recollections, the reason is, that Gen. Lee himself required a modification; and the story is told, in its essential features, in Gen. Lee's *own words*, as written down in an autograph letter of his, which I have in my desk. You see, in this case I was cornered; and could not avoid yielding to his account.[19]

One final question remains to be asked. If Lee did write an inaccurate narrative of the Boteler's Ford incident, why did he do so? Faulty memory may well be the whole explanation. If Lee was suffering from exhaustion that morning, this might tend to blur his memory. Furthermore, the mind inclines to forget or alter facts that wound the ego. Lee may have written an inaccurate narrative in perfect sincerity.

On the other hand, Lee must have read Jackson's and Pendleton's official reports; in fact, one would expect him to examine them carefully in preparing his own comprehensive report, which he transmitted to the Adjutant and Inspector General on August 19, 1863. And of course he read Hill's version of the incident in Dabney's manuscript. One cannot ignore the possibility that Lee, when he wrote his narrative for Mrs. Jackson, may have succumbed to the temptation to show himself in a better light than his knowledge of the facts warranted. If so, the narrative is perhaps the only evidence known to history that Robert E. Lee ever failed to measure up to his well-deserved reputation as an honorable man.

IX

DISSENSION IN THE HIGH COMMAND

Aʟᴛᴇʀ ᴛʜᴇ ᴇɴɢᴀɢᴇᴍᴇɴᴛ at Boteler's Ford, the Confederates enjoyed a respite from Federal pursuit. Lee moved his forces up the Shenandoah Valley by easy marches and went into camp near Winchester. Thanks to McClellan's slow preparation for another offensive, fall was a season of rest and recuperation for the Army of Northern Virginia.

Harvey Hill used the time for recruiting and getting his division in fighting trim. This entailed much reorganization, for at South Mountain and Antietam he had lost some 2,316 killed and wounded, nearly one half of all the men taken into action. In reporting this to Lee he declared, "The unparalleled loss of the division shows that, spite of hunger and fatigue, the officers and men fought most heroically in the two battles in Maryland." [1]

Lee was concerned in these fall weeks with reorganizing and rebuilding the entire army, and with promoting a number of officers, including Longstreet and Jackson. In the first part of October, President Davis appointed, with the confirmation of the Senate, seven lieutenant generals in the Confederate armed forces. In order of seniority they were Longstreet, E. Kirby Smith, Leonidas Polk, William J. Hardee, Jackson, T. H. Holmes, and John C. Pemberton. Following this, Lee announced the reorganization of his troops into two corps, the First under Longstreet and the Second under Jackson. Hill's division was assigned to Jackson's corps along with Jackson's own division, and those of Richard S. Ewell and A. P. Hill. [2]

These changes took place in an atmosphere of dissatisfaction and acrimony among the high-ranking generals. They were of course patriots, sincerely dedicated, one may believe, to the Southern cause; but they were also proud, ambitious men, practitioners of an aggressive profession who were capable of contending with each other for power and prestige as fiercely as they fought the enemy. Dissension in the high command has been the general military rule since mankind first learned the dubious art of organized warfare, and Lee's army was no exception.

Conspicuous among the various quarrels going on at this time were Jackson's feuds with two of his generals, A. P. Hill and Richard B. Garnett, whom Jackson had earlier charged, on various counts, with improper performance of duty. Hill, spurning Lee's efforts at reconciliation, had filed countercharges against Jackson, and their dispute had reached a kind of stalemate. Garnett was not able to fight back so successfully. The previous March, during Jackson's Valley campaign, he had withdrawn troops from an engagement at Kernstown that ended in the repulse of Jackson's forces. For this Jackson had removed him from command and filed a number of specifications against him under the general charge of neglect of duty. In August the case had been partially tried, but the court-martial had been interrupted by the need to march against Pope. Garnett had been released from arrest and given command under Longstreet. That fall the trial was still incomplete and it was never to be resumed, because of Jackson's death.[3]

That the whole affair had engendered much bitterness is shown by a letter that William Garnett, the father of the general, wrote on November 13, 1862, to "My dear friend," apparently General William Nelson Pendleton. The letter, which contains serious accusations against Jackson, seems to have escaped the attention of historians. In it Garnett explained that his son Richard had visited Colonel William H. Harman, who had commanded the Fifth Virginia Infantry at Kernstown. During the visit Harman had said that he knew nothing of Jackson's charges, but that in his official report of the engagement at Kernstown "he had stated, that his right had been placed [in] position by Genl Garnett, (which it seems contradicted one of Jackson's specifications against Genl G.) but unknown to Col H." The letter continued:

He [Harman] told Richard, that Genl Jackson made three attempts to persuade him to strike out this part of his report, of which he has pub-

lically spoken, and to which he will testify, on oath, when the trial comes
on again. In a civil action, a party detected in tampering with a witness
and persuading him to suppress a part of his testimony, subjects himself,
to a heavy fine and imprisonment; and the rule ought to be still more
stringent, in a military offense of this character, which involves a man's
honor, much dearer to a soldier, than his property. The truth of the matter
is, that Jackson found himself caught in a trap, upon that occasion; and
that instead of passing the rear of a retreating army, as he thought, he
found an enemy of three times his number, prepared to meet him. Under
this condition of things, a scape-goat became necessary, and Genl Garnett
was the selected victim. Again, Genl Garnett had been arrested for several
weeks, and yet no charges preferred, doubtless for the purpose of keeping
him out of service. Finding this to be the case, I wrote to the War Dept,
when Jackson was *ordered* to prefer his charges, at once, or withdraw
them. The latter he declined to do, opining, as his reason, "that he considered *Genl Garnett so incompetent an officer*, that if he were placed in
command of a good Brigade, it would soon become a bad one." Such an
opinion from such a source, can excite no other emotion, in the minds
of men, acquainted with both parties, than that of *utter contempt*, and is
proof positive to my mind of inveterate prejudice on Jackson's part,
against Genl G, or of ignorance or malice and I incline to attribute his
conduct to a combination of all these motives.[4]

Of course the mere existence of this letter does not prove the accusations that William Garnett made against Jackson. The aged
father—he remarked that he was in his seventy-seventh year—was
angry over what he regarded as persecution of his son, and hardly
inclined to take an objective view of the matter. As it stands the document is a fragment of historical evidence which seems to deserve study
by Jackson biographers, who can assign it to its proper place in this
famous soldier's career.

Among the dissatisfied generals who felt that certain of their fellow
officers were being rewarded beyond their just desert was Lafayette
McLaws. He was from Georgia, and his grievance was against Virginians. He believed that a "strong feeling" was growing up in the
army "against Virginia," because of the way Virginia newspapers
exaggerated the deeds of Virginia generals, while minimizing the
achievements of those from other states. In particular, he resented the
praise heaped upon Stuart and Jackson. Eventually he would write
a private denunciation of Virginians, in which he would refer to
Stuart as "a Buffoon" who publicized himself by going about with a

"Banjo player and a special correspondent," and to Jackson as a general who "panders to the religious zeal of a puritanical church, and has numerous scribes writing fancy anecdotes of his peculiarities, which never existed." [5]

As a general to admire, McLaws selected his corps commander, Longstreet, and in this choice Lee doubtless would have concurred. When Longstreet walked into army headquarters after the battle of Antietam, Lee affectionately put an arm around his shoulder, saying, "Here comes my war horse just from the field he has done so much to save!" And on October 2, when Lee recommended Longstreet and Jackson for promotion, he placed Longstreet's name first. [6] Undoubtedly, therefore, he would have been amazed if he could have read the letter that Longstreet wrote to General Joseph E. Johnston on October 5.

This document also seems to have gone unnoticed by historians. Longstreet was replying to a letter from Johnston, who was recovering in Richmond from his wounds at Seven Pines, and anticipating an assignment to command in the western theater. After first thanking Johnston for his letter, and for a photograph of himself that he had sent, Longstreet said:

It has revived a good deal of the old enthusiasm that your old Army has always had at the sight or thought of you. Although they have fought many battles and successfully under another leader, I feel that you have their hearts more decidedly than any other leader can ever have.... I cant become reconciled at the idea of your going west. I command the 1st Corps in this Army. if you will take it you are more than welcome to it, and I have no doubt but the command of the entire Army will fall to you before Spring.

After this extraordinary suggestion, Longstreet briefly discussed army supply problems, and gave news of officers whom Johnston knew. Then he added:

If it is possible for me to relieve you by going west dont hesitate to send me. It would put me to no great inconvenience. On the contrary it will give me pleasure if I can relieve you of it. I fear that you ought not to go where you will be exposed to the handicaps that you will meet with out there. I am yet entirely sound and believe that I can endure anything. [7]

It surely must have occurred to Johnston, when he read these transparent statements, that what his solicitous friend really wanted was to get out from under Lee and exercise independent command. His reply to Longstreet, if he made one, seems not to be of record.

Still another of Lee's dissatisfied commanders that fall was Harvey Hill. He felt that he should have been promoted to lieutenant general, that he deserved the rank more than certain others on Davis's list. For example John C. Pemberton, a departmental commander in South Carolina and a Presidential favorite, had less than a month's seniority over Hill, and had never been in a major Civil War battle.[8]

Jackson also thought that Hill's combat record entitled him to promotion. As Ratchford remembered, Jackson indignantly declared that if he had been treated by Davis as Hill had been, he would have resigned and gone home. To this Hill replied that he was fighting for a principle and for his country, not for President Davis, and if he could not fight as an officer he would do so as a private.[9]

This was also his attitude, at first, in his letters home. When Isabella remarked that the Richmond press was not doing justice to his accomplishments in Maryland, he replied that he wanted "the love of wife and children, and not newspaper puffs." When she complained that other generals were receiving promotion ahead of him, he answered: "I am sorry that you are still so jealous about my reputation and I am afraid *envious* of that of others. The two officers you mention [unidentified] are both deserving, they have higher claims upon the country than I have, let them have it."

Then, of South Mountain, he said, "The battle of Sunday was one of the most creditable in the war. I feel very thankful for it." And of Antietam he boasted: "My own exertions were almost superhuman on Wednesday and I thank God that I was able to make them. Notwithstanding the boast of my friend A. P., his troops were in a full run on Wednesday, when I turned one of my batteries on the columns of the Yankees and broke them. Oh History, History what a tissue of lies thou art!"[10]

Despite his attitude toward newspaper puffs, and his scorn of the army correspondent as a "nuisance" and a "knight of the quill" who "only snuffed the battle afar," he yielded to Isabella's insistence and tried, unsuccessfully, to get the Richmond papers to publish an account of the Maryland battles that his adjutant, Major Archer Anderson, had written. Also, he began to think seriously of resigning from the army. This of course was Isabella's fondest dream, and right after the Seven Days he had told her that "if I can honourably leave, I will do so now." That fall he revived this thought. "I have fully decided to resign next month," he said November 10, "unless some terrible calamity befall the country before that time." A week later he wrote: "I have made up my mind definitely to resign at the beginning of the New Year, if the affairs of the South are in a favourable condition. If all be dark then, I must still hold on to the sinking ship."

His health was a factor in this decision. With the onset of cold wet weather he began suffering severe pain in his spine. His camp in November was near Middletown; his duty, the destruction of the Manassas Gap Railroad; and this often kept him long hours in the saddle. During the day he could not lie down to ease the pain in his back, and at night he suffered from the cold: "I often shiver in bed like a man in an ague. When once chilled, I have not vitality enough to react and a mountain of blankets would not warm me. I simply bear it the best way I can."

But of course the "tentless, shoeless soldiers" were far worse off. Hill was grateful to Jackson for help in getting supplies. "He is near Winchester twenty miles distant. I see him very seldom and only on business. He has treated me very kindly and has done all in his power to add to the comfort of my men. But their suffering is greater by far than that of our Revolutionary sires." [11]

Hill's decision to resign may have been shaped not only by declining health and chagrin over not being promoted but also by a feeling that he was being unfairly blamed for the loss of South Mountain. Whether he was a target of widespread or serious criticism is difficult to determine, but about this time a young artillerist in A. P. Hill's division, John H. Chamberlayne, wrote home that D. H. Hill had failed to hold South Mountain, and added: "People up here are very generally beginning to call D. H. Hill a numskull." Hill also remarked to Isabella, "If people are disposed to find fault and censure me, they do not do so to my face. . . ." [12]

Apparently Hill was not yet being blamed for the Lost Dispatch, for although stories of its discovery had appeared in the New York *Herald* September 15, and in the New York *Tribune* the sixteenth, these accounts were vague and inaccurate and did not mention Hill.[13] He would not be explicitly accused of losing the Dispatch until the summer of 1863.

Lee might have obtained a promotion for Hill had he recommended him. But Lee had told Davis on October 2 that he needed only two corps commanders and therefore only two lieutenant generals. And after naming Longstreet and Jackson he remarked: "Next to these two officers, I consider General A. P. Hill the best commander with me. He fights his troops well, and takes good care of them." [14]

By omission, then, Lee was passing judgment on D. H. Hill, and plainly he rated him below his junior, A. P. Hill. Why? Leaving aside the achievements of Powell Hill, which may well afford the best explanation of Lee's opinion, and passing over McLaws's theory that Virginians preferred Virginians—an idea later publicized by Longstreet [15]—one comes to the image of Harvey Hill that must have formed by now in Lee's mind. What was Lee's estimate of the man who in certain respects was the most enigmatic of his generals?

In all likelihood it was still essentially what he had previously indicated to Davis: Hill was an excellent division commander, but no more than that; he did not have the ability to act on his own that higher rank demanded. Lee of course did not know that at Seven Pines Hill had successfully exercised what amounted to corps command; nor had he been present to witness the lone fight that Hill had waged at South Mountain. He had seen him in action in the battle of Antietam, or Sharpsburg, and in his report of the battle he credited him with helping to hold the line in all three sectors, left, right, and center. But here again Hill had been under the tactical command of Longstreet, and it is interesting to note that although Longstreet in his memoirs called Hill "the hardest fighter at Sharpsburg," in his official report of the battle, dated October 10, 1862, he described the center fighting of September 17 without once mentioning Hill, his brigade commanders, or his brigades! These omissions seem to have been overlooked by Freeman, who calls Longstreet's report "a manly, forthright document . . . modest and fair except that it was ungenerous in failing to credit A. P. Hill fully with the help the Light Division gave in the final charge on the right." [16]

A salient factor in Lee's appraisal of Harvey Hill must surely have been the latter's health. As has been seen, it tended to decline markedly when the weather turned cold and wet, and perhaps also when Hill was mentally depressed. It was undoubtedly a serious handicap to a general in the field.

And then there was Hill's personality. Lee has been paraphrased as saying that "D. H. Hill had such a queer temperament he could never tell what to expect from him," and Hill himself told Isabella, "I am so unlike other folks that you could not understand my feelings if I tried to explain them for a week." He was indeed a bundle of complexities, with many of the admirable qualities hidden inside, and a number of negative ones exposed to the world.

He was often gloomy. His frequent predictions that the Confederacy would lose the war stemmed in part from his shrewd understanding of Northern power, and ultimately they came true, but evidently they annoyed the sanguine Lee, who complained that Hill "croaked." Of course, a man with an aching spine is not likely to be cheerful, nor overly mild in speech. Hill's rough military manner was heightened by his proclivity for sarcasm. Robert G. H. Kean, Head of the Confederate Bureau of War, called him "harsh, abrupt, often insulting in the effort to be sarcastic." Archer Anderson, who admired him, suggested in a postwar tribute to "his great military virtues" that in the final judgment of history, "Hill's just fame will perhaps not suffer from his faults of manner or asperities of speech." [17]

As a commander, Hill seldom complimented anyone for efficient performance of routine work. In his battle reports, he was generous in praising merit as he saw it, whether in his own or another's command, and bluntly explicit in pointing out what appeared to him to be military failures and weaknesses. Though in both praise and blame his pen ran to hyperbole, he was an honest reporter, and not often mistaken in his facts; nor did he ever carry censure to the point of preferring charges against his subordinate commanders, as Jackson did.

His boldest and most tactless criticisms were those he wrote of Lee. In his report of the Seven Days, after describing how he had obeyed Lee and Davis in sending Ripley's brigade against the enemy strongpoint at Ellerson's Mill, he said, "The result, as might have been anticipated, was a disastrous and bloody repulse." He also remarked, "The battle of Malvern Hill might have been a complete and glorious success had not our artillery and infantry been fought in detail." And again of Malvern he commented: "So far as I can learn none of our troops drew trigger, except McLaws' division, mine, and a portion of Huger's. Notwithstanding the tremendous odds against us and the blundering management of the battle we inflicted heavy loss upon the Yankees." [18]

It would have been only human of Lee to resent these cutting phrases. The truth in them made them hurt the more. Quite possibly they aroused feelings that helped give force to Lee's own criticisms of Hill.

Further strictures against Lee, less harshly worded but more fully argued, appeared in Hill's report of the Maryland battles. Hill objected first to the fact that Lee had separated his and Longstreet's divisions at Boonsborough. He concluded his account of South Mountain by saying, "Had Longstreet's division been with mine at daylight in the morning, the Yankees would have been disastrously repulsed," from which it followed that "the battle of Sharpsburg never would have been fought, and the Yankees would not have even the shadow of consolation for the loss of Harper's Ferry."

Next, after describing the fighting at Sharpsburg, he called attention to the inadequate food supplies available to the soldiers of his division:

It is true that hunger and exhaustion had nearly unfitted these brave men for battle. Our wagons had been sent off across the river on Sunday, and for three days the men had been sustaining life on green corn and such cattle as they could kill in the fields. In charging through an apple orchard at the Yankees, with the immediate prospect of death before them, I noticed men eagerly devouring apples.

Finally, he inserted in his report a summary critique of Lee's strategy and policies:

The battle of Sharpsburg was a success so far as the failure of the Yankees to carry the position they assailed. It would, however, have been a glorious victory for us but for three causes:

First. The separation of our forces. Had McLaws and R. H. Anderson been there earlier in the morning, the battle would not have lasted two hours, and would have been signally disastrous to the Yankees.

Second. The bad handling of our artillery. This could not cope with the superior weight, caliber, range, and number of the Yankee guns; hence it ought only to have been used against masses of infantry. On the contrary, our guns were made to reply to the Yankee guns, and were smashed up or withdrawn before they could be effectually turned against massive columns of attack. An artillery duel between the Washington Artillery [under Longstreet] and the Yankee batteries across the Antietam on the 16th was the most melancholy farce in the war.

Third. The enormous straggling. The battle was fought with less than 30,000 men. Had all our stragglers been up, McClellan's army would have been completely crushed or annihilated. Doubtless the want of shoes, the want of food, and physical exhaustion had kept many brave men from being with the army; but thousands of thieving poltroons had kept away from sheer cowardice. The straggler is generally a thief and always a coward, lost to all sense of shame; he can only be kept in ranks by a strict and sanguinary discipline.[19]

Just when Hill wrote this is not certain, for he did not date his report; but internal evidence shows that it was written after October 14, and a remark to Isabella indicates that Hill prepared it in November, 1862.[20] Like the earlier criticisms of Lee, these had much point. Lee himself told a subordinate officer, "My army is ruined by straggling." [21] Hill, if asked why he assumed the role of critic, would probably have replied in all sincerity that he had in mind the good of the service. Still it was most unusual for a division commander to criticize his commanding general as he did, and it is difficult to believe that Lee felt grateful to him for it.

Did a man so ready to point out the faults of others have any friends in Lee's army? Hill occasionally remarked to Isabella that he had not one friend in the world, but this was merely one of his exaggerations. At every stage of his career, the attractive qualities that were liberally intermingled with his prickly traits of character had drawn friends to him, and so it was now in the Army of Northern Virginia. Of this there is abundant evidence in his private papers, in the form of cordial letters written him both during and after the war.

A partial list of friendly colleagues outside his own division would include Jackson, Dabney, McLaws, Early, R. H. Anderson, and Lawton. Of these, Anderson was closest to Hill. In 1867 he addressed Hill as "my dear, good friend," and thanked him for his "assurances of undiminished love and regard." [22] Within his own command Hill had been on exceptionally friendly terms with Garland and G. B. Anderson, and in reporting their deaths he paid eloquent tribute to them. There was also a friendly, though not so intimate, relationship between Rodes and Hill. One of Hill's colonels, William L. De Rosset, addressed him in 1885 as "my honored Division commander," and in the same year Colonel Alfred Iverson wrote him: "After so many years I may say to you that I know of no man whose bearing on the battle field more won my admiration or whose invariable kindness to myself my regard." [23]

Among his staff officers Hill's two closest friends were Archer Anderson and Ratchford. Ratchford said of his chief that the South was defended by "no more able and gallant soldier or Christian gentleman and scholar." Between him and Hill there existed, within the confines of military protocol, a kind of father–son relationship. The youthful chief of staff looked even younger than he was and was quite sensitive about it. He constantly wondered whether older men did not covet his position, and on one occasion he became convinced, by gossip, that Hill would like to replace him with someone more experienced. Thereupon Ratchford went to Rodes, whom he admired though he regarded him as "anything but a Christian man," and applied for a vacant position on Rodes's staff.

Rodes accepted the tender of services, but then asked why his young friend wanted to leave Hill. On hearing the reason he said, with an oath, "You are a fool to leave him. You would have been dead long ago had it not been for General Hill's prayers. He exposes himself and staff so much that nothing but an overruling Providence has saved you. Go back to him and have a clear understanding with him and if things are as you think, come to me."

Acting upon this advice, Ratchford had a talk with Hill, who immediately guessed the author of the false gossip. Ratchford, he said, should have come directly to him. Then he assured his young staff officer that when he wanted to get rid of him he would let him know. Eventually Ratchford did yield his key position to Anderson, but he stayed on Hill's staff until October, 1863. [24]

In his relationships with the men under him, Hill was an unassuming general. With the members of his staff who cared to participate, he regularly held prayer meetings, and with soldiers in the ranks he could be friendly and informal. The Reverend William S. Lacy, a Davidson College graduate, recalled after the war how on one occasion, near Richmond, he was marching past a general on horseback, surrounded by a glittering staff, when suddenly he realized that the general was Hill. Then, with more the instinct of the boy he knew than the soldier in ranks, I stepped aside to speak to him and was forbidden by one of the staff. He looked and recognized me, and to the amazement of his supercilious aide, dismounted, shook hands with the ragged dirty soldier, and talked with me some moments about home and my army service.[25]

This readiness to treat soldiers in the ranks as human beings rather than as so much matériel of war helped to make Hill popular with his troops, to the extent that any officer can be popular who must constantly enforce discipline, and order men into hardship and danger. Apparently the unpretentious fighters in the battle line gave "old D. H.," as they called him, their approval.

His tough military humor had a special savor for combat men. When the members of a brigade band submitted to him their application for a group furlough, he disapproved it with the quip, "Shooters before tooters." And when noncombatant officers of his headquarters staff grew too boastful about their military prowess, he was likely to ride into the combat zone and take them along, "treating" them, as he put it, "to a little airing in a fight." He also had a grimly humorous way with any skirmisher who got too cautious or careless in action. He would ride out to the man, make him stand beside his horse, and give him a leisurely shooting lesson amid the enemy bullets.[26]

His willingness to expose himself to greater danger than his troops had to face was proverbial in the army. It was not in accordance with the rule books, nor, strictly speaking, to his credit as a division commander—major generals were not expendable— but it won the hearts of men suffering their own private little hells under fire. As late as 1889, when Hill was living in Milledgeville, Georgia, Chancellor William E. Boggs of the state university met one of Hill's veterans and remarked to the man, who had lost a leg in the war, that he had recently been in Milledgeville and seen the old general.

"Then you have seen the best part of Milledgeville," exclaimed the veteran. And, face flushing with enthusiasm, he told how he had lain under heavy fire in battle line one day, and how he and his comrades cringed and hugged the ground each time a Minié ball hissed too near or a shell "seemed ready to settle down on a fellow's back." Then came a quiet question, "What's the use of all that dodging, men?" and there was Hill, on horseback, immobile as a bronze statue. The veteran was not quite certain how the magic worked, but he was emphatic in his declaration that "it helped a fellow." [27]

This extraordinary courage, this absolute fearlessness in battle, distinguished Harvey Hill in an army and a war in which brave men were legion. It was the quality most often mentioned when other soldiers spoke of him. It seemed to flow effortlessly from his deep religious faith, and like that faith it was marked by the intensity that ran through his complex make-up like a thread of fire. Whatever he did, whether he was praising his God, criticizing his commander, or risking his life to encourage his troops, he did it with a thoroughgoing intensity that set him apart, and often produced intense reactions in others. Whether his associates liked or disliked him, they had no doubt how they felt. As Ratchford expressed it, Hill was a man of "unusual force of character." Toward him it was not easy to take neutral ground.

His duty in the Valley that fall came to an end late in November, when Lee concentrated his forces at Fredericksburg, in the path of General Ambrose E. Burnside, who had replaced McClellan as commander of the Army of the Potomac. In coordination with Jackson's southeastward movement, Hill was ordered to make an independent march to Fredericksburg, crossing the Massanutton Mountains at New Market. His rebuilt division now numbered some nine thousand men, and although shoes were still in short supply, he was determined to prevent straggling. Instead of resorting to the "strict and sanguinary" discipline that he had advocated to Lee, he relied simply upon strictness, and ingenious organization.

Behind each marching unit he placed a provost guard to pick up stragglers, a surgeon to examine those who claimed to be sick, and ambulances to carry those who really were unable to continue on foot. For allowing any man to fall out of ranks without cause, company officers were liable to arrest. These arrangements enabled Hill to march his division some two hundred miles in ten days, through intermittent snow and rain, with a minimum of straggling.

Accompanying the division was a prisoner corps, and Hill on one occasion sent it ahead to build a footbridge over a river crossing. At the end of the day the captain of the prisoner corps reported to Hill and asked for whisky to warm his men, after their long hours of work in the cold water. Hill ordered that he be supplied. Next morning the provost guard brought a drunk prisoner to Hill, who sternly asked him to explain his conduct. Yessir, came the reply; General Hill furnished the whisky. Hill laughed and dismissed the man, telling him to go and sin no more.

The division reached Fredericksburg in such good condition and with so few stragglers that Lee was both surprised and impressed. Jackson arrived on the evening of November 29, swelling the ranks of a growing army that by early December would number about 78,000. Longstreet's corps was in position on the hills behind the city, and with Jackson's troops Lee extended the Confederate right southeastward along the Rappahannock River, to guard against possible crossings by Burnside's impressive army of about 125,000. D. H. Hill was stationed on the far right, at Port Royal, some twenty miles downstream from Fredericksburg.[28]

Relations between Lee and Jackson at this time were not amicable. Freeman states in his biography of Lee that, "The campaigns of 1862 had developed some friction between Jackson and Lee's headquarters staff...." [29] One of D. H. Hill's letters to Dabney, July 21, 1864, is more explicit. Hill said that at Fredericksburg Jackson told him, "I am opposed to fighting here, we will whip the enemy but gain no fruits of victory." Jackson thought that a stand farther south, on the North Anna River, would afford better possibilities for a counterattack. He said, "I have advised the line of the North Anna, but have been overruled." Further, Hill wrote:

While at Fredericksburg, Genl J's feelings were not kind toward Genl Lee. He thought that the latter had shown partiality to Longstreet in the distribution of guns, clothing, camp and garrison equipage, etc. He had felt this keenly after the battle of Sharpsburg and once said that he feared he would be compelled to resign. I judge however that all this had passed away before his death.[30]

Against this background a sharp exchange of letters between Lee and Jackson at Fredericksburg takes on added significance. To Jackson on December 3 Lee wrote that he noted, "from a report just received from General Pendleton," that Jackson had in his corps 127 guns compared to Longstreet's 117. Also, there was an imbalance of quality. Jackson had fifty-two rifled cannon, and eighteen gun-howitzers of the highly efficient type known as the "Napoleon." Longstreet had only forty-six rifles and thirteen Napoleons.

Moreover, in Jackson's corps the best guns were unevenly distributed. D. H. Hill, in particular, had no Napoleons. He had asked Lee for four Napoleons that his division had captured at Seven Pines; these guns had been assigned to a battery of Longstreet's corps, "whether by my order or General Longstreet's I now do not remember," wrote Lee. He recommended that Jackson distribute the Napoleons and rifles in his corps so as "to give General D. H. Hill a fair proportion," and suggested that Hill could have the guns from Seven Pines provided Jackson would send Longstreet four Napoleons in exchange. Then, in conclusion, he added a one-sentence paragraph that seemed to accuse Jackson of appropriating more than his share of the artillery that he had captured at Harpers Ferry: "I observe, from General Pendleton's report, that more of the captured guns are in your corps than in General Longstreet's."

Although the letter closed in the most courteous form of the times, "I am, with great respect, your obedient servant," Jackson reacted to it as though Lee had jabbed him with a bayonet. His reply, the same day, was curt. "Your letter of this date, recommending that I distribute the rifle and Napoleon guns so as 'to give General D. H. Hill a fair proportion,' has been received," he began. "I respectfully request, if any such distribution is to be made, that you will direct your chief of artillery or some other officer to do it; but I hope that none of the guns which belonged to the Army of the Valley, before it became part of the Army of Northern Virginia, after the battle of Cedar Run, will be taken from it."

In other words, Jackson would not act on Lee's recommendation. If Lee insisted on a distribution of the guns he would have to give a direct order, and he should issue it to Pendleton or some other officer, not Jackson. The angry corps commander was also declaring that he had acquired much of his artillery while leading an independent army, and serving notice that he would not approve an attempt on Lee's part to transfer any of the Valley army guns to Longstreet.

Next he took up Lee's remark about the captured guns. If, since his army had been united with Lee's, "any artillery has improperly come into my command, I trust that it will be taken away, and the person in whose possession it may be found punished, if his conduct requires it. So careful was I to prevent any improper distribution of the artillery and other public property captured at Harper's Ferry, that I issued a written order directing my staff officers to turn over to the proper chiefs of staff of the Army of Northern Virginia all captured stores. A copy of the order is herewith inclosed."

As for Hill's lack of Napoleons, "General D. H. Hill's artillery wants existed at the time he was assigned to my command, and it is hoped that artillery which belonged to the Army of the Valley will not be taken to supply his wants." Freeman has called this statement of Jackson's "a smack at his division commander," Hill, but it seems more likely that Jackson was still swinging at Lee, who, by implication, should have supplied Hill's artillery needs before assigning him to Jackson, and should not now ask Jackson to favor his own brother-in-law by taking guns from men who had fought them in the Valley army.

Whatever Jackson meant, his letter from start to finish left no doubt as to how he felt. It closed with, "I am, general, your obedient servant." Lee's use of the phrase "with great respect" was not reciprocated.[31]

Apparently Lee backed away completely from Jackson's wrath, and turned to Richmond as a source of supply for Harvey Hill. On December 5 he wrote both the Secretary of War and the Chief of Ordnance setting forth the general need of his army for improved artillery and asking that he be sent immediately four Napoleons "for a particular purpose." [32] Had Jackson seen and commented on these letters, he might have said that Lee should have sought additional guns from Richmond in the first place.

One might well ask whether the friction between Lee and Jackson in 1862, which came explosively to the surface in this incident of the guns, does not throw additional light on the strange lack of communication between these two generals during the Seven Days. Was proper communication and coordination lacking during that campaign partly because two proud leaders, each the commander of his own army, felt a sense of rivalry and bent over backwards to avoid stepping on each other's toes? The evidence suggests the possibility.

On the day of Jackson's tilt with Lee, Hill reported to corps headquarters that four Federal gunboats were lying opposite Port Royal, and requested artillery reinforcements for the purpose of bombarding them. Jackson sent him Colonel J. Thompson Brown's reserve artillery battalion, which had twenty-four guns, including one Napoleon and eight rifles, and in the week that followed Hill twice drove gunboats away from Port Royal. Young Alexander S. Pendleton of Jackson's staff wrote home about these exploits of "Rawhide Hill as he is called from having had moccasins [made] for his men." [33]

About this time Hill's military intuition helped to determine the site of the battle of Fredericksburg, which would be fought on December 13. Burnside, as he later reported, had hoped to surprise Lee by crossing the Rappahannock at Skinker's Neck, about fourteen miles below Fredericksburg, but abandoned this plan and crossed in front of the city because the Confederates discovered his preparations at the lower crossing and stationed troops there. It was Hill who discovered Burnside's preparations at Skinker's Neck.

This strait, formed by a prominent bend of the river, was beyond the jurisdiction of Hill's post at Port Royal, but Hill—perhaps in riding along the river—had noticed in the vicinity of Skinker's Neck an obscure crossing called the Hop Yard, or Hop-pole. One day in early December he sent a message to General Stuart, asking whether he was picketing this crossing. Stuart replied that he was. Yet that night Hill felt what he later called "an unaccountable presentiment of evil," and he determined to visit the Hop Yard. Although the next day, Sunday, was bitterly cold, he forced himself and two equally miserable staff officers to ride upriver through snow and sleet to the insignificant little crossing that he could not put out of his mind.

On arriving they found no Confederate pickets, but they did see, on the opposite riverbank, a large number of Federals working on a bridge. Hill immediately wrote Jackson, urging him to send a division to the threatened point. Jackson sent Early's division, and Burnside, realizing that his initial plan had been discovered, decided to abandon it and cross boldly—and, as it proved, disastrously—at Fredericksburg.[34]

Jackson's message summoning Hill to the battle of Fredericksburg reached him just before sundown on December 12. By what Jackson later called "a severe night's march," Hill got his men to the battlefield early the next morning. So strong were the Confederate positions on the hills back of Fredericksburg, with Longstreet holding the left of the long line and Jackson the right, that D. H. Hill was kept in reserve. Through the day his division, except for the artillery, did no fighting. He had only to wait while Burnside attacked, and attacked again, stubbornly and futilely under the Southern musketry and cannon fire, until some twelve thousand soldiers of the Union lay dead or wounded.[35]

From his position on the far right Hill could not see what was happening in Longstreet's sector, and he complained to Lee's aide, Charles Marshall, that "as usual" Jackson's troops were doing all the fighting. Marshall, who had been carrying messages up and down the whole line, assured him, to his great surprise, that more Federal dead could be seen in Longstreet's sector than in Jackson's.[36]

In the afternoon, with Confederate victory assured, Jackson laid plans for moving four divisions of infantry, including D. H. Hill's, down from the wooded defensive heights and across the open plain in a counterattack. This would be risky in the face of the well-posted Union artillery, but Jackson burned to make victory decisive by driving the enemy into the river. He formed his infantry under cover of the woods, and arranged to precede its advance with a sudden bombardment from advanced batteries of artillery. Several of Hill's battery commanders, led by Captain J. W. Bondurant, volunteered for this hazardous duty.

After some delay, the attack began at twilight. As the Confederate batteries dashed out from the woods and opened fire, Jackson and Harvey Hill rode to a vantage point near the crest of a ridge. Below them the infantry columns were pushing through the trees and undergrowth, preparing to follow the artillery.

But in answer to the first Southern cannon shots the Federal guns awoke and rose to a crescendo of fury. Shells crashed thunderously in the woods, and turned the plain that Jackson's divisions must cross into a blazing, exploding inferno. No troops could attack through that concentrated shellfire; it would be suicide.

Call off the attack immediately, Hill urged Jackson. It was a mistake that would cost thousands of lives. Withdraw the advanced artillery, and the enemy would cease firing.

Jackson agreed. "Have you a man who would go for it?"

Hill called for a courier, but the one who responded was only a boy, John Chamblin. Hill could not send him into such danger. He called again for a courier, and again. Chamblin was the only one available.

Jackson wheeled his horse. "I'll go." But Hill caught hold of his coat and restrained him. The Confederacy could not afford the risk. Hill turned to the eager boy.

"Go Chamblin, quickly, and tell the captain cease firing retire immediately, by order of General Jackson."

Over and down the ridge through the crashing shells Chamblin spurred his horse, and delivered the order and returned unscathed. Bondurant brought back the advanced artillery, the Union guns slackened and died away, and the offensive ended before the Southern columns emerged from the woods.

Afterward, Hill sought out his surgeon and friend, Dr. A. R. Mott, and told him what Chamblin had done, adding that he would never have forgiven himself if anything had happened to that boy. From now on, he said, Mott had a new medical courier. Chamblin would never again be sent into danger.[37]

Jackson's canceled attack was the last serious action of the battle. Although the Federals held their lines for two more days, they did not again advance, and during the rainy, windy night of December 15 they slipped back across the river in a brilliantly executed withdrawal that caught the Confederates napping.[38] Lee was chagrined because he had not been able to make his victory more decisive. To his wife on the sixteenth he confided his thoughts about the Federals:

Yesterday evening I had my suspicions that they might retire during the night, but could not believe they would relinquish their purpose after all their boasting and preparation, and when I say that the latter is equal to the former, you will have some idea of its magnitude. . . . They suffered heavily as far as the battle went, but it did not go far enough to satisfy me.[39]

Jackson, too, regretted that the year was ending without a decisive Confederate victory. In a private conversation with Harvey Hill, after Fredericksburg, his thoughts turned to the Maryland campaign and the council with Lee and Longstreet in which Lee had outlined his plans for dividing the army and capturing Harpers Ferry. There was something extremely important that he wanted to tell Hill, but he had some doubt about the propriety of speaking.

He began by asking his old mentor whether an officer had a right to divulge the opinions expressed by him at a council of war, and

Hill in reply named various circumstances that would justify such divulgence. Then, after further hesitation, Jackson said, "At the council held at Frederick, I opposed the separation of our forces in order to capture Harper's Ferry. I urged that we should all be kept together." [40]

That was all, but it was enough. The statement was precise and complete, as though Jackson, at the close of the year's fighting, wanted to enter it in the record of his military career.

X

AT ODDS WITH LEE

O<small>N</small> J<small>ANUARY</small> 1, 1863, Hill carried out his intention of resigning from the army. His letter of this date to the Adjutant General read as follows:

I have the honor hereby to tender my resignation as Major General in the Provisional Army of the Confederate States.

Many motives induce me to take this step; one only need I mention, as it is sufficient and conclusive. My strength and health are not sufficient for the proper discharge of my responsible duties. I have a very feeble frame and have been a great sufferer from boyhood. I have been in service more than twenty months and have been habitually at my post, though I [have] never been free a single moment from pain and that too, often of the most excruciating character.

I have been in eleven pitched battles, besides skirmishes, and have most earnestly tried to do my duty in the field, in camp and on the march. I feel therefore that I have some claim upon the Department for the only favour asked of it.

With great respect
D. H. Hill
Maj Genl [1]

Among the "many motives" not specified in this letter were no doubt the urging of Isabella, and Hill's disappointment over slow promotion. Jubal Early said after the war that Hill left the Army of Northern Virginia because he was not on good terms with Jackson, but there seems to be no evidence to justify the assertion. It will be remembered that in November, 1862, Hill told Isabella that

Jackson "has treated me very kindly." Long after the war he said of his brother-in-law: "Gen. Jackson never spoke an unkind word to me, publically or privately, at any time or in any place." [2]

This statement is borne out by the way Jackson handled the resignation. He forwarded it with the sympathetic remark, "Genl Hill has served the country with great zeal, fidelity and success, and I am satisfied has endured exposure beyond the measure of his health, which from my personal knowledge has been for years impaired." Then at the opportune moment he made an effort to keep Hill in the army. Replying on January 13 to a note in which Hill had asked about the progress of his resignation, he said, "If it should be convenient to call and see me at any time before Genl Lee or the War Dept is heard from I hope you will do so as I would like to have a talk with you upon the subject as to leaving at *this time*." [3] The records do not reveal whether this conversation took place, or what effect it may have had upon Hill.

Lee also tried to retain Hill in the service, with the idea of utilizing his prestige and abilities in North Carolina, where a military crisis seemed to be shaping up. North Carolina was part of the rather amorphous area commanded from Richmond by General Gustavus W. Smith. Its Sound region was still firmly held by Union troops, and in mid-December these forces, under the command of General J. G. Foster, had driven westward in a successful raid against Kinston and Goldsboro. The great port of Wilmington might next be attacked, by an enemy fleet known to be assembling in Hampton Roads. Disaffection toward the Confederacy was increasing among North Carolinians, and Smith was asking for reinforcements.

Lee's policy, however, was to keep all his first-line troops as near at hand as possible, and to stand on the defensive in North Carolina, relying on the state militia to meet emergencies. If Hill could help "inspirit or encourage" his fellow Carolinians Lee was willing to "detach him from this army" for the purpose, and in the first week of January he so wrote President Davis and Secretary of War James A. Seddon.[4]

Neither to Seddon nor to Davis did he explain that the general he was offering to detach had resigned his commission. Apparently he thought that Hill might be persuaded to withdraw his letter of January 1. On the seventh, however, he sent the resignation on to Richmond with the following endorsement:

Respy forwd. Feeling very loth that the country should lose the Services
of so good and faithful an officer I inquired whether leave of absence
during the winter, a stationary Post, or service at the South, would not
enable Genl Hill to remain in the Army. I have been informed by Genl
Jackson that a leave of absence would do no good, and that Genl Hill's
health is worse than he had supposed it. I therefore recommend the acceptance of his resignation. I very much regret the loss of so zealous, and
intelligent an officer, who has laboured conscientiously and arduously in
the defense of his Country.

A week later Hill was ordered to Richmond to report to the
Adjutant General. On the seventeenth, Seddon wrote Governor
Zebulon B. Vance of North Carolina that "Maj. Gen. D. H. Hill
... who is so favorably known to yourself, as indeed to the whole
Confederacy, for his distinguished services with the army in Virginia,
has, to the regret of the Department, been constrained to retire from
his late command by ill health. He has consented for the present not
to resign, but will be for a time at home in North Carolina." Earlier
in the month Seddon had informed Vance of Lee's suggestion about
using Hill in his home state, and he wrote now to urge the governor
to take advantage of Hill's military advice and "deserved influence"
with the people.[5]

Hill, then, had been persuaded to remain in the service. It may
be supposed that the Richmond authorities won his consent not to
resign by appealing to his strong sense of duty and his concern about
the defense of his home state, but his precise reasons for changing his
mind are not revealed in the records. What is clearly shown by
Seddon's letter to Vance is that the Secretary of War thought the
governor needed Hill's advice and support, even though General
G. W. Smith had been in North Carolina since Foster's raid.[6]

As a matter of fact, the Richmond authorities had not placed
full confidence in Smith since the battle of Seven Pines, and now,
toward the end of January, the President received a confidential letter
from Lee conveying information that Smith's performance of duty
in North Carolina was unsatisfactory. Lee thought that General
Edmund Kirby Smith, who had been called to Richmond from
Tennessee, should take charge in North Carolina. Although Kirby
Smith had already been appointed to command in the Southwest,
the order effecting this was rescinded and a new one issued in accordance with Lee's suggestion. But Kirby Smith, declaring that he

did not want to replace his friend G. W. Smith, insisted on the first appointment, and his wish was granted. Davis on January 27 recalled G. W. Smith to Richmond, ordered General S. G. French to take command at Goldsboro, and had Seddon telegraph to Hill: "The President desires to know if the command of the army in North Carolina would be acceptable to you?" [7]

Having retained his commission, Hill was hardly in a position to refuse the offer; however, he evidently had reason to believe that it might involve the supersedure of G. W. Smith by himself. In accepting it, he specified that he preferred a subordinate position under Smith. He both liked and admired his West Point classmate and former colleague in Johnston's army, and like Kirby Smith had no desire to replace him. Nevertheless, G. W. Smith and the Richmond authorities had come to the parting of the ways. Smith for some time had been dissatisfied because his juniors in the army had been promoted over him, and on February 7, the day Hill's assignment to command of the troops in North Carolina was announced, he resigned his commission.

Despite his difficulties at Seven Pines and after, Smith was still held in high esteem by a number of his Civil War associates, who sincerely regretted his departure. Hill, in fact, was so concerned over what was happening to Smith that he delayed assuming his new command. On February 20 he wrote Smith from Goldsboro, "I have just seen the order accepting your resignation and feel much embarrassed by it, especially as General French has read me a letter from you speaking with some feeling of the proposed supersedure of yourself by General E. K. Smith or myself." He then explained that he had told the Secretary of War that he preferred to serve under Smith, expressed "regret at being directly or indirectly the cause of your difficulty," and said that he hoped Smith would reconsider his resignation.

In the course of his argument he wrote, "At present I feel at a loss what to do. I have not yet assumed command and do not wish to do so. I came here with the understanding that I was to serve under you. Honestly and truly I prefer that position and shrink from the other." [8]

In *Lee's Lieutenants*, Freeman quotes this single passage and asserts that it "confirmed all General Lee had written President Davis of Hill's unwillingness to assume exclusive responsibility." Freeman's explanation of why Hill wrote as he did is simply that Hill preferred serving under Smith and "lamented" his departure. There is no mention of the letter that French read Hill or of Hill's desire not to wrong or offend Smith.[9] Thus taken out of context, the passage neatly fits Freeman's basic theory that although Hill was a good divisional commander, he always served reluctantly, indecisively, and ineffectively in important positions of independent responsibility.

So thoroughly, indeed, does Freeman ring the changes on this theory [10] that it cannot be ignored. In appraising its accuracy, due weight must be given to the criticism of which Freeman is so keenly aware: Lee's adverse judgment of Hill's administrative performance in the summer of 1862. Yet it does seem that to portray Hill constantly within the frame of this criticism is to oversimplify his Civil War career. As has been seen, at Seven Pines and South Mountain he bore heavy independent responsibility with considerable success. Nor was he reluctant to accept the greater responsibility that the rank of lieutenant general entailed; on the contrary he very much desired it, and before long would attain it, as a reward for decisive action in defense of Richmond.

Like many another general, he was irked by the frustrations of military administration in theaters of low priority, inadequately supplied with men and matériel; and he did not always perform such duty wisely or successfully. But neither did he always fail at it or invariably try to avoid it. Probably he shrank from Smith's post not only because of genuine regard for a friend, but also because of the vexations involved in what Smith called "the anomalous and mixed organization of this command." [11] Yet in May, 1863, with his friend no longer a factor in the situation, he would accept many of Smith's former duties without protest, and in performing them would not hesitate to oppose his judgment to that of Lee.

His letter of February 20 repaired his friendship with Smith, but could not, of course, restore that unhappy general to the army. Smith went his way, and into his position stepped Longstreet. Lee had heard on February 14 that Burnside's old Ninth Corps was being transferred to Hampton Roads. To protect Richmond from the threat of a sudden enemy drive up the James River, Longstreet was sent to the city with Pickett's and Hood's divisions. On February 25 he was assigned to the vacancy left by Smith, and that same day Hill in Goldsboro formally assumed command of North Carolina troops.[12]

What Hill thought about being once more under Longstreet he apparently kept to himself. The military situation in North Carolina was enough to absorb all his attention and energy. Strategically, the state was vital to the Confederacy. Into its major port, Wilmington, which was defended by Fort Fisher at the mouth of the Cape Fear River and could not be completely blockaded even by a fifty-mile arc of Union ships, poured a stream of military supplies to be sent north by rail through Weldon and Petersburg to Richmond. From its farms came food for Lee's troops, while its young men helped fill the ranks of the Confederate armies. Thousands of North Carolinians were fighting under Lee. In fact, Lee and Davis had so drastically depleted the state of its garrisons in order to supply the Army of Northern Viriginia that this had become a matter of concern to Confederate officers like Hill, with homes and families in North Carolina.[13]

As for the people of the state, they were beginning to ask, in tones of increasing anger, why so many good Carolina regiments were fighting in Virginia when they were needed at home for protection against the Union invaders. Although the Federals had not adequately exploited the strategic value of New Bern, Washington, and other bases in the Sound region that they had occupied, they were a constant menace to residents of the eastern counties, where loyal Confederates were systematically looted of their movable possessions, and lived in fear of destructive raids and the depredations of native Union bushwhackers.[14] Still Lee, with the approval of Davis, held to his defensive policy in North Carolina, assigning only a minimal number of active troops to a few key points, and relying on the militia to strengthen the general defenses of the state.

Actually, the militia was a dubious military resource, used only for emergencies and to enforce the conscript law. Scarcely more effective were the mounted guerrillas known as "Partisan Rangers," which had been created by act of Congress, and organized in North Carolina in the summer of 1862, it will be remembered, by Hill himself with the authorization of Secretary of War Randolph. Far from providing the widespread protection that Hill had envisioned, this guerrilla cavalry had become the refuge of draft dodgers, who usually fled from the enemy so fast that they could not even make an accurate report of his numbers. Although Hill also had a regular cavalry brigade it was one that Lee did not consider good enough for first line service with his army. According to Longstreet its commander, General Beverley H. Robertson, "was not deemed a very efficient officer in the field and was therefore relieved from duty with the Army of Northern Virginia." [15]

Hill advocated strong offensive operations against the enemy both in Virginia and North Carolina. At the time of Foster's raid he had urged that the Federals be driven from his home state, but, as he later complained, "I was unheeded." [16] Evidently he had believed, contrary to Lee, that after the Union retreat at Fredericksburg a sizable detachment from the Army of Northern Virginia could safely be sent to North Carolina.

In February, two days prior to his formal assumption of command at Goldsboro, he revived this idea, suggesting to Seddon that "The troops on the Rappahannock must be inactive for some time and could well be employed here." By now his argument rested on stronger grounds. January and February had brought rain and snow that had mudbound the Union army. Hooker, who on January 25 had replaced Burnside, could be expected to delay a new offensive while waiting for dry weather, reorganizing his command, and formulating new plans. Lee accordingly had placed his army in winter quarters along the Rappahannock. There until late April the infantry would remain inactive, shivering in improvised huts through the cold winter, and suffering severely from inadequate supplies of clothing, meat, and vegetables.[17] Pondering these things, modern students of the war might possibly conclude that although Hill's strategic suggestion was not followed, it should have been; that Lee should have left a holding force on the Rappahannock, moved a good part of his army down the rail line into North Carolina, and cleared that state of the relatively weak enemy while recruiting and supplying his troops in the rich eastern counties.

At any rate, Hill thought so, but he knew well enough that it was not his place to argue grand strategy with Richmond. His suggestion to Seddon was only one sentence dropped discreetly into a tactful discussion of his own need for heavy guns at Wilmington; for another brigade of infantry to be used in supply-gathering operations against the enemy and in protecting planters and farmers; and for a brigade of good cavalry "to keep the Yankees close shut up in their fortifications." Describing Robertson's cavalry as "wonderfully inefficient," Hill asked that it be exchanged for General Wade Hampton's brigade, of Lee's army. "I learn that Hampton is now idle at Gordonsville, recruiting his horses," he wrote. If transferred to eastern North Carolina, Hampton could find "more forage . . . than in the whole of Virginia, and he would protect the planting interest." In fact, he would make the Yankees "hug their gunboats everywhere."

Seddon referred Hill's letter to Davis with the comment, "These views strike me as sensible and timely." Davis agreed. He had previously suggested "the proposed disposition of Hampton's brigade to General Lee," he said, but Lee had "dissented." Perhaps "the views of General Hill will prevail over his objections." [18]

But Hill's views did not prevail. Hampton remained in Virginia. There his horses would recuperate faster, Lee maintained, explaining to Davis that according to the chief quartermaster of the army, corn was abundant in eastern North Carolina but "long forage" was scarce. It would not be more than a month, he added, before Hampton's brigade "will be again wanted." [19]

Neither did Hill receive an additional infantry brigade. He began his North Carolina command with a total force of about eleven thousand, consisting of Robertson's cavalry, two infantry brigades under Generals Junius Daniel and J. J. Pettigrew, a small force of reserve artillery, and the garrisons at Hamilton, Weldon, and Goldsboro. At Wilmington, General W. H. C. Whiting had an additional seven thousand, but he had been reporting directly to Richmond and regarded his command as independent of Hill's.[20]

Hill announced his formal assumption of command by publishing a vehement address to his troops, in which he exhorted them to fight to end the war quickly and protect their homes from Northern marauders. "We must cut down to 6 feet by 2 the dimensions of the farms which these plunderers propose to appropriate," he said. They would have to fight all the harder, he told them, because they would receive no help from the numerous "able-bodied skulkers," who had "dodged from the battlefield" under the provisions of exemption law. "But a day of retribution awaits these abortions of humanity. Their own descendants will execrate their memory. . . ."

Soldiers who distinguished themselves in battle could expect pro-

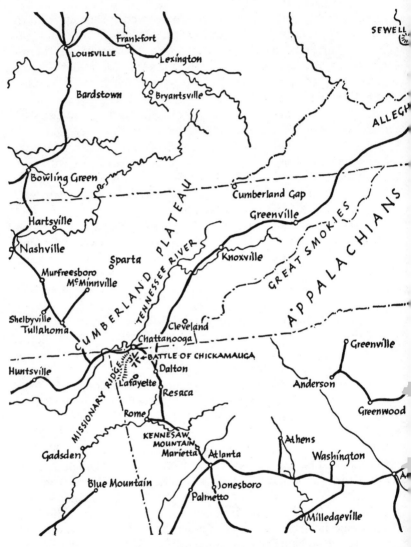

Areas of Hill's Virginia–North Carolina command,

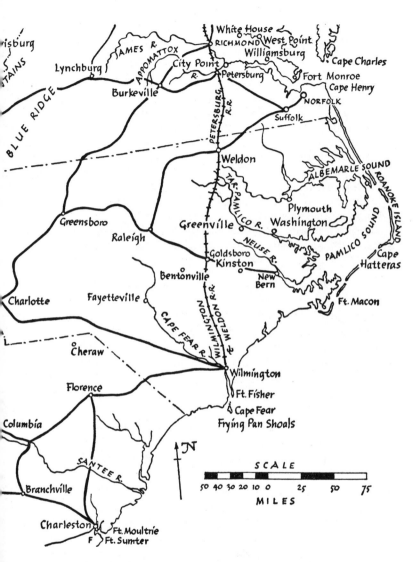

...amauga campaign, and of Hill's military service in 1864–65

motion and public recognition. Those who failed to do their duty would be punished, and regarding this Hill had a special warning for his cavalry:

The cavalry constitute the eyes and ears of the army. The safety of the entire command depends upon their vigilance and the faithfulness of their reports. The officers and men who permit themselves to be surprised deserve to die, and the commanding general will spare no efforts to secure them their deserts. Almost equally criminal are the scouts who through fright bring in wild and sensational reports. They will be court-martialed for cowardice. Many opportunities will be afforded to the cavalry to harass the enemy, cut off his supplies, drive in his pickets, etc. Those who have never been in battle will thus be enabled to enjoy the novel sensation of listening to the sound of hostile shot and shell, and those who have listened a great way off will be allowed to come some miles nearer, and compare the sensation caused by the distant cannonade with that produced by the rattle of musketry.[21]

Cavalry comment on this address has not been found, and should any be discovered it would probably be unprintable. But if Hill meant to stir up his troops and let the civilian population know that their demands for aggressive action against the invader were now to be met, he seems to have accomplished his purpose. "That is . . . the way to talk it," said one pleased North Carolinian, while an infantryman who had served under Hill at Bethel wrote home that the address was "certainly characteristic of the old Gen. . . . hurrah! for old Daniel H." [22]

Hill backed his words with action, and during the four months and more that he remained in control of North Carolina troops, from late February to mid-July, there were no damaging Federal raids in the state comparable to Foster's December exploit. Instead, with help from Longstreet, Hill threw the Federals upon the defensive. He reorganized his forces, tightened discipline, built fighting spirit, and as Ratchford later said, "forced the enemy to stick to the coast where they had fortified foot-holds."

Not all was success, however. Hill never got his cavalry to operate as boldly and efficiently as he wished, and once in exasperation enhanced his reputation as an anticavalry general by offering a reward for "a dead man with spurs on." [23] Neither was he able to dislodge the Federals from their coastal bases, though he made two attempts to do so.

At the beginning of the year Lee had expressed the opinion that offensive operations could not be undertaken with advantage in North Carolina, "as the most we could hope for would be to drive the enemy to his gunboats, where he would be safe"; but by March he saw the need of offensive demonstrations, at least, in order that food supplies badly needed by his army might be gathered in the Sound region.[24] Longstreet and Hill reasoned that while foraging near the enemy coastal bases they might be able to capture them. Since storming operations would be too costly, they planned to employ the tactics of encirclement and bombardment.

In mid-March, Hill tried to capture Foster's headquarters, New Bern, on the south bank of the Neuse River, where it begins steadily widening as it flows into Pamlico Sound.[25] He hoped at first to surround the town with the brigades of Daniel, Pettigrew, and Robertson, reinforced by two more brigades of infantry, General Garnett's from southern Virginia and General Robert Ransom's from Wilmington. To cope with the Union gunboats he tried to borrow one of the three long-range, highly efficient Whitworth rifles that Whiting had at Wilmington.

But Whiting complied neither with Hill's request for the rifle nor with Longstreet's order to "make preparations" for sending Hill troops from Wilmington. To Hill he replied that he needed all three Whitworths to protect blockade runners. To Longstreet he wrote that, far from being able to spare any troops, he needed reinforcements. Moreover, in a tacit assertion of independence from Hill, he requested that he be allowed to act directly under Longstreet as he had previously done under G. W. Smith.

New at his job, and confessedly ignorant of the defense situation at Wilmington, Longstreet did not give Whiting the peremptory order that would have forced him to relinquish the troops and the gun. All that he did was to send him, on March 15, a mild lecture to the effect that it was a mistake to hoard troops against a possible attack when they could be used elsewhere against the common enemy, within supporting distance of Wilmington. This was sound logic. It did not help the attack on New Bern.[26]

Hill, trying to make do with what he had, attacked March 13-15. At the outset Daniel's brigade charged and captured the first line of Union fortifications west of the town, and held the next morning against a weak Union counterattack. But that was the extent of

Confederate success. Everything else that Hill had planned went wrong.

Robertson only partly carried out his mission of cutting the railroad that connected New Bern with the coast, while Garnett, complaining of railroad delays and destroyed bridges along his route, got no nearer to the fighting than Greenville. His failure to arrive reduced Hill's forces to about 8,400 as against Foster's 13,700. Even more serious was the failure of Pettigrew, who had orders to capture a Union fort on the north side of the river and then bombard the enemy shipping and barracks. His chief difficulty was that the four 20-pounder Parrott guns with which he tried to fight the Union gunboats proved to be, in his words, "worse than useless." Half the shells fired from them burst just outside the muzzle; the others flew inaccurately. After one Parrott had broken down and another had burst, wounding three men, one of them mortally, Pettigrew called off his attack.

"The absence of the Whitworth ruined us," he reported to Hill.

Hill agreed, and quoted Pettigrew in a sharp letter that he wrote Longstreet just after returning to Goldsboro. He was angry at having received neither gun nor troops from Whiting. Pointing out that his order of assignment gave him command of all the troops in North Carolina, he declared, "If I am to be cut down to two brigades I will not submit to the swindle." He did not go so far as to tell Longstreet explicitly that he had not been firm enough with Whiting, but the implication was plain. "You were greatly mistaken in supposing that I was indifferent about the Whitworth," he wrote. "I told you that it was too late to get it, but that it was worth all the guns I had. I had tried the Parrotts, and their shells all burst prematurely." [27]

Longstreet replied with a calm discussion of new plans. In a postscript he took notice of Hill's remarks about a "swindle," commented that he presumed "this was not intended as an official communication," and expressed the hope that Hill would "send up another account." [28] Hill did not comply.

The ambiguous command situation was finally clarified on April 1, when orders from the Adjutant General divided Longstreet's command into the Department of Richmond under General Arnold Elzey, the Department of Southern Virginia under General French, and the Department of North Carolina under Hill. Plainly this put Whiting under Hill's control. The orders also stipulated that Longstreet, who had shown signs of thinking himself independent of Lee, was still under Lee's "supervision and general direction." [29]

By this time Hill had undertaken his second expedition against a Federal base—Washington, on the north bank of the Tar–Pamlico River north of New Bern. Neither he nor Longstreet entertained great hope of taking Washington, but a siege of the town would at least facilitate the gathering of food supplies in the vicinity. Longstreet planned at first to have Pickett lead the expedition while Hill stood guard at Goldsboro against a Union counterthrust from New Bern, but soon he changed his mind and placed Hill in charge of the field operations. Hill retained the use of Garnett's brigade, and was supplied with two Whitworth guns. Longstreet also sent him the brigade of General James J. Kemper, and to further strengthen him ordered Whiting, about March 18, to respond to Hill's call for Ransom's brigade. With Longstreet's approval, Hill ordered Kemper to guard Kinston and Ransom to protect Goldsboro while Garnett moved against Washington on the north side of the Tar River and Pettigrew, with Daniel in support, approached from the south.[30]

The siege of Washington began on March 30. Foster, in New Bern, learned of Hill's approach in time to sail to Washington on the twenty-ninth, followed closely by transports bringing reinforcements that increased the garrison to about twelve thousand. Hill's three attacking brigades totaled less than nine thousand, but he advanced boldly and invested the town, drawing his siege lines tight and closing the Tar to Federal shipping by emplacing gun batteries on either bank. When the Federals refused to surrender he ordered women and children removed from the town before he began shelling it. Foster did not attempt a full-scale counterattack, perhaps because Union estimates of Hill's strength ran as high as twenty thousand.[31]

It appeared at the end of the first week that Hill might capture the town, but Longstreet was not certain that he could allow sufficient time. He had decided to lead a similar expedition against Suffolk, Virginia, and he estimated the enemy strength there at perhaps eighteen thousand. "This is considerably more than I can put into the field," he wrote Hill on April 2. "I must therefore call for the brigades of Kemper and Garnett . . . and I also desire that you send the two Whitworth guns. . . . It may be necessary for you to suspend operations in North Carolina until I can send you another force." [32]

When Hill received this letter he wrote Isabella that "Genl Longstreet has called for his Virginia troops and the design upon Washington has to be abandoned. The State will be bitterly disappointed, but not so much as I. Still much good has been done," he reflected. "Instead of lying back at Goldsboro, as though afraid of the Yankees, we have pushed them back everywhere to their fortifications. . . . I will get a great deal of abuse for not effecting impossibilities. Be it so." [33]

But he had already written Longstreet asking for more and heavier guns, and now he argued for a continuation of his siege. Longstreet replied, on the seventh, that he had asked for the return of the brigades and the guns because Hill had previously expressed "but little hope" of being able to take Washington, while Garnett's letters, which Hill had frequently forwarded, had breathed unrelieved gloom. But since Hill now thought he could take the town, Longstreet would let him keep Garnett's brigade and "the six field pieces," which presumably included the two Whitworths. He ended with a compliment to Hill: "I fully appreciate the importance of your success. Besides the bacon and corn that you speak of it ought to give us the coast of North Carolina as far as the mouth of the Chowan at least." [34]

So the siege of Washington continued. Federal reinforcements had appeared on the Pamlico, but could not get past a fort that Hill had constructed below the town. Longstreet thought that the effort to reinforce Washington must have weakened New Bern, and urged Hill to try a secondary attack against Foster's headquarters. Ransom, who had been moved to Kinston, was in a position to invest New Bern, and he was an aggressive general. Ever since being transferred south from Lee's army in early January he had been "smarting under a supposed degradation of position," as Lee put it, and from Kinston he had written Longstreet, "If it be possible to prevent it do not let me be kept only to watch when others are doing better." Now, at Hill's direction, he demonstrated against New Bern, but reported that the enemy there was too strong to attack. He was right. The Federal strength at New Bern was about nine thousand.[35]

Foster, seeing his river reinforcements stopped by Hill's fort, called for an expedition to come overland to his relief, and reluctantly the commanders at New Bern complied with his orders. The expedition marched northward about 6,400 strong, but as it was considered a forlorn hope the command of it was thrust upon an inexperienced brigadier, F. B. Spinola, who was overwhelmed with his responsibility. On April 9 he encountered Pettigrew's brigade, with portions of Daniel's, entrenched at Blount's Creek. He engaged his skirmishers and exchanged artillery fire for nearly two hours, and then retreated to New Bern.[36]

When, four days later, one of Hill's engineers told of this easy victory in a letter home, he also said, "We have silenced the gunboats that were at the town, and hold all the rest at bay below Fort Hill. . . . They have shot at us every day for more than two weeks and have killed, I think, two men in all. . . . They have thrown iron enough at us to build a rail road track, some distance." [37]

As the letter indicated, Southern morale was high, despite cold April rains that soaked the tentless besiegers. The belief that final victory was near made the drab muddy days and the growing food shortages endurable. Yet, for Hill, time was running out. There was a strong possibility that he might soon have to send troops to Charleston, for the Federals' long-threatened sea attack seemed now to be aimed at that port. Even more urgent were Longstreet's wants. Having begun a strong demonstration before Suffolk, he was calling for Hill to send him Garnett's brigade and other units "as soon as it can be done." On the fifteenth he wrote, "We cannot afford to keep the large force that you have watching the garrison at Washington," and suggested that if Hill could not continue the siege with reduced numbers he had better abandon it.[38]

Bursting guns were adding to Hill's difficulties, but the decisive incidents occurred April 12 and 15, when Union supply ships managed to run past the Confederate batteries. Realizing that with fresh supplies the defenders of Washington could hold out indefinitely, Hill raised the siege. Longstreet continued his demonstration before Suffolk until the end of the month. Then on April 30 he was ordered to move without delay to join Lee, who had come to grips with Hooker.[39]

Hill moved back from Washington, as he had predicted to Isabella, amid a chorus of adverse criticism. His disappointed troops grumbled against him, and the Raleigh *Register* called the withdrawal from the town "a disagreeable surprise." In the Richmond newspapers, he and Longstreet both were decried. Yet in all three expeditions whole wagon trains had been filled with food supplies purchased in counties that had long been enemy domain; and, as Seddon assured Longstreet in approving his decision not to attack Suffolk, successful foraging was "the main object." [40]

Hill asked his generals to furnish him with lists of men who had distinguished themselves. "It is due to the poor fellows and justice ought to be done them," he wrote Pettigrew. "The men have shown a noble spirit and I am more than grateful to them for it." On April 24 he formally published his "heartfelt thanks" to his troops, coupled with his most eloquent diatribe yet against men taking advantage of the exemption laws:

How much better is it thus to deserve the thanks of the country by your courage and patience, than to skulk at home as the cowardly exempts do. Some of these poor dogs have hired substitutes, as though money could pay the service every man owes his country. Others claim to own twenty negroes, and with justice might claim to be masters of an infinite amount of cowardice. Others are stuffy squires—bless their dignified souls. Others are warlike militia officers, and their regiments cannot dispense with such models of military skill and valor. And such noble regiments they have. Three field officers, four staff officers, ten captains, thirty lieutenants, and one private with a misery in his bowels. Some are pill and syringe gentlemen, and have done their share of killing at home. Some are kindly making shoes for the army, and generously giving them to the poor soldiers, only asking two months' pay. Some are too sweet and delicate for anything but fancy duty; the sight of blood is unpleasant, and the roar of cannon shocks their sensibilities. When our independence is won, the most trifling soldier in the ranks will be more respected, as he is now more respectable than an army of these skulking exempts.[41]

Officially airing his hates in this manner was a weakness in which Hill repeatedly indulged. On March 24 he had accused Foster, in a personal letter, of being "the most atrocious house-burner as yet unhung in the wide universe," and cited as evidence raids that he said Foster had made when "weary of debauching in your negro harem...." That same day he addressed a sarcastic letter to Edward Stanly, a North Carolinian of Unionist persuasion whom Lincoln had appointed military governor of the state. Stanly replied in kind, and on April 22 the Raleigh *Register* published the correspondence. The editor complimented Hill as a brave and true patriot, but said that he had "condescended when he addressed Edward Stanly, and thereby compromised his own dignity and self-respect." [42]

In the first days of May, before Longstreet reached him, Lee fought and won the battle of Chancellorsville. But disastrously, in the hour of victory, Jackson was fired upon and seriously wounded by his own men, who mistook him for the enemy as he rode back in darkness from a reconnaissance beyond his lines. Though he was taken from the battlefield to a private home where he had the best available medical care, and after a time the personal attention of his wife Anna, pneumonia developed following the amputation of his left arm, and the doctors despaired of his life. He had told Anna long before that he did not fear death, but hoped to have a few hours in which to prepare for it. From this, strange drama ensued:

Sunday, May 10. The doctors tell her this is the day. She comes to his bedside, speaks to him, and penetrates his cloudy consciousness. He must understand that before the day ends he will be in Heaven.

He replies in the religious language of the time that he will be "an infinite gainer to be translated." Still he hardly seems to believe that he is dying.

He rests, and then she comes again, arouses him, and repeats that he will be in Heaven before the sun sets. This time he protests that she is only frightened, that he may yet get well.

Stop, Anna! You have done your religious duty as fully as the most pious could wish. Cease, now, this advocacy of death, and call upon this strong-willed warrior to fight off the Great Adversary, and live. The frail Vice-President of the Confederacy, Alexander H. Stephens, will win as desperate a battle more than once in his lifetime, and the spirit of Stonewall Jackson is no less indomitable. He will live, too.

But she does not hear. She is of the nineteenth century, and not until the twentieth will the Western world grant medical recognition to the power of the mind over the body. Dr. McGuire adds his negative counsel to hers. She presses Jackson to say where he wishes to be buried. And so the directions for dying continue, and at 3:15 P.M. a soldier obeys.[43]

"The great and good Jackson is dead," Hill wrote that day to Governor Vance. "We have lost our *greatest* leader. May God help us. There is none to take his place." With more formality he eulogized Jackson in departmental orders as the general whose "genius and courage have been the chief elements in Southern success," and as the model soldier whose pure, religious life "has taught us that he who most fears God the least fears man.... Let us drop our laurel

upon his bier, but remember that we may best honor him by striving
... with his unwavering trust in God to secure the independence for
which he gave his life." [44]

It was natural for Hill to confide his feelings about Jackson to
Vance; for ever since the end of January, when he had written the
governor, "Your course has elicited the warmest admiration of every
Southern man in the Confederacy," [45] his relations with North
Carolina's bold, vigorous war leader had been frank and friendly.
He and Vance respected each other even though they did not always
see eye to eye in dealing with such problems as disloyalty, desertion,
and calling out the militia.

When Hill would arrest a citizen accused of trafficking with the
Federals, and Vance would let the man go free on a writ of habeas
corpus, Hill would grumble but acquiesce. When Hill would argue,
as he often did, that the governor should call out the militia, Vance
would reply that the militia was virtually useless, as Hill himself admitted, and calling it out would do more harm than good. Actually,
Vance had tried to use militia officers to arrest deserters, but was
inhibited from doing so by a decision of the chief justice of the state
supreme court, Richmond M. Pearson, to the effect that in the
absence of express enactments the governor could not enforce Confederate law in this manner. Publication of Pearson's decision in the
newspapers stimulated desertions among the North Carolina troops
with Lee. The problem was "frightful," Hill wrote to Vance.
"All this proceeds from the pernicious press and judiciary at home.
May God deliver us from such men."

On all these matters he and the governor exchanged blunt opinions, but each expressed the hope that he had not hurt the other's
feelings. In one letter discussing their mutual problems Vance explained that while he wanted to cooperate with Hill he had to deal
with many conflicting factions. "I honestly believe," he said, "that
the worst thing which could now happen to the state would be for
me to lose that popularity with the people which you were kind
enough to say I possessed. I have been heretofore able to coax them
into many things which I believe few others could have done. Excuse
this little boast, which please regard as confidential." [46]

Pressed by Hill, and alarmed by the growth of the desertion evil,
Vance in May attempted once more to check it with militia officers.
He also issued a scorching proclamation against skulks and their

abettors. Hill had been asking for a proclamation that would make "even cowards blush," and Vance's heavy eloquence delighted him. "It is capital, glorious," he wrote the governor. "Please send me a hundred copies to be read on parade to the troops." [47] Yet desertion continued. It would grow worse as the fortunes of the Confederacy declined.

On May 20 Lee recommended that Hill be assigned to the command that Longstreet had been exercising, and eight days later Hill's Department of North Carolina was extended northward to include Petersburg and its environs. Hill did not object, although this gave him heavy new responsibilities. He believed what Grant would later demonstrate—that Petersburg was the key to Richmond. While serving with Jackson the previous November he had remarked to Isabella: "It has long been my opinion that the true base for the Yankees to attack Richmond was Suffolk by the way of Petersburg, but I never could make Genl Lee believe it." [48]

May, 1863, was a time of decision in the Confederate capital. The South was losing the war. Lincoln's issuance of his definitive emancipation proclamation on January 1 had dimmed the hope that antislavery Great Britain would intervene to save the Confederacy from the North's growing military power, which was manifesting itself most dangerously on the Mississippi, where Grant was closing in on Vicksburg. President Davis was perturbed by calls for reinforcements to save Vicksburg, but Lee opposed detaching any of his own troops for this purpose, arguing that he could relieve Union pressure on the Mississippi bastion by invading Pennsylvania. At conferences which he attended in Richmond, May 14 to 17, he won presidential and cabinet approval of the northern venture.[49]

Desirous of strengthening his army for the expedition as rapidly as possible, he wrote Hill from Richmond asking him to send reinforcements. Hill had recently proposed a plan for exchanging his full brigades for Lee's depleted ones, but Lee disapproved on the grounds that this procedure would increase his numbers but weaken his army intrinsically by replacing experienced with inexperienced troops. Hill had also asked Lee how many troops he wanted, and the commanding general answered, "I will state that the extent of the re-enforcements you can send to the Army of Northern Virginia must necessarily depend upon the strength of the enemy in your front."

The Federals, he believed, were preparing to conduct major operations in Virginia. His information indicated that they were "withdrawing troops from South Carolina and the country south of James River," and in his opinion it was best to "do the same." Accordingly he gave Hill discretionary instructions:

If he [the enemy] weakens his force in North Carolina I think you will be able, by using all your local troops, such portion of your regular cavalry and regular brigades as may be necessary, to repulse and restrain his marauding expeditions and protect the railroads and the farming interests of the country you now hold. Every man not required for this purpose I desire you to send to me and rely upon your good judgment to proportion the means to the object in view.[50]

This was both clear and courteous, but it asked Hill to exercise a command function that properly belonged to Lee himself. Hill had no adequate basis for judging his own needs relative to those of the commanding general. He had access neither to Lee's strategic plans nor to the innumerable intelligence reports that poured into army headquarters; yet such comprehensive information was essential to any sound apportionment of troops. It was the commanding general's responsibility to weigh that information and decide how much to weaken Hill in order to strengthen himself. He could share the responsibility with other top officials—particularly with Davis, the ultimate military authority—but he could not properly place it upon Hill.

Hill evidently thought as much, for he declined the discretionary instructions and asked for positive orders. Lee acquiesced.[51] The incident marked the beginning of tension between the two generals, which intensified after Lee had returned to his headquarters near Fredericksburg.

One source of disagreement was the transfer of Beverley Robertson, with two regiments of cavalry, to Lee. When Robertson volunteered to go to Virginia, Hill made no objection and Lee accepted him, though he told Stuart, "I wished to leave Robertson in North Carolina. . . ." Very soon, however, he dropped into a letter to Hill a single, suave sentence: "If you require General Robertson to command or organize the cavalry in your department I will return him to you."

With equal urbanity, Hill replied in a postscript, "I am much obliged to you for the offer of Brigadier-General Robertson, but he has been once in this department."

Thereupon Lee turned to Davis, and in discussing his cavalry needs with the President suggested that Robertson return to North Carolina: "I think it would be better if General Robertson were in command of the cavalry within the State, as he is a good organizer and instructor, but General Hill does not appear to require him."

No doubt Davis knew as well as Lee why Hill did not "require" Robertson. Nothing came of Lee's suggestion. Robertson remained for a time with the Army of Northern Virginia, but eventually was shunted back to Richmond with a recommendation from Lee that he be assigned to a camp for recruiting cavalry "at some point in the rear." [52]

While Lee and Hill were tilting in this manner over Robertson, they were also continuing their argument over which and how many infantry brigades should be withdrawn from the Department of North Carolina. Both Seddon and Davis were involved in the dispute, which engendered varying degrees of friction from the time of Hill's mid-May request for positive orders until the latter part of June.

In addition to Robertson's two cavalry regiments, Hill sent Pettigrew's and Daniel's brigades to Lee, and received in return A. H. Colquitt's—an exchange of about 7,000 effective troops for some 1,500. This left Hill with a total departmental strength in May of about 22,000 effectives, including seven infantry brigades, totaling a little less than 16,000 and commanded by Generals Colquitt, Thomas L. Clingman, John R. Cooke, J. G. Martin, Micah Jenkins, Robert Ransom, and Joseph R. Davis, a nephew of the President. Of the seven, the best brigades by far were Ransom's 2,900 fighting men, Jenkins's 2,400, and Cooke's 2,200. Hill relied chiefly on these three for the protection of Wilmington and the Wilmington and Weldon Railroad. But all three brigades had served with Lee, and he regarded them as detachments from his army, subject to recall whenever needed.[53]

Lee desired not only to build up his army for the Pennsylvania venture but also to be certain that Richmond was not seized by the Federals while his back was turned. In May he received reports of an enemy movement up the York River to West Point, and on May 25, having concluded that the Federals were probably transferring troops from Hill's department, he ordered Hill to send Ransom's brigade to Richmond and Jenkins's to Pickett's division at Hanover Junction, north of the city. General Elzey, he said, could move Ransom onward if necessary. As for Cooke, Hill might retain him until he was better prepared to do without him. Lee repeated this to Hill on the twenty-eighth, and for some reason did not tell him that on the twenty-seventh he had telegraphed to Seddon recommending that Cooke's brigade be ordered to Richmond and that Hill, if necessary, draw reinforcements from General P. G. T. Beauregard, in Charleston.[54]

Hill did not believe that Federal strength in his department was decreasing. On the contrary, a study of recently captured Federal mail indicated that the number of Union regiments in New Bern had risen by nine to a total of at least thirty-one. He had reported this to Lee on the twenty-fifth, and the more he thought about it the more important the information seemed. When he received Lee's orders of the twenty-fifth he wrote back asking that Ransom be replaced "by one of the shattered brigades, else the railroad can be cut and possibly Wilmington be taken." [55] He also dispatched a letter to Richmond.

On the twenty-eighth, Seddon acknowledged the letter, and said he was surprised to learn that both Ransom and Jenkins had been withdrawn. The day before, when he had received Lee's telegram recommending the withdrawal of Cooke, he and the President had agreed not to act until they had consulted with Hill "as to its effect on the safety of your command." Now Seddon believed that, as Hill had suggested, Lee had not had all the facts on enemy strength in North Carolina when he withdrew Ransom and Jenkins. Accordingly, the Secretary modified Lee's orders, directing Hill to send on Ransom's brigade, which was already in motion, but to retain Jenkins and Cooke, "at least until further communication can be had with General Lee and his counsel taken on the new aspect presented by your statement of the enemy's forces in North Carolina." [56]

Davis himself signed the telegram of May 29 that informed Lee his plans were opposed:

General: Hill says he has reported to you as to condition in North Carolina.

To withdraw Ransom's, Cooke's, and Jenkins' brigades is to abandon the country to the enemy, if last information be correct.

Jenkins' brigade was exchanged for the one which had previously guarded the approach across the Blackwater, and which is understood to have gone up with General Pickett.

Ransom has been promoted, to relieve General French, ordered to Mississippi.[57]

The statement that Jenkins's brigade, on the Blackwater River, had been exchanged, implied that Lee no longer had the right to claim it. The telegram was an unusually blunt message from president to commanding general, and when Lee read it his fighting blood rose. Back over the wires that same day hummed his angry reply:

I gave Genl Hill Discretionary orders from Richmond to apportion his force to the strength of Enemy and send what could be spared. He declined to act and requested positive orders. I gave such orders as I could at this distance. Now he objects. I cannot operate in this manner. I request you to cause such orders to be given him as your judgment dictates. Pickett has no Brigade in place of Jenkin's so Genl Longstreet reports. Genl Hill has retained one Regt. from Pettigrew and one from Daniels.[58]

Lee followed this on May 30 with a letter in which he repeated his grievances against Hill, reviewed the reasons for his orders of the twenty-fifth, and explained that the brigade for which Davis thought Jenkins's had been exchanged was only a temporary one that Pickett had not retained. Since the previous fall, he stated, his army had lost four brigades, including Jenkins's, Ransom's, and Cooke's, and had gained only one. Hooker's army, he believed, had been increased; and he made it plain that he thought Hill had more troops than he needed. Declaring himself "unable to operate" in the face of Hill's objections, he asked to be "relieved from any control" of Hill's department.[59]

Although he did not mention in this letter the question of the captured mail, he did raise the issue in another letter of May 30, addressed to Hill. "I know nothing of the force in your front," he wrote, "but I attach no importance to the estimate of the enemy's forces in New Berne based on the captured mail. These letters only go to show that the writers thought these regiments were in New Berne at the time they wrote." He repeated orders already telegraphed to Hill, to "suspend the execution of my order of the 25th" and await directions from the President.[60]

It was up to Davis, then, to decide what to do. His answer to Lee's angry telegram had been conciliatory. "It is embarrassing to be called on for orders," he had telegraphed, "and when they are given to be met with opinions previously invited, but withheld." He would investigate all the questions at issue, he promised, and ended with the assurance: "But half the case had been laid before me when my telegram was sent to you, and then I supposed you were mistaken." [61]

This certainly was sympathetic to Lee, to the point of making assumptions about Hill's role in the matter that Davis might have been hard pressed to prove. Yet it soon became evident that the President was not yielding completely to his commanding general's wishes. Before receiving Lee's amplifying letter, he had Hill queried as follows:

What force can you spare to General Lee on the basis of his proposition to you? Was a regiment of Pettigrew's and another of Daniel's brigade left in your department? What became of the force on the Blackwater which was substituted by Jenkins' brigade? Did it join Pickett's division and was it a brigade? [62]

Hill replied:

All five of Pettigrew's regiments and battery have gone to him. Four regiments, a battalion, and battery of Daniel's have been sent, leaving one regiment behind. I do not know what troops General Jenkins relieved. I could exchange Cooke's for Ransom's brigade.[63]

Davis then worked out a compromise. Ransom and Jenkins were assigned to the region south of Richmond in Hill's newly enlarged department. The brigades of Cooke and Joseph R. Davis, totaling about 4,600 effectives, went to Lee. Hill thus lost two brigades instead of three, and kept the two that he most wanted, Ransom's and Jenkins's.

To Lee the President explained that he did not regard the reports of the enemy threat at West Point as "quite reliable," and that in any event Ransom could cross the James to protect the city if that became necessary. He also warned him that a third regiment of cavalry he was about to accept from Hill was probably not any good, and taking note of his request to be relieved from command of Hill's department, tactfully denied it. Several times it had occurred to him, he said, that "it would be better for you to control all the operations of the Atlantic slope, and I must ask you to reconsider the matter. I wish I knew how to relieve you from all anxiety concerning movements on the York or James River...while you are moving toward the north and west; but even if you could spare troops for the purpose, on whom could you devolve the command...?" [64]

Lee, of course, accepted these decisions. But he frankly said, "I regret to lose Ransom and Jenkins, both good and tried officers, with veteran troops"; and he also told Davis: "I requested to be relieved from command of the troops between the James and the Cape Fear Rivers because I did not see that I could advantageously exercise it, but, on the contrary, to continue in it might be productive of harm. I could only exercise it beneficially by relying upon the judgment of General D. H. Hill, who declined to act upon discretionary orders, and I thought it best for the service to leave him to his own discretion." [65] With this final slap at Hill in early June the dispute cooled off somewhat, though the competition between the two generals for troops had not ended.

When both the Federal and the Confederate records pertinent to the dispute are examined, it appears that, as might be expected, neither Lee nor Hill had a wholly correct view of the military situation in the Richmond area and North Carolina. The Federals had indeed occupied West Point, with some 5,000 troops, and had held it until the night of May 31, when they withdrew southward; but these men had come from General John A. Dix at Fort Monroe, not from General Foster in North Carolina. Instead of decreasing, as Lee had reasoned, Foster's departmental strength had risen, from about 14,000 reported present for duty on April 30 to some 15,700 on May 31.[66]

On the other hand, Hill was mistaken in supposing from the captured mail that the number of Union regiments at New Bern had increased to at least thirty-one. General Whiting estimated that this figure indicated a total strength at New Bern of "between 12,000 and 15,000 men," and urged Seddon not to endanger Wilmington by stripping the North Carolina defense line to reinforce Lee. That Seddon, Davis, and Hill were also alarmed has been shown. However, the actual number of regiments at New Bern as of May 31 was only twenty-one, and the total strength of the garrison was still what it had been in early April, about 9,000.[67]

Lee's anger and disappointment at the changes in his orders wrought by Seddon and Davis at Hill's instance is understandable;

yet the two harassed officials in Richmond were only exercising the civilian control over the military that was traditional in the history of American warfare. Lincoln exerted similar control over Northern generals. To be sure, neither Confederate leader was a Lincoln in ability. Davis, for all his impressive record as West Point graduate, Mexican War colonel of volunteers, United States Congressman, Senator, and Secretary of War under Franklin Pierce, brought little genius to his role as commander in chief of the Confederate armed forces; while Seddon, a man of reasonable competence with considerable experience in the United States House of Representatives, lacked training in military affairs. Yet in countermanding Lee they were conscientiously trying to do their duty as they saw it, in terms of a traditional system of command that was inadequate for fighting a great modern war.

The farther Lee was from Richmond, the weaker the system was likely to be. Because at Fredericksburg he was remote from North Carolina, and would be more distant still when he moved toward Pennsylvania, he had logic on his side when he wrote Davis that he did not think that he could advantageously continue in command of Hill's department. But when he asked Hill to decide how many troops to send him he was, as has already been suggested, asking a subordinate with a necessarily limited view of the war to assume a function that properly belonged to the top command. "No general likes to take the responsibility of weakening his own front," the distinguished military historian Major General Sir Frederick Maurice has written. "Such responsibility can only be taken by some one who is able to view the theater of war as a whole, and who has authority to decide promptly." If this be correct, Lee's censure of Hill for requesting positive orders was of questionable military soundness.

It appears that what the Confederacy really needed was a general staff at Richmond that could gather reliable intelligence, apportion troops, and provide comprehensive, coordinated direction of the whole Southern war effort. Such a system might have obviated the difficulties over reinforcements that Lee had with Hill and other generals, notably Beauregard in the summer of 1864 when Grant was hammering toward Petersburg.[68] However, it is hard to visualize drastic changes being made in the top command in June, 1863. Davis would have had to be persuaded by Lee, and what was paramount in Lee's mind that month was not command theory but the concrete dangers that faced him as he maneuvered his army into the Shenandoah Valley toward Maryland and Pennsylvania.

He and Hill, meanwhile, continued their duel over troops. On June 4, Seddon upheld Lee's refusal of Hill's offer to exchange Colquitt's relatively large brigade for the smaller, veteran brigade of General Stephen D. Ramseur. Then Lee tried again to obtain Jenkins, and on June 19 Davis ruled that Hill could keep him to protect Petersburg and support other defense positions.[69]

Hill had made Petersburg the headquarters of his expanded department. As he looked eastward toward the Blackwater River where the Federals, as he reported on the eighteenth, had been "feebly attempting" to break his defense line for five consecutive days, he was also mentally facing west, toward Vicksburg, for he had volunteered to Davis his services in Mississippi. No doubt he was influenced by the fact that his old friend General Johnston commanded in that area. Davis had replied somewhat indefinitely that he would be glad to approve the transfer provided Hill could be spared in North Carolina.[70]

In preparing Isabella for this move, Hill did not tell her that he had initiated it, but on the contrary strongly implied that it was the President's idea. Apparently there had been less marital friction since he had given up combat service, but all was not complete harmony. Writing to her on June 14 he stoutly denied her accusation that he had been "scolding" her. Then he scolded her, mildly, for not leaving unhealthful Charlotte to dwell with her father, and ended with a plea for her love:

"More than in the days of courtship do I long to hear you say, 'I love you.' The affection of wife and children is all that I have to live for."[71]

Toward the end of June, Lee crossed the Potomac into Maryland. Keenly debated at the time, the wisdom of this "great gamble" northward while Vicksburg was tottering has remained debatable ever since.[72] Hill privately condemned Lee's venture. On June 23 he wrote Isabella:

I fear that the move Northward is most unfortunate. We will not get 50 men in Maryland and Lincoln will get 20,000. The whole North will pour out its countless host and our poor shattered Army will have to fight ten to one. Well, we must hope for the best, but the folly of the movement is transparent.

And again on the twenty-fifth he told her:

Genl Lee is venturing upon a very hazardous movement; and one that must be fruitless, if not disastrous. It would have been infinitely wiser to have brought his Army back to Richmond and held it with a small force while his main strength went to the relief of Vicksburg. As it is, there seems to be no ground to hope for Vicksburg. The flaming dispatches, we are getting from there, are false.[73]

After the war, he summed up this feeling in a vivid sentence: "The drums that beat for the advance into Pennsylvania seemed to many of us to be beating the funeral march of the dead Confederacy." [74]

Lee's departure increased the vulnerability of Richmond, and the Federals moved quickly to take advantage of the situation. As early as June 14, orders sent from Washington to General Dix at Fort Monroe informed him that "Lee's army is in motion toward the Shenandoah Valley," and directed him to concentrate all his available force, threaten the city, and "do . . . all the damage possible." Dix promptly began sending troops up the York River to West Point and to White House, only twenty-five miles east of Richmond. By the end of the month he had some 19,500 men at White House and 1,000 nearby at West Point. At Yorktown were about 3,800 troops and southward, from Fort Monroe to Suffolk, were nearly 7,000 more.[75]

It was an alarming concentration, and before it had been in progress more than a week Seddon directed Hill to be ready to defend Richmond if necessary. Hill accordingly shifted his troops. Leaving three brigades to protect Wilmington, Kinston, and the railroad, against Foster, who still had about 10,000 men in North Carolina, he sent both Ransom and Jenkins to Richmond. Also on guard near the city were two of Lee's brigades, commanded by Cooke and General Henry A. Wise. Northward at Hanover Junction Lee had still another brigade, under General M. D. Corse.[76]

The commander of the Richmond department, General Elzey, had reacted to proposed reductions in his strength in a manner quite similar to Hill's, and had opposed sending Lee any of his troops guarding the city; [77] but Lee was determined to withdraw Corse's brigade, at least. On leaving for the Valley, he had sent one infantry regiment to relieve Corse's men. About June 25, Corse marched away to Gordonsville, and two days later a strong force of Federal cavalry raided Hanover Junction. Scattering the infantry regiment, they burned a bridge and a quartermaster's depot, and made off with thirty-five army wagons, 700 horses and mules, and more than one hundred prisoners. One captive was none other than Lee's son, General W. H. F. Lee, who was taken from his bed in a private residence where he had been recovering from a leg wound.[78]

That Lee himself had moved too far north to know what was happening in the Richmond area is shown by two letters that he addressed, respectively, to Davis and Adjutant General Samuel Cooper on June 23, two days before he crossed the Potomac. To Cooper he gave marching directions for Corse, and mentioned a special plan that he formally proposed to Davis: General Beauregard was to bring a portion of his troops to Virginia, unite them with "such of the troops about Richmond and in North Carolina as could be spared for a short time," and assemble an army in northern Virginia at Culpeper Court House. This threat to Washington, Lee suggested, "would not only effect a diversion most favorable for this army, but would, I think, relieve us of any apprehension of an attack upon Richmond during our absence." [79]

Davis was with General Cooper when these letters arrived, the night of June 28, and the two must have read Lee's proposal with astonishment. Both wrote replies informing him of enemy power in the Richmond area and of the defense needs that made his diversion plan visionary. Davis, that night, composed a courteous but firm refusal of troops. Cooper, the next day, was plain-spoken to the point of asperity. After reading Lee's letter, he said,

The President was embarrassed to understand that part of it which refers to the plan of assembling an army at Culpeper Court-House under General Beauregard. This is the first intimation that he has had that such a plan was ever in contemplation, and, taking all things into consideration, he cannot see how it can by any possibility be carried into effect. You will doubtless learn before this reaches you that the enemy has again assembled in force on the Peninsula, estimated between 20,000 and 30,000 men, from 6,000 to 10,000 of whom are reported to be in the vicinity of White House and the remainder at Yorktown.

Then he told Lee of the cavalry raid at Hanover, and went on to say, "It was unfortunate that this raid took place only about two days after General Corse's brigade had left.... Had it remained at Hanover Junction, it is reasonable to suppose that most of the enemy's cavalry would have been either destroyed or captured and the property saved from injury." The capital must be protected, he continued, even if it became necessary "to hazard something at other points. You can easily estimate your strength here, and I would suggest for your consideration whether, in this state of things, you might not be able to spare a portion of your force to protect your line of communication against attempted raids by the enemy." [80]

Lee doubtless would have met this final thrust with the statement that he had deliberately abandoned his communications because he lacked troops to maintain them, and had sent notice of this, on the twenty-fifth, to Davis.[81] But he was spared the trouble of answering by a final bit of irony. Cooper's and Davis's letters never reached him; they were intercepted by Federal scouts, and after perusal in Washington were published in the Northern press as revealing evidence of Confederate military weakness.[82]

Another communication of the twenty-ninth was not intercepted, as it traveled a safe interior route from Seddon's office to Cooper's. "General D. H. Hill having come over from Petersburg, whence nearly all of his troops have been withdrawn for the defense of this city, applies for leave to command here," wrote the Secretary. "As the forces consist mainly of troops from his department, this seems to me reasonable, and you will issue an order giving him temporary command of the troops in the field for the defense of Richmond." [83]

That same day Elzey asked to be replaced by Hill and sent to Lee's army for artillery service, and accordingly on July 1 Hill was also assigned temporary command of the Department of Richmond. With some ten thousand regular troops, plus the city militia, for what it was worth, he was in a sanguine mood. Shortly before, he had written Vance, "We have not many troops here, but they are not of the exempt stripe. They will whip five to one with ease," and had joked with Seddon about making Dix "the subject of the cartel which he helped to frame." [84]

But Dix, had Hill only known it, was not of a mind to expose himself either to imprisonment or victory. At White House on the morning of June 29, he had held a council of war with his general officers and all had agreed not to attack but merely to threaten Richmond—a decision that Dix later had some difficulty explaining to Washington. The threatening took the form of raids and demonstrations, which repeatedly alarmed Richmond in early July, but which Hill met north and east of the city and threw back with little more than heavy skirmishing.[85]

These successes were attended by a certain amount of friction between Hill and Elzey, who had remained in his departmental headquarters. On July 2, Seddon explained to Hill that he had just seen the President and found "that I have exceeded his views in the order relieving General Elzey and placing you in temporary command." Davis, he continued, directed that Elzey command the city defenses, Hill the troops in the field. Hill replied that any assignment would suit him that was "definite and fixed," and that he would not "for any consideration, have General Elzey's feelings wounded." However, he strongly urged unified instead of divided authority, and suggested that all orders be issued through Seddon. Instead, Seddon within a few days gave Hill "command of all the troops for the defense of Richmond." [86]

By July 5, Hill was writing the Secretary that the Federal "design on Richmond was not a feint but a faint," and four days later he reported that all danger to Richmond was over.[87] In dark contrast was the news that came of the surrender of Vicksburg and the defeat of Lee at Gettysburg, Pennsylvania. On the tenth, Hill confided his feelings to his friend Vance.

"I wrote to you some time ago that the campaign of Lee would prolong the war through Lincoln's administration. It has turned out as I believed it would.

"God help us," he exclaimed, and then spoke of the need for renewed effort. "A grave blunder has been committed but we must meet the calamity involved with faith and courage. The Yankees were whipped on both roads of their advance to Richmond and are now hurrying off. I think that every available man ought to be sent to save Lee, but I cannot tell what counsels will prevail. I think that we have nothing to fear in N. C. except from raiders." [88]

This last sentence breathed an optimism that Hill often had not felt while in North Carolina, and might not have retained had he returned to his old command. But new scenes awaited him now; his personal fortunes were rising as those of his nation declined. About July 10, Davis visited his camp east of Richmond, congratulated him on his defense of the city, and told him that he was appointed a lieutenant general, with orders to report to Johnston in Mississippi.

The commission was dated July 11. On the thirteenth, Hill with his staff began the journey west, traveling by way of Charlotte. At his home, by telegram, he received new orders. The assignment to Mississippi was canceled. He was now to report to General Braxton Bragg at Chattanooga, for duty as a corps commander in the Army of Tennessee.[89]

XI

CHICKAMAUGA

Past the foothills of Missionary Ridge, through shadowy reaches of pine and oak, the mountain stream wound northward toward Chattanooga and the Tennessee. Its prosaic label on the military maps was West Chickamauga Creek, but Bragg's men called it simply "the Chickamauga," and told each other that in the Cherokee language the name meant "River of Death." They knew, on September 19, 1863, that they were about to prove this meaning.

Hill's corps that morning guarded the Confederate left flank while the Army of Tennessee crossed to the west side of the Chickamauga, moving toward some fifty-eight thousand Federals formed in battle line parallel to the stream under the command of Hill's West Point classmate, General William S. Rosecrans. The crossing had begun the previous day, had been slowed by Union skirmishers guarding the fords and bridges, and now was continuing behind schedule. Hill must have wondered, as the sound of renewed fighting broke out near Reed's Bridge to the north, whether General Bragg knew, this time, what he was about. It was a grim thought to entertain at the start of a great battle, but not one he could easily shake off. Two months of service in this luckless army had instilled in him grave doubt of Bragg's ability.[1]

When on July 19 he had reported to Bragg at Chattanooga, in the pleasant expectation of seeing him for the first time since serving under him at Corpus Christi, he had been shocked by his old friend's manner and appearance. Tall, black-bearded, and ungainly, Bragg had never been handsome; but now his bold, swarthy face bore the stamp of sickness and premature age, and from beneath the heavy brows that met at the bridge of his nose his dark eyes glared with a painfully fierce anxiety. His unconcealed nervousness and despondency impressed Hill most unfavorably, but scarcely dampened the renewed hope and enthusiam for the Southern cause that had been kindled in him by his promotion. Writing to Vance from Chattanooga to thank him for his "great kindness and hearty cooperation" during the North Carolina command, he declared:

"When France and England think our cause almost gone, they will interfere. They will never consent to a reestablishment of the old Union. I notice that even the Yankees themselves take that view . . . spite of all their glorification over Vicksburg." [2]

From Chattanooga he also wrote Adjutant General Cooper, about the need for a more drastic conscription policy.

I would most respectfully call the attention of the President to the vast number of able-bodied young men out of the service. From Richmond Va. to this point, there is not a city, town or village which has not many more in it than before the War. At every spot, there were crowds of young men.

The abolition of the exemption bill would give us 400,000 able-bodied young men; its modification so as not to interfere with the industrial pursuits of the country would give us at least 200,000. As the enemy advances, and occupies our territory, many soldiers desert in order to protect their families. Thus our strength is being daily weakened, and unless something is done speedily to reinforce the Army, the contest will become very unequal.

I hope that the great importance of the subject will justify this informal communication. I thought it most likely that as the President had not been traveling lately, he was not aware of the vast number of drones and laggards in the country.[3]

Not content with this, Hill next drew up a more elaborate and emphatic petition to Davis and dispatched it to Cooper over the signatures of himself and some seventeen fellow officers, including Braxton Bragg. "We, the undersigned officers of the Confederate Army," it began, "being deeply impressed with the belief that unless the ranks are speedily replenished our cause will be lost . . . would earnestly implore the President . . . to take prompt measures to recruit our wasted armies by fresh levies from home." Davis, the letter continued, could do this by "calling upon the respective States for enlarged quotas of troops" or by assembling Congress and modifying the exemption law.

Asserting that the "whole system" of exemption was based upon the "false assumption" that none of the peacetime comforts and conveniences of society should be disturbed "amidst . . . a great revolution," Hill then attacked, one by one, the exemption abuses as he saw them: the disproportionate numbers crowding into exempt occupations; the "more than 150,000 soldiers" who had employed substitutes, "not one in a hundred" of whom had remained in the service; and the "timid and effeminate young men" who used political influence to obtain safe military duty. "We do know certainly," he wrote, "that the detailed and exempted men under forty-five exceed a quarter of a million . . . and we think that the Army can be increased a quarter of a million without more suffering and inconvenience to the country than is to be expected in such a life and death struggle as we are engaged in." Even a "levy en masse" was preferable to the loss of independence. "Early and vigorous measures to recruit our wasted ranks may save us further loss of men and resources, and possibly the existence of the Southern Confederacy itself." [4]

About two weeks later, General Cooper addressed a reply to "General Braxton Bragg and other officers" in which he questioned the accuracy of Hill's statistics—without actually denying what every informed Southerner knew, that the evasion of military service was a Confederate scandal—and stressed the difficulty of obtaining either new legislation from Congress or sufficient arms for large numbers of recruits. Perhaps what he was really saying for the President, for whom apparently he was replying, was that the administration deemed it inadvisable to demand of a people committed to states' rights theory the severe centralized war effort that Hill's petition advocated. It was clear at any rate that military men would have to make do largely with what they had.[5]

Nor could it be said that they were using what they had very successfully. Bragg, especially, seemed uncertain what to do with his army. In Kentucky and Tennessee he had gained a reputation for winning barren victories and retreating, and a little less than two months after Hill's arrival he retreated again, yielding Chattanooga to one of Rosecrans's flanking maneuvers, and moving south about thirty miles to Lafayette, Georgia.

Though he felt that he was forced to withdraw in order to protect his communications, he hoped to convert his movement into an attack on Rosecrans's army, and that September reinforcements to add weight to the attack were on the way. From Virginia, with Lee's approval, Longstreet was moving west over tortuous rail connections with the divisions of McLaws and Hood, while from Knoxville, Tennessee, General Simon B. Buckner was coming south with about six thousand men. From Mississippi, Generals John C. Breckinridge and W. H. T. Walker had already arrived with their divisions. Strategy that might have been more effective earlier in the war was at last being attempted; over inner lines of communication the Confederacy was concentrating troops for a major effort in the western theater.[6]

Of all this Hill gave no hint in his letters home. Indeed, Isabella seemed to have little interest in grand strategy; what concerned her was the fact that Hill had become notorious among exempt men in North Carolina because of his open scorn for them. Not long before the retreat from Chattanooga she wrote him about this and apparently asked him to promise not to publish any more denunciations of exempts. In his reply he described how he had carried out a long, hot inspection trip, though "sick all day with diarrhea," and how on returning supperless after 8 P.M. he had found two letters from her and had "clutched them most eagerly, hoping to find a cordial for hunger and weariness," but had been "inexpressibly shocked when I found out how much you had suffered."

It seemed strange to him, he went on, that she should worry about the opinion of "the cowardly skulkers" at a time when "subjugation is staring us in the face." She ought to think of his criticism as arising not from "want of charity" but from "intense anxiety about our suffering country. It is plain now even to the most ignorant that the exempts must take the field, or the Yankees will conquer the country." Still he did not want her to suffer because of his views, and he ended with the declaration: "My own darling, I will promise any thing you wish. Your happiness is dearer to me than every thing in life."[7]

In a much lighter vein were the letters that he occasionally wrote his children. From the vicinity of Lafayette he told about his friendship with "a little boy near here who calls himself 'Genl Hill and Jeff Davis.' His name is Benny, but he wont let you call him that.

He ... loves to pout. But whenever I see him pouting, I call him 'Abe Lincoln,' and he gets ashamed of pouting." [8]

Perhaps this cheerful note in the home correspondence reflected not only Hill's love of children but also the bright side of his personal military situation. Despite frail health and wearing administrative duties he greatly enjoyed his new command, and handled it well. His corps had formerly belonged to General William J. Hardee, who had been transferred to Mississippi. It consisted, at the time of the withdrawal from Chattanooga, of two divisions commanded by Major Generals Breckinridge and Patrick R. Cleburne, each of whom, in his own way, was famous.

Breckinridge was one of the distinguished civil leaders of the South. He had been Vice-President of the United States under James Buchanan, Congressman and United States Senator from Kentucky, and the presidential candidate of the Southern Democrats in 1860. Appointed a brigadier general at the beginning of the war, he had proved himself an able commander, despite his lack of military training, in such hard-fought battles of the western theater as Shiloh and Stone's River, or Murfreesboro. At forty-two, he was a tall, martial figure, easily recognizable on the battlefield because of the huge, dark, drooping mustachios that waved like banners on either side of his jutting chin.[9]

Cleburne also lacked formal training for his high position, but his natural talents had earned him a reputation as a brilliant combat commander. Born in Cork County, Ireland, in 1828, he had been a corporal in the British army before emigrating to Helena, Arkansas, and entering the legal profession. In the spring of 1861, as a private in the Arkansas State troops, he had begun the military career that had carried him through Shiloh, Stone's River, and other battles of the Army of Tennessee. One of his army associates described him as a "blunt, impassive, rather heavy man," with "dull features," but this was only the surface. His cropped, grizzled black beard hid a sensitive face that had been handsome until a Minié ball disfigured it in the battle of Richmond, Kentucky, while the impassive manner concealed an invincible spirit that habitually caught fire in combat and revealed a leader whom men would follow to the death. "A meteor," Robert E. Lee called him, and Jefferson Davis, among others, dubbed him the "Stonewall Jackson of the West." [10]

In Hill, these two able generals and their subordinates recognized a commander whom they could trust and admire. With the aid of his veteran staff officers, including Ratchford and Archer Anderson, who had taken over as chief of staff, he had quickly made his presence felt as an invigorating force throughout the corps, his first efforts being directed toward paring away military fat wherever he saw it.

He set the example himself in his headquarters organization, beginning with transportation. As Ratchford recalled, "the Generals of the Army of Tennessee were a royal set"; the corps and army headquarters commands transported their equipment and personal possessions in caravans of eighteen to twenty wagons, each wagon pulled by a six-mule team. But when Hill arrived in Chattanooga, he found that he had no wagons at all for his corps headquarters. Hardee, transporting himself in the style to which he had been accustomed, had gone off to Mississippi with eighteen six-mule teams.

Hill had no quartermaster, but detailed an officer to this duty and ordered him to obtain transportation for headquarters. Alas, the unhappy man reported after his first day's search, he had found none. The second day he reported that he still had only six six-mule teams, but that he was doing his best and had the promise of more soon.

"What am I to do with six teams?" Hill asked him.

The quartermaster thought he was being reproved. Quickly he protested that he could do better, and hoped the general would be patient with him. He was much surprised when Hill told him to leave three teams for headquarters and turn the other three over to the troops.

Hill next applied his anti-luxury policy to the officers' custom of using enlisted men as personal servants, by ordering that all soldiers detailed for such menial duty be returned to their commands. Reports on compliance with the order were to be submitted to headquarters, and any officer who in the future used an enlisted man as his servant was to be severely penalized. "Six hundred soldiers," Ratchford later wrote, "were restored to the ranks." He believed that as Hill "gradually came down on officers and men alike requiring all to do their duty," noticeable improvements were achieved in efficiency and morale. "All began to recognize that a master spirit was at the head of the corps." [11]

If this was the bright side of Hill's new command, the dark was his distrust of Braxton Bragg. The foreboding that he brought away from his first interview with the commanding general did not leave him; on the contrary it deepened as he observed Bragg's field operations during the withdrawal from Chattanooga. Nor was he alone in this feeling. Distrust of Bragg was rife among the generals of his army.

There was ample reason for it. Bragg had his share of personal bravery, patriotism, and organizational ability, but these strengths were vitiated by serious weaknesses. He was, as his chief of staff, General William W. Mackall, confided to his wife, a vacillating commander who had trouble deciding when and where to move his troops. Hill thought this wavering attitude stemmed largely from inadequate knowledge of the enemy. Unlike Lee, Bragg seemed to have no well-organized system of independent scouts, but to get his information about Federal movements chiefly from his cavalry, which had difficulty penetrating the enemy's infantry-supported cavalry screen.

His uncertainty was reflected in his orders. They were likely to be ambiguous, and were sometimes "impossible," as Hill termed those which could not be carried out because they ignored the physical realities of the military situation. Worse yet, when Bragg blundered he was prone to look for a scapegoat to bear the blame.

The result of all this was a paralysis of initiative in the high command. Bragg's generals obeyed his orders with extreme caution, because if they acted and then found the orders impossible to execute, or for some other reason failed to attain success, they might be pilloried. Their professional instinct for survival kept them thinking as much about protecting their reputation as about striking the enemy.[12]

In the first months of 1863 Bragg had narrowly escaped being ousted from his command. He had brought the difficulty upon himself when, smarting over what he regarded as unfair criticism of his retreat from Murfreesboro, Tennessee, he had addressed a letter to his corps and division commanders asking them to consult with their subordinates and then write him their "candid" opinion of him. He would "retire without a regret," he said, if he found he had lost "the good opinion of my generals." In reply, Hardee, Breckinridge, and Cleburne advised him to resign. The other corps commander, Lieutenant General Leonidas Polk, was on leave when Bragg issued his rash request, but after returning to the army wrote President Davis, on February 4, informing him of the whole affair and suggesting that Bragg be replaced with Joseph E. Johnston.[13]

Polk could safely take this liberty because he and Davis were old friends, having been comrades at West Point. The unorthodox lieutenant general had moved from West Point and the army into the ministry, had become the Episcopal bishop of Louisiana, and had not returned to military service until the summer of 1861, when Davis commissioned him a major general with the duty of mobilizing Confederate forces in the Mississippi Valley. Polk's later service under Bragg in Kentucky had produced in each general a low opinion of the other. Bragg had blamed his troubles in Kentucky on Polk, and the bishop-general, during a visit to Richmond in November, 1862, had made to Davis the suggestion about replacing Bragg with Johnston that now, on February 4, he put into writing.[14]

Bragg, like Polk, was a presidential favorite, but this dissension in the Army of Tennessee so perturbed Davis that he first ordered Johnston to investigate it and then in early March put him in Bragg's place. For several reasons, however—sympathy with Bragg, the desire to avoid even the appearance of self-aggrandizement, and perhaps also a preference for his old command of the Army of Northern Virginia—Johnston avoided replacing Bragg openly and then, falling ill in April, let the other general step back into power. So in the end, by the very narrowest of margins, Bragg stayed on as army commander. Obviously he had lost the "good opinion" of his generals— indeed Polk again urged Davis, in a letter of March 30, to replace him with Johnston—but he said no more about retiring voluntarily.[15]

Just after his retreat from Chattanooga, his prestige with his subordinates was further diminished by his conduct of operations around Lafayette. In this mountainous region during the second week of September Rosecrans carelessly exposed himself to defeat in detail by scattering his advancing army so that the corps of Generals Thomas L. Crittenden and George H. Thomas became isolated and vulnerable to crushing attack. It was a situation that would have made an able Confederate commander famous, and Bragg did try to take advantage of it, but one by one his opportunities slipped by, in a welter of delayed and confusing orders.

Hill was involved in the first of these failures. On September 9, at 11:45 P.M., Bragg ordered him to "send or take" Cleburne's division to join with General T. C. Hindman in attacking Union forces (belonging to Thomas's corps) that seemed to be trapped in a natural cul-de-sac known as McLemore's Cove. The attack was scheduled for the morning of the tenth, and Bragg's order was discretionary. He wrote: "If unforeseen circumstances should prevent your movement, notify Hindman."

It so happened that a number of circumstances not foreseen by Bragg, who was fifteen miles distant, did keep Hill from moving. Cleburne was sick, four of his best regiments were absent on other duty, and the mountain passes he would have to use were heavily blockaded with timber. Bragg's order had been nearly five hours in transmission, and when Hill received it at his headquarters near Layfayette at 4:30 A.M. on the tenth he estimated that it would be night before he could clear the route and march Cleburne's division a distance of eleven miles to meet Hindman. In his and Cleburne's opinion, it was impossible to carry out Bragg's order. Hill so notified both Hindman and the commanding general. Bragg then directed Buckner, who by now had joined the army, to execute the order originally issued to Hill.[16]

Command of the operation now fell upon Hindman. That night and the next day Bragg confused him with vague orders to attack; alarmed him with reports of other enemy forces moving near him; suggested that perhaps he should retreat; and left it up to him to decide what to do. Hindman delayed and wavered and finally, about midafternoon of the eleventh, made contact with the Federals in the cove. By this time Hill had cleared the passes and put Cleburne's and one other division in position to cooperate, but all that could be achieved was skirmishing with the rear guard of two escaping Union divisions.[17]

Once, during that dragging afternoon, Bragg started Hill on a frontal attack and then called it off, apparently in order to wait for Hindman to gain the Union rear. Perhaps this was sound tactics. Perhaps, on the other hand, it was one more exhibition of the hesitancy and vacillation that so often blighted Bragg's generalship. After the failure in McLemore's Cove he was still in position to smash the other isolated enemy corps led by Crittenden; but he delayed when he should have moved swiftly, then, on the basis of erroneous intelligence, struck out in the wrong direction, then delayed again, and in the end accomplished nothing.[18]

Small wonder that as musketry sputtered along the Chickamauga that crisp fall morning of the nineteenth, Harvey Hill listened to the familiar sound with as much apprehension as confidence. Gone was his initial tendency to discount negative criticism of his old friend, Bragg. Now, like Polk, Cleburne, and the others, he had been convinced by repeated experience that the major weakness of the Army of Tennessee was its commander. He may also have felt that the crossing of the Chickamauga, in contrast to Bragg's dilatory movements of previous days, was too hasty; that since Rosecrans had reconcentrated, Bragg ought now to wait for all his reinforcements to come up. Of the nine brigades that Longstreet was bringing from Virginia, only three, belonging to Hood, had reached the battlefield. Neither Longstreet nor one of his division commanders, McLaws, had arrived.

Hood was up, and had already crossed with his brigades. Longstreet and two of McLaws's brigades would arrive that night; but McLaws himself, with two of his own brigades and two of Hood's, would not get to the field in time to take part in the fighting. The maximum strength accruing to Bragg would be about 66,000 effectives and 198 guns. This was hardly a large enough force to run roughshod over Rosecrans's 58,000, backed by 234 guns.[19]

Yet one thing was perfectly clear—and the Confederate soldiers in the ranks knew it as well as their generals—the time had come to make a supreme effort for the Southern cause. If the Union army could be thrown back and driven, and followed hard and hit again, until it was no longer an effective force, the way would be open for the reoccupation of Chattanooga, and for a northward campaign that would do much to offset the disasters of Vicksburg and Gettysburg. If the war could possibly be won at this late season, now was the time to try—to strive without ceasing for decisive, overwhelming victory.

The men were ready. Lean, ragged, looking like scarecrows under their coating of grime from Georgia's dusty roads, they had long since lost their illusions about war, but not their conviction that they fought on the side of right and that they still could win independence for the South. Their ranks were shockingly thin. Brigades had shrunk to the size of regiments; corps were no larger than divisions at the outset of the war. Hill's corps, for instance, numbered less than nine thousand men.[20] But the soldiers of the Army of Tennessee had never

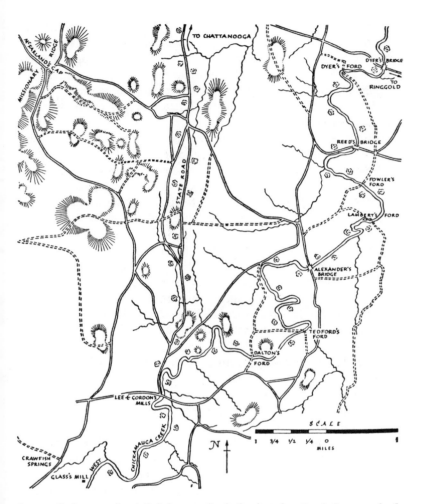

Scene of the two days' fighting, and of the interim Confederate misadventures, along the Chickamauga

lost their will to fight, and the knowledge that their total numbers had increased had lifted their morale. Whenever their generals ordered it, they would attack with élan.

So they crossed the Chickamauga, and the men in blue who believed *their* cause was right came to meet them, and underfoot the autumn oak leaves took on a deeper hue. The fighting of the nineteenth began shortly after 7 A.M. when General Nathan Bedford Forrest's cavalry, on the Confederate right flank, encountered units of Thomas's corps reconnoitering toward Reed's Bridge. Forrest skirmished and fell back, the Confederate infantry moved to his support, and the cannon and musketry roared into full-scale battle, which spread desultorily from right to left, as Bragg fed units piecemeal into the melee.[21]

All morning and into the afternoon Hill's corps stood idle except for one diversionary artillery attack that Hill, on his own initiative, made across the stream. Then Bragg summoned him to a conference and directed him to move Cleburne's division northward and to attack with it on the far Confederate right. Cleburne marched six miles, crossing the Chickamauga at one of the numerous fords, and got into position after sundown. As night came on Hill sent him forward, in concert with General Benjamin F. Cheatham's division, moving on Cleburne's left by order of General Polk. Heavy fighting ensued, with each side firing in the darkness at the flashes of the other's guns, and did not end until some time between 9 and 10 P.M., after Hill had enfiladed the Union line with artillery, and the Confederates had advanced perhaps half a mile.[22]

While this last action of the day was in progress, Bragg at his headquarters was conferring with Polk about plans for Sunday battle the next morning. To the courtly bishop-general, an impressively martial figure in battle-stained uniform and full gray beard, he announced the division of the army into two wings. Longstreet and Polk, as the two senior lieutenant generals, were to be the wing commanders. Longstreet had not yet arrived, but had sent word that he had reached Ringgold, to the east. He had changed from train to horse and was riding with two of his staff officers to the battlefield.

On the premise that Longstreet would safely complete his journey, though no guides had been sent to conduct him through the night over the unfamiliar roads, Bragg was assigning him the left wing, consisting of Buckner's corps, the divisions of Hindman and General Bushrod R. Johnson, and five brigades under Hood. Polk's right wing comprised Hill's corps, the division of General B. F. Cheatham, and a temporary reserve corps of two divisions under General W. H. T. Walker. Bragg gave Polk oral orders to resume the battle at daylight. Hill's far right division would attack first, and the others would follow successively from right to left in a general advance of the whole battle line.[23]

Bragg's reorganization of the army conformed fairly closely to the existing situation. Polk had commanded on the right that day, and Longstreet's troops, under Hood, had been concentrated on the left. With similar feasibility Bragg might have provided equal status for his other lieutenant general, Hill, by employing a tripartite organization, with Hill commanding the right, Polk the center, and Longstreet the left. General Polk, according to the biography of him by his son, William M. Polk, felt that the two-wing arrangement was a "needless affront" to Hill. "It came out in the conference," writes William Polk, that Bragg was "greatly irritated" with Hill because on the morning of September 10 he had not marched to join Hindman at McLemore's Cove. Another cause of irritation was Hill's " 'querulous and insubordinate spirit in general,' " as Bragg later phrased it. Bragg "left the impression," the author continues, that "to save himself contention in the emergencies of the battle," he would "ignore" Hill.[24]

Although William Polk served as an aide to his father at Chickamauga and presumably got his inside information from General Polk, this account of how Bragg felt about Hill the night of the nineteenth might be questioned for a number of reasons. The author does not give the source of his knowledge, and when he tells how Bragg's feelings were revealed he uses vague phraseology. Neither does he indicate whether he wrote from notes, years after the war and his father's death, or simply from memory. The writings of Hill and Bragg indicate that Bragg did not grow hostile toward Hill until some days after the close of the battle of Chickamauga. Moreover, Polk's biography reveals the bias of the son for the father and against those who differed with him, as Bragg had long before the nineteenth and Hill would on the twentieth and after. Still the fact remains that Bragg did ignore Hill not only in the reorganization of the army but also with regard to informing him what had been done. Hill, as William Polk points out, should have received notice from both Bragg's and Polk's headquarters that he had been detached from Bragg's immediate command and placed under Polk; but apparently Bragg left the notification entirely to the new commander of the right wing.[25]

Hill was well aware of his need of orders for the next day, and after Cleburne's night advance had ended and he had made his line secure he began a ride of four miles and more up the Chickamauga to Tedford's Ford, where the orders of the day stated Bragg's headquarters would be. Accompanied by his aide, Lieutenant Reid, and by another staff officer, Captain J. Coleman, he wearily guided his horse along the rutted country road that meandered beside the stream. Since dawn he had been in the saddle, and fatigue weighed heavily upon him.[26]

The night was frosty, the moon bright. Through the woods all around the soldiers had kindled campfires by the thousands against the growing cold. The smoke mingled with mist from the Chickamauga to create a thickening haze, diffusing the moonlight and the red glow of the fires, against which the forms of men and horses moved in wavering silhouette. The effect was weird, bewildering. Hill and his companions might have been wandering through some unearthly forest of black enchantment, where the wind in the shell-blasted trees mingled its soft rustlings with the sobbing cries of men whose flesh had been unmercifully torn, and the ground in the clearings revealed a ghastly fallen fruit: the grotesque forms and pale accusing faces of the dead.[27]

Before Hill saw the end of this eerie night, before the hands of his watch pointed to the hour of sunrise, 5:47 A.M.,[28] he would play his part in a bizarre drama of misadventure along the Chickamauga that would draw a sword of controversy across his military career. Unknowing, he went about the routine performance of duty. Learning from some soldiers on the way to the ford that Breckinridge had come up from the left, he sent Reid to find him and guide his division without delay to Cleburne's right. Then he and Coleman rode on.

They lost their way, rode too far and crossed at the wrong place, and did not get to Tedford's Ford until 11 P.M. or after. Bragg was not there and could not be found. His exact whereabouts seemingly is one of the mysteries of that most unusual night. What is known is that after Polk had left him he received Longstreet at his camp. Longstreet and his escort had also got lost, had blundered into Federal lines and escaped from hasty picket fire, and finally, after some vivid conversation about their thoughtless host, had managed to locate Bragg about 11 P.M., asleep in his headquarters ambulance.[29]

Awakened, he gave Longstreet his battle orders and instructions and then presumably returned to his bed. Near his campfire the new arrivals lay down to sleep. Hill could hardly have reached this spot around 11 P.M. without finding either Longstreet or Bragg. Perhaps Bragg had moved away from Tedford's Ford to a quieter campground for the night. Possibly Hill never reached his destination, but mistook another of the numerous river crossings for it. Yet he and several of his staff officers later testified he was at Tedford's, and surely they were familiar with the place that had been army headquarters that day.

Some time after the unsuccessful search for Bragg, Archer Anderson arrived at the ford with another staff officer, a kinsman of Hill's, Lieutenant R. H. Morrison. Anderson had encountered Polk in the road about 11 P.M., had been told of the new wing command, and had received from him an important oral message which he now delivered: "Tell General Hill I wish to see him tonight at my quarters as the fate of the country may depend upon the attack tomorrow." The message also directed Hill to go to Alexander's Bridge, where a courier would be posted to guide him to Polk.[30]

Alexander's Bridge was downstream, perhaps three miles off to the north as the roads wound, and Hill decided to rest before making the trip back. Was he suffering from the spinal pain that sometimes forced him to lie down until it diminished? He did not say, afterward, but wrote simply in his official report, "I was much exhausted, having been in the saddle from dawn till midnight, and therefore resolved to rest until 3 o'clock." [31] This was a mistake. Either he should have obeyed Polk's summons immediately or, if physically unable to comply at once, should have so notified Polk, preferably in writing. Instead he delayed without sending any message.

About this time Reid rode up, and reported that he had found Polk and Breckinridge together. When Breckinridge had learned of Reid's mission to guide him into battle position that night, he had said that his men were going into camp and that he preferred to let them rest, as they were greatly fatigued, but he promised to have them in position before daylight. Polk then said that he was in command of the right wing, and authorized Breckinridge not to move his division till near day.[32]

Hill, on hearing this, told Reid to start again on his mission at 2 A.M. Then the general and his staff officers rested and perhaps slept—while a courier searched for Hill, bearing orders dispatched by Polk.

From his conversations with Breckinridge and Hill's staff officers, Polk had gone to his quarters beyond Alexander's Bridge, on the east side of the Chickamauga, and had issued these orders under date of September 19, at 11:30 P.M. They directed Hill to "attack the enemy with his corps to-morrow morning at daylight." Cheatham, on Hill's left, was to "make a simultaneous attack." Walker's corps was to act as reserve.

In thus calling for a simultaneous movement of three divisions, Polk was hardly following Bragg's plan of attacking by successive divisions, starting first with the one on the extreme right. His orders took the form of a circular to Hill, Cheatham, and Walker. The various copies were given to couriers. One courier made delivery to Cheatham and returned, and Walker came to Polk's camp and received his orders in person.

The sealed envelope addressed to Hill was handed to a courier named John H. Fisher, an enlisted man. He later swore in a written deposition that after receiving the orders, about midnight, along with the information that Hill was "near" Tedford's Ford, he started his search immediately. During the search, he testified, he met both Cheatham and Breckinridge, who could not tell him Hill's whereabouts. "After going in every direction and inquiring of all the soldiers I met of his and other commands I returned to headquarters, after a search of about four hours, unable to find General Hill," he stated.

Nowhere in the deposition did he say explicitly that he *did go to Tedford's Ford*, and perhaps this is sufficient explanation of why he failed to find Hill. He concluded with the statement that he did not report this failure to the assistant adjutant general who had dispatched him, Lieutenant Colonel Thomas M. Jack, "as I understood from his clerk (Mr. McReady) that I was not to disturb him upon my return." This is an interesting commentary on the efficiency of staff work at Polk's headquarters.[33]

Polk himself was not at his best that night. Two couriers at least, responsible staff officers, should have been dispatched to Hill, one to move about in search of him, the other to await him on his battle line. Also, from the beginning, positive orders should have been given the headquarters staff that efforts to deliver the vital dispatches were to be not merely kept up but if necessary redoubled throughout the hours of darkness, until it was known for a certainty that all three generals had them in hand.

Moreover, the couriers posted to point the way to Polk's quarters could have been handled more effectively. To reach the general's camp, which also served as wing headquarters for the night, visitors from the battle area had to cross Alexander's Bridge to a point one half to three fourths of a mile beyond it, then turn onto a side road and go about one hundred yards into the woods. Without directions, anyone seeking the camp before daylight might be unable to find it; therefore Polk stationed one courier at the bridge and another at the fork of the road with orders to keep up fires and act as guides. After the courier at the bridge, J. A. Perkins, had guided General Walker to headquarters, Polk told him to return to his post to watch for Hill, and to remain there "for an hour or so." This is what Perkins later swore, under oath, and he further testified that he left his post about 2 A.M.

Of course guides should have been kept at the bridge until Polk returned to the battlefield Sunday morning. As commander of the whole right wing he might have been sought after 2 A.M., not only by Hill but by other officers or couriers bearing important dispatches. The courier at the fork of the road, L. Charvet, testified that he was "especially instructed not to move from that place until Generals Walker and Hill would have passed." He did not state how long he actually stayed. Polk's son, in his biography, said that all the couriers were withdrawn at 2 A.M.[34]

At 3 A.M. Hill, in accordance with his previous decision, left Tedford's Ford with Anderson, Coleman, and Morrison and rode to Alexander's Bridge. Coleman, who was acting as guide, rode ahead and searched about in the foggy darkness for Polk's couriers. When he reported he could find no one, Hill went on to his battle line, after ordering Morrison to locate Polk and inform him of this. What Morrison did afterward seems lost to the record. There is no indication that he found Polk in time to affect the course of events.[35]

By the time Hill reached his line it was a little after daylight. Reid had obeyed his orders to start again at 2 A.M. and guide Breckinridge, whose division was now in the process of filing into position on Cleburne's right. And still not one of Hill's officers had any idea that Bragg expected them, at daylight, to lead the whole army in attacking the enemy. Although Breckinridge had spent the latter part of the night at Polk's quarters, Polk had not told him of Bragg's orders. According to Breckinridge, the only reference to an attack was made as he was leaving, "some two hours before day light." Polk "expressed a wish that the attack should be made as soon as possible and expressed a fear that the Enemy would attack us." This must have sounded to Breckinridge like mere speculation as to what Bragg's plans might be.[36]

Hill could see for himself, as the light strengthened and the sun rose, that the right wing was hardly in condition to move forward. Cheatham's division was not properly aligned. Hill's own line ran from north to south, paralleling the Federal position in front, but Cheatham's line, instead of continuing southward from Cleburne's left, angled off to the west, so that Cheatham's left flank was turned toward the enemy. Cleburne, who rode up and down his divisional line more than once studying the situation, concluded that an angle of little more than ninety degrees was formed by the juncture of General James Deshler's brigade on his left with General Preston Smith's brigade on Cheatham's right. Hill noted that another of Cheatham's brigades, General John K. Jackson's, was also running east and west. Polk, he decided, ought to examine the whole line.[37]

Meanwhile, commissary wagons had arrived on the field bringing cooked food supplies of bread and meat. As the men had not eaten breakfast, and some regiments had been without food for twenty-four hours, Hill ordered that the rations be promptly issued.[38]

And now there appeared a galloping courier. It was Captain J. Frank Wheless of Polk's staff. He bore unorthodox orders, fresh and urgent from the commander of the right wing.

Polk, some time between daylight and sunrise, had suddenly become aware that Hill had no orders and that the battle had not begun. He himself should have been on his line much earlier to make certain his orders were properly executed, and now he should have mounted his horse and ridden posthaste with his staff to start the action. Instead, he sent word to Lieutenant Colonel Jack to write new orders to Generals Cheatham, Breckinridge, and Cleburne. These were produced, dated September 20 at 5:30 A.M., and handed to Wheless, who must have spurred his horse hard as General Polk, remaining behind, urged him to go "in a hurry." On the way to Hill's line Wheless had given Cheatham his copy of the orders.

The galloping captain was an earnest and rather officious assistant adjutant general. He thought that Hill must surely have been called to the conference between Bragg and Polk, that Hill had known all along of the plan for the daylight attack, and that Polk's written orders to him were simply confirmation of this knowledge. Therefore when he found Hill just back of his line, warming himself at a campfire and talking calmly with Cleburne and Breckinridge, he could scarcely contain his indignation.

Dismounting, he announced that he had orders from General Polk.

Hill held out his hand to receive them.

"These orders," said Wheless, "are for Generals Breckinridge and Cleburne," and he gave the dispatches to the division commanders, remarking to Hill that, "General Polk has had a staff officer [sic] hunting for you since twelve o'clock last night."

Cleburne and Breckinridge rapidly scanned the orders. One of the two then handed his copy to Hill with the remark, according to Wheless's later statement, "that the men could not go into the fight until they had their rations." Hill read the orders:

Major-General Cleburne,
Major-General Breckinridge:

Generals: The Lieutenant-General commanding, having sought in vain for Lieutenant-General Hill, gives you directly the following orders:

Move upon and attack the enemy so soon as you are in position.

Major-General Cheatham, on our left, has been ordered to make a simultaneous attack.

That was all, signed "respectfully" by Lieutenant Colonel Jack. There was no mention of Bragg, his orders, or his battle plan. Ironically, after all the order-giving, chance meetings, and riding about that had occurred since the close of the previous night's combat, Hill and his generals still did not know that Bragg had ordered an advance of the entire army, to start on the far right of the Confederate line at daylight.

What was clear was that Polk wanted Cleburne and Breckinridge to start an attack by the right wing "so soon" as they were in position. They were, tactically, in position, Breckinridge having completed the formation of his line after sunrise; but Hill thought of the morale of his hungry soldiers, of Cheatham's unsound tactical position, and of the fact that the Federals had built log breastworks, which ought to be flanked rather than assaulted frontally. He asked Wheless to take a note to Polk.

Wheless replied that if Hill had anything he wished to say he would "take pleasure in reporting it to the General."

Hill asked him again to take a note.

Wheless answered that if General Hill preferred writing what he desired to say, he would take a note for him.

Hill then sat down and composed his message upon a small square of paper:

September 20

General: I could find no courier at Alexander's Bridge, and therefore could not find you. My divisions are getting their rations and will not be ready to move for an hour or more. Breckinridge's wagons seem to have got lost. . . . It will be well for you to examine the line from one end to the other before starting. Brigadier-General Jackson is running from east to west. My line is from north to south. General Cleburne reports that the Yankees were felling trees all night, and consequently now occupy a position too strong to be taken by assault. What shall be done when this point is reached?

Respectfully,

D. H. Hill
Lieutenant-General

Wheless grew impatient as Hill slowly wrote the message, and said afterward that he was "about to call his attention" to the delay, when Hill rose and handed him the note. "Without the loss of a moment," as Wheless expressed it, he was on his horse and galloping back toward Polk's headquarters.[39]

Polk, meanwhile, had undergone an embarrassing experience. Toward 7 A.M. one of Bragg's staff officers, Major P. B. Lee, arrived at the camp beyond Alexander's Bridge and in behalf of the commanding general inquired why Polk's attack was delayed. Polk had to admit that he did not know, and that he had not been to the battlefield that morning. Bragg, describing the incident two days later in a letter to his wife, said that Polk was found "two miles from his troops sitting in a rocking chair at a house, waiting his breakfast," an accusation that was denied after the war by Polk's son.[40]

Whatever the descriptive details, Polk must have realized that he had got into a most awkward situation. He now set out for the battle-field, and on the way met Wheless, who gave him Hill's note. After reading it he dispatched a message of his own, bearing the time notation "7 A.M.," to Bragg's chief of staff, General Mackall:

General: I am this instant in receipt of my first communication from General Hill, who informs me that he will not be ready to move for an hour or more, because his troops are receiving rations and because his wagons were lost last night. The attack will be made as soon as he is prepared for it.[41]

This was hardly a full summary of Hill's reasons for delay. Nothing was said of the statements about Cheatham's misaligned troops, yet Polk now proceeded to take Hill's advice, and to inspect the line of the whole right wing, from left to right. When he reached Cle-burne, about 7:25 A.M., he asked him why he did not advance. Cle-burne answered that General Hill had ordered him not to advance until after the rations were issued. To this Polk made no objection, either to Cleburne or to Hill, who was also present. Thus Polk sanc-tioned Hill's delay. Neither did he mention Bragg's plan for a day-light attack. Perhaps he thought that Wheless had told Hill about it.[42]

What he and Hill did discuss was the alignment of the troops in the right wing. Hill declared that Cheatham's line adjoined his at very nearly a right angle. This matter was still unsettled when about 8 A.M. Bragg arrived—at last. Far better for all concerned would it have been if he had gone to the right wing at daylight to see his orders executed. Now he asked Hill why he had not begun the day-light attack, and Hill replied in surprise that he was hearing of these orders for the first time. Bragg then burst out angrily against Polk, saying, according to Hill's recollection long after the war, "I found Polk after sunrise sitting down reading a newspaper at Alexander's Bridge, two miles from the line of battle, where he ought to have been fighting." [43]

Hill felt, however, that Bragg ought also to share responsibility for the delayed attack. He argued in his official report that the army as a whole was not anywhere near ready to attack at daylight, that up to the hour of Bragg's arrival "the essential preparations for battle had not been made . . . and, in fact, could not be made without the presence of the commander-in-chief." Specifically he declared:

The position of the Yankees had not been reconnoitered. Our own line of battle had not been adjusted, and part of it was at right angles to the rest. There was no cavalry on our flanks, and no orders had fixed the strength or position of the reserves.

Moreover, he contended, the left wing needed so much adjustment that it was not ready to support the right when the attack finally did begin.[44]

In a number of ways the evidence sustains Hill's argument. Forrest received no instructions that morning with regard to the operation of his cavalry on the right, until Hill, sometime toward 8 A.M., sent one of his staff officers, Major A. C. Avery, to him with the request that he protect the right flank of Breckinridge's division, a request with which Forrest promptly complied. That the left wing was unready to support the right also seems plain. Indeed, Longstreet said as much in his official report. After telling how, at dawn, he went to find his troops, and how he shifted his line to the right and formed his brigades in a column of attack, he wrote: "Before these arrangements were completed the attack was made by our right wing about 10 o'clock." [45]

The question of the angle at which Cheatham's line adjoined Hill's seems to have been one that could not be settled at a glance in that undulating, wooded terrain. Polk, though he did not challenge Hill's view immediately following his own inspection, argued after the battle that Cheatham's main line nearly paralleled Hill's, and that Cheatham had only one brigade at an angle, a reserve unit, Jackson's, which Hill mistook for the front line. Presumably Bragg also inspected Cheatham's alignment, for he pronounced it correct.[46]

Yet the weight of the evidence sustains Hill's opinion that not only was Jackson's brigade misaligned but Smith's brigade of Cheatham's right formed an angle of nearly ninety degrees with Deshler's brigade of Cleburne's left. Hill after the battle collected certificates from Cleburne, two staff officers, Colonel A. J. Vaughan, Jr., who commanded Smith's brigade on the twentieth, and Captain Rhoads Fisher, who commanded skirmishers on Deshler's left. Collectively these documents, which are still extant, support Hill's opinion and show that when the two brigades advanced, Deshler's brigade passed over Smith's. Deshler, who was killed that day, believed with Cleburne that the angle was close to ninety degrees, and expressed this belief, before the battle, to both Hill and Polk.[47]

Bragg, of course, was burning with anger and impatience to begin fighting. The longer the delay, he reasoned, the stronger the Federals could make their breastworks. Hill believed that the best way to deal with the breastworks was to flank them by shifting the whole Confederate line about a mile northward under cover of the woods. He wrote afterward in his official report that "a simple reconnaissance before the battle would have shown the practicability of the movement and the advantage to be gained by it,"—referring apparently to the reconnaissance that he accused Bragg of not having made prior to 8 A.M. He also reported that about 8:30 A.M., after he had driven back Federal skirmishers on his right, he personally reconnoitered in that direction and found the Federal left flank unguarded by cavalry.

Bragg in his report mentioned no prebattle reconnaissance on the twentieth by himself, his staff, or his cavalry. He did mention Hill's reconnaissance, without referring to Hill by name, and said it proved that on the Confederate right the "main road to Chattanooga" was open. Thus his report, inadvertently no doubt, supported Hill's argument. But one of Bragg's military traits was tenacity in clinging to any battle plan he had adopted. He made no change that morning in the orders that would send his army straight toward the breastworks.[48]

More fortunate than the other units in the long Confederate line were the two northernmost brigades of Breckinridge's division. Reaching to a point on the extreme right some two miles northwest of Reed's Bridge, they extended beyond the Federal barricades, thanks to Hill's order of the previous night placing Breckinridge in position for a flank attack. Breckinridge's line from right to left consisted of the brigades of Generals Daniel W. Adams, Marcellus A. Stovall, and Benjamin H. Helm. Then came Cleburne's three brigades, commanded on the right by Polk's nephew, General Lucius E. Polk, in the center by General S. A. M. Wood, and on the left by Deshler. Across the whole Confederate front, paralleling it north and south, ran the state road from Chattanooga to Lafayette. It marked the general line of the Federal positions, which bulged out east of it in Hill's sector and receded west of it in Longstreet's; but owing to the thick woods and undergrowth the road, the breastworks along it, and the Union infantry and artillery waiting behind the log barricades were hard to make out from the Confederate side.[49]

The morning was growing warm as the sun climbed above the smoke haze and dispelled the last remnants of fog and frost. Hill's men, intently studying the shadowy outlines of the enemy wherever open space permitted, awaited with the stoic fatalism of veteran combat troops the order to advance. It came about 9:30 A.M., and Breckinridge's line went forward. Fifteen minutes later Cleburne followed, in accordance with Bragg's original plan for attack by successive divisions. Yet apparently in the haste to get started there was faulty staff work, for neither division commander understood that the divisions were not to move simultaneously, as Polk had ordered. Breckenridge was puzzled by Cleburne's absence on his left, while Cleburne scrambled to catch up and comply with what he later reported as an order to "dress on the line of General Breckinridge." [50]

After Cleburne had started, Deshler's brigade, as previously noted, passed over Smith's of Cheatham's division. Cheatham also discovered as he straightened out his angled line that the right portion of the left wing, formed by General Alexander P. Stewart's division, overlapped and blocked him. Such was the result of Polk's failure to take Hill's advice about Cheatham and of Bragg's neglect of the proper adjustment of the whole Confederate line. Apprised of this predicament, Bragg took Cheatham's division out and put it in reserve. The left wing did not move. Hill's corps advanced alone, except for Forrest's cavalry on the flank.[51]

Moreover, it advanced in a single line, for Polk had provided no supporting brigades. Hill looked on with deep misgiving and sent a note to Polk, "reminding him," as he later said, "that the corps was in a single line without reserves, and if broken at one point was broken at all points." No support, however, was immediately forthcoming.[52]

As Breckinridge's men swept forward, driving the Federal skirmishers rapidly before them, Hill followed with his staff. To his right, well beyond Breckinridge's line, he saw more Confederate troops advancing on foot.

"What infantry is that?" he asked a passing officer.

"That is Forrest's cavalry."

Hill had heard of the growing fame of the cavalry commander who had risen from private to brigadier and would eventually become a lieutenant general, but was unfamiliar with Forrest's unorthodox habit of dismounting portions of his troops and fighting them as infantry.

"Can I see General Forrest?" he asked.

The officer escorted him to the brigadier, who saw them coming and rode to meet them, a lithe, swarthy giant with iron-gray hair and black chin beard.

Hill, lifting his hat in a gesture of respect, said, "General Forrest, I wish to congratulate you and those brave men moving across that field like veteran infantry." Back east, he continued, he had become unpopular with the cavalry by joking about the scarcity of dead men with spurs on. But now he would aver that "no one can speak disparagingly of such troops as yours."

Forrest acknowledged the compliment with a modestly correct, "Thank you, General." Then with a wave of his hand he wheeled his horse, and galloped away with the tribute that was to become a favorite story of Forrest's Cavalry.[53]

Hill returned to his command. Most of Breckinridge's line was making good progress toward the Federal flank, but the regiments on the left of Helm's brigade had encountered breastworks. Helm— a Confederate brigadier with Union ties in that he and Abraham Lincoln had married half-sisters—had a reputation for combativeness and courage, and he now led an unsuccessful assault against the barricades, sustaining heavy casualties. He himself fell mortally wounded. His shattered brigade was sent to the rear by Breckinridge, who then, with Hill's approval, swung the rest of his line around the Union flank. Here the front ranks of the defenders broke, but without reserves Breckinridge was unable to press his advantage.[54]

Cleburne's troops, meanwhile, had come up against barricades on their right and right center, and had been stopped by canister and rifle fire from the unseen enemy.[55] Perhaps the better part of an hour had elapsed since Hill's line had started forward, and as yet no other infantry unit of Bragg's army had moved into combat. Hill saw blue-coated riflemen slipping into the gap on the left of Stovall that had been created by the withdrawal of Helm's brigade. That gap had to be closed! The Federals must be driven from it before they could find strong positions in the thickets and rolling terrain, and mount a deadly enfilade fire against the Confederates. Hill was aware that the brigade of General S. R. Gist, newly arrived from Rome, Georgia, was in his rear, and he sent a staff officer riding full speed to bring it up.

To his surprise, Walker and Polk and Walker's two divisions came

up with Gist. Walker later said in his report that Hill had sent for
him, whereas Hill said that his request for Gist's brigade was misunderstood. Walker had been marching to the right "by the flank"—
that is, in column of fours—when he learned of Hill's call for assistance, and he deployed his corps in battle line before hurrying it
forward. This must have taken time, considerably more time than
would have been consumed by the quick response of one brigade. Hill
indicated in his report that it allowed the Federals to get "securely
posted in the gap." [56]

Gist had been assigned to Walker by Bragg; and now on the
battlefield, as the fight raged between Breckinridge's brigades and
the newly reinforced Federal left, Walker put Gist in command of
his (Walker's) division, which then consisted of Gist's brigade,
under Colonel Peyton H. Colquitt, and of two others under General
Matthew D. Ector and Colonel Claudius C. Wilson. Walker's other
division, under General St. John R. Liddell, comprised Liddell's
brigade, under Colonel Daniel C. Govan, and the brigade of General
Edward C. Walthall.

Hill meanwhile asked Polk for permission to put Walker's divisions into the battle, and also requested another brigade to help
drive the Federals from the gap. Polk assented, saying he would get
the brigade. The one chosen was that of General John K. Jackson
of Cheatham's division; but Jackson, who received orders to advance from both Bragg and Polk, moved with great caution and
failed to reach the gap. Hill attacked without this additional
aid.[57]

He first ordered Colquitt to lead Gist's brigade into the gap and
support Breckinridge. Then, as Colquitt moved forward, Gist was
directed to follow and support him with the rest of the division. Thus
Hill formed a column of attack, consisting from front to rear of the
brigades of Gist, Wilson, and Ector. But all to no avail. Breckinridge
was driven back before Gist's brigade could reach him, and the canister and musketry from the breastworks, augmented now by enfilading
fire from the riflemen in the gap, wrecked the column of attack. Hill
ordered Gist to withdraw to a defensive position.[58]

Meanwhile on the far right, following the repulse of Breckinridge,
Hill had attempted a second flanking attack with Liddell's division.
Polk, however, had intervened, detaching Walthall's brigade and
sending it off to the left to support Lucius Polk. The remaining

brigade, under Govan, lacked sufficient force to accomplish much on the right, and retreated after a brief initial success.[59]

It was now past noon, and once more Hill had failed to breach the enemy defenses. But his efforts were actually not as fruitless as they seemed. The overlapping, flanking assaults that he had directed against the Federal left had caused General Thomas, who held that portion of the line, to call repeatedly for help, and had so alarmed Rosecrans that he had weakened his right in order to send Thomas reinforcements. During the resultant reshuffling of troops, ambiguous orders and confused maneuvering had created a gap in the Union right, a wide and fatal opening.

This occurred about 11 A.M., just as the Confederate left wing finally moved forward under orders from Bragg sent directly to each division commander. Into the gap by sheer chance swept eight Southern brigades, Longstreet's main column of attack commanded by Hood. The Union right crumbled. Some half dozen blue brigades, including General Philip H. Sheridan's entire division, reeled back under overwhelming flank fire and fled in whole or in part from the field. Rosecrans himself took horse for Chattanooga.

Yet the battle was far from over. Flying troops were rallied around their color-bearers and a new right wing was formed facing south on an east–west spur of Missionary Ridge. The left was still that strong north–south curve of breastworks that had stopped Hill's charges. Along these two disjointed lines the general on whom the Union field command had devolved, Thomas, began the stout afternoon stand that would change his military nickname from "Old Pap" to "Rock of Chickamauga." [60]

Hill must have listened with keen interest to the tumult of battle resounding in the woods off to his left, though he could not tell whether it presaged Confederate success or failure. He had charge of the troops in his sector, Polk having gone elsewhere, and shortly after the repulse of Govan's brigade he received news of a Union threat to his right. Forrest reported that he was skirmishing with a heavy Federal column coming down from the north and that prisoners he had captured identified it as "Granger's corps." Soon blue-coated skirmishers from the column engaged Hill's. There was every indication that the battleworn troops of the Confederate right would have to meet a flank attack.

Walker strongly urged Hill to retreat, but Hill decided this would simply invite the attack. He ordered the reluctant Walker, who was already angry because he thought his prerogatives as a corps commander had been ignored that morning, to stand firm on a north–south line, facing the breastworks, while Breckinridge swung around to an east–west position and confronted the enemy column. It passed by, harassed by Forrest's and Breckinridge's artillery, but a portion of it drove toward Cleburne. He opened with his guns and the attack ended. The enemy column, which proved to be General James B. Steedman's division of General Gordon Granger's reserve corps, moved on to the aid of Thomas. Then, while Hill's lines still held the right-angle formation against the possibility of further Union reinforcements from the north, an aide from Polk rode up. Escorted to Hill, he announced that General Polk had directed him "to order General Hill peremptorily to advance immediately on the enemy." [61]

Back of this surprising command were the activities of Bragg. He had evidently received word of the threat against Hill's sector, for about 2 P.M. he ordered Cheatham to march with his remaining four brigades to the support of Cleburne. Instead, Cheatham moved to the extreme right, well north of Cleburne, and apparently did not confide his specific assignment to Hill. Bragg meanwhile had gone to his left, had directed his checked forces there to continue their attacks, and had dispatched a written message to Polk, ordering him "to again assault the enemy in his front with his whole force." Polk's reaction was to send an aide galloping with the peremptory order to Hill.[62]

This neatly thrust upon Hill the responsibility for any delay, but it was one thing to order an immediate assault and another to be prepared to carry it out. In reply, Hill pointed out that the gap between Cleburne and the rest of his forces was still held by Federal riflemen, who could enfilade any Confederate advance unless they were first driven out and the gap closed. Polk then came up for a consultation.

According to the postwar reminiscence of one of Polk's aides, who witnessed this conference from some distance, learning nothing of what was discussed, it "lasted some time," was "not harmonious," and ended with Polk declaring warmly, as he left, that things would be done his way. Another of Polk's aides, his son-in-law, W. D. Gale, recalled in 1884 that "more than once" Polk exclaimed, "Oh! This man Hill! He is enough to drive me mad!" [63]

Be all this as it may, the fact remains that the attack was delayed while the gap was filled. Hill, by repeated orders, forced the still cautious General Jackson to bring up his brigade, driving the Federal skirmishers ahead of him, and Polk himself ordered Cleburne, about 3:30 P.M., to move forward and connect his right with the left of Jackson's brigade. Cleburne, too, had to drive Federal riflemen as he advanced.[64]

Another interesting fact is that Hill emerged from the consultation in immediate command of the whole right wing. Polk remained on the field, and gave at least one more order to Cleburne, but the official reports of the division and brigade commanders show that Hill was in charge. He himself later said that he was, by order of Polk, while Breckinridge went further and declared that this was the pattern of the whole day. Shortly after the battle he wrote Hill, with regard to the afternoon advance, "I did not hear Gen Polk direct you to assume command of all the attacking forces. I did receive the impression (from occurrences on the field) that you were during the greater part of the day in the immediate command of the columns of the right wing actually engaged in the attack." [65]

As for the plan of attack that was now followed, it was the type of operation that Hill had been advocating all along. Cleburne was ordered to bombard the Union line at the point where the barricades began angling back to protect the Federals' extreme left. Simultaneously, the rest of the right wing would attack the Union left flank in an assault column four lines deep. This column was formed on Jackson's right. Hill put Walker's corps in front, with Liddell in the lead, followed by Gist. He then asked Cheatham to attack with his fresh brigades in place of Breckinridge's riddled division, but Cheatham replied with a statement that offers an intriguing contrast to the order that Bragg had given him. He said, as Hill recalled, "My division was sent by General Polk as a support to General Breckinridge, and under my orders I can do nothing more than support him."

Time was passing. Hill spent none in argument, but went quickly to Breckinridge, told him what Cheatham had said, and asked whether his troops were ready to attack again.

"Yes, I think they are," said Breckinridge.

"Well, then," said Hill, "move promptly and strike hard."

Breckinridge then formed the third line in the column with Cheatham behind him.[66]

Once these dispositions had been made, action followed swiftly, the attack starting about 4 P.M. On the far left of the front line, Cleburne went forward and opened with his heavy batteries. Lucius Polk's brigade, moving in concert with Jackson's, came up against the breastworks near the target angle. A terrible volley from the barricades stopped the charge and drove the Southern line to cover behind the crest of a ridge. Polk called for volunteers to bring up batteries by hand—men could live where horses could not. It was done, and at a distance of less than two hundred yards double charges of canister blasted the Union line, which was already under enfilade and reverse fire from batteries belonging to General Buckner, on the Confederate left. Seeing the blue ranks waver, Polk ordered another charge. With a yell, his men sprang forward and overran the first line of breastworks. Jackson's brigade charged too, and joined in the savage fighting.

Union supporting columns came up fast. Cleburne drove them back with guns massed on a rise of ground. Seeing their support fail, the front ranks retreated, yielding two more lines of barricades to Polk's screaming men. The end was near. On the right, Hill's assault column reached the state road, where various brigades met stout opposition and fell back, only to re-form under the protection of Forrest's artillery and advance again, Breckinridge's men overrunning the north end of the barricades. To the south also, in Longstreet's sector, hours of bloody fighting had broken the Union defenses. Thomas saw both wings crumbling, and ordered a general retreat. It quickly became a rout.[67]

Hill, riding close behind his advancing lines, scarcely dared believe that the enemy was abandoning the field. As he entered the woods west of the state road, a messenger reported that strange troops were approaching. Hill spurred to the left to investigate—and caught sight of Buckner. The two Confederate wings had met.

When the troops realized this, the shout went up. Loud and wild and exultant, it rolled in floods of sound down the long lines and back again, echoing and reechoing in the darkening forest.[68] In the joy of it, men forgot thirst and fatigue and pain, forgot the blood-drenched nightmare they had lived through, stretched lips that were black from biting open powder cartridges, and shouted. Victory! Victory at Chickamauga.

XII

ENEMIES IN GRAY AND BLUE

IT WAS SUNDOWN when Hill and Buckner met and realized that the Federals had completely yielded the field of Chickamauga. In the fading light, Hill halted his troops along the line of the state road. He thought it unwise to pursue until the condition of the enemy was better known, and he wanted to be sure that Confederate units did not attack each other in the darkness.

After the moon had risen brightly, and scouts had reported no Union forces lurking in the forest, further action against the enemy might possibly have been undertaken had Bragg been present to make the decision. But he seems to have been nowhere near his victorious army. Indeed, if Longstreet remembered correctly long afterward, the Confederate commander, acting as though he thought the battle lost, had ridden off to his headquarters at Reed's Bridge as early as 3 P.M., and had not returned. Longstreet noted in his memoirs that this made him the senior general on the field. He did not follow the retreating Federals, he explained, because he "thought night pursuit without authority a heavy, unprofitable labor, while a flank move, after a night's rest, seemed promising of more important results." [1]

Hill believed that a "pell-mell" pursuit straight into Chattanooga the next day would wrest that important base from Rosecrans's demoralized forces and open the way into Tennessee. He went to bed with his corps prepared to move at dawn. The sun rose and the orders came: Bury the dead and gather up arms and equipment from the battlefield! [2]

Incredibly, Bragg was not pursuing. He certainly knew that his army had won the field, for if the shouts of the exultant troops had not convinced him of this, Polk had confirmed it first by messenger to Bragg and then in a midnight report that he made personally at Bragg's request. W. D. Gale accompanied his father-in-law to headquarters, and told afterward how the commanding general got out of bed to listen to the report, how Polk urged prompt pursuit before the routed enemy had time to reorganize and fortify at Chattanooga, and how Bragg demurred. As Gale remembered, Bragg "refused to believe that he had won a victory." [3]

Longstreet said in his official report that Bragg conferred with him early on September 21 and agreed to his suggestion of a flanking movement north of Chattanooga. Bragg in his report disputed this, asserting that "such a movement was utterly impossible for want of transportation." The suggestion, he declared, "was not even entertained." [4]

Whatever plan Bragg may have considered, whether Longstreet's flanking operation or direct pursuit, the fact is that he consumed several precious days in moving his army slowly and cautiously toward Chattanooga. Not until September 23 did he establish his headquarters on Missionary Ridge, overlooking the city. By this time Rosecrans, who had been completely unnerved by his defeat and had apparently been contemplating a retreat across the Tennessee, had pulled together his disorganized army and settled down to withstand a siege of Chattanooga behind strengthened fortifications. It was plain that he could not be easily dislodged, if at all, and that the Confederate advantage gained at Chickamauga had been lost.

The great two-day battle had been fought at terrible cost to both sides—16,550 in total losses for the Federals and 17,800 for the Confederates, with percentage losses in some Southern regiments reaching the astonishing figures of 60 to 68 per cent. But for all the good it had done the Confederacy, this ghastly drama of blood and death might as well not have taken place. Chickamauga had become a barren victory. [5]

The man chiefly responsible for this, in the opinion of many in the Army of Tennessee, was Bragg. Private and general alike blamed him for his slow movement after the beaten enemy, particularly his failure to pursue on the day after the victory. This was Hill's view. Rendering his final judgment after the war he said, "Whatever blunders each of us in authority committed before the battles of the

19th and 20th, and during their progress, the great blunder of all was that of not pursuing the enemy on the 21st." [6]

This feeling led Hill, shortly after Chickamauga, into derogatory criticism of his commander. He was "drawn out," as he later said, "by Gen Bragg's own officers, who had served long with him and knew him well," and certainly Polk, Cleburne, and Buckner, among others, were so dissatisfied with Bragg they were ready to get rid of him. Hill might also have added that a recent arrival, Longstreet, was openly disparaging the commanding general.[7] Yet in the old army game of caustic comment few could match Hill's sarcastic wit. His remarks got back to his old friend, and very likely for the sensitive Bragg they carried a special sting.

Just at this time Bragg was looking about for scapegoats to bear the blame of the fruitless Chickamauga campaign. Already he had demanded of Hindman an explanation of his conduct at McLemore's Cove, and now on September 22 he called on Polk to explain his failure to attack at daylight on the twentieth.[8] Next, on September 25, he wrote Davis, reviewing his recent operations. "Want of transportation for our increased force has seriously incommoded us and has caused delay," he said. "But our greatest evil is *inefficient commanders*. We failed to capture two Divisions of the enemy in McLemore's Cove on the 10th, first, by Genl Hill deciding the movement I ordered from his command, fifteen miles from me, impracticable, and failing to execute, then by a direct failure of Genl Hindman to obey my orders after a force under Buckner had taken the place of Hill."

He went on to blame Polk for failing to attack at daylight on the twentieth, and to characterize the bishop-general as "gallant and patriotic," but "luxurious in his habits," and slow and opinionated. "He has proved an injury to us on every field where I have been associated with him."

Nor was Hill any better. "Genl Hill is despondent, dull, slow, and tho' gallant personally, is always in a state of apprehension, and upon the most flimsy pretexts makes such reports of the enemy about him as to keep up constant apprehension, and require constant reenforcements. His open and constant croaking would demoralize any command in the world. He does not hesitate at all times and in all places to declare our cause lost."

Bragg concluded this attack with the declaration, "I write freely and candidly because the safety of our cause is involved, and but for the errors exposed we should now have no enemy in our front." In short, he was not to blame for anything; Hindman, Hill, and Polk had ruined his campaign.[9]

His letter was unfair to all three, and glaringly so to Hill. The difference in wording in the descriptions of Hill's and Hindman's conduct did not reveal the all-important fact that Bragg had given Hill discretionary orders to attack at McLemore's Cove, nor was there any hint of Hill's reasons for availing himself of the discretion allowed. Moreover, the assertion that Hill was "always in a state of apprehension," making alarming reports of the enemy on "flimsy pretexts," is not borne out by the *Official Records*, which contain an abundance of messages sent and received by Bragg's generals, including Hill. One charge, "croaking," does ring true, but it cannot be demonstrated that Hill's gloomily realistic appraisals of the South's military plight had demoralized his command. The evidence is all to the contrary.

In the letter, Bragg made complimentary references to Longstreet, Buckner, Hood, and Cleburne. Hood had suffered the battlefield amputation of a leg. His desperate wound removed him from a rapidly developing controversy. As for the other three, Bragg doubtless would have been less favorable toward them had he known that they would soon petition for his removal as army commander.

In that last week of September, it was his lieutenant generals, Longstreet, Polk, and Hill, who were most active against him. About the twenty-sixth, they got together and decided that the Richmond authorities should be informed of the need for a new commander. Longstreet then wrote Seddon, declaring Bragg incompetent and asking that he be replaced by Lee, while Polk wrote Davis of "the incapacity of General Bragg" and advocated his replacement "by General Lee or some other." Polk shortly afterward informed the President that "General Hill concurred in the necessity of this measure." [10]

In addition, Polk and Longstreet wrote Lee, urging him to put the Army of Northern Virginia on the defensive under a subordinate, and come west to command the Army of Tennessee. Rather ironically, Lee was writing Longstreet about this time, congratulating him on the Chickamauga victory, saying it was "natural to hear of Longstreet and Hill charging side by side," and expressing the hope that "Genl Bragg will be able to reoccupy Tennessee." The receipt, shortly afterward, of Longstreet's and Polk's pleas for a personal rescue operation must have come as an unpleasant shock. Lee waited weeks before replying, and then sent polite letters of declination.[11]

While trying to oust Bragg, Polk was also formulating his explanation of the failure to attack at daylight. He and Hill discussed events leading up to it, including the question of whether Polk had told one of Hill's staff officers about Bragg's orders for a daylight attack. Polk stated that "on meeting your staff officer in the road on the night of the 19th I communicated to him my orders." Hill replied, "If you communicated them to him, they were not communicated by him to me." [12] He was not in a position to say more, for he had not yet collected from Anderson and his other staff officers the certificates that disputed Polk's contention.

After this discussion, Polk sent his explanation to Bragg, under date of September 28. In it, he detailed his activities on the night of the nineteenth and the morning of the twentieth, with significant alterations and omissions, as follows:

1. He said that he communicated his orders that night to a staff officer of Hill's, unnamed, but did not mention Hill's statement that the orders had not been passed on to him.

2. He said that he posted two couriers as guides at Alexander's Bridge, but did not say when they were withdrawn. Neither did he mention a side road, and the courier posted to guide persons down it to the headquarters in the woods.

3. He said that the courier sent to find Hill, at Tedford's Ford, searched for him "through the night," and "returned about daylight, saying that he could not find him." Actually Fisher had searched from about midnight to about 4 A.M., and daylight on the foggy, smoky twentieth was very close to sunrise, 5:47 A.M. Polk did not say that Fisher did go to Tedford's Ford. He did not say that Fisher, on returning, had not reported his failure to find Hill.

4. He told of his direct orders to Cleburne and Breckinridge "to make the attack at once," but did not say that these orders contained no reference to Bragg's plan for a daylight attack.

5. In summarizing Hill's message to him on the morning of the twentieth, he mentioned nothing but Breckinridge's lost wagons and the delay due to the distribution of rations. He did not mention Hill's statement that he could find no courier at Alexander's Bridge. He

did not say that Hill had advised him to examine his line; neither did he reveal that he had followed this advice.

6. By the sequence of his statements, he indicated that he had first learned of Hill's concern over the angle in the line after he arrived on the scene. This was a "misapprehension" on Hill's part, he said. Hill had mistaken Jackson's reserve brigade for Cheatham's front line.

7. He gave no indication that after arriving in Hill's sector he had sanctioned Hill's delay, but simply explained the "misapprehension" and concluded briskly, "The order to attack was then repeated and executed." [13]

Some of these discrepancies may have resulted simply from carelessness; Polk had not yet obtained written depositions from his couriers and staff officers. But carelessness alone could hardly have produced so thorough an exculpation of Polk, and so neat an indictment of Hill. Hill's word for the explanation was "ingenious," [14] and perhaps that is the kindest term that can be applied to it.

Still Polk could not satisfy Bragg, who had firmly in mind certain other things not mentioned in the explanation, such as Polk's failure to go to the battlefield before 7 A.M. On September 29, he suspended both Polk and Hindman from command, and ordered them to Atlanta, Georgia, to await further orders. Shortly afterward he also preferred charges against each general, to the effect that Hindman had disobeyed orders to attack at McLemore's Cove on the eleventh, and that Polk had been similarly disobedient, as well as negligent, at Chickamauga on the twentieth.[15]

In suspending his two subordinates from command, Bragg had exceeded his authority, which was limited to arrest and the preferment of charges. Davis quickly called his attention to this, and also came strongly to the defense of his friend Polk. On September 30, after he had received Bragg's letter of the twenty-fifth, and telegraphic notice of the suspension of Hindman and Polk, he sent back over the wires his view of Polk's case. The "evil resulting from delay" should have been pointed out to Polk, and "confidence preserved by abstaining from further action. It is now believed that the order in his case should be countermanded." What should be done with Hindman, Davis did not say.

Bragg countered with the argument that Polk had furnished "an unsatisfactory written explanation" of the delay, and that his case was "flagrant and but a repetition of the past. If restored by you to his command," he added pointedly, "the amnesty should extend to all." He then suggested that Polk might be exchanged for Hardee. "Our cause is at stake.... My personal feelings have been yielded to what I know to be the public good, and I suffer self-reproach for not having acted earlier."

Davis now retreated slightly, remarking in a letter of October 3, "You have a much better knowledge of the facts than myself." However, he had not changed his mind regarding Polk, and the bulk of his letter argued the wisdom of avoiding damaging controversy by leniency toward the bishop-general, who seemed to possess "the confidence and affection of his corps." Taking high ground, Davis declared:

It must be a rare occurrence if a battle is fought without many errors and failures, but for which more important results would have been obtained, and the exposure of these diminishes the credit due, impairs the public confidence, undermines the morale of the army, and works evil to the cause for which brave men have died, and for which others have the same sacrifice to make.

Taking not-so-high ground, he continued:

I am at a loss to see how the delay of one general should be regarded as a higher offense than the disobedience of orders by another officer of the same grade [Hill], especially when to the latter is added the other offenses you specify, each giving point to the disobedience charged.[16]

Here, for Hill, was ominous portent. Clearly Bragg's attack upon him in the letter of September 25 had borne fruit.

Like the President, Polk was thinking hard about the safety of General Polk, and of what should be done next to secure it. Before leaving for Atlanta, he began seeking written depositions and statements from those individuals, including Hill, who had been involved in events leading up to the delayed attack. On September 29 he wrote Hill, asking him a series of questions designed to draw from him a full and explicit account of his conduct on the night of the nineteenth and the morning of the twentieth. Hill returned his answers in writing the next day, and in them presented an accurate report of what had happened, except that he placed the receipt of the direct order to Cleburne and Breckinridge later in the morning than this event seems to have occurred.

With regard to the time of receipt he said, "I think the order reached them about 7.30 A.M." Actually, Hill's note replying to this order seems to have been in Polk's hands by 7 A.M. Since Hill on the thirtieth had still not begun to collect his own written evidence (judging by the dates on the statements he later obtained) his memory could have been at fault. If so, it worked to his advantage, for the later the receipt of Polk's direct order to attack, the shorter the delay occasioned by Hill's instructions to proceed with the issuance of rations to the men.

On another point, Hill returned a truthful answer but one that did not tell all that had happened. To Polk's query, "Where were your quarters on the night of the 19th instant?", he replied that he was at Tedford's Ford "from 11 till 3 on the night of the 19th." He did not explain, as he later did in his official report, that he stayed at the ford until 3 A.M. because he decided to get some rest.

By the time he wrote his answers, Hill may have read Polk's explanation to Bragg, a copy of which was furnished him on the thirtieth,[17] and have decided that it would be wise to expose as little surface as possible. He might have been even more wary of Polk could he have read the letter that general wrote his wife shortly after reaching Atlanta. In it Polk confided that "General Walker . . . says it is ridiculous to suspend me for the omission of Hill," and he also wrote: "General Hill said to me: 'I take the blame of the omission to attack.' "[18] At what time or upon what occasion Hill said this, Polk did not specify. Certainly the remark does not appear in either his or Hill's official statements, and, as quoted by Polk, without qualification or explanation of any kind, it conflicts with everything that Hill wrote upon the subject.

In effect, then, the two lieutenant generals had become antagonists, but meanwhile feeling continued to run high against Bragg. It showed in a letter that Longstreet's chief of artillery, Edward Porter Alexander, wrote on September 30 to his father, telling how he had got everything ready the previous afternoon to carry out Longstreet's orders for a bombardment of the enemy lines around Chattanooga. The young colonel declared that "we could have made them leave the town but last night Gen Bragg countermanded the order and we are today in statu quo and no prospect of Braggs making up his mind what to do at all."

With the thought, indignation seemed almost to overcome Alexander, and losing a word here and there he scribbled an outburst against his commanding general that was far removed from the calm prose in which his classic *Military Memoirs of a Confederate* would be couched.

Every body—Lieut Genls even seem to feel disgusted at his incapacity which has let Rosecrantz's Army take its own time to retreat behind his works at Chattanooga, and allowed the fruits of a bloody but *decisive* and *complete* victory slip thro his hands. Gen Longstreet says the rout at Bull Run was no worse than that of the Yankees here and from it all we have gained but some 40 pieces of Arty and a few thousand prisoners— altogether not worth Hoods leg.[19]

Reading this, one might wonder whether Alexander had not caught a good deal of his indignation from Longstreet. Much more restrained, but revealing in its way, was the brief comment on the news of Polk's suspension that Corporal John Euclid Magee of Cheatham's division jotted down in his diary: "The wrangling has commenced. Old Bragg wants to vent his spite on some one." Bragg's quarrelsome ways were well known to his soldiers, who hated him as a merciless martinet.[20]

Among the generals, opposition to Bragg continued strong, and various fragments of evidence indicate that if any one general served as chief inciter it was Longstreet. McLaws flatly declared that Longstreet at this time headed a conspiracy against Bragg with the object of obtaining independent command for himself. It should be noted that the assertion was made privately in 1864, after Longstreet had preferred charges against McLaws for alleged military delinquency. Another witness, General Mackall, wrote his wife on October 10, 1863, that Longstreet was "talking about" Bragg "in a way to destroy all his usefulness." Three days later Mackall confided to his friend, General Johnston: "I think Longstreet has done more injury to the general than all the others put together. You may understand how much influence with his troops a remark from a man of his standing would have to the effect that B. was not on the field and Lee would have been." [21]

Further evidence appears in a note that Longstreet sent Hill on October 4. After informing Hill that the President's aide, Colonel James Chesnut, had just visited his headquarters, Longstreet wrote:

In a ten minutes' conversation I told him of our distressed condition, and urged him to go on to Richmond with all speed and to urge upon the President relief for us.

I suggest that it would be better for you and Buckner to see him and hurry him on. My interview was so short that I had not time to tell him we should have more troops. I think that I said enough of other matters, but it would be well if you and Buckner would also talk with him.[22]

This also indicates that now that Polk had gone, Hill and Buckner were Longstreet's chief allies. Hill seems to have been motivated simply by the desire to oust Bragg. In view of his previous experience with Longstreet, it can hardly be supposed that he was trying to make his old colleague of Seven Pines commander of the Army of Tennessee; and it is even more improbable that he entertained any delusion that he himself might replace Bragg. In all likelihood his preference for Bragg's replacement was his former commander, Johnston.

Army opposition to Bragg found expression that first week of October in a written petition for his removal from command which was signed by a number of generals. Addressing President Davis under date of October 4, the petitioners described the unfavorable military situation that had resulted from the "complete paralysis" that had stricken the Army of Tennessee after the victory of Chickamauga, asked for more troops to offset Federal reinforcements at Chattanooga, and politely requested the removal of Bragg for the "sufficient reason, without assigning others," that "the condition of his health unfits him for the command of an army in the field." Admitting their procedure to be "unusual amongst military men," they declared that they acted as patriots, from "a sense of public duty," and concluded with a plea for "such speedy action as the exigencies of the situation demand." [23]

The author of the petition and the full list of its signers seem to have remained a historical mystery down to the present day. In 1890 the federal government published in the *Official Records* what appears to be a copy of the original document. The copy does not show the names of the signers, but bears the following endorsement by William M. Polk: "Supposed to have been written by Buckner. Signed by Hill, Brown, Preston, and others." [24]

This has not been considered conclusive evidence of Buckner's authorship, for Hill has also been named as the writer of the petition.[25] He repeatedly denied, after the war, that he did write it, though he admitted, "I signed it willingly." His contentions were summed up in a letter that he wrote Longstreet in 1888, in response to Longstreet's request for information on the petition, to be used in his memoirs. "You may say on my authority, if you choose," Hill stated, "that Gen Polk suggested it and that Gen Buckner wrote it. I was ... the least prominent and active in the movement."

Eight years later, after Hill's death, Longstreet published in his memoirs this assertion with regard to the petition: "It was written by General D. H. Hill (as he informed me since the war)." [26]

The whole account in which this sentence appears is misleading, for Longstreet indicates that he had nothing to do with the petition though in fact he signed it, as the original document, preserved among Hill's papers, reveals. It is a four-page letter to Davis, the last page ending near the top, leaving space below for signatures. Just after the close, in the place where the writer of an ordinary letter would sign it, Buckner's signature appears with his rank of major general abbreviated beneath it—the customary official style, used by all the signers, of whom there are twelve. Longstreet's signature is boldy written just to the left of and slightly above Buckner's, so that the names of these two officers stand out as the leading signatures on the page. (See photocopy.)

There is only one signature beneath Longstreet's, that of Brigadier General Bushrod R. Johnson, a division commander in Longstreet's corps. Beneath Buckner's, nine other signatures form a column down the right side of the page, reading from the top as follows, with the added information of each officer's command given, where necessary, after his name and rank: William Preston, brigadier general, commanding a division in Buckner's corps; Archibald Gracie, Jr., brigadier general, commanding a brigade in Preston's division; Hill; John C. Brown, brigadier general, commanding a brigade in General Alexander P. Stewart's division, newly attached to Hill's corps; Marcellus A. Stovall, brigadier general; Randall Lee Gibson, colonel, commanding a brigade in Breckinridge's division; Lucius E. Polk, brigadier general; J. A. Smith, brigadier general, commanding two regiments in Polk's brigade; and finally, at the very bottom of the page, Patrick R. Cleburne, major general. Breckinridge had declined to sign on the grounds that his enmity toward Bragg was so well known that his motive in signing might be misconstrued.[27]

The position of the signatures supports Hill's statement that it was Buckner who wrote the petition. Hill further maintained, "I did not canvass for it or discuss it." Even so, he seems to have rendered special services to this anti-Bragg movement by acting as the custodian of the petition. It was left with him to be signed, one of his staff officers said long afterward, because "his headquarters were located at a central point on the line." This may well have caused Bragg to assume, when he learned of the petition, with "much distress and mortification," on the night of October 4, that Hill was its author and chief advocate.[28]

A somewhat cryptic note by Longstreet indicates that he had the petition in his possession at least part of the time. On October 12 he wrote Hill: "I don't think that there can be any use in sending this up after our conversation of last night. So I return it to you. The other officers who have signed it may desire to use it though I think that they will not." [29]

Longstreet did not say what he was returning, but presumably it was the petition. If so, considerable doubt is thrown upon his statement in his memoirs that this letter was "framed and forwarded to the President." Apparently the signing process consumed a number of days, and in the end the petition was kept by Hill, being filed among his military papers. Davis later indicated that he never saw it.

The decision not to submit it to Davis seems to have stemmed from his arrival at Bragg's headquarters to make a personal investigation of the controversy. Colonel Chesnut had telegraphed him, "Your immediate presence in this army is urgently demanded," and he had taken a special train from Richmond. Stopping overnight in Atlanta on October 8, he conferred with Polk. Since Polk on the sixth had written him another letter which not only excoriated Bragg but also laid the blame for the failure to attack at daylight wholly and emphatically upon Hill, it is probable that Davis went on from Atlanta with fresh doubts about Hill added to those that Bragg had already put in his mind.[30]

He reached Bragg's headquarters the night of the ninth. Bragg

*solely by a sense of public duty, pray that Your Excellency
will grant such speedy action as the exigencies of the situation
demands.*

*We are Respectfully
Your Excellency's
Obedient Servants*

Photocopy of signatures on the petition to President Davis, October 4,
1863, asking that General Bragg be relieved of command of the Army
of Tennessee.

discussed his troubles with him, and asked to be relieved of command, but Davis would not say immediately what he would do.[31] His next move was to summon the corps commanders of the army to a council. It was held in Bragg's headquarters tent, and must surely have been a most awkward gathering—Hill, Buckner, Cheatham, who was temporarily commanding Polk's corps, Longstreet, Bragg, and the President, an unbending Southern gentleman who looked very much the statesman, but whose gaunt, chiseled face, with tight-pressed lips and bunched jaw muscles above the wispy chin beard, betrayed the high tension with which he bore the burdens of office.

Maintaining now an amiable composure, he led the conversation from a discussion of military generalities to the question of whether Bragg should remain in command, and called for an expression of opinion by each of the corps commanders, then and there in Bragg's presence. Longstreet answered first, stating as he afterward put it, "that General Bragg did not seem the man altogether suited to command." Buckner and Cheatham followed with similar opinions. Then Davis questioned Hill, whose response was later described by Longstreet, in a letter written to Hill on the subject of the conference:

You who had been seated in rather a retired position from the circle was [sic] then called, when you moved your seat more into position forming the circle, [and] stated in substance, that you were particularly pleased when assigned to General Braggs Army, as you had served with him in the 3d artillery and had been favorably impressed by him, as to capacity and fitness for high command. After joining his army you thought that you had seen enough of his operations about Chattanooga to cause a change of your former favorable opinion.

Hill may also have been asked about the petition for Bragg's removal. He said, years later, that he spoke "in defence of it to President Davis," but did not specify whether this was in the conference or on some other occasion during Davis's visit. His action must have further inclined Davis and Bragg to regard him as the main instigator of the petition.

Through the conference, Bragg listened passively to the successive statements that he was incompetent, saying not a word but looking, as Buckner remembered, "a little confused." [32] Certainly it was a humiliating experience, yet he emerged from it triumphant, for Davis's final decision was to retain him in command!

In the face of the cumulative evidence that Bragg could neither win fruitful victories nor command the respect of his generals, the decision was indefensible. Davis, shortly afterward, sought to explain it to Polk, who in a letter of October 17 summarized the President's words as follows:

He says to me it is because of his difficulty in getting a successor. He is not satisfied to take either Beauregard, Johnson [Johnston], or Longstreet, and is not prepared to pass them all by to take a man of lower grade. He takes Bragg as he thinks as the best alternative and as he confessed with a very heavy responsibility, and he does it with his eyes open.[33]

How much Davis was influenced by lack of confidence in the generals he mentioned to Polk, and how much by his durable faith —for all his sense of "heavy responsibility"—in his old friend and favorite, Bragg, is a matter of conjecture. Having made the decision to retain him, he had to make others regarding the corps commanders. One tentative decision he had already made, and that was to find a corps command in Bragg's troubled army for another favorite, Lieutenant General John C. Pemberton, who had become anathema in the South as the surrenderer of the Vicksburg garrison of more than thirty thousand men. Davis had actually brought Pemberton and his staff with him to Bragg's camp, but gave up his unrealistic idea after inquiry revealed that no division in the army would suffer Pemberton as its commander.[34]

Another decision had to be made about Polk. When Davis left Atlanta to go on to Bragg's camp, he still hoped to smooth over the Bragg–Polk difficulty, and Colonel Chesnut remained behind and talked with Polk about returning to his corps command. Vociferously Polk declared that one of the few things he would not do to serve his country was to subordinate himself again to Bragg, whom he denounced as a "weakling," and a man whose "integrity of character and military capacity" were "of the lowest order." To this stand Davis acquiesced. When he came back through Atlanta he indicated to Polk that the charges against him would be dismissed and that new duty would be given him.[35]

Still another decision, whether necessary or not, was made with regard to Hill. It was to relieve him from command. Under date of October 11 Bragg addressed to Davis, at army headquarters, the following request:

His Excellency the President:

Sir: With a view to the more efficient organization and command of this army, I beg you will relieve Lieutenant-General Hill from duty with it. Possessing some high qualifications as a commander, he still fails to such an extent in others more essential that he weakens the *morale* and military tone of his command. A want of prompt conformity to orders of great importance is the immediate cause of this application.

Davis's brief reply was made while he was still with the army, and was dated October 13, the day of his departure for Richmond:

General: I have received your application of the 11th instant, for the removal of Lieut. Gen. D. H. Hill from a command in the Army of Tennessee. Regretting that the expectations which induced the assignment of that gallant officer to this army have not been realized, you are authorized to relieve General D. H. Hill from further duty with your command.[36]

Aside from the place notations showing that Bragg and Davis were together at army headquarters, there was nothing in this correspondence to indicate collaboration in the decision to remove Hill. The different dates suggest that Bragg had independently decided to make his request, and that Davis had independently pondered and approved it. But was the deed really done that way?

Hill did not think so. He believed ever afterward that an attempt had been made to form a "coalition" against him—that Bragg had proposed to make him "responsible for Polk's supposed delinquency," and to give his corps to Pemberton while returning Polk to command, thus doubly pleasing the President and at the same time acquiring a scapegoat. "Pemberton," he said, "was actually tendered my corps." He was convinced, however, that Polk never agreed to the scheme, and that "Pemberton also declined, when he found the Division Commanders adverse to him." Evidently he discussed this view with his division commanders, for on October 26, after he had been relieved and had gone home, he wrote Breckinridge to say that in Atlanta he had met Polk, "who professed much friendship and kindness," and that he regretted having spoken "unkindly" of Polk in regard to the coalition. "Please mention the matter to Genl Cleburne," he wrote, "and tell him that I am now convinced that Genl Polk never became a party to it." [37]

Hill's concern here not to wrong Polk stands in marked contrast to the statements about Hill that Polk had made to Bragg and Davis. As for Hill's coalition theory, it harmonizes with the fact that Polk did rebuff efforts to persuade him to return to his command; and furthermore, while the standard historical interpretation of the Pemberton incident has been that Pemberton was offered Polk's corps, there seems to be no evidence that he could not also have been offered Hill's. Also in harmony with Hill's view is a bit of information written by Mackall, on October 13, to his friend Johnston: "Pemberton consulted me about staying here in command of a corps. . . . He told me B. wanted him to stay." [38]

After Hill's letter to Breckinridge had been published in a historical magazine in 1872, Bragg furnished Davis with a copy whereupon Davis wrote him a somewhat different version of the Pemberton incident. Without explicitly calling Hill's view erroneous, Davis indicated that it was he who had taken the initiative in seeking a corps for Pemberton—which corps was not specified—and that Bragg from the first was dubious of the idea. He also remarked that his decision to retain Bragg had made "other changes" necessary, and added: "I found then as on other occasions that your views and recommendations rested on facts which had been developed and pointed only to the efficiency of the army as the object." [39]

On balance, then, it appears that Hill may not have been correct in every detail of his coalition theory, but probably did grasp a considerable amount of the truth. In any case, the fragmentary evidence of an attempted coalition, or of the degree of collaboration between Bragg and Davis, is not so important as the surface facts: that these two high officials did agree to remove Hill, alone of the corps commanders remaining in the army, and that they carefully recorded the decision in official correspondence that provided a severe, secret indictment of his military competence. It was no trivial matter to accuse a lieutenant general of weakening "the morale and military tone of his command," and of failing in "prompt conformity to orders of great importance." Such charges, made by the commanding general and accepted by the President, were enough to destroy the reputation of any officer in the army. Yet Bragg did not believe in them sufficiently to stand on them in a face-to-face conversation with Hill.

Hill of course did not know that the charges existed. What had surprised and disturbed him was the sudden issuance from headquarters of special orders, dated October 15, which relieved him from command and directed him to report to the Adjutant General in Richmond.[40] He went to Bragg on the sixteenth to ask what it was all about, and prudently took Archer Anderson with him as a witness. According to an official certificate that Anderson wrote and signed immediately afterward, paraphrasing the conversation in full detail, Hill began it by asking why he had been relieved, and Bragg replied

that it was in pursuance of an application which he made to the President after his arrival here, when he ascertained that he was to retain command of this army, for authority to relieve Genl Hill upon the ground that his removal would contribute to the harmony and efficiency of the Service; that he stated at the time to the President that he made no charge or imputation against Genl Hill.

No charge or imputation! To be sure, Bragg had not openly preferred charges, based on precise specifications, as he had done with Polk and Hindman; but he had made charges nonetheless, and his accusations, formally presented and accepted over his and the President's signatures, rested securely in the official military records of the Confederacy.

Hill was not satisfied with Bragg's reply. He asked what was meant by the words, "contribute to the efficiency of the service." Bragg answered that "he distinctly disclaimed making any charge or imputation of military offense," but added that there had been times when he thought his orders to Hill "had not been executed as they should have been," and gave as an example the McLemore's Cove incident. Significantly, he did not mention the battle of Chickamauga. Instead he went on to say that the incidents which had displeased him "had been passed by at the time and he did not intend to make them the subject of complaint—his request to the President to relieve Genl Hill was based upon the idea that a commander could not successfully conduct operations, if he was not sustained by the cordial co-operation of his Subordinates, and upon the belief (founded upon recent occurrences, and reports he had received of previous expressions on the part of Genl Hill of want of confidence in him) that he could not expect such support from Genl Hill: he had known there was dissatisfaction with himself, and had asked the

President to relieve him from the command of the army: that he had been refused, and the only course left for him was the one he had taken."

Hill was not disposed to accept this explanation. As Anderson recorded, he "inquired why he had been singled out for removal from those officers who had expressed want of confidence in the commander of the Army. To this question I heard no reply."

The answer, however, seems fairly clear. Bragg had long been unpopular in the South, and fruitless Chickamauga had not helped him with the public. He could not now remove all four of the officers who had criticized him to the President, Longstreet, Hill, Buckner, and Cheatham, without revealing to the public how completely he had lost the confidence of his senior generals, nor could he continue to blame Polk for Chickamauga—Davis would not allow it. By removing Hill alone he safely got rid of a hated critic whom he seemed to regard as responsible for the petition against him, and he acquired another scapegoat in place of Polk.

Hill went on to say that if Bragg was referring to the petition requesting "that the command of the most important Army in the Confederacy might be committed to Genl Lee or Genl Johnston" he would admit that he had signed "that paper with great reluctance and as a matter of simple duty." This was evidently his own interpretation of a passage in which the petitioners had asked Davis to "assign to the command of this army an officer who will inspire the army and the country with undivided confidence." Hill said no more on the matter, but continued with the declaration that he had not expressed a lack of confidence in Bragg "prior to the battle." This was

impossible, as he had never felt want of confidence until on the morning of the battle he found the General in Chief had failed to protect his flank by cavalry, had made no reconnoissance before ordering the attack and had not arranged his lines in person, thereby causing the unnecessary loss, in his [Hill's] opinion, of ten thousand men.

By now Hill may have been speaking pretty heatedly. The assertion that he had "never felt want of confidence" in Bragg prior to Chickamauga seems more emphatic than accurate, and surely it was the very essence of tactlessness to accuse Bragg to his face of causing ten thousand unnecessary casualties. Hill further declared that he had not executed the order to attack at McLemore's Cove because "it was impossible," and then asked Bragg to clarify his charges. Bragg, he argued,

must be sensible that to relieve an officer immediately after a great battle upon the vague statement that his removal would promote the harmony and efficiency of the service—and this with the sanction of the President, would very seriously damage his reputation, and that the very vagueness of the reason assigned would give rise to a thousand imputations: cowardice, mutiny, want of conduct or skill, etc.

He therefore requested that the reasons for removal be put in concrete form, so that he could defend himself.

Here Genl Bragg repeated that he had no charges to prefer against Genl Hill, and distinguished his case from that of Genl Polk and another officer against whom he had preferred charges: he then added that he would not have asked for Genl Hill's removal for anything which occurred up to the close of the battle.

Genl Hill requested that he should put this in writing.

Genl Bragg replied that he would do it when application was made in writing through the proper official channel.

So the conversation ended. According to Ratchford, when Hill got back to his own headquarters he said to Anderson: "General Bragg is not going to give me that statement in writing, and I want you to sit down and write out our conversation just as it occurred and sign it officially"—which Anderson did. Hill's prediction proved correct. Although that same day he sent his application through channels, requesting that the reasons for his removal be furnished him in writing, Bragg declined to do so.[41]

Thus were Hill's efforts at self-defense blocked, and thus did Braxton Bragg repeatedly deny his own belief in the grave charges he had written into his request for Hill's removal. His intent to deceive Hill in their interview is obvious, yet the evidence strongly indicates that he told the truth when he said he would not have asked for Hill's removal "for anything which occurred up to the close of the battle." After all, his first formal accusations had been made not against Hill but against Polk and Hindman, and he had preferred charges against Polk *after* receiving the explanation in which Polk attempted to throw all blame on Hill. When ultimately he did move against Hill—after it was clear that a new scapegoat was needed

—he made his charges secretly and concealed from Hill their true nature. Moreover, as will be seen, when he later commented officially, in writing, on the reason for Hill's removal he ascribed it mainly to Hill's post-battle opposition to him, implying that he held him chiefly responsible for the petition to Davis.[42]

Further evidence, which harmonizes well with Anderson's certificate, is given by Lafayette McLaws. On learning of Hill's removal, McLaws went to army headquarters to say a good word for his old friend. In view of Bragg's reputation for vindictiveness this was an act of courage, but the commanding general seemed willing enough to explain his action. As McLaws wrote Hill several months later:

He told me that you had been removed at his own personal request . . . that the President had informed him that he must remain in command . . . and Genl Bragg then told him that if he was to remain, you must leave, and the President confirmed the order. Genl B. told me that personally he had the kindest feelings towards you, that he had no charges to make against you, but that you and himself could not be together, and more of this import. I spoke of your past services and your reputation as a gallant soldier, etc., but he turned the subject.

From the conversation McLaws concluded that Bragg had not removed Hill for his conduct at Chickamauga but for "your opposition to him as Commander of the army." He further wrote:

You were, as you always are, open and outspoken and made no secret of your opposition to him—and you were looked on as the head and front of the coalition against Genl B. I have no doubt but that all your sarcastic remarks, if you made any, were repeated to Genl Bragg, and that he felt personally aggrieved at your conduct—I remarked to Genl B. that such were your characteristics, and that you often made biting speeches, not in any malicious spirit or to create discontent, but that it was your humor and those who knew you well, did not regard but . . . he again turned the subject and I bade him good morning.

Finally, in this letter, McLaws made an interesting suggestion about Longstreet: "You may be able to trace back Bragg's opposition to you, to a probability that Genl Longstreet excused his opposition to Bragg by quoting your judgment and sayings as having influenced him, in forming his opinion." Again it should be noted that by the time McLaws wrote this he and Longstreet were enemies, yet the thought acquires additional weight when considered in the light of what Longstreet said of Hill in his memoirs.[43]

If it be concluded, from all this evidence, that Bragg did not much believe in the charges he leveled against Hill, why did he make them? They were not necessary for Hill's removal, for Bragg and Davis had ample authority to relieve him from command without mentioning any reasons. Probably Bragg made them partly to strengthen his request to Davis; partly to protect himself more completely by branding Hill in writing as his scapegoat; and partly to obtain revenge.

In the whole affair Hill was not blameless. It does seem logical to take the blame for Chickamauga from his shoulders, for the slow, uncoordinated attacks on the morning of the twentieth cannot be ascribed to his slackness any more than to that of Bragg, Polk, or Longstreet, and on the positive side he contributed greatly to an overwhelming victory, of which Bragg failed to take advantage. After the battle, however, he had as a matter of simple fact—whatever his patriotic motives—openly opposed his commanding general and thus made himself liable to punitive action. If Davis had decided on equal punishment for Hill, Polk, Longstreet, and all the others known to have cooperated in trying to oust Bragg, one might question the wisdom of the decision yet still see justice in it. A presidential reprimand to each of these subordinates would have maintained even justice and bolstered Bragg without revealing to the public the extent of his troubles with his generals.

But Davis, who of course made the ultimate decisions in the matter, did not administer even justice. On the contrary, he allowed Bragg to stigmatize Hill before the public as the one officer to blame for the terribly costly, barren victory of Chickamauga. The removal of Hill only, while Polk was cleared, was enough to brand Hill as the culprit, and surely Davis was not blind to the fact that this provided a scapegoat for his two close friends, Bragg and Polk.

Singling out Hill in this manner was not justified, even though Davis may have regarded him as the chief instigator and author of the petition against Bragg. The President could hardly be certain that Hill had played these roles, and even if he felt sure that he had, why should he attach more culpability to the petition than to the letters against Bragg that Longstreet and Polk had written?

Could Davis have reasoned that all the others who had attacked

Bragg were at least able generals, whereas Hill was not only a trouble-maker but an officer of doubtful competence? Perhaps; for both Bragg and Polk had assured him that Hill was guilty of serious failures as a commander. But if this was what Davis thought, why did he condemn Hill without proper investigation? Though he had only slight personal acquaintance with him, he had seen him risk his life for the Confederacy in battle after battle, compiling a long, distinguished record as a field commander; and he personally had promoted him to the high rank of lieutenant general. He owed it to him—the Confederacy of which he was President owed it to him—to provide the most careful investigation before pronouncing him incompetent.

Yet apparently Davis during his visit to the army made no effort to obtain from Hill and his subordinates *their* accounts of Hill's conduct in the Chickamauga campaign—a procedure that would surely have revealed that Bragg and Polk had not reported the whole truth. Apparently he derived his information almost entirely from the conference with the senior generals, from what Bragg and Polk wrote and told him about Hill, and—perhaps—from what others said against Hill when they saw that Bragg was to remain in command. One of Hill's generals, Breckinridge, did go to Davis and strongly endorse Hill, but seemingly such statements, even from a man of Breckinridge's stature, could not move the President to probe further into Hill's side of the controversy.[44]

If this was inadequate inquiry, affording Hill little opportunity to speak in his own behalf, it was in keeping with the peculiar nature of the allegations filed against him. These rather vaguely worded, cleverly destructive accusations, presented and accepted not as formal charges but as remarks incidental to the request for Hill's removal, could be technically interpreted as not amounting to action against which Hill would have the right to defend himself in military court; and of course the secrecy of the whole procedure made it virtually impossible, at the outset, for him to challenge Bragg. In effect, without even knowing that it had happened, he had been accused, tried, convicted, and sentenced to professional disrepute in the official records of the Confederacy and in any history that might be written from them. As severe punishment with maximum safety and minimum effort for the punishers it could hardly have been excelled. It enabled Bragg and Davis to turn to other affairs in the comfortable knowledge that Hill would never appear in military court to ask embarrassing questions about Bragg and Polk and the President who championed them. That had been forestalled and the case was closed, with no loose ends, except possibly a few in the realm of conscience.

On the day of his futile interview with Bragg, Hill issued a brief, appreciatory farewell to his troops in which he declared it to be his "honest conviction that the corps has no equal in the service"; and about forty-eight hours later he left the Army of Tennessee. "It pained me inexpressibly to part with the Corps," he admitted, but at least he could take comfort from the warm testimonials to his ability that came from his fellow officers.[45]

Breckinridge sent Hill a note expressing "sincere regret at our separation," and stating, "I have had more than one occasion to express my admiration of your fidelity to duty, your soldierly qualities and your extraordinary courage on the field." Another note came from Longstreet, who said in part: "I am surprised and grieved to learn that you have been relieved from duty with this army. We have stood side by side in so many severely contested battlefields that I have learned to lean upon you with great confidence."

And there were numerous other letters and testimonials from the other two division commanders, Cleburne and Stewart, and from most of the brigadiers in the corps. All wanted to tell Hill that they still had full confidence in him and regretted losing him as their commander, and in saying this a number of the writers allowed considerable feeling to show through formal military style. Cleburne, after thanking Hill for his "uniform kindness," wrote:

Allow me . . . to express to you the sincere regard and high confidence with which in so short a time you succeeded in inspiring both myself and, I believe, every officer and man in my command. . . . Though your connection with this army has ended you still retain undiminished the love, respect and confidence of Cleburne's division.

And Stovall declared:

I had frequent opportunities of witnessing the energy, promptness, and judgment displayed in the discharge of the duties of your responsible office, the care for the welfare and comfort of your men, the coolness and skill manifested by you in the disposition of your troops on the battle field; all of which has won for you the confidence and esteem of both the officers and privates of this Brigade.

And Lucius E. Polk said:

In behalf of myself and brigade, allow me to express to you our high appreciation of your uniform kindness in all of your official intercourse with us, and to say to you that although you have not been long with us, you have gained our love, confidence and respect.... Our confidence in you as a soldier, gentleman and patriot has not been in the least diminished. We part with you, General, with the greatest regret, and hope some new field may be given you for the display of that generalship that led us to victory at Chickamauga.

So, one after another, the spontaneous tributes piled up— "Actual observation . . . has convinced me of your excellence as a commander, and worthiness as a man"— "The warm devotion that has been created in so short a time will not die while memory lives"—in all, an extraordinary outpouring of affection and esteem.[46] What other corps commander on either side in the Civil War ever received a more impressive endorsement from officers he had led in battle? And yet materially it availed Hill nothing. He was leaving the Army of Tennessee as the scapegoat of Chickamauga, officially condemned as an officer who had weakened "the morale and military tone of his command," and had, in general, failed as a corps leader.

His apparent guilt was accentuated by the favorable treatment accorded Polk and Hindman, both of whom had countered Bragg's charges by formally requesting courts of inquiry into their respective cases. Polk was relieved from duty with the Army of Tennessee and sent to Johnston's Department of Mississippi in exchange for Hardee. Davis then wrote him on October 29 that both his application for a court of inquiry and Bragg's charges against him were dismissed, ending the personally signed letter with a statement of confidence in Polk: "Your assignment to a new field of duty, alike important and difficult, is the best evidence of my appreciation of your past service and expectations of your future career." Next, Bragg wrote Davis, expressing satisfaction with the action in Polk's case and asking similar treatment for Hindman, whom he now praised as a distinguished fighter at Chickamauga and a gallant soldier possessing "my fullest confidence." The request was granted, after which the understandably distrustful and still dissatisfied Hindman was sent back to duty under Bragg.[47]

Meanwhile the newspapers of the Confederacy were explaining that the general really to blame for the barren victory of Chicka-

mauga was Hill. Southern readers were told that he had delayed the
Sunday morning attack three hours by refusing to fight until he had
fed his men, an act for which he deserved to be "cashiered." The
proof of his delinquency was his removal from command following
the President's personal investigation. Some of these stories, in Hill's
opinion, were inspired by "Polk and his friends for him"; but whether
the army correspondents got their information from Polk or Bragg
or talkative headquarters clerks and staff officers or from all combined the result for Hill was the same: professional disgrace in the
eyes of the Southern people.[48]

The first weeks of November found him in Richmond trying to
obtain new duty and to salvage his reputation. On the thirteenth he
addressed to Adjutant General Cooper a formal application for a
court of inquiry, basing his request not on Bragg's charges, of which
he was still ignorant, but on the "implied censure" inherent in his
removal from command "immediately after a great battle." [49] About
the same time he obtained a private interview with Davis. As he
stated his case to the President, he exhibited his collection of documents showing what had really happened at Chickamauga with
regard to Polk's orders for the daylight attack, the angle in Polk's
line, the feeding of the troops, and the lone fight waged by his own
corps before any other infantry advanced.

Davis grew irritated. Hill pressed his argument. As he later described it, he told the President that

he had made an unjust discrimination between me and Genl Polk. I said
that we had both been relieved on the same ground, but that he had
quashed the charges against Polk, written him a complimentary letter and
given him a new command, while he had kept me out of the field and
thus virtually sustained Polk's statement that the fault at Chickamauga
was mine and virtually endorsed Bragg's treatment of me. I tried to be
calm and respectful and think that I was so, though my language was
plain and earnest. He became very angry and was insulting in language
and manner. He was not only impolite, but ungentlemanly in his rudeness.

Hill also told Davis, in this stormy session, that Bragg had "stated
that he had no fault to find with me as a soldier." To this Davis
seems to have retorted that Bragg had written him to the contrary.
Hill later said, with reference to Bragg's letter requesting his removal, "I became aware of the existence of this letter in my conversation with Mr. Davis." [50]

Perhaps it was only coincidence that soon after this heated interview Hill received a disappointing notification from the Adjutant General. Under date of November 16 Cooper wrote:

General: Having applied for a position equivalent to your rank, on being relieved from duty with the army under General Bragg, I regret to inform you that there is no command to which you could at this time be assigned without displacing other officers already in command.

Until a suitable opportunity is offered for placing you on duty according to your rank, you will consider yourself authorized to dispose of your time in such manner as may best suit your convenience, reporting your address monthly to this office.[51]

That same day, in a long letter to Davis, Hill detailed his arguments for a court of inquiry. "I deeply regret that I was so unfortunate as to give offense in the interview the other day," he began. "I do not wish to seem ungrateful for past kindness and favor. But the refusal to grant me a Court of Inquiry must seriously affect me in the eyes of the country; in regard to it, I would make this appeal to your well-known sense of justice." He then pointed out that he alone had been removed from command although other generals "had equally expressed want of confidence in Bragg," and that the difference in the way he and Polk had been treated branded him before the public as "the real delinquent in the Sunday morning affair. If so," he continued, "I ought to be punished for it and the Court is necessary to establish the facts. If not, my innocence ought to appear and a Court is equally necessary." However, if Davis would not grant the Court, Hill was willing "to abide by your written expression of opinion in regard to my conduct while with the Army of Tennessee."

In the course of his argument he declared that he had been removed from command "for expressing want of confidence in Genl. Bragg," adding that Bragg himself "told me that I was not relieved for any thing that occurred up to the close of the battle." Bragg's charges against him he dismissed as "frivolous objections" and "after-thoughts."

Though he had written some tactful passages, his analysis of Davis's discrimination against him was bluntly explicit, and contained such statements as, "Justice should be even-handed." Abraham Lincoln might have forgiven such language. Jefferson Davis was less likely to do so. In all probability Hill's whole unvarnished argument further angered the Confederate President, who had already demonstrated, in long-standing quarrels with Beauregard and Johnston, and in his relations with other political leaders, that he was a most sensitive, proud, and contentious man.[52]

His reply to Hill on November 17 was coldly polite:

Sir: Yours of yesterday has just come to hand, and I hasten to reply that the conversation, before it closed, removed every impression which was personally disagreeable, and the whole matter was restored to its official character, so far as I am concerned. I am not sure whether you intended your letter to be an application for a court of inquiry, or whether you had made at a previous time such a request. The latter is to be inferred from the language employed, but I am not informed as to the application or the "refusal," if one was made, and cannot judge of the grounds taken in either.

These last two statements contrast oddly with the way Hill had referred, in his letter of the sixteenth, to "the refusal to grant me a Court of Inquiry," as though he felt sure that Davis knew all about it. Hill had not yet received Cooper's reply to his application of the thirteenth for a court. Therefore the reference indicates either that he felt Davis had refused the court in the interview, or that he had learned through the headquarters grapevine that a refusal was imminent, and saw Davis back of it. His whole letter appears to be an effort to alter a decision not to grant the court which he thinks Davis has made. Yet Davis states that he does not even know whether Hill has applied for a court! In view of his conversation with Hill, his tight personal control of the War Department, and his own involvement in Hill's case, this is hard to believe.

Granting that somehow Davis may have remained as uninformed as he said he was, one might still ask why he indulged in so much written speculation as to whether Hill had applied for a court and whether the application had been refused. Why did he not send a messenger over to Cooper's office and *find out* what had happened before he wrote Hill? In effect he was telling Hill that he was not enough concerned about him to bother to find out. It was contemptuous treatment indeed of a general of Hill's high rank and long service to the Confederacy.

In the remainder of his letter, Davis denied that Hill had been relieved of command for expressing a want of confidence in Bragg.

"That reason was not given to me in the note through which General Bragg recommended your removal, and on which I authorized him to relieve you," he wrote, after which he sharply rejected Hill's argument about discrimination between him and Polk:

Need I repeat that no charges were preferred against you, and that no application for a court of inquiry by you was before me, and again call your attention to that difference between your case and that of General Polk. If you have not forgotten my reply to you when you first referred to my note to General Polk, I am surprised that you should again adduce it in your list of grievances.[53]

That was all, and it was perfectly clear that Hill would receive no presidential support. On November 17, just before going home from Richmond, and probably after reading Davis's letter, he wrote presidential aide G. W. C. Lee, requesting "a copy of General Bragg's note to the President asking for my removal from the Army of Tennessee," but received no immediate answer. On the twentieth, Cooper addressed to him a refusal of his application for a court of inquiry. He told Hill that he lacked "adequate cause" to justify an order for a court: "No charges have been preferred by your commanding general or others against you, and no complaint even of your military conduct has been addressed to the Department." Hill had been "simply relieved from duty," not accused of military delinquency. "Indeed, with an officer of your past service and approved gallantry," wrote Cooper, "military delinquency is a presumption not to be indulged by any one, and certainly not in the absence of all charge or complaint sanctioned by the Department." [54]

Yet, the War Department was under the direction and control of the President, who had sanctioned Bragg's charges of military delinquency, and these accusations rested in the official files of Secretary of War Seddon. When War Department Clerk J. B. Jones learned of Hill's request for a copy of them, he commented in his diary that the charges were so severe that they might provoke a duel between Hill and Bragg. Can one suppose that Cooper, an intimate of Davis, really believed what he wrote in his letter of refusal? And though the *Official Records* show only Cooper and Seddon collaborating on this decision against Hill, can one imagine that Davis had nothing to do with it? [55]

At least the courteous and complimentary wording of Cooper's letter provided an official endorsement, and Hill published it in the newspapers together with an account of his interview with Bragg, and of the Sunday morning action at Chickamauga. He also wrote Seddon on November 25, expressing gratitude "for the kind manner in which my application for court of inquiry has been denied," and the hope that it might be reconsidered. To show how his reputation was being damaged, he enclosed an extract from one of the newspaper attacks upon him. "Whether this matter be reconsidered or not, I will feel grateful to the Department for past kindness," he wrote. Seddon replied, "I do not think the interest of the service will allow the court of inquiry requested, and that decision will not be shaken.... You can interpose the shield of your well-earned reputation to such petty assaults." [56]

On that same November 25, five days after the writing of Cooper's letter refusing Hill the court, presidential aide Lee informed Seddon that Davis was willing to let Hill have a copy of Bragg's note, and on the twenty-seventh the copy was sent him. One glance at it must have destroyed any remaining illusions about the Richmond authorities who had been so friendly to him the previous summer. But he did not write back immediately; there were good reasons for waiting before demanding a court on the new grounds of Bragg's accusations.

For one thing, the command situation was fluid. Bragg, to the further ruin of his reputation, had been driven from the heights about Chattanooga, and in early December, at his own request, was relieved of his command. Hill anticipated that it would be given to Johnston, as it was, and probably hoped to be returned to his corps under his old commanding general. Another consideration was his promotion. He was well aware that the Senate, which reassembled in December, had not yet had an opportunity to confirm his July appointment as lieutenant general; and to raise the issue of Bragg's note to Davis just as the President was preparing to send the Senate his appointment list would not be politic.

So Hill waited, all through December. In January, a long list of appointments was confirmed. Hill's name was not on it. In early February, Davis appointed Hood, Hill's junior, a lieutenant general and quickly obtained confirmation. [57] It was now evident that he intended to let Hill revert to his former rank of major general. No other Confederate officer had been so humiliated.

On February 8, four days after the confirmation of Hood's appointment, Hill addressed to Cooper another request for a court of inquiry. "My former application was refused upon the ground that Genl Bragg had presented no charges against me," he wrote. "At that time, I was ignorant of the existence of his letter to the President asking for my removal." Bragg, he said, had never expressed disapproval of him "until he took up the erroneous impression that I was the head and front of the combination against himself." But obviously the letter to Davis did contain "allegations against me," and these charges could be proved false in a court of inquiry.

It was a courteously worded but strong application. Any denial of it would plainly rest more upon legal technicality and arbitrary decision than upon justice. Perhaps that is why the only answer that Hill received was silence.[58]

On February 9, Hood was assigned to corps command in the Army of Tennessee, precluding the possibility that Hill might be restored to such duty. That same day General Beauregard, commanding the Department of South Carolina, Georgia, and Florida, telegraphed Richmond about his need for "a competent officer" at Charleston to exercise command in South Carolina. Hill was his first choice, provided rank would not keep him from taking a post that ordinarily called for a major general. He also telegraphed Hill, informing him his services were applied for and asking, "Can you aid in the matter?"[59]

At this time Hill's elder brother was visiting him. William Randolph, or Colonel W. R. Hill, as he was now called, by reason of an honorary title, had enjoyed success as a lawyer, state legislator, and Mississippi cotton planter, and early in his career had attained a reputation for outstanding ability and integrity. Harvey Hill regarded him as "the soul of honor," and still accorded him the great love and respect that he had felt toward him as a boy.[60] Colonel Hill had decided of his own initiative, as he later said, that he would go to Richmond and talk with his personal friend, President Davis, about his brother's case. This was probably the chief reason for his visit. While in Charlotte he carefully ascertained what Harvey Hill thought about taking command as a major general, since that would be his rank as soon as the current session of Congress expired. When he resumed his journey, he may or may not have known of Beauregard's telegram, which had been addressed to Hill at Raleigh.[61]

In Richmond he talked privately with Davis on February 15, and with Cooper on the seventeenth. According to a written statement that he prepared several weeks later, this is what occurred:

Davis said that he had not had Hill's appointment as lieutenant general confirmed because the army had too many generals of that rank, but did not answer when Colonel Hill asked why, if that were so, Hood had been promoted. The President praised Hill as a soldier and declared that he did not intend to censure him for his past military conduct. Mentioning the Charleston post, he said that he had instructed Cooper to query Hill about serving as second in command to Beauregard with his former rank as major general. If Hill would not serve at the lower rank there was no place open for him.

Colonel Hill replied that his brother had told him he placed service to his country above rank or "private feeling," and was willing to take command as a major general provided he could do so with a clear record that would ensure him the respect of his troops. If, in the order assigning him to duty, undiminished confidence in his capacity as an officer could be expressed, Hill would feel that his record was clear.

Davis answered that he saw no objection to this; he would consult with Cooper the next day, and would give his reply at 2 P.M. if Colonel Hill would call again. Of all this Colonel Hill wrote afterward: "I cannot say that the President gave a distinct and unqualified promise that such a record would be granted, but the tenor and tone of his conversation was such as left no doubt on my mind." So confident was he that Hill would be relieved of the blame for Chickamauga that he telegraphed him the next morning advising him to accept the tendered command.

That afternoon he kept his appointment with Davis, but found him in conference. Seeing that the President was busy with matters incident to the closing of Congress, Colonel Hill decided not to bother him again but to call on Cooper instead. Next morning, the seventeenth, he talked with the Adjutant General. Cooper first told him that he had conferred with the President, who had spoken of him, and had expected to see him the previous day, and then read him a letter, dated February 16, that he said had just been mailed to Hill. It concluded with an order directing Hill to go to Charleston, but nowhere in it was there an expression of undiminished confidence.

Colonel Hill immediately called attention to the missing phrase, and explained why Hill wanted it. Cooper said he was willing to provide it. Praising Hill's character and past services, he declared that any such wording that would soothe his pride as a soldier would be granted. "Tell him," he said, "to write the order himself and forward it to me; or he may telegraph it to me."

Colonel Hill suggested that it be written immediately, so that he could take it to his brother. No, said Cooper; he wanted "to give it all the strength possible," and accordingly would submit it to the President "for his sanction," as soon as Davis was free from the pressure of Congressional affairs. Meanwhile Hill could go on to Charleston knowing that the revised order would be sent him. So assured, Colonel Hill left Richmond the next morning in the belief that he had obtained for his brother the clear record that he desired above all else.[62]

The letter that Cooper had mailed to Hill did not reach him until the night of February 22. It was a strange composition. Cooper said that under the law authorizing the appointment of lieutenant generals, they could only command army corps. Then, lamely, he wrote:

The President, desiring that the public should not lose the service of an officer whose zeal and gallantry have been so conspicuous as your own, has deemed it better not to ask for your confirmation in the rank of lieutenant-general, in order to leave you in that to which you have been already confirmed, and has directed me to offer to you service as a major-general in the Department of South Carolina, Georgia, and Florida. You will, therefore, with as little delay as practicable, repair to Charleston and report to General Beauregard, commanding that department.[63]

Hill, seeing nothing here that would clear his record, telegraphed Cooper on the twenty-third that, "The command at Charleston is impracticable at present; reasons given in full by mail." But his brother had returned by now, and before the letter was written that day he persuaded Hill to go to Charleston, arguing that Davis and Cooper would send new orders containing an expression of undiminished confidence. Accordingly, Hill first wrote Cooper a long letter and then telegraphed him, on the twenty-fourth, "I will repair at once to Charleston and there await, before entering on duty, the clear record promised me. The command is otherwise impracticable."

In the letter he reviewed the harsh treatment he had received from Bragg and Davis, ending with his demotion and the appointment of his junior, Hood, above him. "However," he wrote, "I cordially concur in the preference for this mutilated hero and unhestitatingly admit his claims to promotion to be stronger than my own; and I would feel in like manner with reference to the promotion of R. H. Anderson, A. P. Stewart, Early, and others." Still it all added up to a grave reflection on his military capacity, and it was "reasonable to suppose that the soldiers will view with distrust one who has been treated as no other Confederate officer has been. Unless, then, the assignment to duty be accompanied by an unequivocal expression of undiminished confidence in my capacity, gallantry, and fidelity, I can accept no position that may be tendered." [64]

Hill might also have added that over and above his desire to ensure the respect of his troops he wanted to clear himself, once and forever, of the blame for Chickamauga. He reasoned that if, without the expression of undiminished confidence, he accepted an *offer* of command as major general, as distinct from a peremptory order to serve at the lower rank, he would be voluntarily sanctioning Davis's treatment of him and thus admitting that he deserved degradation for his conduct at Chickamauga. Like virtually every combat officer who felt the stigma of military delinquency in any way—like Jackson, A. P. Hill, Hood, and Polk, to name only a few—he had determined to draw a firm line in defense of his professional reputation. In addition he was refusing to say to the Southern people, "I am the culprit who rendered useless the eighteen thousand Confederate casualties at Chickamauga."

But against the power of the presidency he was at a disadvantage, to say the least. Davis, without replying to Hill's telegram of February 24, allowed him to go to Charleston, where Beauregard was awaiting his arrival before leaving on a trip south to meet a Federal threat to his coastal defenses. Then, after Hill had taken actual but not formal command, in Beauregard's absence, he received a letter from the presidential mouthpiece, Cooper, under date of February 29. The President, said Cooper, had considered Hill's letter of the twenty-third, had decided that Hill had already been sufficiently complimented in the letter assigning him to Charleston, and "therefore declines to accede to your demand. He would scarcely have offered you the command in question if he did not feel confidence in your capacity, gallantry, and fidelity, and does not conceive it is necessary or proper to announce the same in orders." [65]

Here Davis ignored the fact that what was asked was an expression of *undiminished* confidence to offset demotion, and that this had not been granted, although W. R. and Harvey Hill had been led to expect that it would be. It is difficult to see what harm the insertion of one such phrase in official orders of assignment could have done to the service, but if Davis really did deem this too improper to be allowed, there was nothing to prevent him from writing Hill a letter like the one provided Polk—nothing but the controlling factor which for the sake of his own reputation he would never admit, his determination to degrade Hill and make him more than ever the scapegoat of Chickamauga.

The evidence indicates that were it not for this determination, employment as a lieutenant general could have been found for Hill. That Davis did not really think he had too many lieutenant generals in the army is shown not only by Hood's promotion but by Davis's approval, on February 17, of an act of Congress empowering him to appoint lieutenant generals in the provisional army "when, in his discretion, it shall be deemed necessary for the command of any one of the military departments." Obviously this act negated the letter of the sixteenth telling Hill that lieutenant generals could only command army corps. It had been published February 10 and had received final passage the night of the sixteenth. Davis must have known of its progress through Congress; moreover, the Senate did not adjourn until noon, February 18. Why, then, could not Davis have obtained confirmation of Hill's appointment as a lieutenant general, and sent him with that rank to the post of second in command to Beauregard, a full general over an important department?

True, Hill would have had more rank than the position ordinarily called for, but what law or military rule would this have violated? Davis, according to Hill, actually submitted the name of Lieutenant General Pemberton for the Charleston post. And no high-ranking

officer in Charleston could have outranked his job more than Lieutenant General Polk did at the outset of the "important and difficult"
command that Davis had so eloquently bestowed on him in October.
On December 8 Polk's son-in-law and staff officer, Gale, had mourn-
fully written his wife:

The truth is there is nothing for us to do. The precise nature of your
father's command is this. He has charge of collecting and organizing the
paroled prisoners of Port Hudson and Vicksburg. I think there is one
Brigade.... This Brigade ought to be the best drilled of any in the Confederacy as it has a Brigadier General, a Major General, a Lieutenant
General, and a General over it.[66]

Hill knew the army too well to accept Davis's arguments at face
value. He had gone to Charleston on his brother's assurance that
Davis and Cooper together had promised the expression of undiminished confidence, and he protested now, in repeated letters to Cooper
in March, that he still relied "upon the sacredness of that promise."
Also, W. R. Hill wrote Cooper, on March 25, expressing "astonishment" at having learned that "the authorities at Richmond" had
repudiated "the assurances I had received," and appealing to "your
justice, and sense of right." [67]

Cooper, in an embarrassed letter of April 4, replied to Hill: "It
would seem from the letter of your brother, Mr. W. R. Hill, to me
and from his statement which accompanies your letter, that I had
made that promise. I must state in reply that your brother, in be-
lieving I had made the promise, certainly misunderstood my remark to him." He had merely expressed appreciation of Hill, he said,
"and a disposition to gratify, as far as I could, the pride of an officer
who considers himself placed in a false position." All that he had
promised was to lay before the President any revised order that Hill
cared to submit. As the President had given the original order, only
he could change the wording. Cooper had no power to revise it, and
"with the knowledge I possessed of the views of the President,"
would never have promised to do so. "To express in orders 'undiminished confidence' in an officer would be unprecedented in military
history." [68]

Hill refused to accept the argument that the President had not
sanctioned a revised order. To Isabella he wrote:

I have at last got a reply from Genl Cooper. Poor old man, he was afraid of Davis and has made a miserable quibble. Brother was too honest and unsuspicious to deal with the shuffling set at Richmond. I warned him against trickery and deceit, but he scouted the idea of treachery in Davis.[69]

And to Cooper, on April 9, he retorted: "You are perfectly right in your view that an expression of undiminished confidence could only be given by the direction and sanction of His Excellency the President. That is the quarter from which it is expected, and from which, with all deference, I suggest it is due." He went on to argue that Cooper and Davis together, by their statements to his brother and by letting him come to Charleston, had clearly accepted his proposal as to the desired expression, and then for some reason had changed their minds. As for the objection that such an expression in orders would be unprecedented in military history:

It may be equally unprecedented in history that an officer who had fought his way up to the highest rank in the Provisional Army should be relieved from command after a battle, banished for months from the field, and reduced in rank upon vague allegations made by another officer, the investigation of which has been constantly refused, either because the commander-in-chief regards them as frivolous or because the officer making them shrinks from subjecting them to the trying ordeal of a court.

Having construed Cooper's letter of February 16 as a tender of service, he had not formally assumed command and would only do so on receipt of the promised expression, or of a peremptory order, to which he would "of course, yield a prompt compliance." [70]

Though such an order would not have been wholly satisfactory to Hill, it would at least have enabled him to go on duty without sanctioning Davis's treatment of him. Beauregard joined in the debate with messages saying that he needed Hill and that Hill would promptly obey a peremptory assignment to duty. Then Davis, on April 23, wrote a brief endorsement to Hill's letter of April 9: "If General Hill does not willingly accept the offer of command, it is not deemed well for the service to force him to such high and responsible duty as that proposed." This decision was not even communicated to Hill; Davis and Cooper simply maintained silence and Hill went home.[71]

While in Charleston he had received a number of sympathetic

letters from friends and colleagues. One letter came from Longstreet, who had experienced military failure in eastern Tennessee.
Dated March 21, 1864, it is significant for what it reveals of the
writer. Longstreet remarked that an open expression of sympathy
by any of Hill's friends would only make matters worse. "I don't
sympathize much however. I rather envy you," he wrote. His own
troubles weighed on his mind. He said that "the authorities" were
trying to find a plausible reason to "put an end to me," and that he
would accept such a development as "a great relief." Then he declared:

I came to the South because I feared that it might not be able to do
well without me. I had more experience in battle, or thought that I had,
than any other man North or South and was apprehensive that our
people could not get along without me. I had no ambition to gratify nor
have I any now more than to discharge my duties. . . . If I had confidence
in our success without me I would go home to my dear little family in
spite of authority and the Service.[72]

Hill also thought that the authorities, specifically Davis, wanted
to put an end to him. He believed that Davis had hated him ever
since their November interview, and would like him to resign from
the army. He was determined not to resign under a cloud, but to
remain in the service and try to clear his record. To Isabella he confided his hope of being able to defeat "that malignant old man J.D."
and "save my own honor." [73]

No sooner did he arrive home from Charleston than he wrote
Beauregard, "Wishing to share with my countrymen in the dangers
and hardships of the grand campaign now opening, I offer my service to you in any capacity, in which you may be pleased to employ
me near your person." Beauregard, who had recently been transferred to departmental command over North Carolina and Virginia
south of the James, promptly asked Cooper for permission to make
Hill a volunteer aide on his staff. The assignment was approved by
Davis, who evidently was exercising personal control over all matters pertaining to Hill's military career, and on May 5 Hill, with his
old rank of major general, entered on his new duties, which under
army regulations constituted not active but informal service. [74]

In May and June, Grant, now general in chief of the Union armies,
hammered Lee across northern Virginia toward Petersburg. As one

military emergency after another developed, Hill ably and energetically served the Confederacy, acting as a kind of roving trouble shooter and general supervisor for Beauregard. On May 7 he informally commanded about 2,600 men in the repulse of a Union force that was trying to cut the Richmond–Petersburg Railroad near Port Walthall Junction. On May 16, when Beauregard's forces defeated Benjamin F. Butler's army of twenty-two thousand in the battle of Drewry's Bluff just south of Richmond, he maneuvered the division of Whiting in combat, and the next day took temporary command of it at the request of Whiting, who had suffered near collapse from fatigue and nervous strain. In the weeks following the battle, he supervised the location and construction of the famous three-mile line of earthworks by means of which Butler's army was sealed off and neutralized between the James and the Appomattox rivers. Then, in mid-June, he hurried westward to Lynchburg, where he and Jubal Early repulsed a Federal diversionary attack. After that, in response to Beauregard's urgent summons, he returned to Petersburg, now a beleagured city defended by Beauregard and Lee, and began a long, hot, daily grind as Beauregard's inspector of trenches.[75]

In all this he enjoyed the most cordial relations with Beauregard, though according to Lee the debonair Creole privately complained of his croaking. As for the men and officers he informally commanded, they soon made it plain by the way they obeyed that his old fame as a combat commander and his evident skill and courage in the field were enough to win him the confidence of his troops, despite the treatment he had received from Davis. One front-line captain later said of his activities at this time: "General D. H. Hill impressed me as a zealous, unselfish patriot and great soldier, who knew not fear and shrank from no duty. . . . He could always be found at the most dangerous place in the line, doing what he could to encourage and also protect the men." [76]

One might think this service to the Confederacy in time of worsening crisis would have earned Hill a presidential pardon, but not so. Davis showed no inclination to summon him to duty, even though the war by now had taken so heavy a toll of generals that officers with a dangerous lack of combat experience were being assigned to high command.[77] And if Davis's attitude was not enough to maintain the ban, Braxton Bragg was at the President's elbow. Davis had brought this discredited general to Richmond to be his military adviser, with the resounding title of Commander-in-Chief of the Confederate forces.[78]

Repeatedly, requests by other generals for Hill's services as a commander were refused. After the battle of Drewry's Bluff, Beauregard issued orders assigning Hill to the command of Whiting's division, having first asked Davis to put Hill on active duty. Davis had replied, during a personal visit to Beauregard's army, that Hill could have a command as soon as he asked for one in writing. "As I had no guarantee that he would keep his promise," Hill said afterward, "I told Genl Beauregard that I had already told His Excellency that I would obey any order that he would give me. If he needed me, he could order me upon duty, but that I would not descend to the humiliation of begging him for a position." The result of this stand could have been foreseen. Beauregard had to relieve Hill of command. Shortly afterward he wrote him a letter saying he would be happy to have him as a division commander whenever that became possible and acknowledging his "valuable service" as aide, especially his supervision of the defense lines that had blocked Butler.[79]

Johnston also failed in an effort to employ Hill. The application for assignment to the Army of Tennessee was made and declined without Hill's knowledge. And again at the time of the attack on Lynchburg a request for Hill's services was refused. Early telegraphed Bragg that battle was imminent and that he needed Hill as a temporary commander of troops. Bragg replied that another general was being sent from Richmond.[80]

Hill well knew that he was inviting such treatment by standing on his distinction between volunteering for duty and being ordered to it, a distinction which his brother Albert Potts Hill frankly described to him as "too nice for practical minds." He felt, however, that his professional honor, important alike to himself and his children after him, was at stake. He insisted, too, that when he took formal command of troops he wanted to "go to them with an untarnished name. . . . I think that I feel on this subject as every soldier must feel and no one understands it better than Mr. Davis himself." [81]

In his personal war with the President he solicited and received support from the Congressional delegation of North Carolina, led by Isabella's uncle, Senator William A. Graham. He told Graham that what he wanted was a clear record, not promotion—especially not at the expense of any of "the glorious heroes" serving under Lee.

Graham however, in a letter of June 1 to Davis, recommended that Hill be promoted to lieutenant general and given "a suitable command, in the present trying circumstances of the country." Five other North Carolinians signed the letter with him: Senator William T. Dortch, and Congressmen B. S. Gaither, John A. Gilmer, W. N. H. Smith, and R. R. Bridgers.[82]

Davis, a president notably resistant to congressmen whose views crossed his, simply referred this letter to Seddon, who replied to Graham:

Major Genl. Hill has not reported to the Department for duty, and there is reason to believe, from some peculair view of his position, is unwilling to do so. In this state of things, it is not seen how he can be appropriately *sought* after and requested to take a command. His past services and capacity are appreciated, but such attitude assumed to the Department can not be indulged or disregarded.[83]

Hill considered the objection that he had not reported for duty a mere quibble. Only officers on leave were ordinarily required to make monthly reports of their whereabouts. He was not on leave but awaiting assignment to command, and the Richmond authorities certainly knew he was in Petersburg with Beauregard. When Isabella suggested that perhaps she should urge his promotion upon the President he told her, "That malignant man Davis will pay no attention to the Delegation from a great State, which has one half the troops in Lee's Army now defending him from the gallows. How idle then to suppose that any letter of yours can move his heart." Besides, he added, he did not want promotion ahead of men who by now had fought more battles than he. "All I wish is to have a clear record for the past." [84]

Graham's reaction to Seddon's letter was to go in person to the President and inquire about Hill. In this interview Davis said, in effect, that Hill had put himself in limbo by refusing the Charleston command, and declared that he would have to tender his services again or be "dropped." Reporting this in a letter to Hill, Graham said Davis had averred that if he had any prejudices they were in Hill's favor. "The President seemed frank, and his whole manner seemed to indicate that he thought you had taken offense when none was intended." Hill should tender his services to Cooper again, in a conciliatory manner, Graham continued. To make this easier for him, he enclosed a letter to Hill from the members of the North Carolina delegation expressing confidence in him and urging him to apply for active duty.

In reply Hill declared himself "truly grateful" for the members' "very kind letter" and "flattering appreciation." Of Davis he wrote angrily:

Poor an opinion as I have of his truthfulness, I hardly thought that he would have ventured upon so many quibbles.... How does an officer's declination to accept a proffered command put him out of the service? What law requires a relieved officer to report for duty? What law authorizes Davis to drop an officer for failing to do that which no law requires him to do? ... When apparently most frank, he is most crafty and insincere.[85]

He also furnished Graham a copy of the note, dated June 13, that he had written to Cooper. In it he said that he was at Petersburg awaiting orders from the Department as he had been "for the last seven months," and that although reports of this nature were not required of him by army regulations, he would continue to make them "as often as the Department may require." [86] It was a restrained but argumentative communication, not the conciliatory tender of services that Graham had suggested. To it Davis returned his unanswerable counterargument, silence.

Meanwhile, the political support that Hill was receiving from Graham and his colleagues was making another North Carolinian, Bragg, uncomfortable. In self-defense Bragg informed Graham through an intermediary, Senator Thomas J. Semmes of Louisiana, that he had not prejudiced Davis against Hill. When Graham told Hill of this, Hill replied that Bragg had "descended to absolute falsehood." [87] Then on June 11 he wrote Bragg:

In an interview with me after my removal from the Army of Tennessee you said that you had no fault to find with me up to the close of the battle of Chickamauga and you placed my removal upon personal grounds. I learn that you have made a similar statement through Senator Semmes to Senator Graham. You promised at Missionary Ridge, in the presence of Lieutenant-Colonel Anderson, to put this statement in writing, but upon reflection declined to do so. I have been kept out of the field eight months and reduced in rank. This satisfaction is full enough to gratify most men, and I trust that no reason now exists for withholding the promised paper.

He went on to suggest that by furnishing the statement Bragg could relieve himself of the blame "for the severe treatment I have received," and ended with an avowal:

While making this appeal to you for simple justice, I must candidly tell you that I do not regret my course whilst connected with the Army of Tennessee. I acted solely from a sense of duty and, with a full knowledge of all the suffering attendant upon the act, would renew it again.

Bragg passed this letter on to Davis after first appending to it an endorsement in which, as though driven by an inner compulsion to confess, he revealed the basic truth of Hill's argument:

In the personal interview to which the general refers, he demanded to know on what charges he was removed from his command, and was distinctly informed I had made "no charges against him." As I consider no human "faultless," the general's desire for exculpation must have given coloring to his understanding of my reply. He can but know that the immediate cause of his removal by yourself was his own act, not mine. Having taken active steps to procure my removal in a manner both unmilitary and unofficer-like, in which he failed, after a full personal investigation by yourself (though I aided his efforts by an expression of my desire to retire) he was, at my request, transferred from that army as a necessary consequence of the line of conduct he had pursued. His having been kept from the field for eight months and reduced in rank was certainly no act of mine, but, as I learn since my arrival here, resulted from his declining to go on duty when ordered without conditions which the Department could not grant.

When Davis read this he wrote a second endorsement, dated June 17, which was nothing less than a rebuttal to Bragg:

General Bragg:
The request you preferred that General Hill should be removed from your command for the reason that it would conduce to the public interest was connected in my mind with events previously communicated, some of which preceded the battle of Chickamauga and all of which, taken in connection with the fact that he had been promoted and assigned to duty in the army then under your command without previous service with [it] and without your recommendation, formed in my mind a sufficient justification for your request. The attempt to which you refer, to have you removed, was not officially known to me, and, as rumored, involved many others, some of whom were not removed and none, so far as I was concerned, for that specific reason. The withdrawal of Lieutenant-General

Hill from the command of a corps without ability to assign him to another corps prevented his nomination to the Senate for that grade, and consequently left him in the grade to which he had been confirmed. The law permitted no other result.[88]

Thus Davis thrust back upon Bragg and away from himself any blame that might attach to what they had done to Hill. Bragg in his endorsement had incautiously revealed the deceit he had practiced in answering Hill's question about charges. Moreover, he had emphasized the petition against himself as the main reason for Hill's removal by himself and the President. In rebuttal Davis was reminding Bragg that in his letter of September 25 about McLemore's Cove and in the request for removal that he had "preferred" (an interesting verb), he had in fact accused Hill of military delinquency in battle, and was declaring that he, Davis, had sanctioned the removal largely because of these charges and not at all because of the anti-Bragg petition. Plainly this argument clashes with Davis's statement in his letter of November 17 to Hill, "Need I repeat that no charges were preferred against you," and with Cooper's denial of Hill's application for a court on the grounds that no charges had been preferred. The dubiousness of Davis's argument that he had to demote Hill has already been shown.

Clearly Bragg's endorsement corroborated Hill's reiterated contention that Bragg attached little if any importance to his written charges, and if Davis was acting justly and honorably, rather than dishonestly and vindictively, in this controversy, one would expect him now to entertain at least a reasonable doubt of Hill's guilt and to reopen the case with a view toward righting any wrong that might have been done. Instead, having washed his hands in cold legalistic phrases, he left everything as before.[89]

In the trenches of Petersburg, where the air was, in Hill's phrase, "like a heated furnace," and the stench of steadily accumulating filth made soldiers reckless about exposing themselves to vigilant enemy sharpshooters, Hill carried out daily inspections from sunrise to noon, and afterward studied reports from army engineers on work in progress. Though his title had risen to "Inspector General of Trenches," he concluded, finally, that he was "doing the duty of a Lieutenant," and that, as his friends told him, he ought not to remain at Petersburg "in a false position." In the latter part of July, after first inquiring as to the wishes of the North Carolina delegation, he parted cordially with Beauregard and went home.[90]

From July through December he was in the military doldrums, though he stayed in close touch with Graham and occasionally received a letter from a former colleague like General Wade Hampton, who told Hill that as "a son of South Carolina" he had "worthily sustained the reputation of our State on . . . many battlefields," and added, "I trust that you will again have the opportunity to strike, as you have done." By August 1, his report of the entire Chickamauga campaign, exhibiting Bragg's discretionary orders to him for the attack at McLemore's Cove, and showing what had happened before and during the battle of Sunday, September 20, was in Davis's hands. Longstreet's report, which corroborated the contention of Hill that his corps had moved to the Sunday morning attack perhaps an hour in advance of any other infantry, had been on record since October, 1863. That same month Cheatham had submitted a report that also corroborated Hill's, both as to the time of Hill's advance and the confusion in Polk's line. Yet Hill continued to bear the blame for all delay and failure at Chickamauga and to go without a command. His report was suppressed, though Congress asked that it be published.[91]

In October, 1864, Hill asked Vance to query Davis about him, and offered his services "in any capacity" to the governor if Davis did not call him to duty. Vance accordingly wrote Davis on October 25, stating that Hill, "an officer whose abilities in the field are highly esteemed in North Carolina," was "without employment," and proposing that Hill be assigned to command of the eastern portion of the Department of North Carolina. "Should it not be your pleasure to give him this or some other command," Vance wrote pointedly, "I propose giving him such employment myself as I can find for him to do. Like a good and gallant soldier, he expresses to me his great desire to serve anywhere or how his country." [92]

But Bragg was in eastern North Carolina, having been sent to command at Wilmington, and Lee, whose advice was asked, suggested that Bragg and Hill might clash. Davis, as though there were no other command possible for Hill, let Vance's letter go unanswered until January 6, by which time an answer was no longer needed.[93]

By November 1, Hill had toned down his correspondence with Cooper to, "I have the honor to renew my monthly statement that I am awaiting orders at this place and prepared to obey promptly," and in return had the honor of being completely ignored.[94] Perforce, he could only look on while the South met crowding military disasters: the loss of Atlanta to General William Tecumseh Sherman, the ruin of the Army of Tennessee under Hood, whom Davis had put in Johnston's place, and Sherman's smoking march from Atlanta to the sea.

But in Richmond Senator Graham was still active in Hill's behalf. He had succeeded in getting a copy of Hill's Chickamauga report sent to the Senate, and in December, at a private meeting of senators called by those who wanted to force Davis to return Johnston to command, he presented Hill's case. On December 23 one of the senators who had heard him, Robert W. Barnwell of South Carolina, went to Davis and asked him to order Hill to Charleston. Davis replied with praise of Hill, but said Barnwell ought to see Seddon, who was not so favorably disposed toward Hill as he. And then there was another thing that needed explanation. Barnwell could tell Graham about it if he wanted to. What about this matter of Lee's lost order in Maryland? [95]

Davis knew that McClellan had stated in his report that the order was addressed to Hill. He also knew an exaggerated version of a newspaper story which had first appeared in the *Savannah Republican* of June 5, 1863. Sent from Richmond under date of June 1, and written by the army correspondent "P.W.A."—probably P. W. Alexander—it emphasized the importance of the lost order and suggested that Hill had "dropped [it] in his tent." Other newspapers had picked up the story; Hill had heard of it and had written Isabella from near Chattanooga on September 29: "I wrote to you that some of the papers were saying that Genl Lee's failure in Maryland was owing to my losing an order from him dated at Frederick. Please look among my papers and see if it is not among them." The search had revealed Jackson's copy of the order, which caused Hill to think, until after the war, that he had the only copy sent him. He had tried to get an explanation published in the press but had failed. By December, 1864, the story had been exaggerated into the theory that because Hill had disapproved of Lee's order he had thrown it on the ground! [96]

It was this patently absurd version of the story that Barnwell heard from Davis on December 23—after Davis had finished praising Hill. Moreover, Barnwell got the impression from what the President said that this version was officially accepted. As Graham wrote Hill that day, "Mr. B. draws the inference that the officials believe you did not approve the order and threw it on the ground, though your brother when here, upon its being mentioned, said he thought you had Lee's original order in your possession."

In his conversation with Barnwell, Graham declared that the idea of Hill's throwing away the order was an absurdity, and Barnwell went on to Seddon's office to argue Hill's assignment to Charleston. Graham asked Hill for his explanation of the story of the lost order, but expressed the opinion that in reality Davis and his associates attached little importance to the whole affair. It "dates so far back, and beyond subsequent approvals of your conduct," he wrote, "that it can be regarded as but a make-weight and as evidence of temper." [97]

On the day that Graham wrote this, a long-heralded Union attack on Wilmington's main bastion, Fort Fisher, began. Hill swallowed the remnants of his pride and dispatched a note to Cooper:

In view of the invasion of my own state and my belief that I could be useful at the point of attack, I have the honor to renew the expression of my desire to be placed in any position, which will confront me with the enemies of my country.

Before the day ended, Cooper telegraphed him orders to go to Charleston. Doubtless this was not the result of his note, which seems to have been sent by ordinary mail, but of the pressure that Graham had built up, culminating in the efforts of Barnwell, a political leader who had helped to make Davis President.[98] In any event, it seems clear that Graham had been correct in discounting Davis's emphasis on the Lost Dispatch.

Though Cooper intended to employ Hill in South Carolina, his telegraphic orders were ambiguous. The result, after Hill arrived in Charleston, was a typical army mix-up and Hill's eventual assignment to command of the District of Georgia, with headquarters at Augusta. Here, under the general direction of Beauregard, now commanding the Military Division of the West, he remained through January and February, receiving units from Hood's shattered army and directing cavalry operations against Sherman's advancing columns. He remained keenly aware of his reduced rank and the stigma of Chickamauga, and clung to the futile hope that Graham might be able to obtain a congressional resolution in his favor; but he worked zealously at his administrative duties, improving the performance of his cavalry until in the end he was complimenting instead of criticizing its commanders.[99]

And the end came quickly. Sherman, aided by Beauregard's failure to concentrate his widely scattered forces, swept irresistibly northward toward juncture with Grant, bypassing Augusta and plunging on to Columbia. Near the end of February, Hill was ordered to field duty in North Carolina. In that state, in March, there was a reunion of Confederate friends and enemies—Johnston, Hill, Bragg, and others—and a last surge against the bluecoats at Kinston and Bentonville. Then came news of Lee's surrender, and on April 26 Johnston yielded to Sherman the forces that included a division commanded by Hill.[100]

So ended the military activities of a versatile and talented individualist, whose fighting career, marked by great achievement as well as great controversy, strongly suggests, when seen in full, that Harvey Hill was one of the ablest of Lee's lieutenants. With more men of his skill, patriotism, and fortitude the Confederacy might have endured, and altered the history of America and the world far more than it did during its brief, tortured existence.

"A GLORIOUS CHRISTIAN VICTORY"

CHARLOTTE, under Radical Reconstruction. A roistering crowd of drunken soldiers and carpetbaggers blocks the board sidewalk and spills over into the street. A small, sandy-haired boy edges by.

"That's General Hill's boy! Let's scare him."

A shot rings out; a bullet ricochets off the sidewalk, and Joseph Morrison Hill, the general's youngest son, is taken home with a flesh wound in the hip.[1]

As this carelessly cruel little incident indicates, Hill was a well-known opponent of Reconstruction in the postwar South. He accepted the defeat of the Confederacy as a fact and as God's will, but he would neither repudiate the cause for which he had fought nor condone the Radical Republican rule of force. His "great sin," he admitted, was "hatred of the Yankees."[2]

He expressed his views in print, at first rather circumspectly as the founder and editor of a monthly magazine, *The Land We Love,* which he published in Charlotte from 1866 to 1869, and then with scorching emphasis in the 1870s as the editor and publisher of a Charlotte weekly newspaper, *The Southern Home,* which helped to bring about the restoration of Conservative government in North Carolina. Before his friend Vance led the Conservatives to a Democratic party victory in the gubernatorial contest of 1876, Hill shrugged off many a threat of assassination.[3]

His goals for the rehabilitation of the South also included industrialization, though not at the price of knee-bending to "the Northern Baal"; education for young Southerners in the mechanical arts; and the practice of scientific agriculture. This agrarian aim he emphasized in both his magazine and his newspaper. In addition he joined the Granger movement, and both as writer and orator campaigned with considerable success for better farm laws.[4]

In his magazine his lifelong interest in literature and his Southern cultural nationalism found an outlet. One of the main themes of *The Land We Love* was Southern literature. Hill published the writings of Fanny Downing, Francis Orray Ticknor, and Paul Hamilton Hayne, and by 1868 was producing, in the critical judgment of William Gilmore Simms, "the best magazine now published in the South." Hayne, who would later inherit Simms's position as the South's foremost literary representative, wrote Hill in February, 1869, in acknowledgment of advance payment for book notices, "Thanks for your great kindness. If all proprietors of Southern journals ... only resembled *you* in the little matters of promptitude, and fairness, what a different aspect Southern Literature would be assuming to day!" And when Hill wearied of annual travel through the South in search of subscriptions, and sold out to the *New Eclectic* magazine of Baltimore, it was Hayne who expressed "something like a *pang*" at the passing of *The Land We Love,* and lamented the fate of the Southern literary man:

I *had* hoped that our People would sustain a monthly so ardently devoted to their interest and honor!

But they are incorrigible in this particular. "Ephrahim has turned to his idols, let him alone!"

As for mere *Literateurs* like myself, we are *forced* into writing for Yankee papers etc. If, in time, we degenerate into Bohemians, and *"free* Lances" of the press *whose* is the fault? Notwithstanding Dr. Johnson's savage sarcasm on the subject, a man must *live;* to live he must eat and drink; to procure the means wherewith to get physical pabulum, Greenbacks are necessary.[5]

Probably it was not so much belles-lettres that accounted for Hill's initial publishing success as another of his dominant interests and editorial themes, Confederate military history. He conceived of his magazine as "the organ of the late Confederate Army," and so advertised it in the Southern press, with the endorsement of Beauregard, Johnston, Hood, and numerous other generals.[6] Biographical sketches of military heroes like Jackson, official reports of battles, including his own on Chickamauga, and army anecdotes sharpened by his vigorous style appeared regularly in *The Land We Love*, and appealed strongly to Southern readers just after the war. As magazine editor and later as a writer for the *Century*, he preserved valuable information on Civil War battles and leaders. And his outlook was not only Southern, but North Carolinian. To Graham he commented in 1875:

I think that some effort should be made to get a correct Confederate history of our State written. North Carolina did the fighting and Virginia has written the history and from that history it is difficult to discover that our State took any part in the Confederate struggle.[7]

One of his rules as a military historian was charity toward those who had been killed in battle or had died before he wrote about them. Just as he tempered criticism of Lee after his death, and forbore to connect A. P. Hill with the Lost Dispatch, so did he eschew negative discussion of Polk, who had been killed by a cannon shot while serving with Johnston in 1864. In a *Century* article on Chickamauga written after Bragg's death, he did present a searching analysis of Bragg's weak generalship, but never, apparently, did he attempt a full exposé of his old enemy.

Although, like many another Confederate he regarded Davis as the chief architect of Southern ruin, and although the memory of Chickamauga and its aftermath was a sore burden, he also thought of Davis as a martyr who had suffered unjust postwar imprisonment and had become the scapegoat for the Confederacy. Accordingly, his criticism of the former President was restrained, and was balanced by praise of Davis's virtues as he saw them. When he heard that Davis was pleased by the favorable attitude of his magazine, he wrote him in 1867 asking him to clear his record of the Chickamauga stigma. It was the beginning of a campaign that was carried on, intermittently, as long as Hill lived.

Davis was willing to eulogize Hill's gallantry and patriotism, but not to revise the records on Chickamauga. As late as 1886 Hill was still asking for "a frank, fair statement." "But whether you relieve me of this odium or not," he wrote, "I will never forget that you were the head of the Confederacy, the Representative of truth and right and the Recipient of all the shafts of malice intended for our people." Apparently Davis replied with another eulogy but not the desired statement. His final judgment of Hill, written shortly after Hill's death, was that "a more pure vigilant and gallant soldier did not serve the Confederate cause." [8]

With another illustrious Confederate, Lee, Hill's postwar relations were not so cordial. One more clash of opinion between the two generals occurred in 1868 when Hill published in his magazine a refutation of the story that he had thrown the Lost Dispatch to the ground, and sent Lee a copy of what he had written. He argued not only that he had never received the lost order but also that McClellan had learned nothing from it that he could not derive from ordinary sources of intelligence, and in fact had been deceived by it into thinking that Longstreet was stationed at Boonsborough, and that Jackson had returned there from Martinsburg. As a result, McClellan had attacked slowly and cautiously instead of immediately brushing aside Hill's little force and going on to cut Lee's army in two. "It was this error which saved Lee from destruction," wrote Hill, "and in the inscrutable Providence of God the loss of the dispatch prolonged the Confederate struggle for two more years."

As has been seen, Hill's theory had point but was not entirely correct. When Lee read how the loss of the order had saved him from destruction, he got angry, and exclaimed to a friend that according to Hill's reasoning one more Lost Dispatch would have brought the South victory in the war! To Hill he wrote a long, icy letter of rebuttal, in which he concluded that the loss of the order had been not beneficial but injurious to the Southern cause. Plainly he was not one of Hill's admirers, and the feeling was mutual. More than a decade later Hill remarked to Longstreet, "My impression of Genl Lee is not so enthusiastic as that of most men who served under him." [9]

From 1877 onward, Hill's career assumed an entirely different pattern. He sold his newspaper and returned to the college campus, this time not as professor but as president, first of Arkansas Industrial University, the future University of Arkansas, from 1877 to 1884, and then of the Middle Georgia Military and Agricultural College at Milledgeville from 1885 to 1889. The detailed story of these presidencies cannot be told here. Suffice it to say that in Arkansas, at the cost of broken health from endless overwork, Hill managed to build the enrollment, increase the funds, and improve the scholarly standards of the university, and then resigned partly because of his health and partly because he found that the trustees were no longer willing to support his strict system of student discipline. The duties of his second presidency were less strenuous; his son, D. H. Hill, Jr., was professor of English in the college and could help with administrative tasks.[10]

Nine children in all had been born to Hill and Isabella. When they established their new home in Milledgeville, five were living—Harvey Jr., Eugenia, Randolph, Nancy, and Joseph—all of them grown, now, and beginning families or careers of their own. In the impoverished South the three boys had experienced delay and financial difficulty as they tried to advance themselves professionally; but Harvey Jr. would eventually be president of the North Carolina State College of Agriculture and Engineering, and a Civil War historian; Randolph, a well-known physician; and Joseph, Chief Justice of the Supreme Court of Arkansas.

Hill and his children were bound to one another with strong bonds of affection. In his relations with them he was usually at his best, encouraging rather than critical, merry rather than sarcastic, and unselfishly, unfailingly loving. They saw not only his worldly accomplishments but also his inner religious life and his private charities. "The dear Father," they called him, and they said of him, admiringly, "Father never stops work and never does anything except with all his might." [11]

In Georgia Hill had regained good health, except for the chronic spinal ailment that never left him, and although his little college was poverty-stricken and paid him a very low salary for his combined teaching and administrative services, he might have passed the most tranquil years of his life in Milledgeville except for one thing, one terrible thing that came upon him like an enemy in the night. Cancer. At first he called it dyspepsia, but by the spring of 1888, though he was still unwilling to speak about cancer of the stomach, there could be no doubt that he was seriously ill.

General Grant had died of throat cancer in 1885. Hill had admired the gallant way he had worked to the last in order to complete his memoirs, so that they could be published for the financial benefit of his family. Hill had also paid tribute to one of Isabella's sisters who had died of cancer, and had written of her to Joseph: "Never once did she murmur against the pain, and it was her religion that sustained her. Her death was *a glorious Christian victory*, which agnosticism cannot ignore and atheism cannot explain."

Now he had begun a similar ordeal. His health rapidly declined, and soon he was describing himself as "little better than a stack of skin and bones," yet he did not quit work. He was not wholly dependent on his salary, having made investments that brought him a modest annual income; but this was not enough to support him and Isabella, and he did not want to be a burden to his children. "Besides," he remarked, "I doubt whether I could be happy in idleness. It looks more manly to die in harness."

So by night Isabella nursed him— "She is always great in time of trouble," he said—and by day he attended to his college duties. Actually, he was still not ready to admit that he had incurable cancer or that death was rapidly approaching. After all, he had fought disease all his life, and he was used to winning his battles. He was able to go on working after school started again in the fall of 1888, because it was mainly at night that he was afflicted with the torments of his steadily worsening illness: the stomach cramps, the heavy sweats, and the chills, which were sometimes followed by partial paralysis. On November 13 he said, "I have not missed a single duty this Term and hope that God will help me to go through till the close of the Session."

When the cramps got too severe, his doctor would administer morphine, but nothing seemed to ease the outbreaks of stinging rash that began in 1889. By March of that year he was getting only four hours of sleep at night. To Joseph, who was engaged in legal practice in Arkansas, he wrote:

The skin where the stinging is becomes as cold as that of a corpse. My veins become distended like whip-cords and they are full of lumps. A vigorous rubbing with a stiff hair brush for half an hour or less time will give relief for the time. But before that point is relieved there will be stinging in several others, may be, six or eight. . . . The suffering is endurable, if not in the feet. Then it is almost maddening. . . . I cannot gain any strength so long as I lose so much sleep.

And still he continued working. The night of April 14, after a stomach cramp and heavy chill, he was unconscious for two hours. Next morning he attended a faculty meeting and taught his classes as usual. "The reaction seems to be complete," he remarked.

On June 14 he wrote Joseph: "Thanks be to a merciful God, I got through the Commencement exercises without a break-down. I resigned, the Board refused to receive the resignation but instead gave me an *indefinite* leave of absence." He added that he was planning a trip to North Carolina. Perhaps a visit to the seacoast would help.

He went, and derived no benefit. As he grew weaker through the summer, the stinging rash dwindled in intensity, "and for that I cannot be too thankful to Almighty God," said he.

August came. He again submitted his resignation and this time the board accepted with regret. In a formal resolution they proclaimed that the people of the South honored his achievements "as a Soldier and as a Teacher."

He did not go back to Georgia that September, but was taken to the home of a relative in Charlotte. "Pray for my life," he wrote Joseph. "It is not a question of health, but of life. Dear boy, cling to the cross of Christ always." [12]

Three weeks of September passed. Isabella, Harvey Jr., and Nancy were with him. On Saturday the twenty-first Harvey Jr. noted a change for the worse, but on Sunday Hill walked out on the porch and sat talking cheerfully in the sunshine for about an hour. [13]

On Monday he slept a great deal and in waking moments spoke indifferently of his approaching death. Tuesday, September 24, was a day of clouds and gathering storm. That morning, at his bedside, Harvey Jr. and Isabella thought they heard him murmur, "Nearly there." By afternoon it seemed that he was free of pain. The storm broke over the city, and for a time the thunder crashed like the artillery at South Mountain. Then the sky cleared, the sun came out, and Harvey Hill went to meet his God.

NOTES

In citations to manuscripts, DU signifies Duke University Library; HFP, Hill family papers in the possession of Miss Pauline Hill of Raleigh, North Carolina, and Mr. and Mrs. David R. Williams of Mulberry Plantation, South Carolina; LC, Library of Congress; NCA, North Carolina Department of Archives and History, Raleigh; SHC, Southern Historical Collection, University of North Carolina Library; UTS, Union Theological Seminary Library, Richmond; VSL, Virginia State Library, Richmond; and Hill, Daniel Harvey Hill.

The main printed source, *War of the Rebellion: A Compilation of the Official Records of the Union and Confederate Armies*, Washington, 1880–1901, is cited as OR, with arabic numerals for volumes and parts of volumes, and with no series indicated unless it is other than Series I.

Prologue: I CANNOT CRITICIZE LEE NOW

1. Hill to "Editor of Century," Jan. 28, March 27, 1885, Century Collection, New York Public Library. Quotation from letter of Jan. 28.

Chapter I. THE ATTACKERS

1. Lee to his wife, April 22, 1862, Robert E. Lee Papers, LC.
2. Letter, April 24, 1862, HFP.
3. Johnston to Hill, May 22, 1885, copy in Hill's hand, Hill Papers, NCA.
4. Hill to Johnston, May 25, 1885, HFP. On Johnston's defense line see Douglas Southall Freeman, *Lee's Lieutenants: A Study in Command*, New York, 1942–44 (cited hereafter as LL), I, 148, and Gilbert E. Govan and James W. Livingood, *A Different Valor: The Story of General Joseph E. Johnston, C.S.A.*, Indianapolis, 1956, pp. 109–110.
5. LL, I, 151, 170–171; OR, 11, pt. 3, pp. 448, 482–483; Hill to his wife, April 27, 1862, HFP.
6. OR, 11, pt. 1, p. 602, pt. 3, pp. 473, 486 ff.; *Southern Historical Society Papers*, Richmond, 1876–1944 (cited hereafter as SHSP), VIII, 283, X, 38.
7. SHSP, VIII, 284–285; Joseph E. Johnston, *Narrative of Military Operations, Directed, During the Late War Between the States*, New York, 1874, pp. 119–120.
8. OR, 11, pt. 1, pp. 535–538.
9. J. A. Early, *Lieutenant General Jubal Anderson Early, C.S.A.*, Philadelphia, 1912, p. 69; OR, 11, pt. 1, pp. 603, 607; Johnston, *Narrative*, p. 122.
10. OR, 11, pt. 1, pp. 538, 603, 607; SHSP, VII, 368, VIII, 290; LL, I, 86.
11. OR, 11, pt. 1, pp. 539, 550, 603; Early to Hill, May 7, 1862, Hill Papers, VSL.

12. OR, 11, pt. 1, p. 603; Hill to James Longstreet, Aug. 31, 1885, James Longstreet Papers, DU.

13. OR, 11, pt. 1, pp. 540, 603, 604, 610, 611; SHSP, VIII, 292, 294, 295.

14. LL, I, 188, and n. 67.

15. OR, 11, pt. 1, pp. 275–276, 565, 603, 607; Early, *Early*, p. 69; James Longstreet, *From Manassas to Appomattox*, Philadelphia, 1896 (cited hereafter as Longstreet), p. 78; Johnston, *Narrative*, p. 122. H. C. Wall said that in a conversation held several years after the war Johnston told him that he had consented to the attack "only after repeated requests from General Hill." Walter Clark, ed., *Histories of the Several Regiments and Battalions from North Carolina in the Great War, 1861–65*, Raleigh, 1901 (cited hereafter as Clark), II, 199.

16. OR, 11, pt. 1, pp. 565, 603, 604–605; Longstreet, p. 78; Johnston, *Narrative*, p. 122.

17. OR, 11, pt. 1, pp. 608, 611; Early to Johnston, April 10, 1872, Joseph E. Johnston Collection, Huntington Library; Dunbar Rowland, ed., *Jefferson Davis, Constitutionalist: His Letters, Papers and Speeches*, Jackson, Miss., 1923 (cited hereafter as Rowland), VIII, 18–25; SHSP, VII, 370–372, VIII, 295–296.

18. SHSP, VII, 370; OR, 11, pt. 1, pp. 539–540, 550–551, 552, 554–555; Letter, Oct. 13, Jubal A. Early Papers, LC.

19. OR, 11, pt. 1, pp. 276, 605; Hill to his wife, May 11, 1862, HFP.

20. J. W. Ratchford to D. H. Hill [Jr.], Paint Rock, Texas, no date, pp. 17–18, Daniel Harvey Hill, Jr. Papers, NCA. This lengthy, paginated letter, containing Ratchford's recollections of Hill from 1858 through the Civil War, was probably written in 1890. Cited hereafter as Ratchford ms.

Chapter II. WHENCE THE WARRIOR

1. Hill to Bradley T. Johnson, May 18, 1887, Bradley T. Johnson Papers, DU; Hill to General S. Cooper, Jan. 1, 1863, Confederate Records, Correspondence of the Adjutant General, National Archives.

2. Hill, "Family and Personal History," ms. in Charles Carrol Simms Collection, South Caroliniana Library, University of South Carolina, access to ms. granted the author through the courtesy of Mary C. Simms Oliphant; *Dictionary of American Biography*, IX, 27; ms. genealogy of Hill family in Hill Papers, SHC.

3. Nancy Hill to Hill, Feb. 11, 1846; Hill to his wife, Jan. 26, Oct. 4, 1862, HFP.

4. A. C. Avery, *Life and Character of Lieutenant General D. H. Hill* (pamphlet), Raleigh, 1893 (cited hereafter as Avery), p. 6.

5. Hill, "Family and Personal History"; D. H. Hill [Jr.], *Col. William Hill and the Campaign of 1780* (pamphlet), n.p., n.d.; Joseph M. Hill, *Biography of Daniel Harvey Hill* (pamphlet), Arkansas History Commission, n.p., n.d., p. 8.

6. Register of Cadet Applicants, Engineer Department, 1837–38, War Records Branch, National Archives; Descriptive Lists of New Cadets, 1838–68, United States Military Academy Archives, West Point; Hill to his brother Albert, June 1 and 2, 1839, HFP; *Official Register of the Officers and Cadets of the U. S. Military Academy*, West Point, 1839–42, *passim*; George W. Cullum, *Biographical Register of the Officers and Graduates of the U. S. Military Academy* . . . Boston, 1891, II, 109–152.

7. Sketch of Hill in the New York *Herald*, Oct. 27, 1862; Hill to John W.

Phelps, July 19, 1849, Hill Papers, NCA; Robert U. Johnson and Clarence C. Buel, eds., *Battles and Leaders of the Civil War*, New York, 1887–88 (cited hereafter as *B&L*), II, 359.

8. Nancy Hill to Hill, March 6, [1845], Feb. 11, 1846, HFP.
9. See Hill's service records, and his correspondence with the Adjutant General for these years, in Records of the War Department, Office of the Adjutant General (Record Group No. 94), National Archives. Cited hereafter as Hill, NA.
10. *B&L*, II, 360, III, 639.
11. Hill, "Family and Personal History"; official endorsement to letter, Hill to R. Jones, Dec. 18, 1845, Hill, NA; *Southern Quarterly Review*, IX, 434–457; Justin H. Smith, *The War with Mexico*, New York, 1919, I, 452–453; Daniel K. Whitaker to W. R. Hill, July 16, 1848, Hill Papers, NCA.
12. Hill, Mexican War Diary, SHC. Cited hereafter as Diary.
13. Diary, *passim*; brevet commissions in Hill Papers, NCA.
14. Diary, Sept. 10, 1847; copy of T. J. Jackson to G. J. Pillow, May 11, 1854, Jackson file, Davidson College Library.
15. Diary, Sept. 14, 1847; Hill, "Family and Personal History"; statement of Barnard Bee in Avery, p. 7.
16. Diary, Sept. 14, 1847; Hill, "Family and Personal History"; copy of Jackson to Pillow, May 11, 1854, Jackson file, Davidson College Library; Hill to R. L. Dabney, July 11, 1864, Robert L. Dabney Papers, UTS.
17. Hill's commission as first lieutenant, dated March 25, 1847, is in Hill Papers, NCA. On his newspaper articles see Diary, Dec. 4, 1846, and Charleston *Mercury*, Oct. 12, Nov. 13, 1846, Feb. 25, 1847. Hill also published in the *Mercury* of Jan. 5, 1847, an "Actor" article on Mexican folkways in which he criticized Roman Catholic priests for living "in open concubinage." The second *Review* article is in XIV (July 1848), 183–197. The South Carolina legislature awarded Hill an honorary sword for his Mexican War heroism. Avery, p. 7.
18. See Diary, *passim*, and Dec. 9, 1846 to Jan. 8, 1847.
19. Joseph M. Hill, *Hill*, p. 10; D. H. Hill and A. W. Miller, *Memorial Sketches of Rev. Robert Hall Morrison, D.D.* (pamphlet), Charlotte, 1889, pp. 9–14; "Declaration of Widow for Pension," Dec. 20, 1889, Mexican War pension papers of Hill, National Archives; Hill to his wife, Nov. 20, 1868, HFP; Robert Hall Morrison to James Morrison, June 13, 1843, Robert Hall Morrison Papers, SHC.
20. Hill to his mother, June 2, 1849, HFP; "Declaration of Widow for Pension"; *B&L*, II, 580.
21. William Couper, *One Hundred Years at V. M. I....*, Richmond, 1939, I, 189.
22. On Hill's resignation see General Thomas Gardner to General R. Jones, April 27, 1849, and endorsement, Hill, NA. His college activities can be traced in trustee and faculty minutes preserved at Washington and Lee University and Davidson College. He is characterized as a teacher in C. D. Fishburne to D. H. Hill, Jr.. Feb. 8, 1890, Daniel Harvey Hill, Jr. Papers, NCA. Cited hereafter as Fishburne reminiscence.
23. See, at Davidson College, Faculty Minutes, April 14, 1854, Dec. 21, 1854—Jan. 16, 1855, and Trustee Minutes, Oct. 15, 1853, Aug. 10, Sept. 26, 1854, Jan. 24, 1855. See also Fishburne reminiscence and Cornelia Rebekah Shaw, *Davidson College*, New York, 1923, pp. 77–78, 86–87. Hill's "primacy" at

Davidson is discussed in Henry E. Shepherd, "Gen. D. H. Hill—A Character Sketch," *Confederate Veteran*, XXV (Sept. 1917), p. 411. On Hill as "controlling spirit," see Ratchford ms., p. 1.

24. Hill to R. L. Dabney, July 11, 1864, Robert L. Dabney Papers, UTS; Daniel Harvey Hill, "The Real Stonewall Jackson," *Century*, XLVII (1893–94), 624–625; copy of Jackson to Pillow, May 11, 1854, Jackson file, Davidson College Library. The nursing incident was related to the author Aug. 13, 1955, by Miss Isabel Arnold of De Land, Florida, daughter of Eugenia Hill Arnold.

25. Conversation, Aug. 13, 1955, with Miss Isabel Arnold.

26. Hill to his wife, July 5, 1861, HFP.

27. Hill, *Elements of Algebra*, p. 322 and *passim*; Fishburne reminiscence. See also Hal Bridges, "D. H. Hill's Anti-Yankee Algebra," *Journal of Southern History*, XXII (May 1956), 220–222.

28. Hill, *Sermon on the Mount*, pp. 152–153; Hill to William Alexander Graham, Dec. 2, 1856, William Alexander Graham Papers (hereafter cited as Graham Papers), SHC. On the military education movement see John Hope Franklin, *The Militant South*, Cambridge, Mass., 1956, pp. 156–157.

29. Robert Hall Morrison to James Morrison, Jan. 5 [?], 1858, Robert Hall Morrison Papers, SHC; Hill to Governor Thomas Bragg of North Carolina, Feb. 25, 1858, Hill Letters, New-York Historical Society; Davidson College Trustee Minutes, July 12, 1859. The author is indebted to Miss Mary Graham of Charlotte for supplying information on Hill's home in a letter of Jan. 14, 1958.

30. Henry E. Shepherd, "Gen. D. H. Hill—A Character Sketch," *Confederate Veteran*, XXV (Sept. 1917), p. 412; *Private Laws of the State of North Carolina . . . 1858–59*, Raleigh, 1859, pp. 383–384; *Catalog of the North Carolina Military Institute . . . 1859–60*, Charlotte, 1860, pp. 3–7; *Regulations for the North Carolina Military Institute*, Charlotte, 1860, pp. 1–10.

31. Ratchford ms., pp. 5–6.

32. John W. Ellis to Hill, April 24, 1861, Hill Papers, NCA; Clark, I, 125–126; OR, 2, p. 93.

33. LL, I, 16; Hill to his wife, May 30, 1861, HFP.

34. Ratchford ms., pp. 10–11. Hill wrote in his official report, OR, 2, p. 94, "We were aroused at 3 o'clock . . . for a general advance on the enemy," and then described his march with no mention of further orders from Magruder. Magruder in his reports said nothing at all about the Confederate advance. OR, 2, pp. 91–93.

35. OR, 2, pp. 82, 94–97; Clark, I, 88; William Gaston Lewis to Miss Mittie Pender, June 12, 1861, William Gaston Lewis Papers, SHC. These papers were called to the author's attention by Manly Wade Wellman. See also his *Rebel Boast*, New York, 1957, p. 53.

36. OR, 2, p. 95.

37. Letters of June 11 and June 20 in HFP. Compare LL, I, 21.

38. Hans Louis Trefousse, *Ben Butler*, New York, 1957, p. 81, tells of Butler's disgrace. Good examples of the extravagant newspaper stories that lauded Hill and Magruder can be found in the Richmond *Dispatch*, June 13, 1861, and the Raleigh *Register*, June 19, 1861. Hill's promotion is recorded in Marcus J. Wright, *General Officers of the Confederate Army*, New York, 1911, p. 56.

39. OR, 51, pt. 2, p. 144; OR, 4, pp. 662, 682, 700; OR, 9, p. 188.

40. Robert Stiles, *Four Years under Marse Robert*, Washington, 1903, p. 67.

41. Hill to Stuart, Dec. 22, 1861, James E. B. Stuart Collection, Huntington Library; OR, 5, p. 1063. Burke Davis, *Jeb Stuart*, New York, 1957, pp. 88–89, quotes President Davis; see also p. 265.
42. Hill to his wife, Dec. 30, 1861, Jan 10, 19, 26, Feb. 1, 18, 1862, HFP.
43. Hill to his wife, Dec. 26, 1861, Jan. 17, 27, Feb. 9, 27, 1862, HFP. On the fall of Fort Donelson see Robert S. Henry, *The Story of the Confederacy*, Indianapolis, 1931, pp. 81–86.
44. Hill to his wife, Jan. 17, March 19, Feb. 28, 1862, HFP.
45. Hill to his wife, Dec. 14, 17, 1861, Jan. 26, March 19, 1862, HFP.
46. See for example Hill to his wife, June 2, 1861, and Feb. 1, 1862, HFP.
47. Hill to his wife, Feb. 3, 21, 1862, HFP.
48. Frank E. Vandiver, *Mighty Stonewall*, New York, 1957, pp. 186–195.
49. See also Stiles, *Four Years under Marse Robert*, p. 72, for comment on Hill's admiration at this time for Jackson's military genius.
50. OR, 5, p. 1095.
51. Vandiver, *Stonewall*, p. 199; LL, I, 140; Johnston, *Narrative*, p. 108.
52. Letters of March 9, 19, 1862, HFP.
53. Hill to his wife, March 19, 30, 1862, HFP. Hill's official commission as major general is in the Hill Papers, NCA.
54. OR, 11, pt. 3, pp. 461, 464.

Chapter III. SEVEN PINES

1. OR, 11, pt. 1, p. 276, pt. 3, p. 502.
2. Letters of May 10 and 11, 1862, HFP.
3. Henry, *Confederacy*, pp. 139–146.
4. Govan and Livingood, *Johnston*, pp. 139, 146; OR, 11, pt. 1, p. 872.
5. OR, 11, pt. 1, p. 943; Johnston, *Narrative*, pp. 132–133.
6. OR, 11, pt. 1, p. 933; Gustavus W. Smith, *Battle of Seven Pines*, New York, 1891, pp. 19–22, 177–178, and *Confederate War Papers*, 2nd ed., New York, 1884, pp. 166–169; B&L, II, 228, 242–244; LL, I, 225–228.
7. OR, 11, pt. 1, pp. 943, 944, 951, 961, 971; Edward Porter Alexander, *Military Memoirs of a Confederate*, New York, 1907, p. 80.
8. B&L, II, 226–227.
9. OR, 11, pt. 1, pp. 933–934, 937, 942; B&L, II, 228, 244; LL, I, 166, 235.
10. OR, 11, pt. 1, pp. 872, 873, 913; B&L, II, 242.
11. Hill to Longstreet, Aug. 5, 1879, Oct. 12, 1885, Longstreet Papers, DU.
12. Longstreet, pp. 93–94; OR, 11, pt. 1, pp. 943, 971.
13. OR, 11, pt. 1, pp. 943, 961–962.
14. OR, 11, pt. 1, p. 943; Thomas H. Carter to Hill, July 1, 1885, Hill Papers, VSL.
15. OR, 11, pt. 1, pp. 943, 973.
16. E. A. Osborne to Hill, June 18, 1885, Hill Papers, VSL; *Extracts of Letters of Bryan Grimes to His Wife ...*, compiled by Pulaski Cowper, Raleigh, 1883, p. 14; OR, 11, pt. 1, p. 956.
17. Carter to Hill, July 1, 1885, Hill Papers, VSL.
18. OR, 11, pt. 1, pp. 874, 943; SHSP, XIII, 263.
19. OR, 11, pt. 1, pp. 982, 986.
20. LL, I, 239–240; Govan and Livingood, *Johnston*, p. 152; OR, 11, pt. 1, pp. 939–940, 943–944, 971, 982.
21. OR, 11, pt. 1, p. 934.

22. OR, 11, pt. 1, pp. 940, 944; Carter to Hill, July 1, 1885, Hill Papers, VSL; John Chamblin to Hill, May 18, 1885, Hill Papers, NCA; Longstreet, pp. 94–96; *LL*, I, 240–243, 258–259.

23. OR, 11, pt. 1, p. 944; Ratchford ms., pp. 19–20.

24. OR, 11, pt. 1, pp. 944, 947–949, 951; John Bratton to Hill, July 22, 1885, Hill Papers, VSL.

25. OR, 11, pt. 1, pp. 813–814, 838–840, 889, 915, 944, 973–974; Longstreet to Hill, Nov. 27, 1877, Hill Papers, NCA; Daniel Harvey Hill [Jr.], *Bethel to Sharpsburg*, Raleigh, 1926, II, 68. For Hill's ride between the contending forces, see David Macrae, *The Americans at Home*, New York, 1952, I, 249–250. The place of the incident in the sequence of events is conjectured.

26. Govan and Livingood, *Johnston*, pp. 154–156.

27. OR, 11, pt. 1, p. 945; Hill to Longstreet, Oct. 19, 1885, Longstreet Papers, DU.

28. OR, 11, pt. 1, pp. 982, 986; Longstreet, p. 104; Hill [Jr.], *Bethel to Sharpsburg*, II, 83–84.

29. OR, 11, pt. 1, pp. 782, 787, 945, 982.

30. OR, 11, pt. 1, p. 945; Ratchford ms., pp. 20–21; Thomas I. Moore to Hill, May 11, 1885, Hill Papers, VSL; Clark, I, 657, 693–694.

31. Ratchford ms., pp. 21–22; Hill to Jubal A. Early, Jan. 15, 1884, Early Papers, LC.

32. See Hill's and Wilcox's reports, OR, 11, pt. 1, pp. 945, 988–989, and Wilcox to Hill, June 17, 1885, Hill Papers, VSL. From Hill's brief, telescoped account of the action of June 1, it might appear that the withdrawal orders were sent before the Federal attack began on the left. But Wilcox, whose report has been accepted as probably the more accurate on this point, stated that Hill's order to him mentioned Mahone's retreat.

33. OR, 11, pt. 1, pp. 945, 983–984; John Chamblin to Hill, May 18, 1885, Hill Papers, NCA; R. H. Anderson to Hill, Nov. 14, 1867, Hill Papers, NCA.

34. For Lee's activities from the evening of May 31 to 1 P.M. June 1, see Douglas Southall Freeman, *R. E. Lee: A Biography*, New York, 1934–35 (cited hereafter as *Lee*), II, 72–76. Davis's notice to Lee, dated June 1, without indication of the hour, is in OR, 11, pt. 3, pp. 568–569. Smith discusses his prostration in *B&L*, II, 261.

35. For the incidents here discussed see Jefferson Davis, *Rise and Fall of the Confederate Government*, New York, 1881, II, 128–129; Smith, *Confederate War Papers*, 205–206, 211–212; *Lee*, II, 74–77. Smith repeated his story of the transfer of command in his *Battle of Seven Pines*, p. 137. See also, on Smith's collapse, OR, 11, pt. 3, pp. 685–686.

36. Longstreet, p. 109; OR, 11, pt. 1, p. 945, pt. 3, p. 570; Smith, *Battle of Seven Pines*, pp. 139–140.

37. OR, 11, pt. 1, pp. 946, 953, 966, 976; Alexander, *Memoirs*, pp. 82, 89.

38. Johnston to John Page Nicholson, April 14, 1875, John Page Nicholson Collection, Huntington Library; Carter to Hill, July 1, 1885, Hill Papers, VSL.

39. OR, 11, pt. 1, pp. 939–941, 943–946.

40. OR, 11, pt. 1, pp. 933–935; Smith, *Confederate War Papers*, pp. 166–171.

41. OR, 11, pt. 1, pp. 935–939; Hill to his son Joseph, June 12, 1886, HFP; C. M. Wilcox to Hill, June 23, 1885, Hill Papers, VSL.

42. Johnston, *Narrative*, pp. 132 ff.; Hill to Longstreet, Aug. 5, 1879, Longstreet Papers, DU; Longstreet to Hill, Jan. 9, 1878, Aug. 25, 1879, Hill Papers, VSL; Longstreet to Hill, Nov. 27, 1877, Hill Papers, NCA.

43. Smith, *Battle of Seven Pines*, pp. 64–67; OR, 11, pt. 3, p. 580.

44. Longstreet, pp. 81 ff. Compare p. 108 of these memoirs with Longstreet's, Hill's, and Wilcox's official reports, OR, 11, pt. 1, pp. 940, 945, 989, and with Wilcox to Hill, June 17, 1885, Hill Papers, VSL.

45. LL, I, p. 238. Nowhere does Freeman in his account of Seven Pines, pp. 225–260, point out the great extent to which Hill exercised the tactical command that Johnston had assigned to Longstreet. For Wilcox's statement see OR, 11, pt. 1, p. 989. See also H. J. Eckenrode and Bryan Conrad, *James Longstreet*, Chapel Hill, 1936, p. 55.

Chapter IV. RED FIELDS AROUND RICHMOND

1. Hill to his wife, June 4, 7, 10, 16, 1862, HFP. Criticism of Lee is summarized in *Lee*, II, 86. The letter to Randolph is in OR, 11, pt. 3, p. 587.
2. Hill to his wife, June 10, 1862, HFP.
3. LL, I, 268–273.
4. OR, 11, pt. 2, pp. 484–485; B&L, II, 580; LL, I, 240, 247.
5. Clark, I, 266; Cullum, *Biographical Register . . . U. S. Military Academy*, p. 480.
6. LL, I, 248–249.
7. *Dictionary of American Biography*, IV, 315.
8. Clement A. Evans, ed., *Confederate Military History*, Atlanta, 1899, V, 418; Cullum, *Biographical Register . . . U. S. Military Academy*, pp. 157, 170; LL, I, 273.
9. Hill to his wife, June 10, 16, 22, 1862, HFP.
10. Hill to his wife, June 10, 1862, HFP; *Lee*, II, 95–104.
11. This account of the conference and of Lee's strategy and battle plans is based upon B&L, II, 347; OR, 11, pt. 2, pp. 491, 498–499; Sir Frederick Maurice, *Robert E. Lee the Soldier*, Boston, 1925, pp. 109–116; *Lee*, II, 32, 108–118; and LL, I, 494–497, wherein Freeman discusses objections that Harvey Hill may possibly have raised against Lee's plans.
12. Longstreet to Hill, Nov. 5, 1877, Hill Papers, VSL; D. H. Hill, "The Battle of Gaines's Mill," *Century*, XXX (May–Oct. 1885), p. 294; Longstreet, pp. 121–122. Lenoir Chambers, in *Stonewall Jackson*, New York, 1959, II, 23, takes note of Hill's account.
13. OR, 11, pt. 1, p. 49.
14. James Cooper Nisbet tells of army contempt for "hospital rats" in *Four Years on the Firing Line*, Chattanooga, n.d., p. 127. An official copy of Hill's order, dated June 24, 1862, is in the James W. Eldridge Collection, Huntington Library.
15. OR, 11, pt. 2, pp. 485, 629, 756; *Lee*, II, 122–125.
16. Douglas Southall Freeman and Grady McWhiney, eds., *Lee's Dispatches . . .*, new edition, New York, 1957, p. 15; Clark, I, 138.
17. OR, 11, pt. 2, pp. 623, 654; B&L, II, 352.
18. OR, 11, pt. 2, pp. 623, 835, 841.
19. OR, 11, pt. 2, p. 835.
20. B&L, II, 328; *Lee*, II, 133.
21. OR, 11, pt. 2, pp. 647, 835, 841, 878, 897, 899. For Lee's order to hold and not attack, see LL, I, 514.
22. OR, 11, pt. 2, pp. 647–648.
23. B&L, II, 361; Robert E. Lee [Jr.], *Recollections and Letters of General Robert E. Lee*, New York, 1904, p. 415; Sir Frederick Maurice, ed., *An Aide-de-Camp of Lee*, Boston, 1927, p. 94.

24. OR, 11, pt. 2, p. 623; Hill [Jr.], *Bethel to Sharpsburg*, II, 107; *Lee*, II, 132.
25. OR, 11, pt. 2, pp. 623, 899.
26. OR, 11, pt. 2, pp. 38–39, 623, 648, 656, 658, 976, 983; Alexander, *Memoirs*, p. 121. Incomplete and conflicting official reports force the student of the action at Ellerson's Mill to reconcile differences and deal in probabilities. Freeman's interpretation in *LL*, I, 515, would seem overly to minimize Lee's and Davis's responsibility for Ripley's attack and to exaggerate the responsibility of D. H. Hill. In *B&L*, II, 361, Hill states: "Ripley's brigade was sent to the assistance of Pender, by the direct order, through me, of both Mr. Davis and General Lee."
27. See detailed description of their movements in *LL*, I, pp. 506–513.
28. OR, 11, pt. 2, pp. 222–223, 399–400.
29. *B&L*, II, 353; *Lee*, II, 140–141.
30. *Lee*, II, 138; OR, 11, pt. 2, p. 624; William E. Ardrey Diary, June 27, 1862, DU.
31. OR, 11, pt. 2, pp. 483–484, 553.
32. See the reproduction of one of the Confederate maps in *Lee*, II, facing p. 138. See also Richard Taylor, *Destruction and Reconstruction*, edited by Richard B. Harwell, New York, 1955, pp. 99–100, and *B&L*, II, 361 and n.
33. OR, 11, pt. 2, p. 492; *LL*, I, 520–521; Alexander, *Memoirs*, p. 123.
34. This account of the battle of Gaines' Mill or First Cold Harbor is based on OR, 11, pt. 2, pp. 491–493, 553, 624–626, 631, 640–642; *Lee*, II, 146–157; *LL*, I, 518–534; William E. Ardrey Diary, June 27, 1862.
35. Letter of June 28, 1862, Lafayette McLaws Papers, SHC.
36. See the reports of Federal participants in the battle, OR, 11, pt. 2, pp. 223 ff., and of the Confederate participants, *Ibid.*, pp. 491 ff. See also *B&L*, II, pp. 334–335, 340, 355–357, 363; John B. Hood, *Advance and Retreat . . .* , New Orleans, 1880, pp. 25–28; Longstreet, p. 129; and *LL*, I, 535. Wilcox's letter to Hill, June 17, 1885, is in Hill Papers, VSL.
37. OR, 11, pt. 2, p. 626; *B&L*, II, 357.
38. OR, 11, pt. 2, p. 626; *B&L*, II, 360–361; Ratchford ms., pp. 25–28; Edward J. Nichols, *Toward Gettysburg: A Biography of General John F. Reynolds*, Pennsylvania State University Press, 1958, pp. 100 ff. While a prisoner, Reynolds wrote his sisters an account of his capture that said nothing about going to sleep in a little house. See *Ibid.*, pp. 96–97.
39. OR, 11, pt. 2, p. 626; Henry, *Confederacy*, p. 160; Vandiver, *Stonewall*, pp. 310–311.
40. Vandiver, *Stonewall*, pp. 311–312; *LL*, I, 553–555.
41. *LL*, I, 540–541; OR, 11, pt. 2, p. 495.
42. Copy, in R. L. Dabney's hand, of R. L. Dabney to Hill, Jan. 8, 1886, Charles W. Dabney Papers (including Robert Lewis Dabney Papers), SHC.
43. *LL*, I, 568–587, 659; Alexander, *Memoirs*, 156.
44. OR, 11, pt. 2, pp. 495–496, 627–628; *B&L*, II, 391; Wilcox to Hill, June 23, 1885, Hill Papers, VSL.
45. OR, 11, pt. 2, pp. 495–496, 557, 558, 566, 607, 668, 811, 818; *B&L*, II, 412.
46. OR, 11, pt. 2, pp. 496, 627–628.
47. OR, 11, pt. 2, p. 627; *B&L*, II, 392; John B. Gordon, *Reminiscences of the Civil War*, New York, 1903, pp. 67–68; Ratchford ms., p. 29.
48. McLaws to "Dear General," Nov. 30, 1885, James Longstreet Photoprints, SHC. The wording of this letter indicates that the addressee is not Longstreet.

49. Alexander, *Memoirs*, p. 157; OR, 11, pt. 2, pp. 496, 628, 669, 677; B&L, II, 392.
50. OR, 11, pt. 2, pp. 627–628, 653; B&L, II, 412; LL, I, 596.
51. OR, 11, pt. 2, p. 628; B&L, II, 393; LL, I, 595–596, 616–618. Freeman suggests that Pendleton was largely to blame for the nonemployment of the reserve artillery. For a defense of Pendleton see Jennings C. Wise, *The Long Arm of Lee*, Lynchburg, Va., 1915, I, 225–229.
52. OR, 11, pt. 2, pp. 485–487, 628; LL, I, pp. 621–623; T. C. De Leon, *Belles, Beaux and Brains of the Sixties*, New York, 1909, pp. 83–84.
53. OR, 11, pt. 2, pp. 628, 643, 650.
54. OR, 11, pt. 2, p. 634.
55. OR, 11, pt. 2, pp. 558, 628; G. F. R. Henderson, *Stonewall Jackson and the American Civil War*, authorized American edition, New York, 1949, p. 388.
56. OR, 11, pt. 2, pp. 628, 634, 643.
57. B&L, II, 394.
58. Pleasant A. Stovall, *Robert Toombs*, New York, 1892, pp. 254, 256–257.
59. LL, I, 597–603.
60. See OR, 11, pt. 2, pp. 496, 558, 566–567, 629, and Henry, *Confederacy*, p. 162.
61. Hill [Jr.], *Bethel to Sharpsburg*, II, 178; OR, 11, pt. 2, pp. 559, 618–619; B&L, II, 394.

Chapter V. "LEE HAS MADE A GROSS MISTAKE"

1. Hill to his wife, July 3, 1862, HFP; Jackson to Hill, July 3, 1862, Hill Papers, NCA; OR, 11, pt. 2, pp. 497, 629.
2. Alexander, *Memoirs*, p. 171; OR, 11, pt. 2, p. 629.
3. Hill to his wife, July 3, 9, 1862, HFP; OR, 11, pt. 2, pp. 493, 496, 554, 557.
4. Toombs to Hill, July 6, 1862, Hill Papers, VSL, and July 13, 1862, Hill Papers, SHC; Hill to Toombs, July 15, 1862, Hill Papers, VSL; Stovall, *Toombs*, pp. 254–258; SHSP, XXVIII, 294. Toombs's letter of July 13 is not in Stovall's biography, which gives in full the rest of the correspondence.
5. OR, Series II, 4, pp. 174, 177, 265–268, 815–816, and vol. 6, pp. 647–648; J. G. Randall, *The Civil War and Reconstruction*, Boston, 1937, pp. 437–439.
6. OR, Series II, 4, p. 825; OR, 9, p. 476; OR, 11, pt. 3, p. 646; OR, 12, pt. 3, p. 917; LL, I, 631–632.
7. General Order No. 35, July 29, 1862, Thomas Lanier Clingman Papers, SHC; OR, 12, pt. 3, p. 917; OR, Series II, 4, 825–826.
8. OR, 9, p. 476; General Order No. 35, July 29, 1862, Thomas Lanier Clingman Papers, SHC.
9. OR, 51, pt. 2, p. 601; OR, 9, p. 477.
10. OR, Series II, 4, 826; OR, 11, pt. 3, p. 663; OR, 11, pt. 2, p. 939; Hill [Jr.], *Bethel to Sharpsburg*, II, 198–199.
11. OR, 11, pt. 2, pp. 934–946, quoted statements on p. 938.
12. OR, 11, pt. 3, pp. 660 ff.
13. OR, 51, pt. 2, p. 1075.
14. OR, 12, pt. 3, p. 938; OR, 19, pt. 1, p. 1019.
15. Horace Montgomery, *Howell Cobb's Confederate Career*, Tuscaloosa, Ala., 1959, pp. 13–26, 68.
16. Henry, *Confederacy*, pp. 172–178; OR, 19, pt. 1, p. 1019.
17. OR, 19, pt. 1, pp. 144–145, pt. 2, pp. 592, 603, 604, 605.

18. *LL*, II, 149–152, 154; *Lee*, II, 359; *OR*, 19, pt. 1, pp. 145, 1019.
19. *OR*, 19, pt. 1, pp. 145, 148, pt. 2, pp. 603–604.
20. The quoted phrase is Lee's. See Hal Bridges, ed., "A Lee Letter on the 'Lost Dispatch' and the Maryland Campaign of 1862," *Virginia Magazine of History and Biography*, vol. 66 (April 1958), pp. 161–166, quoted phrase on p. 165.
21. See *B&L*, II, 663; Longstreet, 201–203.
22. See the monthly magazine edited and published by D. H. Hill in Charlotte from 1866 to 1869, *The Land We Love* (cited hereafter as *LWL*), IV, 274. The copy of the order made by Jackson for Hill is in the Hill Papers, NCA.
23. Jubal Early to Hill, Aug. 2, 1885, Hill Papers, VSL; *OR*, 19, pt. 1, pp. 145, 829, 1019.
24. *OR*, 19, pt. 1, pp. 1021–1022.
25. *OR*, 19, pt. 1, p. 148.
26. *B&L*, II, 606.
27. *OR*, 19, pt. 2, pp. 270–271.
28. *OR*, 19, pt. 1, pp. 44, 45, pt. 2, p. 287; *OR*, 51, pt. 1, pp. 822–823; *B&L*, II, 570.
29. McClellan to Hill, Feb. 1, 1869, Hill Papers, VSL; *B&L*, II, 603; *OR*, 19, pt. 1, pp. 42–43.
30. *OR*, 19, pt. 2, p. 281; Kenneth P. Williams, *Lincoln Finds a General: A Military Study of the Civil War*, New York, 1949–59, I, 370.
31. Ratchford ms., pp. 34–35; *LWL*, IV, 270 ff.; *SHSP*, XIII, 420.
32. Marshall to Hill, Nov. 11, 1867, Hill Papers, VSL.
33. See Hill to his wife, Sept. 29, 1863, HFP; McClellan to Hill, Feb. 1, 1869, Hill Papers, VSL; Hill to R. H. Chilton, Dec. 11, 1867, Hill Letters, Confederate Museum, Richmond; Hill to Longstreet, Feb. 11, 1885, Longstreet Papers, DU.
34. Ratchford ms., p. 35; *B&L*, II, 570; Hill [Jr.], *Bethel to Sharpsburg*, II, 346.
35. The two ms. statements are in Hill Papers, VSL; see also Allan Nevins, *The War for the Union*, Volume II: *War Becomes Revolution*, New York, 1960, p. 219, n. 10. Crawford wrote his statement to Hill under date of Aug. 22, 1868, and accompanied it with a certified true copy of the original letter from Marcy in his possession. For Colgrove's statement, see *B&L*, II, 603.
36. See Hill to John Esten Cooke, Oct. 5, 1868, Hill Papers, DU.
37. Some of the most useful discussions relative to the losing of Lee's famous order can be found in these sources: R. H. Chilton to Hill, June 22, 1867, Hill Papers, NCA, and to Robert E. Lee, July 26, 1867, Robert E. Lee Headquarters Papers, Virginia Historical Society; R. H. Anderson to Hill, Nov. 14, 1867, Hill Papers, NCA; *LWL*, IV, 273–275; *LL*, II, Appendix I; Walter H. Taylor, *Four Years with General Lee*, New York, 1878, p. 67, n. 1; Bridges, ed., "Lee Letter," *Virginia Magazine of History and Biography*, vol. 66 (April 1958), p. 164; Ratchford ms., pp. 35–36.
38. For Hill's postwar reasoning on the misleading effect of the order, see *B&L*, II, 570.
39. *OR*, 19, pt. 1, pp. 45, 374, 417; *B&L*, II, 584.

Chapter VI.   HOLD AT ALL HAZARDS

1. Hill to Longstreet, Feb. 11, 1885, Longstreet Papers, DU; A. H. Colquitt to Hill, July 4, 1885, Hill Papers, NCA; *OR*, 19, pt. 1, pp. 48, 816–817, 1019, 1052; *B&L*, II, 560.

2. OR, 19, pt. 1, p. 1052; Colquitt to Hill, July 4, 1885, Hill Papers, NCA.
3. OR, 19, pt. 1, pp. 817, 1052; Thomas L. Rosser to Hill, July 10, 1883, Hill Papers, VSL; maps in *B&L*, II, 568, and in OR, *Atlas*, Plate XXVII, 3.
4. OR, 19, pt. 1, pp. 145, 817, pt. 2, p. 604. For map of route taken by army see *Lee*, II, 364.
5. OR, 19, pt. 1, pp. 816–817.
6. Colquitt to Hill, July 4, 1885, Hill Papers, NCA. Although Freeman in *LL*, II, 171, accepts the story that the Federals revealed themselves to Colquitt after dark by lighting large numbers of campfires, such military folly hardly seems in keeping with the care they took to conceal their numbers from Stuart. Freeman's source is the reminiscence of Judge George D. Grattan in *SHSP*, XXXIX, 31–44, story of campfires on p. 36. This reminiscence, when checked against Colquitt's letter and other documents, appears not very reliable on the battle of South Mountain.
7. Colquitt to Hill, July 4, 1885, Hill Papers, NCA; Clark, II, 219.
8. *LL*, II, 171, 718, 721; OR, 19, pt. 1, p. 817, pt. 2, p. 607; *B&L*, II, 560; Hill to Longstreet, Feb. 11, 1885, Longstreet Papers, DU. In this letter Hill emphasized that Lee suggested, and did not specifically order, the conference with Stuart at Turner's Gap.
9. Bridges, ed., "Lee Letter," p. 165; *LL*, II, Appendix I.
10. Bridges, ed., "Lee Letter," p. 165.
11. See Lee's report, OR, 19, pt. 1, p. 146.
12. For the message to McLaws, see OR, 19, pt. 2, p. 608. It is paraphrased in *Lee*, II, 369. The message to Stuart is in the James E. B. Stuart Collection, Huntington Library. The Captain Blackford mentioned in it is evidently Stuart's engineer, W. W. Blackford. The hour was not noted on either message.
13. OR, 19, pt. 1, pp. 146, 817, 1019.
14. Hill to Longstreet, July 30, 1885, Longstreet Papers, DU.
15. Hill to Longstreet, Feb. 11, June 5, 8, 1885, Longstreet Papers, DU; Hill to C. C. Buel, Dec. 10, 1885, Century Collection, New York Public Library; *B&L*, II, 561–562.
16. OR, 19, pt. 1, pp. 1019–1020. Freeman in *LL*, II, 174–176, places the calling up of these units later in the morning, after a reconnaissance that Hill made toward Fox's Gap; but in so doing he seems to have fallen into an incorrect sequence of events—the result, apparently, of confusing Hill's examination of Turner's Gap with his later reconnaissance toward Fox's Gap. The ordering up of Ripley's regiment is related in the text in accordance with Hill's report, cited. Ripley reported that he was ordered on the "evening of September 13" to send the regiment at daylight on the 14th to occupy the pass, and that he did so. OR, 19, pt. 1, p. 1031.
17. OR, 19, pt. 1, pp. 1019–1020; *B&L*, II, 564, 565. See also Hill [Jr.], II, 365. An acquaintance of Lee recorded Lee as saying in a postwar conversation that Hill should have had all his troops up at the mountain. See *LL*, II, 718. Lee at the time was angry over an article that Hill had published on the Lost Dispatch. The brief paraphrase of this comment by Lee does not indicate his thinking with regard to just when Hill should have brought up all his troops, nor does it indicate whether Lee took account of Hill's concern over a Federal move to his rear through the lower gaps. This factor in the situation seems to have been overlooked by Freeman, who indicates that Hill left part of his division at Boonsborough simply because he was overly concerned with the part of his orders that directed him to prevent escape from Harpers Ferry. See *LL*, II, 174–176.

18. OR, 19, pt. 1, p. 1019. See maps, B&L, II, 568, and OR, Atlas, Plate XXVII, 3.
19. B&L, II, 562, 586; Rosser to Hill, July 10, 1883, Hill Papers, VSL; OR, 19, pt. 1, pp. 210, 461. Compare LL, II, 174–175. Hill's statement in B&L, II, 562, that Rosser got to the heights after the Federals conflicts with the official records, and seems to be a misinterpretation of Rosser's letter of July 10, cited above. Rosser speaks of seeing the enemy on the road in his front, but does not specify at what time, or just where on the road the enemy was.
20. B&L, II, 562, 563.
21. J. F. Johnston to Hill, May 28, 1885, Hill Papers, VSL; B&L, II, 564–565. In B&L, Hill's description of this incident begins with the phrase, "A little before this," which is used ambiguously. This makes it difficult to fit Hill's visit to the lookout station into the sequence of events, but Johnston's letter indicates pretty clearly that Hill went to the station while Garland was moving toward Fox's Gap. Hill's published article on the battle of South Mountain should be used with care as a source, for Hill described it as "badly mutilated" and "quite unsatisfactory to me." Hill to his son Joseph, May 17, 1886, HFP.
22. Apparently these orders were sent about 8:30 A.M. Allowing, as Freeman does, about an hour for the courier to perform his duty, the orders would have been delivered around 9:30 A.M. Ripley reported, one week after the battle, that he got his order "soon after" 9 A.M. Calvin Leach, a soldier in Ripley's brigade, noted in his diary under entry of September 14, [1862], that his regiment, the First North Carolina, started toward the sound of the cannon "today at 10 o'clock. . . ." (Calvin Leach Diary, SHC). This correlates pretty closely with Ripley's report, for of course it must have taken Ripley some time after receiving his order to put his brigade in marching column on the turnpike. Rodes reported, one month after the battle, that "toward noon" he was ordered to follow Ripley's brigade. This vague indication of the hour could mean any time after mid-morning. Ripley's and Rodes's reports are in OR, 19, pt. 1, pp. 1031, 1034. Had Freeman seen the Leach diary entry, he might have modified his suggestion in LL, II, 179, n. 40, that Hill did not dispatch orders to Rodes and Ripley before 10 or 10:30 A.M. Freeman interprets Rodes's "toward noon" as 11–11:30 A.M., and rejects Ripley's "soon after" 9 A.M. because later in his report Ripley said he was taking position when General Thomas F. Drayton arrived, and Drayton came up not earlier than 3:30 P.M. Ripley's report, however, is not reliable for what happened after he reached the scene of action, for he moved his regiments from place to place and avoided fighting, and later wrote a largely fictional version of what he saw and did on the mountain. In proof of this, three mss. corroborate one another: the Leach diary, under entry of September 14; S. A. Thruston to Governor Zebulon B. Vance, Sept. 27, 1862, William L. De Rosset Papers, NCA; and William L. De Rosset to Hill, June 18, 1885, Hill Papers, VSL.
23. Vague and varying records make it difficult to say exactly when Anderson arrived, but apparently it was before 10 A.M. J. F. Johnston to Hill, May 28, 1885, Hill Papers, VSL, indicates that Anderson was up by the time Garland's brigade was routed, and the Federals seem to have driven it by 10 A.M. See editors' note, under map, B&L, II, 568. Hill reported, in OR, 19, pt. 1, p. 1020: "Anderson's brigade arrived in time to take the place of the much-demoralized troops of Garland." Colonel D. K. McRae, who succeeded Garland in command, wrote in his report of two of Anderson's regiments reaching Fox's Gap before the final rout of Garland's brigade. See OR, 19, pt. 1, p. 1041. See also B&L, II, 587. All this indicates a considerably earlier hour of

arrival for Anderson than that suggested by Freeman, who writes in *LL*, II, 180: "Before 2 o'clock, that stalwart Brigadier, George B. Anderson, had climbed to the pass and had filed to the right."

24. J. F. Johnston to Hill, May 28, 1885; D. K. McRae to Hill, Aug. 21, 1885, Hill Papers, VSL.

25. Rosser to Hill, July 10, 1883, Hill Papers, VSL; OR, 19, pt. 1, p. 1040; Hill [Jr.], *Bethel to Sharpsburg*, II, 366.

26. Hill [Jr.], *Bethel to Sharpsburg*, II, 367, 369; OR, 19, pt. 1, pp. 461, 1040–1041; Clark, I, 627; B&L, II, 563–564; D. K. McRae to Hill, Aug. 21, 1885, Hill Papers, VSL; Thomas Ruffin to Hill, Aug. 4, 1885, Hill Papers, VSL.

27. OR, 19, pt. 1, pp. 1040–1042; McRae to Hill, Aug. 21, 1885; Alfred Iverson to Hill, Aug. 23, 1885, Hill Papers, NCA; J. G. de Roulhac Hamilton, ed., *The Papers of Thomas Ruffin*, Raleigh, 1918–20, III, 262–263; Rosser to Hill, July 10, 1883; Hill to C. C. Buel, Dec. 10, 1885, Century Collection, New York Public Library.

28. OR, 19, pt. 1, p. 1020. Hill's discussion of this part of the battle, in B&L, II, 566–567, contains statements about Anderson's not coming up until after the rout of Garland's brigade. These statements have not been accepted, because they conflict with the abundant evidence, already given, that Anderson was up in time to support Garland's brigade. Various explanations of inaccuracy on Hill's part suggest themselves; perhaps the most probable is that, like many another writer of memoirs, he was tricked by his memory and failed to check the records carefully.

29. OR, 19, pt. 1, pp. 459, 1020; B&L, II, 567, 587. Freeman in LL, II, 180, finds this lull "incredible" and "well-nigh miraculous," and comments that Hill was "luckier than he deserved to be." In his narrative Freeman does not mention Anderson's morning counterattack; his thesis, as previously noted, is that Anderson arrived some time before 2 P.M. Neither does he take account of Hill's use of a large number of guns, nor of the Federals' apprehensions about Longstreet.

30. The time of arrival, which is not given in the records, has been conjectured from Ripley's and Rodes's reports (OR, 19, pt. 1, pp. 1031, 1033–1034), the Calvin Leach Diary, entry of Sept. 14, and OR, Atlas, Plate XXVII, 3. Ripley was stationed immediately northeast of Boonsborough, and had to march about two miles up the turnpike to reach the Mountain House. Rodes was about half a mile west of Boonsborough, and had to march about three miles on the turnpike. Part of the route was flat; for perhaps the last mile and a half the pike slanted upward in a fairly straight line to the Mountain House, about one thousand feet above the plain. No doubt Hill, after seeing most of McClellan's army from the lookout, ordered Ripley and Rodes to come up with all possible speed; and over the two- and three-mile distances, including the moderate upgrade, the field-hardened, well-rested, and lightly equipped men of the two brigades were capable of marching, one would think, at a rate of at least three miles per hour. Thus Ripley, if he started his march at 10 A.M., as Leach noted, could have reached the Mountain House well before 11 A.M.; and if hard-driving Robert Rodes also started about 10 A.M., which seems likely, he could have arrived by 11 A.M. He states that just before reporting to Hill he overtook Ripley on the mountain, an indication that Ripley may not have pushed his men very hard, and that both brigades arrived about 11 A.M. Hill reported, "Rodes and Ripley came up soon after Anderson." OR, 19, pt. 1, p. 1020. The foregoing analysis conflicts with Freeman's theory that the two brigades did not arrive before 2 or 3 P.M., and with his censure of Hill for

failure to get all of his division on the mountain "until after midday." *LL*, II, 179, 183.

31. *OR*, 19, pt. 1, pp. 186, 187, 189–191, 214, 267, 1020; *B&L*, II, 567–569.
32. *OR*, 19, pt. 1, p. 1020. The nature of Longstreet's message is not given in the record; in the text it has been assumed that Longstreet was reporting his progress.
33. *OR*, 19, pt. 1, pp. 908–909, 1020–1021; see also the three mutually corroboratory mss. cited at the end of note No. 22, this chapter.
34. *OR*, 19, pt. 1, pp. 908–909, 922, 1021.
35. *OR*, 19, pt. 1, pp. 220–222, 267, 1021, 1034–1035; *B&L*, II, 571–574.
36. For the first of these incidents, which may have occurred earlier in the battle, as the time of its occurrence is not given, see Clark, I, 166, where the quoted accolade to Hill is also to be found. For the story about the rocks, which was told of Hill after the battle, see Stiles, *Four Years under Marse Robert*, p. 66.
37. *OR*, 19, pt. 1, pp. 460, 1021; *B&L*, II, 571.
38. *OR*, 19, pt. 1, pp. 215, 247–248, 1020, 1053; Hill to Longstreet, Feb. 11, 1885, Longstreet Papers, DU; *B&L*, II, 575–576, 580.
39. This account of the council of war and Hill's opinion of the battle is based upon Hill to Longstreet, Feb. 11, 1885; *OR*, 19, pt. 1, p. 1021; and *Lee*, II, 372–374. Hill's letter indicates that the council of war was held earlier than the hour of 9 P.M. that Hill recalled in *B&L*, II, 571.
40. *Lee*, II, 374–377; *LL*, II, 190–192.
41. *Lee*, II, 372.
42. Ratchford ms., pp. 38–39.

Chapter VII. "THE LONGEST, SADDEST DAY"

1. *Lee*, II, 378–387; Vandiver, *Stonewall*, p. 392; *OR*, 19, pt. 1, pp. 217–218, 1022. In *Lee*, II, 381, Freeman states the reasons for Lee's decision to stand at Sharpsburg. The decision has been sharply criticized. See for example Alexander, *Memoirs*, 242–249.
2. Hill to his son Joseph, June 12, 1886, HFP.
3. Ratchford ms., pp. 41–43. Ratchford is vague as to the exact time of this incident of the 17th, and the time given in the text is conjectured.
4. *OR*, 19, pt. 1, pp. 149, 1022–1023; *LL*, II, 206–210; Warren W. Hassler, Jr., *General George B. McClellan*, Baton Rouge, 1957, pp. 273–280.
5. *Lee*, II, 391; Gordon, *Reminiscences*, p. 84.
6. *OR*, 19, pt. 1, p. 1023; McRae to Hill, Aug. 21, 1885, Hill Papers, VSL.
7. *B&L*, II, 671.
8. This account of the fighting in Hill's sector is based upon *OR*, 19, pt. 1, pp. 61–62, 149–150, 323–324, 845, 1023–1024, 1030, 1037–1038; Gordon, *Reminiscences*, pp. 84–85; Bruce Catton, *Mr. Lincoln's Army*, New York, 1951, pp. 295–304; Hassler, *McClellan*, pp. 273, 280–285; *LL*, II, 211–217.
9. *OR*, 19, pt. 1, pp. 150, 425; *LL*, II, 217–221; Hassler, *McClellan*, pp. 286–289.
10. *OR*, 19, pt. 1, p. 1024.
11. *OR*, 19, pt. 1, pp. 845–846; Longstreet, p. 261; *LL*, II, 221–222; Hassler, *McClellan*, p. 289.
12. *OR*, 19, pt. 1, pp. 150, 1025, 1031.
13. *OR*, 19, pt. 1, pp. 426, 886–887, 981.
14. *Lee*, II, 398, 402, 403–404; Hassler, *McClellan*, p. 290; Henry Lord Page King, Diary, Sept. 17, 1862, SHC; Wise, *Long Arm of Lee*, I, 323.

15. *Lee*, II, 405.
16. See OR, 19, pt. 1, pp. 141, 148, 150, 951, 955, 957, 981; *LL*, II, 199–202, 204, 217, 221–222; *Lee*, II, 379, 382, 398–402, 414. Freeman in *Lee*, II, 382, notes that on the 16th Lee expected Hill to arrive during the day, and that during the evening he ordered him to come up, but the matter is not explored further.
17. Calvin Leach Diary, Sept. 17, 18, [1862], SHC.

Chapter VIII. A CONFLICT OF TESTIMONY

1. OR, 19, pt. 1, pp. 142, 151, 152, 831, 833, 957, 972, 981.
2. Hill to R. L. Dabney, July 19, 1864, Robert L. Dabney Papers, UTS; Ratchford ms., pp. 46–47; OR, 19, pt. 1, p. 957.
3. OR, 19, pt. 1, pp. 339–340, 833–834.
4. Lee to Mrs. T. J. Jackson, Jan. 25, 1866, copy taken from Lee's letterbook, R. E. Lee Papers, Confederate Museum; copy of R. E. Lee to Mrs. T. J. Jackson, Jan. 25, 1866, Robert L. Dabney Papers, UTS. This latter document is marked by Dabney's son, Charles, "copy of a copy made by my father." Except for minor variations, in abbreviation of names, punctuation, etc., the copies in the two depositaries are identical regarding the Boteler's Ford incident.
5. Both Freeman and Vandiver recognize the conflict. See *Lee*, II, 407–408, n. 20, and Vandiver, *Stonewall*, pp. 402–403, 525, n. 6.
6. *LL*, II, 228.
7. OR, 19, pt. 1, pp. 972–973.
8. OR, 19, pt. 1, pp. 151, 957, 981.
9. OR, 19, pt. 1, p. 841; Longstreet, p. 263.
10. OR, 19, pt. 1, pp. 831, 833–834.
11. OR, 19, pt. 2, p. 612.
12. OR, 19, pt. 1, p. 834.
13. Susan P. Lee, *Memoirs of William Nelson Pendleton, D.D.*, Phila., 1893, p. 214; quoted in *LL*, II, 232.
14. Longstreet, p. 264.
15. Chambers, *Jackson*, II, 232.
16. OR, 19, pt. 1, p. 142.
17. OR, 19, pt. 1, pp. 340, 973, 1025.
18. R. L. Dabney, *Life and Campaigns of Lieut.-Gen. Thomas J. Jackson*, New York, 1866, pp. 577–578.
19. R. L. Dabney to Hill, March 2, 1869, Hill Papers, SHC.

Chapter IX. DISSENSION IN THE HIGH COMMAND

1. Ratchford ms., pp. 47–48; OR, 19, pt. 1, p. 1025.
2. *LL*, II, pp. 247, 248 and n. 36, 250–269.
3. *LL*, I, 312–314, II, 146–147, 244–245, 326; Chambers, *Jackson*, I, 474.
4. Letter in William Nelson Pendleton Papers, SHC. See also OR, 12, pt. 1, pp. 391–392, and *LL*, I, 318.
5. McLaws to "Miss Lizzie" [Ewell?], Feb. 18, 1863, R. S. Ewell Papers, LC. Quoted in Burke Davis, *They Called Him Stonewall*, New York, 1954, p. 387.
6. G. Moxley Sorrel, *Recollections of a Confederate Staff Officer*, 2nd ed., New York, 1917, p. 116; OR, 19, pt. 2, p. 643.
7. Longstreet to Johnston, Oct. 5, 1862, Longstreet Papers, DU.

8. *Dictionary of American Biography*, XIV, 415; John C. Pemberton, *Pemberton, Defender of Vicksburg*, Chapel Hill, 1942, pp. 25–35.
9. Ratchford ms., pp. 72–73.
10. Hill to his wife, Oct. 8, 18, 1862, HFP.
11. Hill to his wife, July 3, Nov. 10, 17, 1862, HFP.
12. C. G. Chamberlayne, ed., *Ham Chamberlayne—Virginian*, Richmond, 1932, p. 134; quoted in *LL*, II, 274; Hill to his wife, Nov. 17, 1862, HFP.
13. *Herald*, p. 1, col. 6; *Tribune*, p. 4, col. 6. For information on the location of these stories the present writer thanks Professor J. Cutler Andrews of Chatham College, author of *The North Reports the Civil War*.
14. OR, 19, pt. 2, p. 643.
15. Longstreet, p. 332.
16. Longstreet, p. 332, n.; OR, 19, pt. 1, pp. 149–150, 840; *LL*, II, 240.
17. *LL*, II, 721; Hill to his wife, Oct. 8, 1862, HFP; Edward Younger, ed., *Inside the Confederate Government: The Diary of Robert Garlick Hill Kean*, New York, 1957, p. 81; SHSP, XXXIII, 25.
18. OR, 11, pt. 2, pp. 623, 629.
19. OR, 19, pt. 1, pp. 1022, 1025, 1026. Compare *LL*, II, 274–275, 282.
20. Letter of Nov. 17, 1862, HFP.
21. See *Lee*, II, 409–411; SHSP, XIII, 13.
22. Letter of Nov. 14, 1867, Hill Papers, NCA.
23. Hill on Garland and Anderson is quoted in *LL*, II, 250, n. 1, 251, n. 4. See also Rodes to Hill, March 22, 1863, Hill Papers, NCA; De Rosset to Hill, June 18, 1885, Hill Papers, VSL; Iverson to Hill, Aug. 23, 1885, Hill Papers, NCA.
24. Ratchford ms., pp. 43–45, 77.
25. Quoted in Shaw, *Davidson College*, pp. 110–111.
26. Ratchford ms., pp. 53–54; Stiles, *Four Years under Marse Robert*, p. 66.
27. William E. Boggs to Hill, March 19, 1889, HFP.
28. Ratchford ms., pp. 48–51; Ratchford to Hill, July 20 [?], 1886, Hill Papers, NCA; *Lee*, II, 438, 441; Vandiver, *Stonewall*, p. 420.
29. *Lee*, II, 489.
30. Robert L. Dabney Papers, UTS. See also OR, 21, pp. 1097–1099, especially the statement by Quartermaster General A. C. Myers, p. 1099: "General Jackson's corps is said not to be so well supplied as General Longstreet's."
31. For the two letters, see OR, 21, pp. 1043–1044. Freeman's interpretation of the incident is in *LL*, II, 323–324.
32. OR, 21, pp. 1046–1047, 1048.
33. OR, 21, pp. 642–643; T. J. Jackson to Hill, Dec. 4, 1862, Hill Papers, SHC; A. S. Pendleton to his mother, Dec. 11, 1862, William Nelson Pendleton Papers, SHC.
34. OR, 21, pp. 87, 630, 1042–1043; Hill to R. L. Dabney, July 21, 1864, Robert L. Dabney Papers, UTS; Early, *Early*, p. 477; Dabney, *Jackson*, p. 597.
35. Henderson, *Jackson*, p. 590.
36. Maurice, ed., *An Aide-de-Camp of Lee*, p. xvii.
37. OR, 21, pp. 634, 643; *LL*, II, 369–373; John Chamblin to Hill, May 25, 1885, and A. R. Mott to Chamblin, June 29, 1885, copy made by Hill, Hill Papers, VSL.
38. OR, 21, pp. 547–548; Chambers, *Jackson*, II, 304–305.
39. Letter in Robert E. Lee Papers, LC.
40. Hill to R. L. Dabney, July 21, 1864, Robert L. Dabney Papers, UTS.

Chapter X. AT ODDS WITH LEE

1. Hill to General S. Cooper (see also endorsements), Confederate Records, Correspondence of the Adjutant General, National Archives.
2. *LL*, II, 274, n. 29; Hill to C. C. Buel, May 5, 1885, Century Collection, New York Public Library.
3. Jackson's note to Hill is in Hill Papers, VSL.
4. OR, 18, pp. 54–59, 810–815, 819–820; Freeman and McWhiney, eds., *Lee's Dispatches*, pp. 68–70.
5. OR, 18, pp. 831, 847, 851.
6. OR, 18, p. 107.
7. OR, 18, pp. 856, 861; Joseph Howard Parks, *General Edmund Kirby Smith*, C.S.A., Baton Rouge, 1954, p. 251.
8. Smith, *Confederate War Papers*, pp. 299–301, 333–342; OR, 18, p. 872.
9. See *LL*, II, 427.
10. See for example *LL*, I, xxxvi, II, xxviii, 54–55, 182, 211, 469–470, 475.
11. Smith, *Confederate War Papers*, p. 302.
12. *LL*, II, 467–469; OR, 18, pp. 894–895.
13. *LL*, II, 428.
14. J. G. de Roulhac Hamilton, *North Carolina since 1860*, Chicago, 1919, p. 23.
15. Clark, III, 549, IV, 645; OR, 18, p. 900.
16. OR, 18, p. 189.
17. OR, 18, p. 891; Alexander, *Memoirs*, pp. 314–318.
18. OR, 18, pp. 890–891.
19. Freeman and McWhiney, eds., *Lee's Dispatches*, pp. 72–73.
20. OR, 18, p. 901.
21. OR, 18, pp. 894–895.
22. Kenneth Rayner to Thomas Ruffin, March 8, 1863, in Hamilton, ed., *Papers of Thomas Ruffin*, III, 303; George Whitaker Wills to his sister, Lucy Cary Wills, March 5, 1863, George Whitaker Wills Papers, SHC. See also Wellman, *Rebel Boast*, p. 104.
23. Ratchford ms., pp. 54–56.
24. OR, 18, pp. 819, 926–927.
25. OR, *Atlas*, Plate LXVII, 3.
26. OR, 18, pp. 188–189, 819, 898, 902–903, 905, 907–908, 910–911, 913, 920.
27. OR, 18, pp. 188–198, 547, 901; Hill to J. J. Pettigrew, March 14, 1863, J. J. Pettigrew Papers, NCA. Compare Freeman's account of the New Bern expedition, *LL*, II, 473–476.
28. OR, 18, p. 931.
29. OR, 18, p. 953.
30. OR, 18, pp. 925, 926–927, 931, 932, 941, 942.
31. OR, 18, pp. 211, 594, 915–916, 941, 961; OR, *Atlas*, Plate XXIV, 5; Raleigh *Register*, April 8, 1863.
32. OR, 18, p. 956.
33. April 5, 1863, HFP.
34. OR, 18, pp. 968–969.
35. OR, 18, pp. 594, 820, 856, 961, 969, 973, 986.
36. OR, 18, pp. 247–252, 974.
37. William Gaston Lewis to Miss Mittie Pender, April 13, 1863, William Gaston Lewis Papers, SHC. See also Wellman, *Rebel Boast*, p. 106.
38. OR, 18, pp. 987, 990, 991.

39. OR, 18, pp. 215, 1007, 1032. Compare Freeman's account of the siege of Washington, LL, II, 478 ff.
40. John T. Ellis to Charles Ellis, Jr., April 25, 1863, Munford-Ellis Papers, DU; J. G. de Roulhac Hamilton, ed., Papers of Randolph Abbott Shotwell, Raleigh, 1929–36, I, 462; Raleigh Register, April 22, 1863; Lafayette McLaws to his wife, April 26, 1863, Lafayette McLaws Papers, SHC; OR, 18, p. 999.
41. Hill to Pettigrew, April 23 [1863], J. J. Pettigrew Papers, NCA; OR, 51, pt. 2, p. 694.
42. OR, Series II, 5, p. 389; Raleigh Register, April 22, 1863. The Hill-Stanly correspondence also appears in Frank Moore, ed., The Rebellion Record, New York, 1862–71, VI, 474–476.
43. This account of Jackson's death is based upon Dabney, Jackson, pp. 722 ff.; LL, II, 678 ff.; Chambers, Jackson, II, 444 ff.
44. Hill to Vance, May 10 [1863], Zebulon Baird Vance Papers, NCA (cited hereafter as Vance Papers); OR, 18, p. 1073.
45. Jan. 30, 1863, Hill Letters, New-York Historical Society.
46. See, on these matters, Vance to Hill, April 23, 1863, Zebulon Baird Vance Letter Book, NCA, and April 28 [1863], Hill Papers, VSL; Hill to Vance, May 1, 1863, Vance Papers; Vance to Hill, May 4, 1863, Hill Papers, VSL (quoted); Hill to Vance, May 31, 1863, Vance Papers (quoted); OR, 51, pt. 2, p. 709.
47. OR, 51, pt. 2, pp. 706–708, 709; OR, 18, p. 1011; Hill to Vance, May 12, 1863, Vance Papers.
48. OR, 18, pp. 1066, 1077; Hill to his wife, Nov. 17, 1862, HFP.
49. Govan and Livingood, Johnston, pp. 196–197, 207; Lee, III, 18–19.
50. OR, 18, p. 1063.
51. OR, 25, pt. 2, p. 832.
52. OR, 27, pt. 3, pp. 1006–1007; OR, 25, pt. 2, pp. 820–821; OR, 18, pp. 1071, 1075, 1088.
53. OR, 18, pp. 1063, 1071, 1075, 1079, 1086. The "effective" total used by Hill and Lee in their correspondence was "total enlisted men present, less sum of enlisted men sick and on extra duty." OR, 27, pt. 3, p. 947.
54. OR, 18, pp. 1071, 1075, 1076.
55. OR, 18, pp. 1073, 1074–1075.
56. OR, 18, p. 1076. Hill's letter does not appear in the records; some indication of its content can be gained from Seddon's reply.
57. OR, 18, p. 1077.
58. Freeman and McWhiney, eds., Lee's Dispatches, pp. 99–100.
59. OR, 18, pp. 1078–1079.
60. OR, 18, p. 1079.
61. OR, 51, pt. 2, p. 718.
62. OR, 18, p. 1079.
63. OR, 18, p. 1082.
64. OR, 18, pp. 1083–1085.
65. OR, 18, p. 1088.
66. OR, 18, pp. 678, 701, 707, 736; OR, 27, pt. 3, pp. 6–7. Foster did not report "effective" strengths, which of course would have produced smaller totals.
67. OR, 18, pp. 736–737, 1081.
68. This discussion of the command system draws upon Frank Vandiver, Rebel Brass: The Confederate Command System, Baton Rouge, 1956, pp. 23–25, 54–55; Maurice, Lee the Soldier, p. 253; T. Harry Williams, Lincoln and His

Generals, New York, 1952, pp. 3, 8, and *P. G. T. Beauregard*, Baton Rouge, 1955, p. 225.

69. OR, 51, pt. 2, p. 720; OR, 27, pt. 3, p. 904.
70. OR, 27, pt. 2, p. 790; OR, 51, pt. 2, p. 724.
71. Hill to his wife, June 14, 25, 1863, HFP.
72. For sympathetic analysis of Lee's reasons for the movement see Maurice, *Lee the Soldier*, pp. 189–193, and *Lee*, III, 18–19. The phrase "great gamble" is Freeman's, *Lee*, III, 24. For some adverse views see Alexander, *Memoirs*, pp. 364–365.
73. Letter of June 23 in Hill Papers, NCA; letter of the 25th in HFP.
74. B&L, III, 639 n.
75. OR, 27, pt. 3, pp. 111, 453–454.
76. OR, 27, pt. 3, pp. 455, 912; OR, 27, pt. 1, pp. 75–77.
77. OR, 27, pt. 3, pp. 904, 931.
78. OR, 27, pt. 1, pp. 19, 75–77; *Lee*, III, 32, 139.
79. OR, 27, pt. 3, pp. 924–925.
80. OR, 27, pt. 1, pp. 75–77.
81. OR, 27, pt. 3, p. 931.
82. Younger, ed., *Diary of Robert G. H. Kean*, p. 88.
83. OR, 27, pt. 3, p. 945.
84. OR, 51, pt. 2, p. 728; OR, 27, pt. 3, pp. 939, 948; Hill to Vance, June 25, 1863, Vance Papers.
85. OR, 27, pt. 3, pp. 412, 949 ff.; John W. Graham to his father, July 5, 1863, Graham Papers, SHC; Younger, ed., *Diary of Robert G. H. Kean*, pp. 77–78.
86. OR, 27, pt. 3, pp. 956–957, 969, 970–971.
87. OR, 27, pt. 3, pp. 972, 990.
88. Vance Papers.
89. Avery, pp. 32–33; Ratchford ms., pp. 56–57; commission in Hill Papers, NCA; OR, 27, pt. 3, p. 1003.

Chapter XI. CHICKAMAUGA

1. OR, 30, pt. 1, pp. 55–56, pt. 2, pp. 31–32, 524; Alexander, *Memoirs*, p. 452; OR, *Atlas*, Plate XLVI, 1.
2. B&L, III, 639; Hill to Vance, July 25, 1863, Vance Papers.
3. July 20, 1863, Confederate Records, Correspondence of the Adjutant General, National Archives.
4. OR, Series IV, 2, pp. 670–671. A rough draft of the letter, in Hill's hand, is in Hill Papers, VSL.
5. OR, Series IV, 2, pp. 695–696. For a summary discussion of the evasion of military service in the Confederacy, see E. Merton Coulter, *The Confederate States of America, 1861–1865*, Baton Rouge, 1950, pp. 314–327.
6. OR, 30, pt. 2, p. 23, pt. 4, pp. 610–611; Henry, *Confederacy*, pp. 306–307; Stanley F. Horn, *The Army of Tennessee*, Indianapolis, 1941 (cited hereafter as Horn), pp. 242–248. For an adverse critique of Bragg's abandonment of Chattanooga, see Hill in B&L, III, 641.
7. Hill to his wife, Aug. 14, 1863, HFP.
8. Hill to one of his sons, fragmentary letter apparently written near Lafayette in the first part of Sept. 1863, HFP.
9. Nash K. Burger and John K. Bettersworth, *South of Appomattox*, New York, 1959, pp. 81–92.

10. Thomas R. Hay, "Pat Cleburne," in *Cleburne and His Command*, by Irving A. Buck, edited by Thomas R. Hay, Jackson, Tenn., 1959, pp. 14, 19–22, 35; Biography of Cleburne by Calhoun Benham in *Kennesaw Gazette* (Atlanta, Ga.), Jan. 1–Nov. 15, 1889.

11. Ratchford ms., pp. 57–59. Hill's question to the quartermaster has been restored to the first person. Ratchford gives it in the third person.

12. On Bragg's weaknesses see William W. Mackall, *A Son's Recollections of His Father*, New York, 1930, pp. 178–179; B&L, III, 640, 641, 644, 646; Horn, pp. 249–250.

13. OR, 20, pt. 1, pp. 698–699; Horn, pp. 222–224.

14. William M. Polk, *Leonidas Polk: Bishop and General*, new edition, New York, 1915 (cited hereafter as Polk), I, 74–75, 350–358, II, 165; OR, 16, pt. 1, pp. 1088 ff.

15. Horn, pp. 224–227; Govan and Livingood, *Johnston*, pp. 178–186.

16. OR, 30, pt. 2, pp. 28, 138, 297–300; affidavits of Archer Anderson and J. H. Erskine, medical director of Hill's corps, Oct. 15, 1863, Hill Papers, NCA; Cleburne to Hill, Oct. 15, 1863, Hill Papers, VSL.

17. OR, 30, pt. 1, pp. 327–328, pt. 2, pp. 29–30, 138–139, 293–298.

18. Horn, pp. 252–254.

19. B&L, III, 640; Alexander, *Memoirs*, pp. 450–452, 455; OR, 30, pt. 2, pp. 451–453; Horn, pp. 259–260. Estimates of the strengths of the two armies vary considerably. Livermore's figures are used in the text. Horn, p. 273, considers them too low for Rosecrans and too high for Bragg.

20. B&L, III, 644–645.

21. OR, 30, pt. 1, pp. 56, 400, pt. 2, pp. 453, 524; B&L, III, 649–650.

22. OR, 30, pt. 2, pp. 32, 79, 140, 154; B&L, III, 651–652.

23. Polk, II, 254–256; OR, 30, pt. 2, p. 33; Sorrel, *Recollections*, p. 188; Horn, pp. 259–260.

24. Polk, II, 255.

25. Polk, II, 258–259.

26. OR, 30, pt. 2, p. 140. Hill and other Confederate officers, in their official reports, spelled the name of the ford "Thedford's."

27. Physical details of the battlefield that night can be found in William D. Gale to his wife, Sept. 28, 1863, Gale Papers, SHC, and in the John Euclid Magee Diary, entry of Sept. 20, 1863, DU.

28. Polk, II, 263–264, n.

29. OR, 30, pt. 2, pp. 64, 140; certificates of Reid, undated, and of Coleman, Oct. 13, 1863, Hill Papers, NCA; B&L, III, 653; Sorrel, *Recollections*, pp. 188–189. It should be noted that occasionally, throughout this account of the night of the 19th, it is necessary to reconcile varying hours or approximations of hours given by different witnesses.

30. See OR, 30, pt. 2, pp. 33, 47, 63, 140, and the undated certificate of Archer Anderson (who by now was a lieutenant colonel) in Hill Papers, NCA. Polk said later that he told "a staff officer" of Hill's, whom he did not name, of Bragg's order for a daylight attack. Anderson certified that Polk did not mention the daylight attack to him. General Breckinridge witnessed the interview between Anderson and Polk, and wrote Hill on Oct. 16, 1863: "I do not recollect that Lt. Gen Polk directed Col Anderson to order you to attack at day light." Letter in Hill Papers, NCA. Reid was also present at the Polk-Anderson interview, and Major A. C. Avery of Hill's staff came up while Polk was talking with Anderson and Reid. Both Reid and Avery certified that they heard no mention of a daylight attack. These signed staff officer certificates,

without date or place, are in Hill Papers, NCA. The weight of the evidence indicates that Polk's recollection of what he told Hill's staff officer was faulty. Probably, since he expected to see Hill soon, he waited to communicate his top-secret battle order to him in person.

31. OR, 30, pt. 2, p. 140.
32. Certificate of Reid, Hill Papers, NCA.
33. See OR, 30, pt. 2, pp. 47–48, 52, 57–59.
34. OR, 30, pt. 2, pp. 58–60; Polk, II, 257–258. Charvet also testified that at an unstated hour, which seems to have been shortly after 11 P.M., he directed two of Hill's staff officers to Polk. As neither Polk nor Hill mentioned this afterward, it seems to have been an immaterial occurrence. Judging from Reid's certificate, the unsubstantiated identification of one of the staff officers as Reid in Polk, II, 258, seems to be in error.
35. OR, 30, pt. 2, pp. 64, 140–141; certificates of Coleman and Anderson, Oct. 13, 1863, Hill Papers, NCA. Compare the account of Hill's actions that is given in Polk, II, 259.
36. See the certificate of Reid, and Breckinridge to Hill, Oct. 16, 1863, Hill Papers, NCA. Polk also told Breckinridge he was to be on Cleburne's right, and one of Polk's staff officers helped guide him to this position. OR, 30, pt. 2, p. 198.
37. OR, 30, pt. 2, pp. 53, 141; Cleburne to Hill, Sept. 30, 1863, Hill Papers, NCA; Hill to William A. Graham, June 13, 1864, Graham Papers, SHC.
38. OR, 30, pt. 2, pp. 141, 176.
39. For the facts, messages, dialogue, etc., used in the narrative of events beginning with the appearance of Wheless, see OR, 30, pt. 2, pp. 52, 53, 58, 60–62; J. Frank Wheless to Colonel W. D. Gale, Oct. 8, 1867, Leonidas Polk Papers, SHC; certificate of Reid, Hill Papers, NCA.
40. OR, 30, pt. 2, pp. 55–56; Bragg to his wife, Sept. 22, 1863, Braxton Bragg Papers, Library of Congress; quoted in Don Seitz, Braxton Bragg, Columbia, S.C., 1924, p. 359. William Polk's denials can be found in B&L, III, 662–663, and in Polk, II, 265–266, n. 1. His attempt to show that General Polk was on the line of battle at sunrise, and his description of Polk's camp, would seem to be outweighed by the evidence already cited.
41. OR, 30, pt. 2, pp. 53, 61–62. Hill maintained that Polk's attack orders to Breckinridge and Cleburne were received about 7:25 A.M., a time that obviously conflicts with the hour of 7 A.M. on Polk's note to Mackall. See Hill's statements in OR, 30, pt. 2, pp. 64, 141. Hill seems to have confused the time that the orders were received with the time, about 7:25 A.M., that Polk first came up to him on the battle line.
42. OR, 30, pt. 2, pp. 60, 62, 141; Wheless to Gale, Oct. 8, 1867, Leonidas Polk Papers, SHC; Captain H. C. Semple to Hill, Oct. 13, 1863, Hill Papers, NCA; certificate of Major W. C. S. Duxbury, Charlotte, N.C., Nov. 6, 1863, Hill Papers, VSL. Semple and Duxbury were present when Polk arrived and conversed with Cleburne and Hill. Semple was Cleburne's acting chief of artillery. Duxbury was Hill's chief ordnance officer.
43. OR, 30, pt. 2, pp. 64, 141; certificate of Major Duxbury, cited in note immediately preceding this; B&L, III, 653.
44. OR, 30, pt. 2, p. 141.
45. On Forrest see the certificate of Major A. C. Avery, Morgantown, N.C., Nov. 3, 1863, Hill Papers, NCA; OR, 30, pt. 2, p. 525; Robert Selph Henry, "First with the Most" Forrest, Indianapolis, 1944, p. 188. On the unreadiness of the left wing see OR, 30, pt. 2, p. 288.

46. OR, 30, pt. 2, pp. 47–48, 141.
47. The documents, in the Hill Papers, NCA, are P. R. Cleburne to Hill, Missionary Ridge, Sept. 30, 1863; certificate of Captain J. T. Hawood, "In Field," Sept. 23, 1863; certificate of Colonel A. J. Vaughan, Jr., n.p., Oct. 13, 1863; certificate of Major A. C. Avery, Hq., Hill's Corps, Oct. 13, 1863; certificate of Captain Rhoads Fisher, n.p., n.d. See also OR, 30, pt. 2, p. 188.
48. OR, 30, pt. 2, pp. 33, 141, 143, 154. Hill's view of the advantages to be gained by flanking the breastworks to the north is echoed by the Federal general and military historian John B. Turchin in his *Chickamauga*, Chicago, 1888, pp. 100, 174. Longstreet, p. 455, says that Bragg was "advised of the opportunity," but rejected Hill's suggestion.
49. OR, 30, pt. 2, pp. 141–142, 157.
50. OR, 30, pt. 1, pp. 57–58, 277, pt. 2, pp. 141, 154, 198–199; B&L, III, 655.
51. OR, 30, pt. 2, pp. 79, 363; B&L, III, 653.
52. OR, 30, pt. 2, p. 141. Polk, II, 267, admits that the lack of support for Hill's line was faulty, but ascribes the difficulty to Bragg.
53. John Allan Wyeth, *Life of General Nathan Bedford Forrest*, New York, 1899, pp. 252–253.
54. OR, 30, pt. 2, pp. 142, 199–200. See also, A. D. Kirwan, ed., *Johnny Green of the Orphan Brigade: The Journal of a Confederate Soldier*, University of Kentucky, 1956, pp. 94–96.
55. OR, 30, pt. 2, pp. 154–156, 157. Cleburne also had difficulty with his line, in that Deshler's brigade had got entangled with the right of the left wing, and had been thrown out of position.
56. OR, 30, pt. 2, pp. 142, 241. On p. 241 and also on p. 245 will be found some rather cryptic paraphrased dialogue that may indicate that as soon as Walker came up, sharp words passed between him and Hill over Hill's request for Gist's brigade.
57. This account attempts to reconcile the somewhat confused and conflicting evidence found in OR, 30, pt. 2, pp. 79–80, 84–85, 142, 144, and in B&L, III, 657. Hill's official report seems not wholly reliable with regard to the actions of Cheatham's and Walker's troops. The reports of Cheatham and Walker, and probably those of their subordinates, were not submitted to Hill, and he wrote his own report after being separated from the Army of Tennessee. His account in B&L, III, 657, seems inaccurate with regard to the duration of Breckinridge's fight, and refers to Gist's brigade without mentioning the rest of the division under Gist.
58. OR, 30, pt. 2, pp. 200, 245–246, 249.
59. OR, 30, pt. 2, pp. 252–253, 259, 274–275; B&L, III, 657. Walker in his report, pp. 241–242, argued that he would have accomplished much more than Hill, if Hill had permitted him "to fight my Reserve Corps according to my own judgment." He said that Hill "disintegrated" the corps and fought it by brigades, but the reports of the division and brigade commanders, already cited in this note, show that Hill ordered attack by unified divisions. William M. Polk echoes Walker's charges, in Polk, II, 272–273, basing his assertions upon Walker's report.
60. OR, 30, pt. 1, pp. 58–60, 489–490, 635, pt. 2, pp. 288, 303, 363–364, 457; B&L, III, 657–658, 661, 663–664.
61. OR, 30, pt. 1, pp. 854–855, 860, pt. 2, pp. 144, 241. On p. 241, Walker gives the paraphrase of Polk's order that is quoted in the text. He also states that he proposed to retreat in order to regroup and then advance. Hill dis-

puted this in *B&L*, III, 660 and n. Breckinridge in his letter to Hill of Oct. 16, 1863, endorsed Hill's decision to stand firm.

62. Braxton Bragg Letterbook, 2 P.M., Sept. 20, 1863, in William P. Palmer Collection, SHC; OR, 30, pt. 2, pp. 34 (where Bragg gives the quoted paraphrase of his order to Polk), and 80.

63. For the conference, see the account by W. W. Carnes in *SHSP*, XIV, 403. See also W. D. Gale to William M. Polk, Dec. 15, 1884, Leonidas Polk Papers, SHC. Hill's reply to Polk about the gap has been inferred from the known situation, the orders that followed, and Carnes's and Gale's comments, in the sources here cited, about Hill's concern for his flank and the delay that occurred while the gap was filled.

64. OR, 30, pt. 2, pp. 85, 144, 156. Polk did not write an official report of the battle. In Hill's report there is a hiatus with regard to what happened between the repulse of Govan's brigade (mistakenly called Walker's corps) and 3:30 P.M. Hill's article on Chickamauga for the *Century* editors also omits mention of afternoon friction with Polk (who had been killed in combat in 1864), and places the approach of Granger at 3 P.M., considerably later than it actually occurred. This bridges the time that apparently was consumed by the ironing out of differences between Polk and Hill. See *B&L*, III, 660–661. It should be noted that the article was altered by the editors. Hill said they deleted one third of it and made it obscure in places. Hill to Longstreet, March 12, 1887, Longstreet Papers, DU.

65. OR, 30, pt. 2, pp. 85, 156, 200, 241, 253; Breckinridge to Hill, Oct. 16, 1863. Hill states in *B&L*, III, 661: "At 3:30 P.M. General Polk sent an order to me to assume command of the attacking forces on the right and renew the assault." There may be here some further telescoping of events. Carnes, in *SHSP*, XIV, 404–405, gives a colorful account of Polk in immediate command of the afternoon advance, and William M. Polk has drawn on this narrative in describing the battle in Polk, II, 277 ff. The conflict between Carnes's reminiscence and the evidence already cited is obvious.

66. The plan of attack and the formation of the right wing can be discerned by cross-checking the statements of the various commanding officers in OR, 30, pt. 2, pp. 80, 85, 144, 156, 162, 177, 189–190, 200, 217, 231, 241, 246, 249, 259, 275. The quoted dialogue is from Hill's endorsement to Breckinridge's report of the battle. This endorsement does not appear in the OR, but was published in *SHSP*, VII, 167–168. Hill in his report, cited at p. 144, ascribed the delay between 3:30 and 4 P.M. to Jackson's slowness. W. D. Gale took the view that all delay in the right wing that day was simply the result of Hill's recalcitrance. Gale to William M. Polk, Dec. 15, 1884, Leonidas Polk Papers, SHC. William M. Polk's view is much the same. He writes that, "The order to advance was given to Hill at 3:30, and had to be twice repeated before he moved." He brushes aside Hill's difficulty in getting Jackson into position by saying that "this was not an essential to [Hill's] movements," an assertion that can hardly be accepted in the light of the evidence already given in the notes and text. See Polk, II, 277 and n.

67. OR, 30, pt. 1, pp. 279, 291, 296, 470, 475, pt. 2, pp. 85, 144, 156, 177–178, 200, 246, 253, 259–260, 525. See also Archibald Gracie, *The Truth about Chickamauga*, Boston, 1911, pp. 80–101.

68. *B&L*, III, 661; *SHSP*, XVIII, 264.

Chapter XII.   ENEMIES IN GRAY AND BLUE

1. OR, 30, pt. 2, pp. 34, 145; Horn, pp. 270, 272; Longstreet to Hill, July 5, 1884, Hill Papers, VSL; Longstreet, pp. 456, 457–458.
2. Hill to his wife, Sept. 25, 1863, HFP; OR, 30, pt. 2, p. 145.
3. Polk, II, 280–281.
4. OR, 30, pt. 2, pp. 37, 289–290.
5. OR, 30, pt. 2, p. 145, pt. 4, pp. 680 ff., 698; Horn, pp. 264, 273, 277–278, 281; Robert G. Athearn, ed., *Soldier in the West: The Civil War Letters of Alfred Lacey Hough*, Philadelphia, 1957, p. 151, n. 13.
6. Kirwan, ed., *Johnny Green*, p. 99; B&L, III, 662. See also John C. Brown to Longstreet, April 14, 1888, Longstreet Papers, DU.
7. Hill to the editor of the *Daily Picayune*, of New Orleans, Aug. 18, 1887, Hill Papers, NCA; OR, 30, pt. 4, p. 742.
8. OR, 30, pt. 2, pp. 54, 307.
9. See Bragg to "My Dear Sir," Missionary Ridge, Sept. 25, 1863, Georgia Portfolio, II, p. 120, DU. Content clearly identifies the addressee as Davis.
10. OR, 30, pt. 2, p. 67, pt. 4, pp. 705–706.
11. OR, 30, pt. 2, p. 69, pt. 4, p. 708; OR, 52, pt. 2, p. 549; Lee to Longstreet, Sept. 25, 1863, Charles W. Dabney Papers, SHC.
12. OR, 30, pt. 2, pp. 62–63.
13. OR, 30, pt. 2, p. 47.
14. Hill to William A. Graham, June 13, 1864, Graham Papers, SHC.
15. OR, 30, pt. 2, pp. 55–56, 298, 310, pt. 4, p. 731.
16. For the Davis-Bragg correspondence, see OR, 30, pt. 2, p. 55, and OR, 52, pt. 2, pp. 533–535.
17. See OR, 30, pt. 2, pp. 56–57, 62–63, 64.
18. Polk, II, 298.
19. Edward Porter Alexander Papers, SHC.
20. John Euclid Magee Diary, entry of Sept. 30, 1863, DU; Thomas F. Berry, *Four Years with Morgan and Forrest*, Oklahoma City, 1914, p. 246; Sam R. Watkins, "Co. Aytch," edited by Bell Irvin Wiley, Jackson, Tenn., 1952, pp. 70–71.
21. McLaws to "Miss Lizzie" [Ewell?], Feb. 29, 1864, R. S. Ewell Papers, LC; Mackall, *A Son's Recollections*, pp. 183–184; OR, 30, pt. 4, p. 742.
22. OR, 30, pt. 4, p. 728.
23. Original document in Hill Papers, VSL.
24. OR, 30, pt. 2, pp. 65–66. The copy differs slightly from the original in wording and paragraphing.
25. Horn, p. 286; Arndt M. Stickles, *Simon Bolivar Buckner*, Chapel Hill, 1940, pp. 233–235.
26. Rowland, IX, p. 498; Hill to Longstreet, Feb. 11, 1888, Longstreet Papers, DU; Longstreet, pp. 464–465.
27. For the commands given, see OR, 30, pt. 2, pp. 12, 13, 15, 16, 17, pt. 4, p. 721. Avery, p. 36, gives Breckinridge's statement.
28. Rowland, IX, 498; Avery, p. 35; Mackall, *A Son's Recollections*, pp. 181–182. For a story, based on a recollection of another recollection, to the effect that Hill hesitated to sign the petition until the other generals convinced him it was his duty to do so, see Joseph M. Hill, *Hill*, pp. 23–24.
29. Longstreet to Hill, Oct. 12, 1863, Hill Papers, NCA.
30. OR, 52, pt. 2, pp. 535, 538, 678; Polk, II, 299; OR, 30, pt. 2, p. 67.
31. Mackall, *A Son's Recollections*, pp. 182–183; Rowland, VII, 321.

32. This account of the conference is based upon Longstreet to Hill, July 5, 1885, Hill Papers, VSL; Hill to the editor of the *Daily Picayune* of New Orleans, Aug. 18, 1887, Hill Papers, NCA; Horn, pp. 287–288; Stickles, *Buckner*, pp. 235–236.
33. Polk to "My Dear Rogers [?]," Atlanta, Oct. 17, 1863, Gale Papers, SHC. Though the signature has been cut out of this letter, the peculiar handwriting and the content identify Polk as the writer.
34. Rowland, VII, 321; OR, 30, pt. 4, pp. 735, 742.
35. See letter cited in Note No. 33, this chapter.
36. Bragg's request and Davis's reply are in OR, 30, pt. 2, pp. 148–149.
37. Hill to General John C. Breckinridge, Oct. 26, 1863, Hill Letters, New-York Historical Society. The quotation about Pemberton's being offered the corps is taken from Hill to William A. Graham, May 28, 1864, HFP.
38. For comments on Pemberton's objective see OR, 30, pt. 4, pp. 735, 742, and Horn, p. 287. See also, on Polk and Bragg, Polk, II, 300.
39. Rowland, VII, 321.
40. OR, 30, pt. 2, p. 149.
41. See Anderson's certificate in Hill Papers, NCA. See also Ratchford ms., pp. 66–68; OR, 30, pt. 2, p. 149; Bragg to Hill, Oct. 18, 1863, Hill Papers, NCA.
42. See OR, 52, pt. 2, pp. 534, 677. In a letter to a friend, dated Feb. 8, 1873, Bragg accused Hill of military delinquency at McLemore's Cove and Chickamauga. The letter contains a number of inaccuracies, such as the assertion that Bragg did not learn of Polk's direct orders of Sept. 20 to Cleburne and Breckinridge until after he had suspended Polk from command. By comparing Bragg's letter with the OR, the various inaccuracies can easily be detected. They are not pointed out in Polk, II, 296, 308–314, wherein the author first quotes at length from this letter and then publishes it in full.
43. McLaws to Hill, Jan. 23, 1864, Hill Papers, NCA.
44. Hill to William A. Graham, Jan. 30, 1865, Graham Papers, SHC.
45. OR, 30, pt. 2, pp. 148–149; Longstreet to Hill, Oct. 18, 1863, Hill Papers, VSL; Hill to Breckinridge, Oct. 26, 1863, Hill Letters, New-York Historical Society.
46. These testimonials are in Hill Papers in NCA and VSL. A number have been published in Avery, pp. 37–39.
47. OR, 30, pt. 2, pp. 68, 70, 309, 310–311, 312; OR, 31, pt. 3, p. 582; OR, 52, pt. 2, p. 547.
48. Raleigh *Register*, Oct. 23, 1863; Richmond *Dispatch*, Oct. 20, 1863; Mobile *Advertiser*, Oct. 27, Nov. 6, 1863; story from the Charleston *Courier* of Oct. 26, 1863, published in OR, 30, pt. 2, p. 152; Hill to William A. Graham, June 2, 1864, HFP.
49. OR, 30, pt. 2, p. 150.
50. Hill to William A. Graham, May 28, 1864, HFP, and May 27, June 13, Dec. 7, 1864, Graham Papers, SHC.
51. OR, 31, pt. 3, p. 701. This letter seems to be the sole basis for Freeman's assumption that Hill had become newly jealous of his rank. See LL, III, 317–318 and n. 22.
52. Hill's letter to Davis of Nov. 16, 1863 (either the original or a signed copy in Hill's hand), is in Hill Papers, NCA. For a discerning analysis of Davis see Bell Irvin Wiley, *The Road to Appomattox*, Memphis, Tenn., 1956, Chapter I.
53. OR, 52, pt. 2, p. 562. This letter is not mentioned by Freeman in his discussion of the Bragg-Davis-Hill controversy (LL, III, 317 ff.).
54. OR, 30, pt. 2, p. 151.

55. J. B. Jones, *A Rebel War Clerk's Diary*, new edition, edited by Howard Swiggett, New York, 1935, II, 106; Younger, ed., *Diary of R. G. H. Kean*, pp. xxiii, xxiv.
56. OR, 30, pt. 2, pp. 151, 152, 153. An undated and unidentified newspaper clipping of Hill's "card" in defense of himself is in the HFP.
57. LL, III, 318 and n. 24.
58. Hill's copy of the application, erroneously dated 1863, is in Hill Papers, NCA. See also Hill to William A. Graham, Dec. 7, 1864, Graham Papers, SHC.
59. OR, 35, pt. 1, p. 581.
60. Maurice Augustus Moore, *Reminiscences of York*, pamphlet, n.p., n.d., *passim*; Hill to J. Starke Sims, Nov. 1, 1866, Hill Papers, NCA.
61. Harvey Hill did not get his brother to carry to Richmond a letter dated Feb. 23, as Freeman supposes in LL, III, 320. The order of events, as discussed in LL, III, 319–321, is confused.
62. Certified true copy of W. R. Hill to Hill, March 10, 1864, Hill Papers, VSL. Davis refers to this interview with "my friend, your Brother, W. R. Hill," in a letter to Hill of Dec. 4, 1867, Hill Papers, NCA.
63. OR, 42, pt. 3, p. 1165.
64. OR, 53, pp. 312–313; W. R. Hill to General Samuel Cooper, March 25, 1864, Hill Papers, NCA.
65. OR, 35, pt. 1, p. 323; OR, 42, pt. 3, pp. 1165–1166.
66. See James M. Matthews, ed., *Public Laws of the Confederate States of America, Passed at the Third [–Fourth] Session of the First Congress, 1863 [–1863–4]*, Richmond, 1863–64, p. 195; clipping of published law, with notation of publication date, in Hill's hand, pasted on back of Cooper's letter of Feb. 16 to Hill, Hill Papers, NCA; *SHSP*, L, 448, 459. Freeman, in discussing Hill's case, mentions the old law for the appointment of lieutenant generals, but not the new. LL, III, 317. On the submission of Pemberton's name see Hill to William A. Graham, May 27, 1864, Graham Papers, SHC. Gale's letter is in the Gale Papers, SHC.
67. Hill Papers, NCA.
68. OR, 42, pt. 3, pp. 1167–1168.
69. April 10, 1864, Hill Papers, NCA.
70. OR, 42, pt. 3, pp. 1168–1169.
71. OR, 42, pt. 3, pp. 1169–1170; Hill to Beauregard, April 26, 1864, Charles W. Dabney Papers, SHC. Freeman has set an authoritative and essentially negative stamp upon the historical character and reputation of Hill, and at this point his treatment of him seems to call for further comment. His account of the Bragg-Davis-Hill controversy is markedly adverse to Hill, affording an interesting contrast to the balanced or even quite sympathetic discussion that he devotes to the adamant stands taken by other officers in defense of their professional reputations (see for example LL, II, 243 ff., 257). In LL, III, 317–322, he quotes Bragg's charges against Hill without assessing their validity; presents Hill's efforts to obtain an expression of undiminished confidence as captious, eccentric, and unreasonably demanding; and accepts Davis's and Cooper's arguments at face value. Had Freeman made more use of Hill manuscripts listed in the bibliography of *Lee's Lieutenants*, he might have modified his interpretations of Hill. However, he has not brought all the pertinent material in the *Official Records* to bear upon his discussion of the Bragg-Davis-Hill controversy; and some of this material, as in OR, 30, pt. 2, pp. 151–152, and OR, 52, pt. 2, pp. 677–678, suggests on the surface that Bragg's charges were questionable, that Davis was unfair to Hill,

and that Hill had good reason for his arguments and actions. As to why Freeman treated Hill as he did—could it be that he developed a blind spot
toward a general who opposed and criticized Lee?

72. This letter, and others more expressive of sympathy and admiration for Hill,
can be found in Hill Papers, VSL.

73. Hill to his wife, March 22, [1864], HFP.

74. Hill to Beauregard, April 26, 1864, Charles W. Dabney Papers, SHC;
Davis to Hill, Dec. 4, 1867, Hill Papers, NCA; OR, 36, pt. 2, p. 960.

75. LL, III, 462–464, 490–495, 526–527; Beauregard to Hill, June 7, 1864,
Hill Papers, NCA; Hill to his wife, May 22, 1864, Hill Papers, NCA; OR,
36, pt. 3, pp. 827, 835; Williams, *Beauregard*, p. 220; OR, 40, pt. 2, pp. 649,
658, 660, pt. 3, pp. 760, 771. For a sharp critique of Lee by Hill, with regard
to the defense of Petersburg prior to the siege, see OR, 36, pt. 3, p. 896.
For Hill's efforts to investigate a questionable order by Bragg affecting the
defense of Petersburg in May, see *Ibid.*, pp. 859–860; copy of Hill to General H. A. Wise, June 1, 1864, Hill Papers, VSL; LL, III, 485 and n. 73.

76. Hill to his wife, May 30, [1864], HFP; LL, II, p. 721; SHSP, XXIII, 197.

77. See LL, III, 512–514, and Hill to William A. Graham, July 7, 1864, Graham
Papers, SHC.

78. Seitz, *Bragg*, p. 410.

79. OR, 36, pt. 2, p. 1022; OR, 51, pt. 2, pp. 939, 943, 954; Beauregard to Hill,
July 24, 1864, Hill Papers, VSL; Hill to William A. Graham, May 28, 1864,
HFP; OR, 36, pt. 3, p. 821; Beauregard to Hill, June 7, 1864, Hill Papers,
NCA.

80. Hill to Johnston, May 25, 1885, HFP; OR, 51, pt. 2, p. 1020; Hill to William
A. Graham, July 7, 1864, Graham Papers, SHC.

81. Albert Potts Hill to Hill, Nov. 11, 1864, Hill Papers, VSL; Hill to William
A. Graham, May 28, 1864, HFP, and June 4, 1864, Graham Papers, SHC.

82. Hill to William A. Graham, May 10, 1864, Graham Papers, SHC. Graham
and associates to Davis is in Confederate Records, Correspondence of the
Adjutant General, National Archives.

83. Letter dated June 6, 1864, in Hill Papers, NCA.

84. OR, 40, pt. 2, p. 650; Hill to his wife, June 4, 1864, Hill Papers, NCA.

85. Graham's letter to Hill, with the first part, including the date, missing, is
in Hill Papers, VSL. Hill's reply to Graham, dated June 13, 1864, is in
Graham Papers, SHC.

86. OR, 40, pt. 2, p. 650.

87. See Hill-Graham correspondence of June 13, 1864, and prior to that date, as
cited in Note No. 85, this chapter, and Hill to Graham, May 28, 1864, HFP.

88. Hill's letter and the endorsements are in OR, 52, pt. 2, pp. 677–678.

89. Horn, p. 284, quotes the next-to-last sentence in Bragg's endorsement to
show how it vitiates Bragg's charges in the request for Hill's removal. Freeman, in discussing Hill's case, mentions neither Hill's letter of June 11 nor
the endorsements to it.

90. Hill to his wife, July 15, [1864], HFP; Hill to R. L. Dabney, July 19, 1864,
Robert L. Dabney Papers, UTS; Hill to William A. Graham, July 7, 1864,
Graham Papers, SHC.

91. Wade Hampton to Hill, Oct. 12, 1864, Hill Papers, VSL; OR, 30, pt. 2, pp.
77, 79, 147, 287, 288; LWL, I, 444. Hill to Graham, Dec. 7, 1864, Graham
Papers, SHC.

92. Hill to Vance, Oct. 13, 1864, Vance Papers; OR, 42, pt. 3, p. 1163.

93. OR, 42, pt. 3, pp. 1163–1164; Rowland, VI, p. 438.

94. OR, 42, pt. 3, p. 1170.

95. Graham to Hill, Dec. 23, 1864, Hill Papers, VSL.

96. Savannah *Republican*, June 5, 1863 (the author thanks Mrs. Lilla M. Hawes, director of the Georgia Historical Society, for furnishing a copy of the story and information on the probable identity of P. W. A.); Hill to his wife, Sept. 29, 1863, HFP; Hill to E. J. Hale, Dec. 23, 1863, E. J. Hale Papers, NCA.

97. Graham to Hill, Dec. 23, 1864, Hill Papers, VSL.

98. Trefousse, *Butler*, pp. 171–172; copy of Hill to Cooper, Dec. 23, 1864, HFP; OR, 47, pt. 2, p. 991; H. J. Eckenrode, *Jefferson Davis*, New York, 1923, p. 110.

99. OR, 47, pt. 2, pp. 991, 1001, 1030, 1051 ff.; Hill to Graham, Jan. 30, 1865, Graham Papers, SHC.

100. Williams, *Beauregard*, p. 246; OR, 47, pt. 1, pp. 1052 ff., pt. 2, p. 1272, pt. 3, pp. 748, 843–844.

Epilogue: "A GLORIOUS CHRISTIAN VICTORY"

1. Incident related to the author on Nov. 30, 1955, by a member of the Hill family who prefers not to be named.

2. Hill to Jubal Early, March 6, 1869, Jubal A. Early Papers, LC.

3. Complete files of *LWL* are available in a number of libraries, including that of the University of Colorado. The most complete files of the *Southern Home* are at DU and the University of North Carolina Library. On threats of assassination, see D. H. Hill, Jr. to Mrs. J. J. Thomson, April 18, 1919, carbon copy, Daniel Harvey Hill, Jr. Papers, NCA.

4. Mss. of Hill's Granger addresses are in Hill Papers, NCA. See also the *Daily Sentinel* of Raleigh, Aug. 31, 1873.

5. Paul Hamilton Hayne to Hill, Feb. 19, 1869, Hill Papers, NCA, and March 5, 1869, HFP. See also Jay B. Hubbell, *The South in American Literature, 1607–1900*, Duke University Press, 1954, pp. 476, 717, 720–721, 743. On Simms's opinion see the Charleston *Courier*, March 4, 1868. For information on Simms the author thanks Mary C. Simms Oliphant.

6. At least one undated advertisement, apparently from the New Orleans *Times*, and numerous letters of endorsement from Confederate generals, are in Hill Papers, NCA.

7. Hill to Graham, April 28, 1875, Graham Papers, SHC.

8. See *LWL*, I, 277–280; Davis to Hill, Dec. 4, 1867, Hill Papers, NCA; Rowland, IX, 499, 500; Hill to his son Joseph, Oct. 8, 1887, HFP; Davis to Joseph M. Hill, Oct. 31, 1889, HFP.

9. Bridges, ed., "Lee Letter"; *LWL*, IV, 278; LL, II, 718–719; Hill to Longstreet, Aug. 29, 1879, Longstreet Papers, DU.

10. Hal Bridges, "D. H. Hill and Higher Education in the New South," *Arkansas Historical Quarterly*, XV (Summer, 1956), pp. 107–124.

11. Numerous letters showing the activities of Hill's children, and his relations with them, are in HFP.

12. Details of Hill's fight against cancer, and his thoughts about it, are found in numerous letters, in HFP, that Hill wrote to his son Joseph from August, 1887 to September, 1889. For the acceptance of Hill's resignation, and the board resolution, see J. N. Moore to Hill, Aug. 8, 1889, Hill Papers, NCA.

13. Details of Hill's death are taken from D. H. Hill, Jr. to Joseph Hill, Sept. 26, 1889, HFP, and the *News and Observer* of Raleigh, Sept. 26, 1889.

BIBLIOGRAPHY

This list is restricted to sources cited in the text and notes.

MANUSCRIPTS

Confederate Museum, Richmond:
    Daniel Harvey Hill Letters; R. E. Lee Papers.
Davidson College:
    Faculty Minutes, 1854–59; Trustee Minutes, 1853–59; [Stonewall] Jackson file, in College Library.
Duke University Library:
    William E. Ardrey Diary; Daniel Harvey Hill Papers; Bradley T. Johnson Papers; James Longstreet Papers; John Euclid Magee Diary; Munford-Ellis Papers.
Henry E. Huntington Library:
    James W. Eldridge Collection; Joseph E. Johnston Collection; John Page Nicholson Collection; James E. B. Stuart Collection.
Hill Family Papers:
    Daniel Harvey Hill Papers, and related mss., in the possession of Miss Pauline Hill of Raleigh, North Carolina, and Mr. and Mrs. David R. Williams of Mulberry Plantation, South Carolina.
Library of Congress:
    Braxton Bragg Papers; Jubal A. Early Papers; R. S. Ewell Papers; Robert E. Lee Papers.
National Archives:
    Confederate Records, Correspondence of the Adjutant General; Mexican War Pension Papers of Daniel Harvey Hill; Records of the War Department, Office of the Adjutant General (Record Group No. 94); Register of Cadet Applicants, Engineer Department, 1837–38, War Records Branch.
New-York Historical Society:
    D. H. Hill Letters.
New York Public Library:
    Century Collection.
North Carolina Department of Archives and History, Raleigh:
    William L. De Rosset Papers; E. J. Hale Papers; Daniel Harvey Hill Papers; Daniel Harvey Hill, Jr. Papers; J. J. Pettigrew Papers; Zebulon Baird Vance Letter Book, 1862–63; Zebulon Baird Vance Papers.
South Caroliniana Library, University of South Carolina:
    Charles Carrol Simms Collection.
Southern Historical Collection, University of North Carolina Library:
    Edward Porter Alexander Papers; Thomas Lanier Clingman Papers; Charles W. Dabney Papers; Gale Papers; William Alexander Graham Papers; Daniel Harvey Hill Papers; Daniel Harvey Hill Mexican War Diary; Henry Lord Page King Diary; Calvin Leach Diary; William Gaston Lewis Papers; James Longstreet Photoprints; Lafayette McLaws Papers; Robert Hall Morrison

Papers; William P. Palmer Collection; William Nelson Pendleton Papers;
Leonidas Polk Papers; George Whitaker Wills Papers.
Union Theological Seminary Library, Richmond:
Robert L. Dabney Papers.
United States Military Academy Archives:
Descriptive Lists of New Cadets, 1838–68.
Virginia Historical Society, Richmond:
Robert E. Lee Headquarters Papers.
Virginia State Library, Richmond:
Daniel Harvey Hill Papers.
Washington and Lee University:
Washington College Faculty Minutes, 1848–54; Washington College Trus-
tee Records, 1848–54.

NEWSPAPERS

Charleston *Courier*; Charleston *Mercury*; *Daily Sentinel*, Raleigh; *Kennesaw
Gazette*, Atlanta; Mobile *Advertiser*; *News and Observer*, Raleigh; New York
Herald; Raleigh *Register*; Richmond *Dispatch*; Savannah *Republican*; *South-
ern Home*, Charlotte.

PRINTED SOURCES

Alexander, Edward Porter. *Military Memoirs of a Confederate*. New York, 1907.
Athearn, Robert G., ed. *Soldier in the West: The Civil War Letters of Alfred
Lacey Hough*. Philadelphia, 1957.
Avery, A. C. *Life and Character of Lieutenant General D. H. Hill* (pamphlet).
Raleigh, 1893.
Berry, Thomas F. *Four Years with Morgan and Forrest*. Oklahoma City, 1914.
Bridges, Hal. "D. H. Hill and Higher Education in the New South," *Arkansas
Historical Quarterly*, XV (Summer, 1956), 107–124.
———. "D. H. Hill's Anti-Yankee Algebra," *Journal of Southern History*, XXII
(May 1956), 220–222.
———, ed. "A Lee Letter on the 'Lost Dispatch' and the Maryland Campaign
of 1862," *Virginia Magazine of History and Biography*, vol. 66 (April
1958), 161–166.
Buck, Irving A. *Cleburne and His Command*. Edited by Thomas R. Hay. Jack-
son, Tenn., 1959.
Chamberlayne, C. G., ed. *Ham Chamberlayne—Virginian*. Richmond, 1932.
Clark, Walter, ed. *Histories of the Several Regiments and Battalions from North
Carolina in the Great War 1861–65*. 5 vols. Raleigh, 1901.
Cullum, George W. *Biographical Register of the Officers and Graduates of the
U. S. Military Academy*. 4 vols. Boston, 1891.
Davis, Jefferson. *Jefferson Davis, Constitutionalist: His Letters, Papers and
Speeches*. Collected and Edited by Dunbar Rowland. 10 vols. Jackson, Miss.,
1923.
———. *The Rise and Fall of the Confederate Government*. 2 vols. New York,
1881.
De Leon, T. C. *Belles, Beaux and Brains of the Sixties*. New York, 1909.
Early, J. A. *Lieutenant General Jubal Anderson Early, C.S.A.* Philadelphia, 1912.
Freeman, Douglas Southall, and Grady McWhiney, eds. *Lee's Dispatches*. New
ed. New York, 1957.
Gordon, John B. *Reminiscences of the Civil War*. New York, 1903.

Grimes, Bryan. *Extracts of Letters of ... to His Wife.* Compiled by Pulaski Cowper. Raleigh, 1883.

Hill, Daniel Harvey (pseudonym, H. S. Foote, Esq.). "The Army in Texas," *Southern Quarterly Review,* IX (April 1846), 434–457.

———. "The Army in Texas—No. 2," *Southern Quarterly Review,* XIV (July 1848), 183–197.

———. "The Battle of Gaines's Mill," *Century,* XXX (May–Oct. 1885), 294–309.

———. *A Consideration of the Sermon on the Mount.* Philadelphia, 1858.

———. *The Crucifixion of Christ.* Philadelphia, 1859.

———. *Elements of Algebra.* Philadelphia, 1857.

———, ed. *The Land We Love.* Monthly magazine. vols. I–VI. Charlotte, May 1866–March 1869.

———. "The Real Stonewall Jackson," *Century,* XLVII (1893–94), 623–628.

———, and A. W. Miller. *Memorial Sketches of Rev. Robert Hall Morrison, D.D.* (pamphlet). Charlotte, 1889.

Hill, Daniel Harvey, [Jr.]. *Col. William Hill and the Campaign of 1780* (pamphlet). n.p., n.d.

Hill, Joseph M. *Biography of Daniel Harvey Hill* (pamphlet). Arkansas History Commission. n.p., n.d.

Hood, John B. *Advance and Retreat.* New Orleans, 1880.

Johnson, Robert U., and Clarence C. Buel, eds. *Battles and Leaders of the Civil War.* 4 vols. New York, 1887–88.

Johnston, Joseph E. *Narrative of Military Operations, Directed, during the Late War Between the States.* New York, 1874.

Jones, J. B. *A Rebel War Clerk's Diary.* Edited by Howard Swiggett. 2 vols. New York, 1935.

Kirwan, A. D., ed. *Johnny Green of the Orphan Brigade: The Journal of a Confederate Soldier.* University of Kentucky, 1956.

Lee, Robert E., [Jr.]. *Recollections and Letters of General Robert E. Lee.* New York, 1904.

Lee, Susan P. *Memoirs of William Nelson Pendleton, D.D.* Philadelphia, 1893.

Longstreet, James. *From Manassas to Appomattox.* Philadelphia, 1896.

Mackall, William W. *A Son's Recollections of His Father.* New York, 1930.

Macrae, David. *The Americans at Home.* 2 vols. New York, 1952.

Marshall, Charles. *An Aide-de-Camp of Lee.* Edited by Sir Frederick Maurice. Boston, 1927.

Matthews, James M., ed. *Public Laws of the Confederate States of America, Passed at the Third [–Fourth] Session of the First Congress, 1863 [–1863–4].* Richmond, 1863–64.

Moore, Frank, ed. *The Rebellion Record.* 12 vols. New York, 1862–71.

Moore, Maurice Augustus. *Reminiscences of York* (pamphlet). n.p., n.d.

Nisbet, James Cooper. *Four Years on the Firing Line.* Chattanooga, n.d.

North Carolina Military Institute. *Catalog ... 1859–60.* Charlotte, 1860.

North Carolina Military Institute. *Regulations.* Charlotte, 1860.

North Carolina, State of. *Private Laws ... 1858–59.* Raleigh, 1859.

Official Register of the Officers and Cadets of the U. S. Military Academy. West Point, 1839–42.

Polk, William M. *Leonidas Polk: Bishop and General.* 2 vols. new ed. New York, 1915.

Ruffin, Thomas. *The Papers of Thomas Ruffin.* Collected and Edited by J. G. de Roulhac Hamilton. 4 vols. Raleigh, 1918–20.

Shepherd, Henry E. "Gen. D. H. Hill—A Character Sketch," *Confederate Veteran*, XXV (Sept. 1917), 411–413.

Shotwell, Randolph Abbott. *The Papers of Randolph Abbott Shotwell.* Edited by J. G. de Roulhac Hamilton with the Collaboration of Rebecca Cameron. 3 vols. Raleigh, 1929–36.

Smith, Gustavus W. *The Battle of Seven Pines.* New York, 1891.

———. *Confederate War Papers.* 2d ed. New York, 1884.

Sorrel, G. Moxley. *Recollections of a Confederate Staff Officer.* 2d ed. New York, 1917.

Southern Historical Society Papers. 50 vols. Richmond, 1876–1953.

Stiles, Robert. *Four Years under Marse Robert.* 2d ed. New York, 1903.

Taylor, Richard. *Destruction and Reconstruction.* Edited by Richard B. Harwell. New York, 1955.

Taylor, Walter H. *Four Years with General Lee.* New York, 1878.

Turchin, John B. *Chickamauga.* Chicago, 1888.

War of the Rebellion: A Compilation of the Official Records of the Union and Confederate Armies. 70 vols. in 128 books. Washington, 1880–1901.

Watkins, Sam R. "*Co. Aytch.*" Edited with an Introduction by Bell Irvin Wiley. Jackson, Tenn., 1952.

Wright, Marcus J. *General Officers of the Confederate Army.* New York, 1911.

Younger, Edward, ed. *Inside the Confederate Government: The Diary of Robert Garlick Hill Kean.* New York, 1957.

SECONDARY WORKS

Burger, Nash K., and John K. Bettersworth. *South of Appomattox.* New York, 1959.

Catton, Bruce. *Mr. Lincoln's Army.* New York, 1951.

Chambers, Lenoir. *Stonewall Jackson.* 2 vols. New York, 1959.

Coulter, E. Merton. *The Confederate States of America, 1861–1865.* Baton Rouge, 1950.

Couper, William. *One Hundred Years at V. M. I.* 4 vols. Richmond, 1939.

Dabney, Robert L. *Life and Campaigns of Lieut.-Gen. Thomas J. Jackson.* New York, 1866.

Davis, Burke. *Jeb Stuart: The Last Cavalier.* New York, 1957.

———. *They Called Him Stonewall.* New York, 1954.

Eckenrode, H. J. *Jefferson Davis.* New York, 1923.

———, and Bryan Conrad. *James Longstreet.* Chapel Hill, 1936.

Evans, Clement A., ed. *Confederate Military History.* 12 vols. Atlanta, 1899.

Franklin, John Hope. *The Militant South.* Cambridge, Mass., 1956.

Freeman, Douglas Southall. *Lee's Lieutenants: A Study in Command.* 3 vols. New York, 1942–44.

———. *R. E. Lee: A Biography.* 4 vols. New York, 1934–35.

Govan, Gilbert E., and James W. Livingood. *A Different Valor: The Story of General Joseph E. Johnston, C.S.A.* Indianapolis, 1956.

Gracie, Archibald. *The Truth about Chickamauga.* Boston, 1911.

Hamilton, J. G. de Roulhac. *North Carolina since 1860.* Chicago, 1919.

Hassler, Warren W., Jr. *General George B. McClellan.* Baton Rouge, 1957.

Henderson, G. F. R. *Stonewall Jackson and the American Civil War.* Authorized American Edition. New York, 1949.

Henry, Robert Selph. "*First with the Most*" *Forrest.* Indianapolis, 1944.

———. *The Story of the Confederacy.* Indianapolis, 1931.

Hill, Daniel Harvey, [Jr.]. *Bethel to Sharpsburg*. 2 vols. Raleigh, 1926.

Horn, Stanley F. *The Army of Tennessee: A Military History*. Indianapolis, 1941.

Hubbell, Jay B. *The South in American Literature, 1607–1900*. Duke University Press, 1954.

Maurice, Sir Frederick. *Robert E. Lee the Soldier*. Boston, 1925.

Montgomery, Horace. *Howell Cobb's Confederate Career*. Tuscaloosa, Ala., 1959.

Nevins, Allan. *The War for the Union*, Volume II: *War Becomes Revolution*. New York, 1960.

Nichols, Edward J. *Toward Gettysburg: A Biography of General John F. Reynolds*. Pennsylvania State University Press, 1958.

Parks, Joseph Howard. *General Edmund Kirby Smith, C.S.A.* Baton Rouge, 1954.

Pemberton, John C. *Pemberton, Defender of Vicksburg*. Chapel Hill, 1942.

Randall, J. G. *The Civil War and Reconstruction*. Boston, 1937.

Seitz, Don. *Braxton Bragg, General of the Confederacy*. Columbia, S.C., 1924.

Shaw, Cornelia Rebekah. *Davidson College*. New York, 1923.

Smith, Justin H. *The War with Mexico*. 2 vols. New York, 1919.

Stickles, Arndt M. *Simon Bolivar Buckner*. Chapel Hill, 1940.

Stovall, Pleasant A. *Robert Toombs*. New York, 1892.

Trefousse, Hans Louis. *Ben Butler*. New York, 1957.

Vandiver, Frank E. *Mighty Stonewall*. New York, 1957.

———. *Rebel Brass: The Confederate Command System*. Baton Rouge, 1956.

Wellman, Manly Wade. *Rebel Boast*. New York, 1957.

Wiley, Bell Irvin. *The Road to Appomattox*. Memphis, Tenn., 1956.

Williams, Kenneth P. *Lincoln Finds a General: A Military Study of the Civil War*. 5 vols. New York, 1949–59.

Williams, T. Harry. *Lincoln and His Generals*. New York, 1952.

———. *P. G. T. Beauregard: Napoleon in Gray*. Baton Rouge, 1954.

Wise, Jennings C. *The Long Arm of Lee*. 2 vols. Lynchburg, Va., 1915.

Wyeth, John Allan. *Life of General Nathan Bedford Forrest*. New York, 1899.

INDEX